Many Identities, One Nation

EARLY AMERICAN STUDIES

Daniel K. Richter and Kathleen M. Brown, Series Editors

Exploring neglected aspects of our colonial, revolutionary, and early national history and culture, Early American Studies reinterprets familiar themes and events in fresh ways. Interdisciplinary in character, and with a special emphasis on the period from about 1600 to 1850, the series is published in partnership with the McNeil Center for Early American Studies.

A complete list of books in the series is available from the publisher.

Many Identities, One Nation

The Revolution and Its Legacy in the Mid-Atlantic

LIAM RIORDAN

PENN

University of Pennsylvania Press

Philadelphia

Printed in the United States of America on acid-free paper

10 9 8 7 6 5 4 3 2 1

Published by
University of Pennsylvania Press
Philadelphia, Pennsylvania 19104–4112

A Cataloging-in-Publication record is available from the Library of Congress.

ISBN 978-0-8122-4001-6

For my parents
Geraldine O'Boyle Riordan
and
John Patrick Riordan

Contents

Illustrations

Tables

"That," he said, a little greasy from bacon, "that was a point that exercised my mind a good deal during your absence. . . . How quickly could he come by a new identity?"

"Identity?" said Jack, comfortably pouring out more coffee. "Is not identity something you are born with?"

"The identity I am thinking of is something that hovers between a man and the rest of the world: a mid-point between his view of himself and theirs of him—for each, of course, affects the other continually. A reciprocal fluxion, sir. There is nothing absolute about this identity of mine. Were you, you personally, to spend some days in Spain at present you would find yours change, you know, because of the general opinion there that you are a false harsh brutal murdering villain, an odious man."

"I dare say they are vexed," said Jack, smiling. "And I dare say they call me Beelzebub. But that won't make me Beelzebub."

"Does it not? Does it not? Ah?"

—*Patrick O'Brian,* Master and Commander

Introduction

Public self-reflection is a necessary (if unsettling) element of historical inquiry if we want it to be more than an antiquarian pursuit. So let me begin by sharing some autobiographical information with a bearing on this book. How does identity shape my own sense of self? I'll start by posing an old, and perhaps tiresome, question. What's in a name? In my case, Liam O'Boyle Patrick Riordan, there's quite a bit of Irishness wrapped up in self-understanding. My childhood memories are replete with public events where ethnicity mattered, like riding in the St. Patrick's Day parade with my father, who served on the local community college governing board, or hearing him give Robert Emmet's "Speech from the Dock" in Golden Gate Park at the annual celebration of the Irish martyr's death (for a photo of me there as a three-year-old, see the *San Francisco Examiner*, March 9, 1970). Later, my first semiprofessional public presentation as an undergraduate historian would come at the Irish Literary and Historical Society of San Francisco. Nevertheless, my sense of being Irish American was far from all consuming. Irish step dancing always struck me as weird. I never attended parochial schools, didn't live in an Irish American neighborhood, and have a strained sense of myself as a Catholic (note how ethnic and religious lines are difficult to untangle). Still, growing up in San Francisco made me very aware that a host of cultural identities (numerous Latino and Asian groups, gay and lesbian cultures, African American urban life, and more) shaped my world. Being Irish American and Roman Catholic gave some purchase, a helpful orientation, in negotiating daily life that in my fortunate case only very rarely imposed themselves as obligations or carried public penalties.

Imagine, then, my surprise when my Guatemala-born, California-raised, German-citizen sister-in-law informed me by chance that my brother did not consider himself to be Irish American! She thought he was in denial, and perhaps I did too, but I was wary about insisting on his proper group membership. If he was "just American," as he later told me, so be it. What, then, separated our self-understandings? I am two and a half years older, but otherwise we are remarkably close. The same parents raised us, we lived in the same household, we traveled together to Ireland twice, and we share professional commitments as teachers. Our main difference regarding ethnic self-identity, perhaps, is that he left the private high school we both attended to go to a public one where he met working-class Irish Americans who were a somewhat rough group. I suspect that these schoolmates gave Irishness a connotation that he wanted little part of, whereas my more sheltered path led to an easier and more genteel embrace of ethnicity.

Our divergent sensibilities resonate as a cautionary tale about casting historical judgment in the subtle arena of cultural identity. If my brother's sense of self surprises me, how can I be certain of how group identity operated in early America? The point is *not* to suggest that my personal experience allows direct access to the issues faced by my historical subjects. Archival research and a close reading of evidence produced in the period are the basis of my claim to any insight. Indeed, as an early American specialist, I am deeply aware of the distance that separates contemporary America from the Revolutionary period that I study. Nevertheless, the art and mystery of the historian's craft arise from exploring the fragile ties of continuity and rupture that bind past and present together. While the transformation of the Revolutionary Delaware Valley examined here is separated from us by two centuries, there are important elements of that world that deserve our careful attention. In particular the fluid processes through which cultural identities are formed and transformed in situational social contexts occurred along an erratic continuum from separatist particularism to assimilation with which we remain familiar today.

The main actors here inhabited a region comprised of eastern Pennsylvania, western New Jersey, and northern Delaware in the period from 1770 to 1830. The dynamism of the Revolutionary Delaware Valley's multicultural society has struck me as its most compelling feature, especially how religious, racial, and ethnic identities there combined, diverged, and infused the shifting popular culture of ordinary people during these decades of rapid change. The most prominent groups and their basic trajectories in this broad Revolutionary period can be quickly limned, but, as the bulk of what follows should plainly indicate, analyzing the oftentimes ambiguous and always contested processes of cultural change requires careful attention to detail in order to properly assess the subtleties of self-understanding and perception as they find public expression.

The most distinctive aspect of the colonial Delaware Valley, and perhaps the reason that it has often been treated as an exceptional place outside the mainstream of early American development, arises from the regional prominence of the Society of Friends. Quakers were a major political force there to the eve of independence and, along with appointed officials who were often Anglicans, fashioned a distinctive regional public culture. These religiously and ethnically Anglo groups occupied the conceptual and geographical center of power in the colonial Delaware Valley.[1] While these groups wielded considerable influence, their declining demographic presence and heated disagreements with each other undermined their hegemonic claims and assumptions. Large waves of immigration in the eighteenth century brought German speakers and Scots Irish people to the region, and the newcomers' primary settlement beyond older English areas made ethnic and religious identity an obvious fact of everyday life. The rapid expansion of colonial society in the Delaware Valley, as elsewhere, was an economic and geographic phenomenon, but it also included a vital cultural diversity that merits closer consideration.

The range of cultural groups in the eighteenth-century Delaware Valley will surprise those who think of early America as the province of Englishmen. As one leading historian has observed of the entire Mid-Atlantic, of which the Delaware Valley was a central component, "more than any other region of colonial British America, the Middle Colonies were a pluralistic society containing a large variety of linguistic, ethnic, and religious groups." However, the implications of this increasingly recognized "mélange of cultural configurations" remain dramatically understudied.[2]

We still know surprisingly little about the multicultural nature of eighteenth-century society in the Delaware Valley. The area's initial colonial settlement by Dutch, Swedes, and Finns; subsequent Anglo colonial policies (including a relatively open legal system, equitable access to land, and an active promotional campaign committed to religious liberty); and its bountiful agricultural potential combined to attract huge numbers of immigrants, who created a remarkably mixed landscape. An impressive scholarly literature about the Delaware Valley, and the Mid-Atlantic more broadly, has begun to question the enduring narratives of early America that place Massachusetts and Virginia at the center of our historical imagination of the early United States.[3] Traditionally, Puritan New England has been portrayed as America writ large, and, in a more compelling version, the black-white racial dualism of the Chesapeake has been deployed as the towering synecdoche of the American dilemma. These classic renderings of early American history gain influence by anticipating the sectional cleavage of the Civil War but wholly avoid the significance of cultural diversity in the large Mid-Atlantic region stretching from New York to Delaware. Cultural diversity powerfully shaped not just the Mid-Atlantic but also the heterogeneous societies of Rhode Island, Maryland, North Carolina, and the expanding frontier zone from Maine to Georgia. Most early Americans experienced cultural diversity as a regular feature of their lives. Close attention to this pluralistic social reality where no single group dominated may offer us a more usable past than the traditional origin myths of Puritan New England and the racialized slave societies of the Chesapeake.

The Delaware Valley's fluid multicultural social reality is recovered here through intense local scrutiny of the interaction of diverse individuals in three river towns—New Castle, Delaware; Burlington, New Jersey; and Easton, Pennsylvania.[4] These towns stand on distinct parts of a 130-mile run of the Delaware River (fig. 1), but several common characteristics make them appropriate for comparative treatment. They shared roughly equivalent size, ranging from about 350 to 3,500 inhabitants during the period under study. All had working waterfronts and shared similar economic functions as market centers at significant crossroads. Finally, each had similar political and judicial functions as seats of county government at the start of the period. In sum, these three modest places are representative of Philadelphia's small-town hinterland and mediated between the region's metropolitan center and the mass of rural people. Most importantly, these towns had decidedly mixed local populations. In Burlington, New Jersey, Quakers and Anglicans dominated local life. In New Castle, Delaware, Scots Irish Presbyterians competed with Anglicans for public leadership in a town with a large number of African Americans. Farther upriver at Easton, Pennsylvania, Native Americans shaped the eighteenth-century frontier town whose Pennsylvania German majority often seemed shockingly foreign to those at the Anglo center of the region. These three towns offer a microcosm of the Delaware Valley's cultural diversity, and the arguments made here would vary only in detail, but not in essential thrust, had different Delaware River towns been selected instead.

An early desire to understand the significance of religious buildings in each town and the people who worshiped in them was critical to deepening my sense of the striking local diversity of these places. Public space in each of them today remains anchored by churches used in the period under study. None possesses the more familiar landscape of New England with a central Congregational church to give the appearance of a homogenous community, nor do they have the characteristic Anglican crossroads church of the Chesapeake to serve as a focal point for people on scattered plantations. Instead, the built environment of the Delaware Valley foregrounds multiple religious communities (pointedly excluding Native Americans) with potentially competing claims as spiritual and social institutions. This focus led me to see that religion occupied a vital center of multiculturalism in the Revolutionary Delaware Valley.

Our first focused look at these towns deserves to begin with their religious buildings, for they can effectively introduce us to the region's diverse inhabitants. As early as 1700, the Dutch Reformed congregation in New Castle had joined with local Presbyterians, and seven years later the Dutch Reformed title to land and property was transferred to the Presbyterian congregation. The new church that they built on the site remains in use today (fig. 2).[5] Scots Irish respectability manifested itself in the maintenance of this church. Its three ministers from 1769 to 1824 were born in Ireland or were of Scots Irish descent and reflected a major ethnic strain in the congregation and local population. New Castle's Anglican church, also still in use today, although reconstructed after a devastating fire in 1980, was built as a modest Society for the Propagation of the Gospel

(SPG) mission in 1703 (fig. 3), but gained a far more imposing physical presence with the addition of an attractive tower and steeple in 1820 (fig. 4). The lack of surviving religious buildings from the period also raises an important issue. New Castle's active Union Church of Africans has no structure surviving from the period. Just as in Delaware's formal politics, where bitter disagreements between Presbyterians and Anglicans never disrupted their common belief that African Americans should be barred from a political voice, New Castle's surviving religious architecture from the Revolutionary era recalls only white religious groups and conceals the local prominence of blacks, who made up as much as a third of the town's population.

Burlington also has two surviving religious buildings used during the Revolutionary period. St. Mary's Anglican Church was a small SPG mission built on the same model as its counterpart in New Castle. Additions in 1769, 1811, and 1821 expanded the original squat structure, but even after those additions its proportions remained just 66 by 33 feet (fig. 5). In the mid-nineteenth century the congregation raised an impressive Romanesque church across the large lot from the original one and chose to preserve the old building. Members of the Society of Friends in Burlington replaced their unique seventeenth-century octagonal meetinghouse with a new two-story brick one in 1787 (fig. 6) that plainly displayed Quaker distinctiveness. Friends rejected the sacral power of a consecrated church in favor of a simple structure that lacked essential features in other Christian churches such as pulpits, altars, and steeples. Yet this understated building for silent worship was carefully constructed of fine material and rigorously maintained. As in so much Quaker material culture, it was "of the best sort but plain."[6]

The placement of religious buildings in these landscapes symbolized each group's relationship to colonial authority. The surviving religious buildings in Burlington and New Castle are located close to one another at the center of each town. In Burlington, the Quaker meetinghouse and Anglican church practically share rear burial grounds, as the street front religious buildings stood around the corner from one another at the town's central crossroads of High and Broad streets. In New Castle, they stand along the town commons close to the once-bustling waterfront. Tellingly of their difference in status, however, the Anglican church stands on the commons itself, while the Presbyterian church is across the street in a mixed residential-commercial row of buildings. Yet the German church in Easton, the town's only permanent structure for formal religious worship until 1818, was built just off the town's central square. Members of Easton's Lutheran and German Reformed confessions banded together in a manner typical of Pennsylvania Germans when they raised a shared "union church" in 1775, where both groups worshipped with separate ministers for the next six decades (fig. 7).

The displacement of the union church from Easton's focal point under-scores the outsider status of Pennsylvania Germans in the colonial period. Whereas in New Castle theological similarities hastened cooperation across ethnic lines between Dutch Reformed and Scots Irish Presbyterians at the start of the eighteenth century, in Easton ethnic bonds facilitated ties among Pennsylvania Germans with distinct theological traditions. Easton's Pennsylvania German union church could not occupy the town center, like its counterparts elsewhere, because the county courthouse had been built on that central site a decade earlier (fig. 11). Nevertheless, the German church was a large and impressive stone structure, enhanced by an imposing brick tower in 1832, which announced a far stronger public presence than that of the Union Church of Africans in New Castle, which, in turn, occupied more central space than displaced Native American spiritual traditions, which lacked any publicly acknowledged structures in these towns.

These varied religious buildings remind us in a very material way that taking the measure of cultural diversity in the Revolutionary Delaware Valley will require careful sifting of local evidence in order to describe that which groups in these towns had in common as well as how they moved in distinct ways. Whom did these structures represent? Did they point toward differences or similarities in the lives of people in each place? How did the locally grounded experiences of individual and group life symbolized by these institutions inform the Revolutionary transformation from outposts in a transatlantic empire to places in an independent nation? Did an emerging national identity reconcile, coerce, or ignore the ongoing traditions expressed by this religious architecture?

If geography—both the multicultural region and its specific expressions in each town—provides one critical axis of analysis, the other is chronology. Examining cultural diversity in the Delaware Valley is especially important in the era of rapid change inaugurated by the Revolutionary War. Although the war itself directly touched the Delaware Valley for a relatively short period from 1776 to 1778, the Revolution must be understood to extend beyond the war, and even beyond such famous postwar political events as Constitutional ratification and the election of Thomas Jefferson, if we are to understand its impact on ordinary people. The Revolution was inseparable from early national public life in these places.[7] The broad cultural transformation examined here did not occur as a result of singular events on precise dates as the traditions of military and political history have often led us to expect. People throughout the new nation experienced the local implications of the American Revolution over the course of several decades, which informed how they created a much more recognizably modern Jacksonian society starting in the 1820s. This expansive chronology leads to a mixed assessment of the interconnected achievements *and* limitations of Revolutionary change in the Delaware Valley, an important stance in trying to understand the Revolution's ongoing legacy for the United States.[8]

Group identity traversed an especially sensitive terrain as a result of the new nation's experiment with representative government. The American Revolution challenged individuals to decide how "the people" were to be understood within a framework of popular sovereignty and republican equality. How were both individual rights and social order to be secured in the Revolutionary nation? This tension has long been recognized as a fundamental question of the period and has received careful scholarly attention.[9] Based primarily on formal political sources, however, this distinguished literature does not reflect the transformation in early American scholarship wrought by social historians of the past generation. A notable gap separates social historians with their tendency to focus on the colonial period and ordinary people in specific places, from political historians of the Revolution and early republic who more often focus on leaders and institutions whose influence transcended particular localities.[10] This cultural history seeks to bridge that gap by applying some of the demographic techniques of the former approach to understand how politics reached local people and how they helped to shape the Revolutionary nation.

The implementation of popular sovereignty in the postwar period through the creation of a nonethnic "civic culture" of American nationalism and citizenship has been widely acknowledged. However, it has too rarely been noted that such an ideologically defined national identity responded to resurgent ethno-religious concerns.[11] National identity required a greater imaginative dimension in the United States than it had in any European polity, as in the United States national identity would always be distinct from ethnicity.[12] The new nation's potential instability encouraged the submersion of ethnic and religious differences in defining citizenship and heightened the salience of "whiteness" as a broadly shared identity for maintaining national order.[13]

Citizens in the Revolutionary nation faced troubling questions about social stability in their postcolonial and postmonarchical society. Sensitivity about the relationship between personal and national identity was particularly problematic in the culturally diverse Mid-Atlantic and received probing attention from its leading creative writers. Washington Irving, for example, created the persona of Diedrich Knickerbocker as the author-preserver of New York's Dutch culture, and his most famous character, Rip Van Winkle, "doubted his own identity, and whether he was himself or another man."[14] Similarly, the Pennsylvania author Hugh Henry Brackenridge's massive satire *Modern Chivalry* (1792–1815) created a lasting comic character in Teague O'Regan, an illiterate Irish immigrant whose ambitious opportunism led to political office. These characters' ethnic associations were critical to their resonance and drew upon widely shared values and opinions that are difficult to recover from the evidence typically given interpretive weight by social and political historians. Even more than Irving or Brackenridge, the Philadelphia-born Quaker Charles Brockden Brown cast unstable identity at the very heart of his work. As one recent critic noted, all Brown's novels "echoed with the crashes of shattering identity."[15] No resident of the towns studied here probably shared Brown's hypersensitivity to the instability of self, but they certainly understood that diverse identities shaped their lives in new ways as a result of the American Revolution. It is no coincidence that these leading Mid-Atlantic creative writers wrestled with the variability of personal identity in the Revolutionary nation.

The American Revolution sets this story in motion because it heightened people's awareness of the public consequences of personal identity. The region's multicultural demography was politicized in a mobilization for war that challenged established authority and contained distinct consequences for different groups. Anglican and Quaker political preeminence in the region was toppled, Pennsylvania Germans and Scots Irishmen were newly assertive, and African Americans seized upon the period's social turmoil and idealistic rhetoric to begin the process of successful emancipation. Perhaps the starkest transformation of group identity occurred for Native Americans, whose peripheral status in late colonial society plummeted to an even more complete exclusion from the nation.

These distinctive group engagements with the region's rapidly changing public culture should be understood as variants of a shared Revolutionary identity politics that arose during the war and that continued to influence public life in the Delaware Valley into the 1820s. In each case, group identity had new consequences as the Revolution dismantled the colonial order. The overlapping relationships among religion, race, and ethnicity reshaped one another throughout the broad Revolutionary period, and their renegotiation informed the national social order that gradually cohered in the region. The upsurge of group consciousness central to Revolutionary identity politics also inspired attempts to restrain the potentially destabilizing consequences of this politicization. The supple nature of these contests over group identity (fought by individuals *within* groups as much as between groups) rarely yielded absolute victors and vanquished, but from the mass of detailed local evidence produced in the struggles to articulate legitimate group claims, an overall pattern of assertion and resistance, followed by rejection and repression and then negotiation and accommodation, can be observed from 1770 to 1830. Placing the public struggles over the proper expression of group distinctiveness in the context of everyday life in three specific towns yields a new understanding of how cultural identification structured the emerging Jacksonian society of the 1820s as a culmination of the Delaware Valley's Revolutionary identity politics.

The examination of ethno-religious diversity in the Delaware Valley during the earliest years of nationhood reveals that a conflicted relationship between varied local identities and national unity has been at the heart of American public thought and social experience since the founding of the republic. Awareness of group distinctiveness has been a persistent feature in national characterization. Similar issues, of course, had also emerged in the colonial period, for colonization was fundamentally defined by the relocation of diverse groups into new settings. In fact, the creation of recognizably "ethnic" distinctions (often based in language, religion, and national origins) accelerated as a result of the colonial experience.[16] However, the rapid reformulation of group relations in the Revolutionary Delaware Valley makes close attention to cultural identity then and there especially fruitful. The changing places of three groups studied here are especially clear. Quakers were pushed from public office and often treated as un-American for refusing to join the patriot movement. Pennsylvania Germans secured a far more central place for themselves as American citizens than they had achieved as provincial British subjects. African Americans made similar claims to public legitimacy only to discover that the benefits of national unity would not include them.

The ways in which individuals took public action as members of self-consciously distinctive groups were extremely varied, and it is imperative that group relations not be treated as static or monolithic. Indeed, the situational variability of identity formation requires the painstaking comparative local methodology adopted here. Awareness of difference arises from specific cross-cultural encounters that are best interpreted with a close understanding of local context. The constructionist view of identities as fluid, situational, and dynamic has come to dominate most recent assessments of cultural identity and quite appropriately levels a searing critique of previous scholarly and popular assumptions that have tended to essentialize the nature of identity. While one must recognize volitional aspects of identities, they simultaneously take shape from a connection to the past and in relationship to external and structural forces that limit their possible forms of expression.[17]

The approach taken here emphasizes cultural identities as contingent historical constructions and aims to preserve the recognition of difference in the past while striving to avoid forcing those often fragile expressions to conform to my own preconceptions about how they should manifest themselves. I hope to do justice to the transcendent qualities of their particularity by considering several groups comparatively and to show how their multiplicity of interwoven experiences marked a constant struggle for mutual interaction. Moreover, my retelling of stories within stories about cultural diversity in the Revolutionary Delaware Valley strives to be a dialogue with people in the past who, like us, struggled to organize their heterogeneity into at least provisional unities that would permit a multicultural and non-exclusionary society. In our ongoing effort to reconcile diversity and unity we often still fail to recognize our high degree of commonality as individuals participating in shared processes of identity formation and assertion.[18]

One clear consequence of the close analysis of local diversity in the Revolutionary Delaware Valley has meant that ethnicity and religion must be assessed alongside European American, African American, and Native American "racial" identities. No study of early American cultural diversity could possibly be complete without considering groups understood to be nonwhite today. While Indians in the Pennsylvania backcountry suffered disastrous losses as a result of the Seven Years' War, and the region never became totally defined by slavery like places to the south, Native Americans and African Americans played critical roles in the Delaware Valley for specific local reasons as well as for important symbolic ones. The simultaneous analysis of these intertwined strands of cultural identity does not imply that white ethnicity and nonwhite racial identity were somehow equivalent. Categorization as black or Indian clearly marked an extreme form of difference and carried more severe social penalties in early America than various forms of white identity. However, to treat (white) ethnicity as wholly different from (black or Indian) racial identity only reinforces the notion of race as a fixed social category. By examining the varied ways that ethnic, religious, and racial identities shaped one another and the dynamic political culture of the Revolutionary Delaware Valley, we can better understand how racial identity's negative connotations became more fixed by the 1820s than they had been in the 1770s.[19] In short, this book seeks to explain how respectable, white, Protestantism came to present itself as normal—and with special claims to being American—by the 1820s.[20] Close scrutiny of specific individuals and groups in carefully bounded contexts reveals this claim to authority to have been more contested by varied local identities than we have recognized heretofore.

The tight focus here on individuals and events in three river towns owes an interpretive and methodological debt to the rich community-study literature that flourished for two decades starting in the 1970s.[21] Assessing multiple overlapping records together can yield a richly layered understanding of everyday life, and the demographic emphasis of community studies is essential for tracing the varied allegiances of individuals and families over time. However, social history, and especially its classic expression in the community-study monograph, has been under siege for some time. The inward gaze of such studies that often celebrate particularity, the growing specialization of academic discourse, and the theme of local diversity tied to social conflict have seemed to many to abandon the telling of a common story that can give clearer meaning to the past.[22]

Committing oneself to studying ordinary people in specific communities need not be the narrowly conceived project that such critics decry. A comparative approach can help avoid the insularity of a single community focus. Calibrating the experiences of individuals from three towns permits larger patterns to emerge and underscores that each town is studied not for its own sake, but to answer a more pressing question about the diversity of its inhabitants. How did individuals experience and understand cultural diversity in a period of nation building? Knowledge about the local context is not an end in itself: it provides the evidence to consider how multiculturalism and nationalism intersected in the Revolutionary Delaware Valley. While the developments in each town studied here may at times seem divergent, the comparative approach allows us to see how different people engaged a shared experience of negotiating their relationship with the new nation in distinct ways.

Historical ethnography provides a second methodological model essential to the interpretation of how personal identity arose from local difference.[23] Because ethnography has been most influential among scholars who examine contemporary societies (especially in the disciplines of anthropology, sociology, folklore, and cultural studies), doing research as an early American ethnographer requires modifying its participant-observer fieldwork method. Although documents and artifacts sometimes reveal the past with startling immediacy, more often their significance surfaces very slowly, and only the gradual compilation of varied evidence begins to point in directions that bear careful scrutiny.

This historical ethnography reconstructs local encounters of cultural difference from both quantitative and qualitative sources. Evidence for this analysis includes a database with more than four thousand individual entries compiled from tax, census, military, and church records from the late 1760s to the early 1830s. This data provides a demographic springboard for interpreting a wide range of material from personal manuscripts and newspapers to folk art, hymnals, clothing, and architecture. Nontraditional historical sources linked to popular culture often contain especially powerful expressions of cultural identity whose meanings take clearest shape when triangulated with other evidence. The attempt here is to illuminate a previous world of experience by assembling words, actions, images, sounds, objects, and built environments from three river towns. The ability of an outside observer to enter such places, interpret specific events, and recognize broader patterns stems from the fundamentally public nature of group identity in these encounters. As these were incidents that were shared at the time, a careful scholar can reasonably hope to recover some of their meanings.

The account that follows unfolds chronologically with an introduction to each town and essential information about colonial development in Chapter 1. The remaining six chapters can usefully be divided into two halves. Chapters 2 through 4 examine the upsurge of the region's conflicted Revolutionary identity politics, first in the war itself and then in postwar political and religious life. At the center of the region's Revolutionary identity politics lay a dramatic expansion of what counted as public and political. From Quaker calls for the non-payment of taxes, to the Pennsylvania German Fries Rebellion, to the formation of the Union Church of Africans, group identity had dramatic consequences for how people understood themselves and their relationship to Revolutionary society. At no time, however, did all members of any one group act with absolute uniformity. Ambiguity and conflict coursed within these groups, and the labels of group identity were used in pejorative ways at least as often as they were employed in a self-affirming manner. Awareness of both the liberating and the repressive potential of identity politics informs this analysis.

The second half of the book explores varied responses to the heightened cultural particularism sparked by the Revolutionary War. The most successful forces that responded to Revolutionary identity politics, and that in many ways borrowed from it, were cosmopolitan evangelicalism and partisan politics, considered in Chapters 5 and 6, respectively. Both these key thrusts of early national public action struggled to reshape the Delaware Valley's resurgent local diversity into American unity. The unheralded persistence of Protestant social reform and permanent political parties, both quite novel in the early nineteenth century, marks an important moment of resistance to and accommodation with the teeming local diversity of the Revolutionary Delaware Valley. Although leaders of the evangelical and partisan movements were often deeply suspicious of one another, both championed the ideal of a unified and strengthened nation under their guidance and depended for their success upon massive grassroots mobilization and firm local allegiances. The gradual growth of national society that they helped to foster never destroyed local diversity, but it did stimulate new commitments in everyday group life by the 1810s and 1820s that are considered in Chapter 7. In sum, this study uncovers how religious, racial, and ethnic expressions gained heightened public significance in the Delaware Valley during the Revolutionary War, shaped public life there in the early national period, and helped form Jacksonian society. This account revisits some of the central concerns of the ethnocultural interpretation of electoral politics, but does so from a local ethnographic perspective that connects the party formation of the 1820s to developments set in motion by the war for independence.[24]

The multiethnic, multiracial, multireligious, and multilingual character of the Revolutionary Delaware Valley suggests that it can provide a useful foil for reconsidering recent largely polemical assertions about multiculturalism in the contemporary United States.[25] Some readers may be unsettled by the idea that multiculturalism could provide a useful interpretive framework for examining early America, but it is imperative to move beyond superficial connotations of that term, one of the most debilitating of which assumes that controversial public awareness about group identity has primarily been a recent phenomenon.[26] Describing the Revolutionary Delaware Valley as a multicultural region highlights that religious, racial, and ethnic identities were widely recognized at the time as having significant social consequences. This subject demands attention precisely because disagreement still rages over how best to reconcile distinctive group identities with national unity. A historical perspective on multiculturalism is essential not only to properly locate cultural diversity as a central theme in American history but also to demonstrate how the politicization of group identity has changed over time. The rich interaction between group identity and cultural diversity needs to be understood not merely as a contemporary "problem," but as a constitutive feature of the societies created from the massive transatlantic migrations that inaugurated the modern world.[27]

We still need studies that focus on lawyers in the courthouse, politicians in the statehouse, and merchants in the counting house. Still more, we need to learn about midwives at a neighbor's house, slave life behind the great house, paupers fleeing the poorhouse, and Iroquois meetings in the longhouse, but this book does not follow those lines of inquiry. Instead, it attempts to unite those sensible divisions to analyze a general transformation in public life during the broad Revolutionary era by following the paths taken by diverse people in three Delaware River towns. Only when a range of overlapping human relationships are understood in their local context can we begin to grasp how power operated and changed in a given society. Awareness of difference represents a fundamental matter of human concern that has increasingly moved along a distinctive trajectory in the modern era. By closely studying individual experiences in a multicultural context, I hope to further our understanding of how certain cultural forms became privileged categories in the creation of the United States.

Figure 1. The Delaware River, today the longest undammed waterway east of the Mississippi, hosted a major area of European colonization. The river integrated the region, and its abundant resources helped Philadelphia to become the largest and wealthiest city in eighteenth-century British North America. The three county seats at the center of this study, each from a different state and a distinct ecological niche along a 130-mile run of the river, are representative of the metropolis's small-town hinterland. Most importantly, studying the diverse inhabitants of each town allows us to recapture the vibrant multiculturalism of the Revolutionary Delaware Valley.

Map by Mike Hermann, UMaine Canadian-American Center Cartography.

Figure 2. Although the rise of Philadelphia anchored Anglo legal and political power in the region, the English were European latecomers to the Delaware Valley. A closer look at the religious landscape of the three river towns studied here demonstrates the multiple cultures that shaped everyday life in each of them. This Presbyterian church in New Castle, Delaware (with later cupola and altered façade), was built in 1707 on the site of an earlier Dutch Reformed church. The initial Dutch presence in the town would persist in elements of local buildings and in the names of old families, yet this structure also symbolizes an importance syncretization of Dutch and Scots Irish Calvinism. By the Revolutionary period, the ministers and congregation here, as well as the population of New Castle County more broadly, had a strong Scots Irish presence.

Presbyterian church, originally built 1707, New Castle. Photograph (1982), Historic American Buildings Survey, DEL, 2-NEWCA, 4-9, Library of Congress.

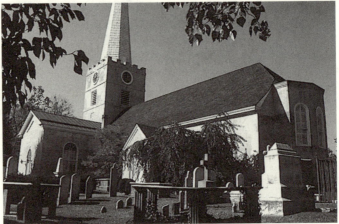

Figures 3 and 4. This Anglican church in New Castle was built in 1703 by the London-based Society for the Propagation of the Gospel (SPG) and sought to counter the rapid growth of Quaker and other religious sects in the region. The building retained a modest physical presence into the nineteenth century, as the 1805 watercolor makes clear (fig. 3, top), although it stood prominently on the commons at the center of town. The Anglican Church was an influential anglicizing force in the colonies, and its conservative Anglo associations were often contrasted with radical Scots Irish Presbyterianism in the Delaware Valley's Revolutionary identity politics. The addition of a clock tower and steeple (fig. 4, bottom), designed by the noted architect William Strickland, reoriented the church in the early 1820s to assert the respectability and prominence of Episcopalians in early national society. The often charged political connotations of Presbyterian and Episcopalian ethnic and religious identities occurred in a town that was about one-third African American. Slavery's power to deny public legitimacy to those it enslaved prevented this important group from being memorialized in the local religious landscape (but see figs. 20–21).

Figure 3: Immanuel Episcopal Church, originally built 1703, New Castle. Watercolor by Benjamin Henry Latrobe (1805). Courtesy of Delaware State Archives, Dover, Delaware. Figure 4: Immanuel Episcopal Church, tower added 1820, New Castle. Photograph by author.

Figures 5 and 6. Moving upriver, passing Philadelphia, and crossing to the opposite bank, we come to Burlington, New Jersey. The Anglican church (fig. 5, top), built in 1703 on the same SPG plan as its counterpart in New Castle, was an essential feature of a well-constituted English colonial capital. Local affluence supported several additions, culminating in the 1834 cruciform plan seen here. This church conveyed a wholly different public message from that of the nearby meetinghouse of the Society of Friends (fig. 6, bottom). This houselike religious building replaced the town's late seventeenth-century Friends' meetinghouse in 1787. The radical theology of Quakers demanded a distinctive way of walking in the world that departed from most other early American Christian groups. Although persecuted as outsiders in England, Quakers were the most influential charter group of English colonization in the Delaware Valley. West Jersey Quakers were especially prominent, and the Friends' Yearly Meeting in the region alternated annually between Burlington and Philadelphia until 1760.

Figure 5: Old St. Mary's Episcopal Church, originally built 1703, Burlington. Photograph (1936), Historic American Buildings Survey, NJ, 3-BURL, 1-6, Library of Congress. Figure 6: Society of Friends' meetinghouse, originally built 1787, Burlington. Lithograph by John Collins (1847). Courtesy American Antiquarian Society.

Figure 7. Heading upriver once more, over the falls at Trenton and into the rolling hills of the piedmont, we find Easton, Pennsylvania, which was settled by Europeans at least a century after the older colonial towns on the coastal plain. This large limestone structure (all the other religious buildings used more refined brick) was built in 1775 to be shared by the local Lutheran and German Reformed congregations. Such "union churches" of the *kirchenleute* (church Germans, as opposed to the less numerous German sects such as the Moravians and Amish) were found throughout the large zone of Pennsylvania German settlement that arced from northern New Jersey through Pennsylvania and into the Maryland and Virginia backcountries. This union church hosted the town's last Indian treaty conference in 1777 and marks the critical location of Pennsylvania Germans as ethno-religious outsiders on the Indian frontier of an English colony with a strong pacifist tradition. The people who worshiped here would forge a more central public place for themselves in the Revolutionary transition from subjects to citizens, symbolized by the partly visible 1832 addition of a large brick tower and steeple, akin to the similar national form of the tower and steeple in Figure 4.

Lutheran and German Reformed union church, originally built 1775, Easton. Photograph by author.

Figure 8. This 1797 view of the New Castle waterfront hints at the major role that maritime commerce played in this port town. Local merchants were among the colony's wealthiest men, but their affluence rested upon the labor of common seamen and dockworkers whose perspectives are much more difficult to recover. The town had an important role as a provisioning stop for outbound ships, and its saltwater port stayed ice free year-round. As a commercial and transportation nexus in the age of sail, New Castle was open to the diverse movement of people and goods throughout the Atlantic world and had especially strong trade connections with the West Indies and Ireland.

Watercolor by Yves Le Blanc (1797). Courtesy of private collector and Historical Society of Delaware.

Figure 9. These adjacent runaway advertisements from a 1787 Delaware newspaper dramatically reveal one way that New Castle's transatlantic setting was manifested in local demography. The iconic quality of these parallel images saps the individual humanity of the property that they seek to recover and provokes us to consider how Irish indentured servants and African slaves were understood to be more similar to one another in the late eighteenth century than our later racial consciousness allows.

Delaware Gazette (October 10, 1787), full page and detail. Courtesy of American Antiquarian Society.

Figure 10. This Burlington street plan from 1797, with its elegant residential water-front depicted in the lower inset, reinforces our sense of the town's affluence. It may have been the most prosperous township in the entire Mid-Atlantic. Such wealth, in consort with strong Quaker and Anglican traditions, made neutrality and loyalism in the Revolution especially strong here. During the war, British forces spared the town, while patriots cannonaded it from the river. Quakers and Anglicans both faced significant hurdles in regaining a prominent place in the Revolutionary nation. Although unable to compete successfully in early national electoral politics, Burlington residents would play a major role in cosmopolitan moral reform.

Engraving by William Birch (1797). Courtesy of Historic Urban Plans.

Figure 11. This 1798 woodcut of Easton's central crossroads reveals an important contrast between cosmopolitan and local sensibilities. As they did in other rural county seats, the Pennsylvania proprietors built the Georgian-style courthouse in the town's main square in 1765 to demonstrate Anglo legal, political, and cultural authority. It continued to outshine the town's more modest vernacular structures at the end of the century, which include notable Pennsylvania German building traditions such as the half-timbered structure in the distant center and, in the left foreground, a log building with horizontal stripes of whitewashed mortar. Even the large union church (fig. 7), built on land granted by the proprietors *off* the central square, lacked the genteel elegance of Anglo-American respectability conveyed by the courthouse. The article that accompanied this image emphasized that the town's "chiefly German" inhabitants had already begun to transform "the gloomy haunts of the rude savage indian."

Woodcut from *Philadelphia Monthly Magazine* (1798). Courtesy of Rare Book and Manuscript Library, University of Pennsylvania.

Chapter 1

The Importance of Place:
Cultural Diversity in Three River Towns

The Delaware River was the region's central corridor and integrated its three colonies and their inhabitants in numerous ways. While the river helped to connect the people along its banks, the three river towns scrutinized here also reveal important differences. The distances between them along a 130-mile run of the river meant that the local character of each town built upon distinct economic, demographic, and environmental conditions. The active seafaring economy of New Castle, Delaware, drew a heady laboring population of African Americans and Irishmen. Burlington was the most refined of the three towns, and its Quaker and Anglican leaders profited from easy access to nearby Philadelphia and rich New Jersey farmland. Unlike the older settlements on the lower river that were both colonial capitals, Easton, Pennsylvania, still faced frontier conditions in the late eighteenth century, and the classic colonial encounter there usually occurred between Native Americans and German speakers. Public life and politics in the colonial Delaware Valley were too multifaceted to be reduced to a simple logic of tripartite racial categories that supposedly separated whites, blacks, and native peoples into distinct and isolated groups. Instead, intersecting lines of religious, racial, and ethnic identity shaped how people understood themselves and their world. African Americans in New Castle provide strong evidence about black racial identity and its relationship to low-status Irishmen. Quakers in Burlington demonstrate the importance of religion as a category of profound difference that caused deep divisions among Protestants in early America. The strength of Pennsylvania German settlement in Easton showcases the cogency of ethnic identity in the Delaware Valley.

This chapter introduces the reader to the diverse local character of each town and puts this definitive quality into motion by examining some of the critical interrelationships among these groups during the Seven Years' War. Examining how this war mobilized people reveals the salience of religious and ethnic identity, including such differences among Indians, in the multicultural Delaware Valley. Traditional historical accounts have often emphasized a close relationship between the Seven Years' War and the American Revolution, a connection also found here from the perspective of war's profound impact upon personal and group identity.

A Journey Upriver: Meeting the People in Three River Towns

Our introduction to the cultural diversity of the Delaware Valley begins with a trip up the river and a visit to each town. The Delaware River is among the eastern seaboard's largest waterways, and it hosted one of the major settlement regions in colonial British America. The river's course is most easily visualized as the political boundary that separates Pennsylvania and New Jersey. While its headwaters lie far into New York, the main river runs 330 miles to Delaware Bay and includes a watershed of nearly 13,500 miles. Taking a journey upriver, New Castle, on the western shore, will be our first stop. Although it lies well inside the long funnel shape of Delaware Bay, looking out from New Castle, one still senses the ocean in the expanse of water that all but fills the horizon. Continuing north past Philadelphia to Burlington, on the eastern shore, the river has narrowed considerably but remains affected by ocean tides, and it was still too broad to be bridged during the period under study. Easton lies considerably farther upriver at the confluence with the Lehigh River, the Delaware's second largest tributary (after the Schuylkill River at Philadelphia), which gave rise to the identification of the immediate area as the "Forks of the Delaware." These locations represent a broad range of eighteenth-century settlement in the Delaware Valley. The varied physical setting of each place contributed to their significant differences, most importantly in the varied people who settled them.

The European founding of each town reveals some of their distinctiveness from one another and reinforces the close relationship between local experience and geographic setting.[1] New Castle's strategic location for the fur trade attracted Swedes, who negotiated with local Indians to purchase a large part of the shoreline in the 1630s, and by 1651 the Dutch had built a military fortification there.[2] Because its saltwater port remained open year-round without freezing, it developed an important commercial function. In the prerailroad era it enjoyed a privileged location as a transportation hub on the fastest north-south coastal route with packet ships on the Delaware and Chesapeake rivers and a rapid land crossing from New Castle to the head of the Elk River in Maryland.[3] Goods and people easily moved from New Castle throughout Delaware, Maryland, and southeastern Pennsylvania. This early settlement and strategic location helped it to serve as Delaware's capital throughout the English colonial period that began in 1664.

New Castle and Burlington were both official colonial ports with royal customs houses, with the Delaware town considerably more active. New Castle's official maritime activity in 1772 included forty-four topsail ships and forty-six sloops that brought 4,363 tons of goods over its docks, while Burlington was visited by only four of the larger topsail ships and eighteen sloops, which altogether transported just 785 tons that year. Trade in both places was dwarfed, of course, by Philadelphia's massive commercial activity, which moved more than 88,000 tons. Although somewhat on the small side, trade in New Castle approached the median for North American ports and was typical, even robust, when compared to more southerly ones.[4] Moreover, these imperial statistics missed the less dramatic local trade and provisioning that were essential to New Castle.

A painting of the New Castle waterfront from 1797 suggests the vibrancy of the small working port (fig. 8). It depicts two piers extending into the river with barrels and wood piled high, and the provisioning house behind them advertised goods for sale on a large sign meant to be read from the water. The image presents a vigorous local economy, with ships in motion and wharves and warehouses filled with goods. New Castle served as the final supply stop for many vessels departing the Delaware River. As one traveler noted, ships leaving Philadelphia generally sailed to New Castle, where they "take in their poultry and vegetables" while waiting for good wind and tide conditions to depart on long journeys.[5] The town's role as a provisioning port supplying thirsty seamen and travelers presumably explains why New Castle imported an enormous amount of Caribbean rum, nearly 140,000 gallons in 1772, almost one-fifth as much as the Philadelphia metropolis, but for a town with just 262 taxpayers.[6]

The West Indies was the Delaware Valley's most important trading region, and twenty-three of twenty-four export ships from New Castle sailed there in 1772. Edible commodities, especially Indian corn, bread, flour, and pickled fish, represented the town's most important exports.[7] The tremendous economic success of all the Mid-Atlantic colonies depended on overseas demand for food, an essential component in the transatlantic economy of the early modern era. On the eve of the Revolution, an active trade had linked the West Indies and the Delaware Valley for almost a century, and New Castle had long been among the multitude of small ports in the vast Atlantic system.[8]

New Castle's active waterfront hosted a large transitory population of working seamen and dockhands that gave the town a rough-and-tumble character. The traveler Benjamin Latrobe described it as "the *Gravesend* of Philadelphia," an unattractive place with "the usual conveniences for the accommodation of seafaring men . . . in plenty and of the coarsest sort. And as a *little* country town it has all the petty scandal, curiosity, envy and hatred which distinguishes little towns all over the world." Not surprisingly, he hoped to escape the dingy port as quickly as possible. "I will not stay a moment longer in the place than I can help."[9]

As a busy port town, New Castle teemed with transient seamen looking for work on outward-bound ships. In a sample of five hundred sailors who registered for citizenship certificates in Philadelphia from 1798 to 1816, eleven identified New Castle as their place of birth, a strikingly high rate for a small corner of the Delaware Valley. Among them was Edmond Morris, a free African American, who was one of the throng of lower-sort sailors whose boisterous presence helped shape the town's character.[10] While New Castle and Burlington shared a great deal as old colonial capitals with transatlantic ports, New Castle and Easton both had large laboring groups that genteel Burlington could often hide.

New Castle also occupied a critical transition zone that separated the predominant indentured and wage-labor system of the eighteenth-century Mid-Atlantic from the slave-labor system of the Chesapeake. As a result, northern Delaware had a considerably larger African American presence than most other parts of the Delaware Valley. Few Euro-American colonists in New Castle showed any scruples about exploiting human bondage, and enslaved people were present in the colony as early as 1639. Delaware's black presence has been estimated at 20 percent of its overall colonial population, and in spite of a sharp increase in the direct importation of enslaved Africans into the region from 1759 to 1765, most blacks in the Delaware Valley by the late eighteenth century had been born in the New World.[11]

Some blacks with personal knowledge of Africa did still live around New Castle in the 1770s. Attachment to the Old World apparently inspired at least one runaway to resist slavery. Congamochu had lived to adulthood in Africa, and his owner described him as having "many large scars on his belly and arms in his country fashion, talks very bad English, [and] has a hole through one of his ears." Commenting on the man's motivations for fleeing, the owner noted that he "was seen at the river shore, near New Castle, the day after he went off," and "as he talked much of his wives, and country, it is thought he will endeavor to get off by water."[12] Such intense attachments to African homelands are difficult to trace in the surviving historical record, but there seems little doubt that the upsurge in public black self-identification as "African" after the Revolutionary War drew upon the memories and traditions kept alive by individuals like Congamochu.

African Americans were one of the largest groups in New Castle, composing 23 percent of the local population in 1800, the earliest year for which detailed local data survives. New Castle Town and Hundred had a total population of 2,438 that year, 555 of whom were African American, and of these 58 percent were free.[13] Nearly one-fourth of New Castle residents were black at the close of the eighteenth century, and their influence on everyday life, with a presence in 150 out of 304 households, was even more profound. Although the majority of local African Americans were free by 1800 according to the census, slavery remained widespread there, with 51 percent of the households with black residents including enslaved people.

Rigid racial segregation was a practical impossibility in a small town like New Castle, where fifty-two local households included both whites and free blacks in 1800. Moreover, skin color and slave status had come unhinged in twenty-nine white-headed households that included both slaves and free blacks. The manuscript census records list each household as the enumerator walked up and down the town's streets, and African Americans clearly lived in every section and on every street. Only once among 304 households did seven residential units appear in a row without a black inhabitant. In contrast to African Americans' dispersal throughout New Castle, however, independent free black households established themselves in close proximity to one another. Nearly half of the exclusively free black households (ten out of twenty-one) were grouped together among thirty-five dwellings, and only one appears in the list more than seven entries away from another free black household.

Three sequential dwellings within the most concentrated free black area of town exemplify the complexity of local domestic life. What did it mean for the three slaves living in Cornelius Hensey's "white" household to know that James Champon's ten-person household and James Davis's four-person one on either side of them were entirely composed of free blacks? Even more puzzling was the separate household of "Moses & Abraham" who shared the same dwelling with the free-black household head James Davis. Although Old Testament names and identification without a surname are classic African American features in early American life, Moses and Abraham were listed in the census as free white men between the ages of twenty-six and forty-five. Were they possibly mixed-race people for whom the census had no category? Did they have a family connection to another neighbor, Abraham Spencer, who headed a free-black household of eight persons? The life histories of Abraham and Moses cannot be reconstructed beyond their sparse census entries, but these free whites exemplify how everyday life regularly transgressed simplistic group boundaries, such as those employed in the census, that attempted to set white and black fundamentally apart.

The majority of blacks in New Castle had attained free status by 1800, but they experienced freedom in a state where slavery would remain legal until the resolution of the Civil War. Indeed, 254 slaves still lived in New Castle County as late as 1860. Notwithstanding the persistence of slavery in Delaware, the 1790s marked a crucial transition in slave status in this northernmost third of the state. In that decade the slave population declined in New Castle County by 28 percent, and the free black population soared by 331 percent. Whereas 80 percent of blacks in New Castle County had been slaves in 1790, 60 percent were free by 1800. Although local census data does not survive to identify the precise situation for New Castle Hundred in 1790, it seems certain that local changes mirrored those in the surrounding county.[14] As local African Americans increasingly became free after the Revolutionary War, all New Castle residents faced a profound transformation in the meaning of racial identity.

The African American presence in New Castle decisively distinguished it from Burlington and Easton. Largely as a result of the oppression that blacks suffered in early America, they formed strong communal bonds that encouraged close cooperation through a widespread, if largely informal and necessarily secretive, social network that connected blacks in New Castle to urban black communities in nearby Wilmington and Philadelphia. Sam, for example, who was owned by the prominent New Castle resident Gunning Bedford, reportedly fled to Philadelphia in the company of a Wilmington slave in 1782.[15] When Philadelphia's free black population boomed after the Revolutionary War, former Delaware slaves contributed notably to the creation of public African American institutions there.[16] Ironically, the regular use of violence essential to the maintenance of slavery simultaneously stimulated a powerful sense of group identity for African Americans that would play a critical role in their attempt to achieve equality in an increasingly race-conscious society in the postwar Revolutionary nation.

While racial difference grew increasingly important throughout the colonial period, a fixed demarcation of black and white as inalienably different had not been established in the late eighteenth century Delaware Valley. Groups of runaways who fled conditions of extreme inequality, for example, sometimes transcended racial boundaries, as when two slaves and a white apprentice escaped from New Castle's jail together in 1799. The jailer suspected that all three were headed toward the home of the apprentice's mother.[17] Although interracial alliances probably were quite fragile, the powerful logic of race that would come to dominance in the nineteenth century (and that persists to the present) should not obscure our ability to recognize that low status often connected black and white individuals, especially in a place like New Castle, with its large population of mixed-race maritime workers and at a time when most local African Americans were rapidly changing status from slave to free.

The possibilities for cross-racial cooperation in New Castle were enhanced by the ethnic identity of many low-status whites there. About half of all Scots Irish immigrants arriving in the Delaware Valley before 1763 first set foot at New Castle, and about two-thirds of them arrived as indentured servants.[18] While a large black population distinguished New Castle from most other Delaware Valley towns of the period, its significant Scots Irish presence (like that of New Castle County more generally) separated it from the overwhelmingly English ancestry of whites in Delaware's two more southerly counties. As the leading historian of early Delaware has noted, by the 1760s "New Castle County had taken on a distinct Scotch-Irish tint."[19] Meanwhile, German-speaking immigrants, who arrived in the region in far greater numbers than the Scots Irish, were prohibited from disembarking at New Castle because immigrants from central Europe had to register and swear an oath of allegiance to the king and to the proprietor in Philadelphia. An unintended consequence of this policy would give downriver New Castle a strong Scots Irish presence and upriver Easton an overwhelmingly German one.

The connections and differences among the Irish, Scots, and Scots Irish in early America make this an especially complex expression of cultural identity. While Presbyterianism often became a powerful unifying force for them in the New World and has led many scholars to use the terms interchangeably, these three labels could also invoke different experiences with divergent social consequences. In this work *Scots Irish* refers to individuals whose Irish or Scottish family traditions combined with Presbyterianism to become a rallying point for self-understanding and group consciousness. Yet, of all the cultural groups examined here, this one commanded the least effective degree of group conformity.[20] Thus we shall find an especially high degree of variation among Scots Irish individuals in the Revolutionary Delaware Valley.

Being identified as "Irish" usually carried decisively negative connotations of boorish and violent behavior in early America. As the most careful recent scholar of Ulster Scots has noted, to many contemporaries in colonial America they were the period's "sordid refuse," and they suffered from the most consistently negative stereotyping of any "white" ethnoreligious group in the Delaware Valley.[21] Given these hostile associations, it is important to recall that Irishness in this period primarily referred to Presbyterians, rather than the more familiar anti-Catholic animus that it would assume by the 1830s.

This pejorative dimension of Irishness often meant that it was explained in relationship to blackness. Although being Irish obviously carried less stigma and had more benign social consequences than being black, we can benefit from considering the two groups in comparison to one another, especially in a place like New Castle, where the two groups lived together closely in large numbers. Take, for example, a joke repeated in a Delaware newspaper about an "Irish gentlemen" landing in Jamaica who was confronted on the quay by "a negro, who, from his intimacy with the Irish, had acquired a perfect familiarity of their language, in which he accordingly addressed the stranger." Stunned by this Irish-speaking "sooty visage," the newcomer retreated to the boat and "declared his intention 'not to stay in that d——d place, where all his *countrymen* turned *blacks*.'" The experience supposedly led the Irishman to permanently settle in London "through the apprehension that he should have turned black in Jamaica."[22] The joke may have turned on the absurdity of Irishmen becoming black, yet it also highlighted the labile nature of cultural identity as defined by malleable material such as language.

The close connection between low-status Irishmen and African Americans forcefully appeared in a pair of runaway advertisements printed in the *Delaware Gazette*. Adam Caldwell of New Castle reported in one of them that Michael Devin had fled from him shortly after having arrived by ship from Derry, in northern Ireland, while a second advertisement offered a five-pound reward for the capture of "Negroman Ned" who had been on the run for more than three months. The crude images that accompanied each advertisement demonstrate how those with unfree status were linked in the public mind (fig. 9).[23] The stock visual representations of each runaway identified them with different key symbols, the Irishman in a distinctive hat with shillelagh and the African in loincloth with staff. The quotidian nature of group representations like these reflected and reinforced the widespread linking of low-status blackness and Irishness in the Delaware Valley. Unraveling how individual African Americans and Scots Irishmen transgressed and reinforced racial and ethnic boundaries in a period that witnessed the local collapse of slavery and indentured servitude is a central challenge for understanding cultural diversity in New Castle.

Although public identification as Irish implied a low social assessment, many Scots Irish individuals attained leading places in the colonial Delaware Valley.[24] Two Anglo leaders in New Castle who left the limitations of their Irish origins behind them demonstrate the complex biographical patterns that underlie the politics of group identity. George Ross, the original Anglican missionary at New Castle, who led the church for more than fifty years, had been born in Scotland and attended the University of Edinburgh, where he trained as a Presbyterian minister. Ross, however, disliked the established Presbyterian Church of Scotland and at the end of his training visited London, where he was soon ordained as an Anglican, much to the shock of Presbyterian leaders in Edinburgh.[25]

Another conservative Anglo leader in New Castle with Irish family roots was George Read Sr. His father had been a wealthy Dubliner before immigrating to Maryland and had had his eldest son educated at the academy run by the Presbyterian minister Francis Alison in New London, Pennsylvania. After training as a lawyer in Philadelphia, Read settled in New Castle and later married Gertrude Til Ross, the Anglican missionary's daughter. Despite the Scottish and Irish backgrounds of these leading New Castle families and their early associations with Presbyterianism, at the point that our narrative begins they were Anglo cultural leaders and prominent Anglicans.

Anglo refers here to people who centrally identified with English culture, often with ties to the Anglican Church; political influence derived from English authority, especially proprietary power; or the cultural superiority widely associated with Britain in the eighteenth century. As evident for Ross and Read, being Anglo was not strictly a matter of geographical or genealogical origins. Rather, the term refers to values that could be particularly useful in seeking or maintaining social ascendance in a colonial society where select English norms informed influential British ways. The leading political, religious, and social roles of Ross and Read in New Castle highlight an important difference between the Scots Irish and Pennsylvania German groups in the late colonial Delaware Valley. The Old World position of the Scots Irish as Britons assisted many of them in becoming colonial leaders much more rapidly than German-speaking immigrants to the British New World. Such personal achievement often included a transition from a primary identification as Scots Irish and Presbyterian to a more assimilated Anglo sense of self. Indeed, one of the great puzzles of the American Revolution is that it occurred in a colonial society that for the better part of a century had been becoming more like Britain in terms of its politics, commerce, and law—a process often referred to as Anglicization.

The cultural distinctions among Britons in New Castle were especially clear in its local religious character. Aeneas Ross, the son of the local Anglican church's founding missionary, was about to enter the third decade of his rectorship there when the Revolution challenged some of the most fundamental practices of his faith. Ross's Presbyterian counterpart, Joseph Montgomery, was the son of Irish immigrants and served as the town's Presbyterian minister from 1769 to 1777.[26] As Presbyterians achieved greater public prominence during and following the Revolutionary War, the religious affiliation of New Castle's wealthiest residents became increasingly Presbyterian, while the late colonial predominance of Anglicans at the top of the social order precipitously declined. It is not necessary to insist on precise correlations when observing that Presbyterianism was closely linked to the Scots Irish and Anglicanism strongly associated with Englishness here. As we shall see in the next chapter, the Scots Irish in Delaware, and Reverend Montgomery in particular, were at the forefront of the radical patriot movement in the region, while Anglican ministers proved more hesitant to sunder the empire.

New Castle thus had sharply bifurcated qualities. It was a rowdy place of seafaring laborers whose ethnic and racial identities often reinforced their low social status. Their toil helped to enrich a small group of elites who dominated the formal politics of the town and colony. In addition to political and legal institutions, the Anglican Church played a major role in the self-understanding and public presentation of this leadership group. Yet, the Englishness at the center of elite Anglo culture was itself fractured by internal difference. While the Church of England might claim official preeminence, a connection that Anglican proprietors especially stressed, Quakers made an effective bid to be the Delaware Valley's normative expression of Englishness throughout the colonial period.

Taking leave of New Castle and heading north on the river for fifty miles, one passes Philadelphia and crosses the river to reach Burlington,

New Jersey. The town's Quaker founders arrived in the Delaware Valley before the establishment of William Penn's colony and capital city. As at New
Castle, other Europeans preceded the English at Burlington, and a small
Dutch settlement, begun in 1624 on an Indian route useful for trade, remained to greet the English Friends who arrived in 1677 and 1678.[27]
While these Quakers might appear as a clearly demarcated ethnic and religious group, they had a different sense of their most prominent group
identities. Two separate groups of Quakers founded the town, and Yorkshire and London Friends carefully distinguished how they took possession of the land. The two groups had initially planned to settle separate
communities apart from one another, but, as a descendent of one founder
explained, "being few and the Indians numerous," they chose to cooperate more closely. Yorkshire Friends settled on town lots along the eastern,
or upriver, side of central High Street, while London Friends established
urban residences on the western side.[28] These distinctions among Burlington's English Quakers soon faded. From the outset of the colonial venture,
New World conditions spurred a rearrangement of group boundaries.
Nevertheless, the difference between the two founding groups in local
place names persisted into the nineteenth century, with the Yorkshire
Bridge on the eastern road out of town and the London Bridge on the
western one.

Burlington was the seat of the Quaker West Jersey proprietors, and the
Delaware Valley's Yearly Meeting of the Society of Friends first met in
Burlington and then rotated annually between here and Philadelphia
until 1760. Although religious variety among Protestants is often muted in
contemporary thinking about multiculturalism, Quaker distinctiveness
was a prominent and unmistakable feature of early American society. The
religious beliefs and social practices of the Society of Friends placed them
on a far margin of Christianity in the early modern world. Born of social
and religious upheaval in northwestern England starting in the 1640s,
Quakers' principal values and practices derive from the central tenet that
a divine spark of Christ resides within every individual as an "inward light"
that must be cultivated as the ultimate authority for human behavior.
From this core belief a number of key Quaker practices followed, especially religious meetings as silent worship without an ordained minister
where both men and women could be moved to speak with equal spiritual
legitimacy. Female religious authority among Friends was only the most
heterodox of numerous social practices—like nonviolence—that highlighted Quaker distance from more mainstream group values in early
America.[29]

While commitment to the inward light of Christ threatened to spawn
anarchistic individualism among Friends, an institutional structure of
Quaker meetings contained this potential through rigorous efforts to
maintain common group standards. A hierarchy of preparatory, monthly,

quarterly, yearly, and still other meetings grew over time in an attempt to define and enforce appropriate behavior. The need to make decisions by consensus, or, in the Quaker language of the day, "to act in unity with one's meeting," significantly limited the atomistic potential of the inward light. In its most schematic form, being Quaker arose from an accommodation between introspectively informed individual action and the imperative for unity with the collective sense of the meeting.[30]

Friends in the Delaware Valley embodied their collective identity in highly visible ways, from the use of distinctive language and physical behavior to a separate calendar system that rejected pagan names for months and days. A distinctive personal style emphasizing plainness characterized Friends, a manner of self-presentation whose notability sometimes countered its supposed aim of understated withdrawal from conspicuous consumption. The public nature of Quaker identity was so pronounced that a street thief exploited Quaker ways to gain his victims' confidence. As newspaper reports explained, the thief "personated the Quaker in his dress as well as stile," a Quaker performance that included distinctive clothing, language, and bodily movements ("a well imitated Quaker-like nod").[31] Quaker identity had a material dimension that triggered widely shared cultural assumptions.

Above all else, perhaps, Quakers were assumed to be wealthy and conservative in the Revolutionary Delaware Valley. The success of Friends came partly as a result of being the charter group of English settlement in the region. The Smith family of Burlington exemplifies this preeminence. By the late eighteenth century the Smiths had handsomely profited from four generations of trade with the West Indies. Richard Smith, the American family founder, had been among the leading Quakers to establish West Jersey a century earlier, and along with two sons he claimed ownership of 35,000 acres stretching across the colony from the Delaware River to the Atlantic Ocean. From the start, the family held a dominant position in local affairs and achieved prominence in regional political, economic, and social networks. Later, John Smith, a grandson of the founding patriarch, would strengthen such alliances when he married Hannah Logan, the daughter of the powerful Pennsylvania political leader James Logan. John's elder brother, Samuel, demonstrated his accomplishments as a gentleman by eschewing the family mercantile business and developing his skills as a government figure and man of letters who penned the most important history of colonial New Jersey.[32] The Smiths remained the town's leading family on the eve of the American Revolution, with three Smith brothers among the top decile of taxed residents in 1774, with another brother and son joining them in the top quintile. The Burlington Smiths sat atop the colony's social order, one of just two families that dominated its eighteenth-century "age of oligarchy."[33] No family in either New Castle or Easton came close to matching their place among the regional elite.

Although the Smiths were exceptional, they highlight an important quality of Burlington, which was probably the region's most affluent town in the late eighteenth century. As early as 1750 the wealthy Shippen family of Pennsylvania had built a summer house in the pleasant Jersey country town, beginning a tradition of elite summer residency that would continue into the nineteenth century.[34] Tax data from 1774 and 1784 demonstrates that Burlington led all eleven townships in the county in the number and quality of its luxury items. In spite of a middling population among the townships, Burlington ranked highest in marks of elite status, such as the number of merchants, wheeled chaises, and riding chairs. Its concentration of brewhouses and taverns also underscores the urban amenities that it offered travelers and inhabitants from the surrounding countryside. Wealth was especially concentrated in the urban portion of the township, where house lots were assessed at a value 160 percent higher than elsewhere in 1784.[35] Based on an examination of Burlington County probate inventories from 1760 to 1820, Burlington Township residents were among the most prosperous people in the entire Mid-Atlantic.[36]

One traveler praised the town for qualities that clearly flowed from local wealth when he described the "beauty" of the "well-built town," on a riverbank "covered by shade from the hanging branches of weeping willows." It was "paved with wide streets," and "the houses reflect the substance of the inhabitants, peace and quiet, a settlement of Quakers, for in these parts all Americans are Quakers."[37] Burlington served as an unusually elegant connection between the Jersey countryside and an international market easily accessible through nearby Philadelphia, and as a pastoral oasis just beyond the metropolis it attracted several prominent newcomers who would play influential roles in its public affairs after the Revolutionary War.

Notwithstanding the prominence of Burlington Friends, the town was no longer exclusively Quaker even at the start of the eighteenth century. On the whole, the Society of Friends dominated Burlington less than they did much of the rest of West Jersey. Anglicans gained greater influence after East and West Jersey became a single royal colony in 1702, and they had lived in Burlington almost from the town's founding, becoming especially prominent when George Keith, the Quaker schismatic and subsequent Society for the Propagation of the Gospel (SPG) missionary, settled there and brought many local Quaker families into the Church of England.[38] As a permanent SPG mission site beginning in 1703, Burlington had a long-term Anglican presence, and the high social status they shared with Quakers led to notable cooperation among local leaders. On the eve of the American Revolution, Quakers and Anglicans had nearly equal numbers among Burlington taxpayers, at 27 and 26 percent, respectively. Based on conservative figures that probably undercount Friends, Quakers and Anglicans made up 87 percent of the town's wealthiest decile of tax-payers, well above their 53 percent in the full range of taxpayers.[39]

The close relationship between Burlington's two main religious groups is suggested by the fact that its two long-term Anglican ministers during the period under study both married Quakers from wealthy families. This Anglican-Quaker fusion, which required that the women relinquish their membership in the Society of Friends, was especially strong in the case of Ann Kinsey. She married the Reverend Charles Henry Wharton in 1799, and her mother and sister also joined the Episcopal church within the next three years.[40] Quakers generally maintained careful group order, es-pecially through an increasing reliance on disownment procedures in the latter half of the eighteenth century. Nevertheless, in some cases boundaries between the faiths could blur. For instance, John Rogers, the sixth-largest property holder in Burlington in 1774, and his wife, Mary, baptized and buried their firstborn son in the Anglican church in 1769 but raised their next four children as Quakers. When Friends genuinely recanted their departures from the Society's discipline, they could often maintain their membership, especially if they were wealthy.[41]

Burlington's concentrated wealth attracted entrepreneurs in an occupa-tion peculiarly dependent upon those with surplus income and the incli-nation to purchase luxury goods. Two leading artists of the postwar period worked in Burlington at the turn of the century. The French portrait painter Charles Balthazar Julien Fevret de Saint-Memin settled there with his parents and sister during their émigré years from 1798 to 1810, when he painted nine hundred portraits of the national and regional elite. As an excellent recent study noted, Saint-Memin's "distinctive profile por-traits have come to epitomize Federal America."[42] Leaders in all three towns studied here sat for his portraits, mostly in Philadelphia, and the numbers from each town suggest their degree of integration into the lead-ing circle of Delaware Valley society. Eight Burlington residents had their portraits painted, three from New Castle, and only a single person (and a non-German) from Easton (figs. 14–16).

Like Saint-Memin, the immigrant English painter William Birch also took advantage of Burlington's patronage possibilities by producing a de-tailed engraving of the town in 1797 (fig. 10). The main image is a town map that emphasizes the concentrated settlement along High Street, lead-ing away from the river, and on Delaware Street, which borders it. Care-fully documented orchards and gardens in less concentrated areas depict a carefully manicured place, while main roads such as Federal and Wash-ington streets convey its conservative political opinions. A smaller inset view of the waterfront at the bottom of the map also emphasizes Burling-ton's gentility with stately houses, attractive arbors, and three anchored sailing vessels that imply substantial local wealth rather than the sweat and toil of a working waterfront. Finally, a small rowed craft at mid-river carries three small figures, each of whom wears the distinctive broad-brimmed hat of the Quakers. Simultaneously refined and mass-produced, the Burlington engraving aimed for sale to a unique clientele in an afflu-ent town.

Continuing north once more to complete our introduction to the Delaware Valley's cultural diversity, one must travel eighty miles above Burlington along the winding river to reach Easton, Pennsylvania, at the confluence of the Delaware and Lehigh rivers. Situated well above the falls of the Delaware at Trenton, which prevented direct access to transatlantic trade and transportation, Easton would be founded a century after the first permanent European settlement at New Castle and seventy-five years after the Quaker incorporation of Burlington. While the towns in the lower river valley were well-established capitals of their respective colonies by the start of the eighteenth century, Easton remained a frontier town and would host its final major Indian conference in February 1777. Easton may have been the smallest of the three towns in 1770, but it would be the largest of the trio by 1830. Altered by massive canal construction and mul-tiple mills powered by local streams, Easton is a classic example of a com-munity transformed by early industrial development, changes that would largely bypass Burlington and New Castle.

Preliminary surveys of proprietary property at the "Forks of the Delaware" had begun in the mid-1730s, but permanent colonial settle-ment started when William Parsons and Nicholas Scull laid out the town in the spring of 1750. As a proprietary official explained, "the first and only place suited for trade and commerce is at the confluence" of the Delaware and Lehigh rivers.[43] Easton lay at the heart of contested terrain in the infamous Walking Purchase of 1737, whereby proprietary officials manipulated the terms of William Penn's 1686 Indian deed, which itself was almost certainly falsified.[44] All three towns had been built atop Native American trade and spiritual centers before the arrival of Europeans, but only in Easton did the newcomers' transition from infrequent visitors to permanent occupiers remain violently contested in the latter half of the eighteenth century.

Easton's founding coincided with the height of non-British migration to the Delaware Valley, and German speakers were the town's most influen-tial settlement group. German migration to Pennsylvania was dominated by the *kirchenleute* or "church Germans." These Lutheran and German Re-formed adherents understood themselves to be quite different from peo-ple in the varied German-speaking religious sects scattered throughout Pennsylvania, such as the famous Moravian community at Bethlehem, just up the Lehigh River from Easton. In spite of theological and historical dif-ferences separating the German Reformed and Lutheran traditions, these church Germans often banded together in colonial Pennsylvania to form "union churches" that shared a common religious building. These widespread institutions could vary from fully integrated congregations with a shared minister to the more pragmatic arrangement of simply pooling resources to raise a single church.[45]

The term *Pennsylvania German* refers here to the distinctive culture created by church Germans in British North America, which was influential in a large geographic area arcing from northern New Jersey, through Pennsylvania, and into the backcountries of Maryland and Virginia.[46] Pennsylvania Germans represented about a third of all Pennsylvanians in 1790, based on surname analysis of the first census, but in core areas of German settlement such as Northampton County, with Easton as its seat, that figure climbed to 63 percent of the population.[47] Identifying these towns as having prominent Scots Irish, African American, Quaker, Anglican, and Pennsylvania German groups is not meant to suggest that the boundaries of any group, or that the relationships within them, were fixed. Rather, the stage is being set for us to probe more deeply in attempting to understand the meaning of this diversity and how it changed over time.

When planning to create Northampton County out of the northernmost reaches of Bucks County in 1750, Pennsylvania's proprietary and Quaker leaders were quite conscious of the importance of group identity and aimed to restrict the political influence of German settlers in Pennsylvania. Governor James Hamilton and the Quaker assembly supported the proposal of proprietary councilor Thomas Graeme that the boundaries of new counties be drawn to "comprehend to a trifle the whole body of Dutch and consequently forever exclude them from becoming a [political] majority."[48] This scheme sent twenty-six representatives to the assembly from the three English-dominated old counties and Philadelphia, while the five newer counties (including Northampton) elected just ten assemblymen, even though the two areas had roughly equal populations by 1760.[49] At the same time, Quaker and proprietary interests recognized that naturalized Germans could help them to defeat their political adversaries. The proprietors hoped that church Germans would defer to their leadership, a political vision embodied in the fashioning of Easton's built landscape to trumpet proprietary power. Easton was named after the family estate of Thomas Penn's new wife in Northamptonshire, England, and the town's main streets received names that similarly reflected proprietary significance.[50] The county courthouse that occupied the town's prominent central square provided the most obvious expression of proprietary grandeur. Completed in 1766, its elegant Georgian design displayed a cosmopolitan style otherwise lacking in the small country town. In fact, the only praise a genteel visitor from Burlington offered during a short visit to Easton in 1769 was to applaud the "handsome Court House."[51]

Easton's difference from communities in the lower Delaware Valley was partly the result of its later settlement, ongoing frontier conditions, and limited development. Whereas Easton barely had one hundred taxpayers on its rolls in the early 1770s, New Castle and Burlington each had more than twice that number. These physical and economic factors exacerbated the cultural distance that separated people in the large zone of Pennsylvania German settlement such as Easton from those in older colonial towns such as New Castle and Burlington.

The Pennsylvania German town's distance from the Anglo-American center of the Delaware Valley appears clearly in outsiders' comments about it. James Burd condemned Easton as "a doghole of a place, remote from all the world" in 1771.[52] The wealthy Quaker Richard Smith of Burlington offered a more subtle assessment, yet also stressed its limitations. Returning from a long journey into the Indian country beyond New York and Pennsylvania, Smith paused in Easton only long enough "to drink some punch and get shaved." He found the local milieu beneath him and noted that Lewis Gordon was the local "Ferryman, Tavern Keeper, Lawyer, Clerk of the court and Justice of the Peace."[53] The combination of all these roles in a single individual underscores Easton's small size where multiple proprietary favors were granted to a small handful. The proprietary governor appointed justices, and Gordon's profitable ferry and tavern were actually owned by Proprietor Richard Penn, who leased the property and the exclusive right to carry people and goods across the river.[54] In a town where the majority of residents were Pennsylvania Germans, Gordon, an Anglicized Scot, secured its most lucrative appointments. The handful of local elites who depended on proprietary patronage for many of their privileges would face grave challenges when the Revolutionary War came to Easton.

While the only known late eighteenth-century images of New Castle and Burlington depict their differing riverfronts, the only contemporary image of Easton touted its courthouse (fig. 11). The engraving accompanied a boosterish celebration of the town's promise in the *Philadelphia Monthly Magazine* in 1798. Yet the image also offered a clear contrast between the Georgian courthouse at its center and the private buildings lining the street. The two finely built houses closest to the viewer both have large windows, but the remaining structures are small and simple. Whereas the courthouse strikingly achieved the balanced ideal of Anglo-Georgian design that had come to prominence during the latter half of the century in America, none of the private buildings attempted such a scheme.[55] Similarly, the public building's carefully framed and raised entrance notably differs from all the rest, with their doorways on the street level.

The Easton image, like the courthouse itself, celebrated cosmopolitan Anglo-American legal and political authority as the central, stabilizing force in a modest country town. The accompanying article reinforced the point that the courthouse symbolized the town's prospects for future improvement, which rested upon "a constant communication between it and Philadelphia." Ironically, what had been a center for proprietary influence in the colonial period was refashioned in the postwar years as a symbol for national development. The article offers more than a simple paean to Philadelphia-led economic growth, for that explicit aim was contextualized within a racial and ethnic framework as the town moved from the "gloomy haunts of the rude savage indian" fifty years earlier to now boast fourteen hundred "chiefly German" inhabitants.[56]

Easton's ethnic makeup had a material expression in its many Pennsylvania German buildings. The exposed beam, or "half timber," construction of the house at the distant center of the image depicts a common eighteenth-century European building style, but one that had fallen out of favor in Anglo-America. An even more striking example of Pennsylvania German architectural tradition appears in the "striped" house in the left foreground. A traveler who observed such buildings in the countryside north of Philadelphia in 1829 commented that "the whole face of the country look[s] *German*," particularly those houses that "look to the eye like 'Wilmington stripes,' for the taste is to white-wash the smooth mortar between the logs, but not the logs themselves, thus making the house in stripes of alternate white, and dusky wood color."[57] Anglo American and Pennsylvania German style were easy to see in the built environment and lived experience of Easton residents.

William Parsons, the surveyor who later held several proprietary appointments there, thought poorly of Easton's non-Anglo residents. As he explained to provincial authorities in Philadelphia, "this new world has taken a great turn of late and now we must acknowledge that the earth with the fullness thereof belongs to the Dutch, at least they think so."[58] Parsons held a starkly racialized view of Pennsylvania German colonists. Money raised for a local school that aimed to Anglicize German-speaking children led him to wonder "whether it be man or beast that the generous benefactors are about to civilize." Indeed, educating Germans "seems to me like attempting to wash a blackamoor white." This seemingly hyperbolic fusion of Germans and Africans as equally distant from whites was less idiosyncratic than one might initially think.[59] The massive German immigration to Pennsylvania that began in the 1720s, especially when coupled with wartime fears of the mid-1750s, sparked grave suspicions among some Anglo elites about the German presence.

White racial identity had limited utility as a foundation for colonial authority due to the hostility that many elites felt toward Pennsylvania Germans. Benjamin Franklin expressed the fear that many Anglos in the Delaware Valley shared about new German settlers in a frequently reprinted 1755 essay, where he asked, "why should Pennsylvania, founded by the English, become a Colony of *Aliens*, who will shortly be so numerous as to Germanize us instead of our Anglifying them, and will never adopt our Language or Customs, any more than they can acquire our Complexion."[60] Franklin targeted a perennial concern raised by immigration. How would foreign newcomers join society without causing social turmoil? Even more striking, however, was his extreme separation of the swarming "Palatine Boors," as he described Germans elsewhere in this account, and the English. His sense of their fundamental difference went beyond cultural distinctions of language and custom to include "complexion." More than simply learned behavior, in Franklin's view, the embodied difference of Germans prevented them from fully joining Anglo-American society.

Given today's widespread belief that all Europeans are white, Franklin's distinctions may seem puzzling, but he definitely presented Germans as physically different from Englishmen. As he concluded, this "leads me to add one remark: That the number of purely white people in the world is proportionately very small." Even among Europeans, "the Spaniards, Italians, French, Russians, and Swedes, are generally of what we call a swarthy Complexion; as are the Germans also, the Saxons only excepted, who with the English, make the principle Body of White People on the Face of the Earth."[61] Interestingly, Franklin perceived German speakers to belong to two distinct groups. Saxons from the northeast, whose fifth-century invasion of England he implicitly acknowledged elsewhere as shaping the English people, he accepted as white.[62] Meanwhile, he cast Palatines of the southwest and the numerous Rhineland groups that made up the overwhelming majority of German-speaking immigrants to Pennsylvania as swarthy and inferior. The boundaries of whiteness embraced and excluded different groups in the early Delaware Valley than they do today.

Franklin's fear that Germanization might prevail over Anglicization in the broad area of Pennsylvania German influence was sometimes borne out in places like Easton. Robert Traill, for example, had left the Orkney Islands for Philadelphia in 1744 at the age of nine, after the death of his father, a Presbyterian minister. He eventually made his way to Easton where he worked as a storekeeper, taught school, and trained at law with his fellow Scotsman Lewis Gordon. However, unlike Gordon, who never successfully integrated with local people, Traill married Elizabeth Grotz, whose parents were German born. He worshipped in the local German Reformed church, a Calvinistic faith like his natal Presbyterianism, and was buried with a Reformed service in 1816. Traill's religious life included an important degree of assimilation into Pennsylvania German culture, especially because Reformed services were held entirely in German during his lifetime. Moreover, his successful legal practice built upon his bilingualism, which attracted large numbers of Pennsylvania German clients.[63]

The Reformed congregation in which Robert Traill worshipped held its services in the union church building that it shared with local Lutherans. Whereas religious buildings appear at the physical center of both New

Castle and Burlington in close proximity to the county courthouses, in Easton the union church stood a block off the town's central square, on land that had been given to the German congregations by the proprietors in the early 1770s. Perhaps the proprietors simply selected this lot with an eye to preserving lots on the square for more profitable purposes, but given the care with which they had funded the construction of glorious Anglican Christ Church in Philadelphia, perhaps the most impressive building in all the British colonies, the proprietors clearly understood that public architecture provided a unique opportunity for religious, political, and social authority to reinforce one another. Whatever the degree of intentionality in the town's plan, Easton's physical landscape on the eve of the Revolution suggested that the courthouse, with its proprietary-appointed officials, was more important than the recently constructed German union church.

Even though proprietary officials may not have thought highly of Pennsylvania Germans, Easton's union church played a vital role in local life. Both religious groups maintained independent ministers throughout the period, yet their confessional cooperation was impressive, as they shared an organist and schoolteacher and were described together as the "German congregations at Easton" in legal documents concerning union church property. The scant presence of Britons in the town meant that no "English" church, as local people collectively described all European Americans of non-German descent, would be established there until 1818. While less architecturally refined than the courthouse, the large union church was well built from local stone and hosted both congregations until the early 1830s, when Lutherans chose to build a grander independent church. Whereas the county courthouse would fall victim to modernization and be demolished in the early 1860s, the union church building remains in use today as the First United Church of Christ, a direct descendent of the original Pennsylvania German congregations.

People of German descent held an easy majority in Northampton County, although the county seat at Easton had more non-German inhabitants than most parts of the surrounding countryside. Easton's Lutheran and German Reformed congregations included nearly 61 percent of the town's taxed residents in the early 1770s, and only three individuals among the remaining 40 percent (Lewis Gordon, who had married in Philadelphia's Christ Church, and the father and son Michael and Meyer Hart, who were Jewish and of likely Sephardic descent) had any known religious affiliation.[64]

A closer look at religious affiliation in Easton on the eve of the Revolutionary War reveals another striking departure from the other two towns. Only in Easton did a large number of local taxpayers (21 percent) actively participate in two different congregations. The shared union church was more than a pragmatic strategy for pooling worldly resources; it was a co-operative venture in spiritual terms as well. For example, Jacob Opp, an immigrant from Chur-Paltz on the Rhine and a successful Easton innkeeper by the 1770s, was a Lutheran communicant in 1773 and served as that group's treasurer a decade later, yet had several daughters, who later became Lutheran catechumens, baptized by the Reformed minister in the 1770s. When Opp died in 1805, he received a Reformed burial.[65] Many more examples of individuals with richly mixed religious affiliations could be added, but more importantly, the unusually large number of people with mixed religious affiliation in Easton steadily declined after the Revolutionary War. Largely as a result of heightened Lutheran denominational consciousness, fewer Easton residents maintained mixed religious affiliations over time.

This marked alteration of spiritual identity reflected the changing place of Pennsylvania German ethnicity in Revolutionary Easton. In the colonial period, Pennsylvania Germans had cooperated closely with one another as ethnic outsiders—perhaps even as racial outsiders in the formulations of Franklin and Parsons—but during the Revolutionary War they increasingly achieved significant local leadership positions. This upward mobility led to a softening of ethnic solidarity, though it never ended for most, and a growing commitment to religious distinctiveness among German Reformed and Lutheran adherents in Easton. The boundary that separated and connected religious and ethnic identities shifted as people in the Revolutionary Delaware Valley negotiated the transition from a colonial to a national society.

War and the Fault Lines of Diversity

For all their local diversity, residents in colonial New Castle, Burlington, and Easton participated in a shared Delaware Valley political culture in which Quaker influence had long been absolutely central. A Quaker Party, which formed in the Pennsylvania legislature in 1739, used popular and inclusive strategies to build a broad coalition against their proprietary opponents, who controlled the governor's office and its sweeping powers of appointment. Since William Penn's sons had become Anglicans, as more properly befitted their status as proprietors, the main fault line of formal politics in Pennsylvania had a significant religious dimension. The Quaker Party enjoyed great success in the 1740s and 1750s, and, in spite of significant setbacks during the Seven Years' War, the most careful scholar of Pennsylvania's colonial politics finds that an "ideology of Civil Quakerism" retained "unrivaled persuasive power" in the region into the 1770s.[66] Because the subsequent Revolutionary tradition effectively caricatured Quakers as traitors, our view of their early prominence has been clouded, necessitating a brief consideration of Quaker colonial significance. The crisis Friends faced in the Seven Years' War is also a useful precursor to understanding the even more tumultuous changes that would occur when the next major war shook the region in the 1770s. Here we will pay particular attention to how the identities of Quakers, Anglicans, Pennsylvania Germans, and varied Indian groups were set in high relief by wartime conflict.

An Anglo elite, primarily led by Quaker and Anglican men, held most political leadership positions and dominated assumptions about proper authority in the colonial Delaware Valley. Its leaders successfully managed a political culture insightfully characterized as "popular politics" with "an oligarchic temper" that restricted power to those "who belonged 'inside' the political world, along with a determination to respect rather than challenge that limitation."[67] Such values in the gerrymandered creation of Northampton County that attempted to limit German influence in the assembly were noted earlier. Although this political culture has been best studied for Pennsylvania and was most fully articulated there, formal politics in Delaware and New Jersey offered variations on that theme, with weaker opposition to executive authority. Colonial politics in Delaware, under the control of the Pennsylvania proprietor, was much less open to popular influence, while New Jersey elites, particularly those in the heavily Quaker western part of the colony, enjoyed the firmest control of political life in the region.[68]

Residents of each town engaged the Quakerized politics of the colonial center in distinct ways. Burlington inhabitants shared many values of the Quaker Party; however, the structure of royal government in New Jersey encouraged a much stronger elite consensus than existed in embattled Pennsylvania. Burlington enjoyed substantial political advantages as the colonial capital of New Jersey, a status it shared with Perth Amboy in the east. Relying on savvy use of patronage and a strategic alliance with Perth Amboy assemblymen, the old proprietary capitals maintained a successful legislative coalition that cooperated with the royal governor for much of the century. Quaker and Anglican elites in Burlington worked closely together and shared legislative access with four Quakers and three Anglicans holding the town's assembly seats from 1760 to 1776. While individuals from these groups are estimated to have represented 16 percent and 8 percent of the province's total population, they held 37 percent and 20 percent, respectively, of the legislative seats from 1703 to 1776.[69] As the leading Burlington Quaker Samuel Smith noted about provincial politics, "harmony reigns in a considerable degree" and our "publick business is consequently dispatched with ease." The control of the assembly by leading Jersey families such as the Smiths led one historian to characterize the colony's eighteenth-century politics as "essentially elitist and deferential."[70]

Formal politics in colonial Delaware was closely integrated with Pennsylvania. Although the "lower counties on the Delaware" had established an independent legislature in the early eighteenth century, the proprietary governor remained Delaware's executive and traveled to New Castle at least twice a year to attend its assembly meetings. These moments of political prominence for the small capital were largely symbolic, and the proprietors almost never interfered in Delaware affairs before 1770. The governor had very little cause to dispute the Delaware assembly, for, in total contrast to the Pennsylvania assembly that constantly antagonized proprietary interests, the Delaware assembly supported the proprietors. The divergence of the two representative bodies was especially clear during wartime. Delaware's long coastline without defensive fortifications and lack of a prominent Quaker presence meant that its assembly consistently pressed for more aggressive military spending and preparation.[71]

The Delaware assembly sustained its firm alliance with Pennsylvania's proprietors during the Seven Years' War, but almost everywhere else political life changed significantly with the region's first experience of sustained warfare. Residents of Northampton County, on Pennsylvania's northern frontier, shared Delaware's vulnerability to enemy attack. Although Pennsylvania Germans had traditionally supported the popular Quaker Party, wartime conditions enhanced the proprietors' ability to court a potentially decisive voting group. The Quaker Party's reluctance to fund wartime expenses meant that it lost much of its following among church Germans during the war, and its subsequent royalization campaign to end proprietary rule was also viewed suspiciously by most Pennsylvania Germans. Nevertheless, the proprietors' persistent wariness of German outsiders and disdain for the popular techniques used so effectively by the Quaker Party limited the long-term alliance of Pennsylvania German and proprietary interests.

Like all the newer frontier counties with large non-English populations, Northampton County had a minor presence in the Pennsylvania assembly, with only a single representative until the 1770s, and Lutheran and German Reformed individuals filled only 4 percent of seats in the assembly from 1758 to 1775.[72] While Germans were a relatively recent immigrant group and might not be expected to be political leaders in strong numbers, apportionment effectively protected the influence of the older "English" counties of Chester, Philadelphia, and Bucks. Pennsylvania Germans' negligible place in the colonial assembly reflected the peripheral role that Anglo leaders believed Germans should play in formal politics. By the 1750s, Pennsylvania Germans had become an important voting bloc to court, but neither Quaker nor proprietary leaders planned to share substantive power with them.

Elite Pennsylvanians' fears about the loyalty of German speakers during the Seven Years' War stimulated some anti-German feeling, but war itself drove nonpacifistic Anglo and German colonists closer together than ever before, especially in vulnerable frontier locations such as Easton.[73]

In December 1755, William Parsons, Easton's proprietary land agent, described a desperate local situation and warned that without military support the Indians "will very soon be within sight of Philadelphia."[74] In a June 1757 petition requesting munitions from the Governor's Council, Easton residents viewed "their Situation [as] much more Dangerous than any other part of the Province on this side of the Susquehanna . . . [because] every Indian, almost, that comes here says this Town stands upon their Land."[75] Parsons concurred that Easton "stands upon the very Land which the Indians claim, and is upon that Account alone much more in danger of an Attack from the Savages than any other place."[76] Colonists in Easton shared a common understanding about the threat posed to them by Indians.

The Seven Years' War accelerated racial unity among church Germans and other colonists as "civilized" whites who warred against Native American "savages."[77] The Quaker assembly's refusal to establish a compulsory militia and the prohibition on the enlistment of Friends in the voluntary militia opened an important avenue for Pennsylvania German social ascendance. For church Germans, who lacked pacifistic religious tenets, service in Indian wars led to close cooperation with Anglo-American proprietary interests. If military service in a sense allowed many Pennsylvania Germans to prove their whiteness, the same logic suggests that most Quakers simultaneously rejected white solidarity. Many Quakers boldly dissented from the war effort and attempted to fashion an alliance with Delaware Indians, who themselves broke with Iroquois attempts to enforce "racial" conformity among native groups. The massive racial formation that organized the cultural diversity of early America into broad categories of white, black, and red only cohered slowly and incompletely.

War and military mobilization surely hardened racial boundaries, yet martial conflict also exacerbated dissent from the crude logic of race. The varying ways in which war politicized Quakers, Pennsylvania Germans, proprietary allies, Moravians, Delawares, Iroquois, and Christian Indians are especially clear in their interactions at the major treaty conferences hosted at Easton from 1755 to 1762. These meetings attempted to bring the shocking violence of the war to a close and revealed deep division within, not just between, local settlers, colonial leaders, and native groups. Treaty meetings required elaborate efforts to articulate and maintain dependable group boundaries. British colonists and Indians generally opposed one another and had distinct interests at these meetings, but such a dualistic conflict had to be deflected because successful treaties required reconciliation. In order for the work of peace to go forward, treaty conferences needed to nurture shared interests in a ritualistically crafted middle ground.[78] Indians and colonists both sought reliability from the other side at such meetings, hoping that their counterparts might possess greater group solidarity than they knew to exist among themselves.

Wartime diplomacy in Pennsylvania revolved around an Iroquois-proprietary alliance that attempted to stifle dissent by western Senecas, Delawares, and Quakers.[79] Friends had grown so disgusted with the proprietary handling of Indian affairs that they began to meet independently with Native Americans at the Easton conference in July 1756. By the end of the year Quakers had formed the Friendly Association for Regaining and Preserving Peace with the Indians by Pacific Measures. Burlington Friends played the leading role in forming a parallel institution, the New Jersey Association for Helping the Indians, with at least twelve of nineteen founding members from Burlington.[80]

Members of the Friendly Association played a key role supporting, recording, and researching the Delaware leader Teedyuscung's claim to have been defrauded by proprietary misdeeds. As one proprietary ally wrote about Quaker Indian diplomacy, "Our broad brim's Politicians have made a sort of Peace with the Indians at Easton, a part of whom are now & were during the Treaty Scalping in the same County; they are sad dirty Scoundrels; don't think I mean the Indians."[81] Outraged by Quaker interference, Governor William Denny attempted to ban them from future meetings and condemned Friends' interference as having "the worst consequences, as it must tend to divide the king's subjects into different parties and interests."[82] Such prohibitions failed, largely because the Friendly Association added substantially to the gifts given to Indians at the Seven Years' War conferences, an essential contribution to successful diplomacy.

Proprietary and Quaker vitriol complicated Indian negotiations so explosively that when Albany-based British Indian superintendent William Johnson finally attended an Easton conference in 1762, he was stunned by Quaker accusations that he aimed to help the proprietors confirm their illegal seizure of Delaware land. From Johnson's perspective atop the colonial hierarchy of Indian negotiations, such dissent among Englishmen was intolerable. He left the conference complaining that he "would do nothing more in such a Mob and such treatment he never had met before."[83] Johnson was unprepared to cope with the diversity of interests in multicultural Pennsylvania—above all, Quaker advocacy for Delawares.

The Quaker Public Friend Susannah Hatton attended one Easton treaty meeting where she shared a spiritual message with "religious Indians" with the help of translator Job Chilloway. Hatton's ministry enjoyed considerable success, and one Friend described it as "the most Melting season I ever saw among such a number of people."[84] In direct contrast to these civilized Christian Indians, Hatton and her fellow Quakers found Easton residents, "who are mostly Germans," to be "the most thoughtless stuped people that I have seen." After suffering a great deal of rude, noisy, and drunken behavior from local Pennsylvania Germans, Hatton "stood up being cloathed with Authority and reprimanded them closely . . . advising them . . . that those they called Heathen demonstrated by there Conduct that they were nearer the Kingdom [of God] than many of those called Christians."[85]

Just as proprietary forces worked hard to discredit Quaker alliances with Indians, so too the Iroquois struggled to make other Indians conform to their leadership. The upstart Delaware leader Teedyuscung's dissent was just the most flamboyant example of a wide range of disagreements among autonomous native nations during the war. In addition to the Delaware-Iroquois split, the Forks of the Delaware remained home to many Christian Indians. Moravian missionaries, headquartered since 1741 at nearby Bethlehem, carried out the most successful Indian conversion effort in colonial British America.[86] Susannah Hatton's translator Job Chilloway, for instance, was among the Jersey Indians who had been displaced to the Forks and had probably received Moravian baptism like his brother Wilhelm. As a frequent employee of the Pennsylvania government who successfully sued in its courts, and as one of the few Indians to possess a patented title to land in the colony, Job Chilloway confounded an emerging racial logic that supposedly separated whites and Indians.[87]

Christian Indians were a frequent enough presence in Northampton County that their racial status as Indians often went unrecorded. Nevertheless, they lived dangerously in colonial society. For example, Moses Tatamy, a principle convert of the Presbyterian missionary David Brainerd, was unusual in his degree of acculturation, which included a deed to three hundred acres upriver from Easton. But this adaptation to English property holding and his regular work as an interpreter failed to spare his family from tragedy and later economic reversal. His son William was killed while carrying messages to arrange Easton's 1757 conference, and the wife of another son who lived in Easton as late as 1796 was among the town's poorest inhabitants. Far from enjoying a liberated middle ground, Christian Indians occupied a fraught cultural terrain whose hybridity often triggered shock and rejection from colonists and Indians alike.[88] By contesting the demands of racial conformity, Quakers, Christian Indians, and Delawares such as Teedyuscung may have fought a losing battle, but to ignore their struggle would award racial categorization a fixed power that it had not attained in the late colonial Delaware Valley.

The coming together of multiple religious, racial, and ethnic groups in the creation of the colonial Delaware Valley can be observed in the work of cultural brokers who labored to reconcile and stabilize the conflicts that often arose in this multicultural landscape. The most influential of these "go-betweens" may have been the translator and proprietary agent Conrad Weiser. One month after his death in 1761, Weiser would be commemorated at an Easton conference in a manner that highlights the complex relationships among individual and group identity in a multicultural society. In his opening speech, Seneca George presented eight strings, two black belts, and three white belts to stress the need for reconciliation and the difficulty of communicating without Weiser, whom he described as "a great Man, and One Half a Seven Nation Indian, and one Half an Englishmen."[89]

When Governor James Hamilton first spoke after listening to three days of Indian presentations, he immediately returned to Seneca George's powerful invocation of Weiser. Hamilton agreed that Weiser's death marked a major loss and "heartily join[ed] in covering his body with bark," another demonstration of the degree to which colonists and Indians shared symbolic forms. But Hamilton emphasized that Weiser had only been "by adoption one of the Six Nations, though by birth one of us."[90] The governor insisted that colonists who worked closely with Indians could not actually become members of a native group in a fundamental way. Yet Weiser's allegiances were more complex than the governor allowed as Wesier had been born in Württemberg and arrived in New York as a thirteen-year-old immigrant in 1710. Although many probably thought of him as a "Palatine," in the context of Indian negotiations, Pennsylvania's governor insistently embraced him as "one of us."

What, then, does Weiser's example mean for the racial othering of colonial Pennsylvania Germans expressed by varied Anglo Americans such as Benjamin Franklin, Easton's proprietary land agent William Parsons, and Quaker Public Friend Susannah Hatton? As Franklin noted in closing his hostile account about German incompatibility with Englishmen, "perhaps I am partial to the Complexion of my Country, for such Kind of Partiality is natural to Mankind."[91] Examining group identity raises disturbing issues when it uncovers the deep impulse to make sense of the world by recognizing, and often disliking, what you are not. Such group consciousness by negation, more through a rejection of others than a positive assertion of self, is a prominent feature of understanding the meaning of difference in the Delaware Valley. Looking back to the eighteenth century from a distance of more than two hundred years, one is understandably tempted to assume that the central fact of colonial society pitted European Americans against Native Americans. Racial identity and self-interest suggest an obvious opposition, but the experiences of individuals at the time reveal a richer set of local circumstances. Moreover, the very different situation of African Americans in New Castle and of Native Americans around Easton demonstrates the shallowness of "race" as a coherent or useful overarching category. Surely it is more accurate to stress ethnicity whenever possible (although this importantly remains elusive for African Americans here), given that concept's greater openness to local variation and as a term that more clearly puts all early Americans into a shared analytical framework, although never one of equivalent experience or consequences.[92]

Many shy away from multiculturalism as a useful framework for social analysis because they see group identity as an easily exploited façade.

These opponents of ethnic distinction are correct insofar as cultural identities can be manipulated and used coercively. However, to shun ethnic assertions and to fail to grapple with how they have informed individuals'
understandings of themselves, their world, and others reinforces the
seeming permanence of other categories of difference (race, class, and
gender being the most dominant ones recently) as the sole proper forms
for delineating group boundaries. Instead, we will continue to explore
how the complexion of one's country has many additional shades that
deserve close attention. Religious, racial, and ethnic expressions, their in-
tersections with one another and other forces, and especially their relationships with an emerging national identity, are examined here within
the specific local contexts of three Delaware River towns. As we shall see,
the American Revolution ruptured the status quo of colonial society and
unleashed a new Revolutionary identity politics that continued to exert itself into the nineteenth century. If the Seven Years' War had especially
strong reverberations for Quakers, Pennsylvania Germans, and varied native groups, the next war would initiate an even more profound rearrangement of group relationships whose impact would continue to be felt for
many decades. Comparing the trajectories of multiple groups in these
river towns and uncovering the logic of their local circumstances allows us
to gauge what has changed, as well as what has remained consistent, in
America's long engagement with cultural diversity.

Chapter 2

The Crisis of Everyday Life during the Revolutionary War

Residents of Burlington, New Castle, and Easton experienced the American Revolution in distinct ways that highlight basic differences in each town, yet people in all three contended with a shared Revolutionary dilemma. How would individuals and communities respond to the often forceful demand that they be either patriot or loyalist? This powerful new public identity triggered wide-ranging local responses that intertwined with other long-standing forms of self-understanding. The wartime developments in all three towns offer special insight because the period's uncertainties, especially during the large-scale troop movements in the Delaware Valley from 1776 through 1778, led people to document aspects of everyday life that might otherwise have been dismissed as minutiae. Direct exposure to wartime trauma disrupted daily life and made political allegiance a matter of public scrutiny as never before. The wartime experiences in each town reveal how the assault on the colonial social order forced politics beyond traditional boundaries. Furthermore, this Revolutionary experience became a crucial shared memory that shaped local popular culture well into the nineteenth century.

The Revolutionary War's radical potential in the Delaware Valley lay in how its attack on colonial authority required a renegotiation of relationships among its diverse cultural groups. For some colonial outsiders, the Revolutionary experience became a means to claim a more central place for themselves in the new nation. In New Castle, Delaware, Scots Irish Presbyterians played a leading role among radical patriots, and Lutheran and Reformed Pennsylvania Germans in Easton assumed leadership roles as patriots during the Revolution as never before. Meanwhile, Quakers and Anglicans in Burlington, New Jersey, suffered serious dislocation due to their neutral and loyalist leanings. The formation of meaningful new public identities as patriot or loyalist built upon and disrupted preexisting relationships among religious, racial, and ethnic allegiances.

Each town's wartime experience is considered in succession here. The war came directly to Burlington due to its accessibility on the river and along a main land route connecting Philadelphia and New York City. As an affluent Quaker and Anglican town with a leading place in colonial politics and strong attachments to the British Empire, the Burlington example serves to counter narrow patriotic accounts of the Revolution, as the cannonading and raids it suffered were primarily levied by patriots. Neutrality and loyalism enjoyed broad support in Burlington, especially while the British occupied nearby Philadelphia for nine months starting in September 1777. Even with the British army's departure from the Delaware Valley, its control of New York City throughout the war meant that Burlington residents had relatively easy access to British authority.

Ethno-religious political expression only flowered when reinforced by local conditions. Loyalists, for example, had extremely diverse beliefs, so much so that a careful study of loyalist exiles found it "practically impossible to delineate any characteristics common to them all."[1] Focusing on a particular setting, however, allows critical local circumstances to be assessed, and loyalism in Burlington built upon strong Anglican and Quaker foundations. Both groups were far from monolithic, but the clearest examples of ambivalence and outright hostility toward the rebels came from members of these religious groups with strong Anglo attachments.

Whereas patriots harassed Burlington, British naval ships and loyalist privateers attacked New Castle. Although a patriot tenor came to dominate local life, it did not arise from harmonious communal unity. The horrors of war and the immediate proximity of British forces prompted many local men to bold loyalism, which, in turn, stimulated sharp patriot retribution. Lurking beneath this schism in white society lay an even more profound source of potential social change, as patriot ideals of liberty and wartime disruption opened room for enslaved people to seek freedom from bondage. The striking assertion of African rights in the postwar Delaware Valley is best understood as an extension of Revolutionary developments that began to gain momentum during the war.

Revolutionary resistance also caused serious divisions in Easton. Fully committed patriots would eventually force the town's small Scots Irish elite, the main beneficiaries of proprietary patronage there, from power. Unlike New Castle, where the Scots Irish were often radicals, in Easton they tended to be conservatives who hoped to preserve the status quo. The logic of local circumstances determined the public significance of cultural identities. While the Scots Irish in New Castle felt disenfranchised by an Anglo elite, in Easton, key Scots Irish individuals (several of whom had tellingly become Anglicans) enjoyed significant economic, political, and legal advantages over the local majority of Pennsylvania Germans.

Like any group of people bound together by the malleable claims of shared culture, Pennsylvania Germans could be found on all sides of the Revolutionary struggle, from ardent patriots to active loyalists, with the majority among the sensible core of wary people who hoped to avoid war's violence altogether. Just as local conditions led most Scots Irish in New

Castle and Easton to divergent political positions, so too Pennsylvania German culture alone did not predetermine Revolutionary allegiance. Most Pennsylvania Germans in Easton eventually became patriots, but to see how this occurred we need to know more about local conditions there. As in the Seven Years' War, local Pennsylvania Germans' emergence as patriot leaders built upon frontier conditions and the public recognition offered by military service.

The Revolutionary War hastened Pennsylvania German social ascendance in the frontier areas that they dominated and heightened their demands for public consideration in the postcolonial period. This key transition largely occurred as a unifying event in Easton and completes the spectrum of wartime experiences considered here. The Revolution brought a besieged unity to Quakers and Anglicans in Burlington who feared the rebellion and faced major upheavals in local and national life due to patriot success. The polarization that divided New Castle residents would outlast the war and color life there in the early republic. Meanwhile, those in Easton fortuitously avoided the stark choices that confronted people in the battlefield towns. Instead of the divisive experience that direct American-British martial conflict would have brought, Easton residents forged solidarity from their opposition to Native Americans. Indians were beseeched to be neutral at an Easton treaty in 1777, but then demonized as perpetrators of nearby "massacres" and attacked in a large-scale extermination campaign. Easton's Pennsylvania German Revolutionary success story was largely achieved by fighting against what was perceived as a sordid alliance of Indians, tories, and redcoats on Pennsylvania's northern frontier.

These distinct Revolutionary trajectories heightened social conflict in the three towns. Most significantly, it exacerbated preexisting distinctions as religious, racial, and ethnic identities took on sharper significance during the war. The importance of individual allegiance obviously accelerated as patriot and loyalist became meaningful marks of difference in Revolutionary society, and these positions grafted onto preexisting forms of individual and group understanding. Because the Revolution forced people to make public presentations of self that under ordinary circumstances could have remained discrete or hidden, it politicized personal behavior and elevated the everyday to the extraordinary. The patriot movement in the Delaware Valley succeeded by forcing politics beyond the status quo and in the process initiated a Revolutionary identity politics that persisted into the early national period.

Opposing Rebellion in Burlington

Religious identity has been a vital dimension of individual perception, self-understanding, and group life throughout American history. It often intertwines with ethnic, racial, and national identities, which together can provide a significant conceptual framework for understanding the world.[2] The ethno-religious influence upon Revolutionary experience had a strong role in Burlington, where people of mostly English descent gathered in Quaker and Anglican religious organizations that together accounted for 66 percent of all local taxpayers in 1774.[3]

The local prominence of the Society of Friends and the Church of England, alongside additional factors, helped make Burlington a loyalist stronghold. As the capital of West Jersey, Burlington was a focal point for royal patronage, with more direct ties to England than either New Castle or Easton. Only Burlington boasted leading local loyalists such as Governor William Franklin and the Anglican priest Jonathan Odell. The comparative affluence of its residents also intensified their embrace of the colonial order. Finally, the proximity of British forces throughout the conflict also encouraged loyalism. Indeed, the lack of British assaults on the town is quite striking, especially when contrasted with the high damages inflicted by British forces in immediately adjacent townships.[4] The British spared Burlington from direct attack and had good reasons for this decision.

The Reverend Jonathan Odell's arch loyalism, venomous satirical poetry, and dedicated British service during the war (and afterward as a leading official in New Brunswick, Canada) allow us exceptional access to the largely forgotten opposition to rebel leadership. His impassioned loyalism stemmed from deep currents in local life. Precisely because this tradition would be purposefully excised from popular memory by patriot efforts during the war and thereafter, it is important to recover how Odell's rich Anglophilia was fully consonant with American ways as rebellion threatened the region. Moreover, because the daily lives of ministers in the Church of England had particularly freighted political consequences, a brief study of Odell highlights the upsurge of Revolutionary identity politics in the Delaware Valley.

Born in East Jersey, Jonathan Odell descended from early seventeenth-century English immigrants to North America. His father died early with modest property, but enough to ensure that his only son could earn an undergraduate degree from the College of New Jersey in 1754.[5] Odell studied medicine there after graduation and then served with the British army in the West Indies as a physician. As it did for most other Britons in colonial America, the Seven Years' War supercharged his commitment to the empire, as one of his earliest surviving poems attests.

From East to West, and to the frozen Poles
Thy banners are displayed, thy Fame resounds;
Thy *Glory* and the *world's* have equal bounds.[6]

Odell's position as the Anglican minister in Burlington rested upon the support of Benjamin Franklin in Britain and William Franklin, New Jersey's last royal governor, after whom Odell named his only son, William Franklin Odell. Fresh from ordination in London, Odell arrived in Burlington in 1767 to a small congregation in the midst of a strong Quaker community. The young priest optimistically faced his prospects, and, as he explained in a report to his superiors, "Quakers . . . in this Country, [were] of all Dissenters the most friendly to those of our Communion."[7] St. Mary's Church prospered under Odell's leadership so that 26 percent of Burlington's taxpayers participated in Anglican services in 1774. The next year a fellow Society for the Propagation of the Gospel (SPG) missionary commented that the church in New Jersey has "of late become very respectable" and singled out Burlington for special praise.[8]

All was far from comfortable, however, as New England's sniping at British rule turned violent and eventually forced itself upon Burlington. Odell's first direct conflict with the rebels occurred in 1775 when a committee of inspection in Philadelphia seized two letters of his that criticized the new extralegal bodies that had become the infrastructure of the patriot movement. At this point New Jersey's still cautious provincial government chose not to issue a public censure because "this Congress would by no means violate the right of private sentiment, and . . . Mr. Odell's letter does not clearly appear to have been intended to influence public measures."[9] For the moment ordinary social dictates that acknowledged an important difference between private sentiment and public language prevailed.

The Revolutionary collapse of public-private distinctions, however, soon restructured American society and made the ordinary duties of Anglican priests subject to harsh penalties. Odell came under increasing supervision as the Revolution intensified, and, by June 1776, Governor Franklin had been arrested, and Odell, with his pregnant wife and two small children, fled for British protection in New York. Captured on the way by rebels who declared him "inimical to American liberty," Odell was confined to an eight-mile circle from the Burlington courthouse, although this parole hardly stilled his opposition to rebellion.[10]

As British and Hessian troops swept across New Jersey in December 1776, Odell's confidence rose, and he lashed out to denounce the illegal violence of ambitious rebel leaders who misled their foolish followers.

A truce then to all whig and tory debate;
True lovers of Freedom, contention we hate;
For the Demon of discord in vain tries his art
To inflame or possess a true *Protestant* heart.

True Protestant friends to fair Liberty's cause,
To decorum, good order, religion, and laws,
From avarice, jealousy, perfidy, flee;
We wish all the world were as happy as we. . . .

While thousands around us, misled by a few,
The Phantom of pride and ambition pursue,
With pity their fatal delusion we see;
And wish all the world were as happy as we![11]

Odell noted in the margin of his manuscript copy that "Protestant" was a term adopted by his circle of loyalists for whom "decorum, good order, religion, and laws" were conjoined. His politics and religion were deeply interwoven.

After the formal separation of the colonies from Britain, Odell could not carry out his regular religious duties—such as leading his congregation in prayers for the king, who headed the faith—without declaring a political position. Everyday life had become politicized in ways that no longer worked to his advantage. As he explained to SPG authorities, "since the declaration of Independency the alternative has been either to make such alteration in the Liturgy as both honor and conscience must be alarmed at, or else to shut up our churches, and discontinue our attendance at public worship." Like most Anglican clerics in the northern colonies, Odell "suspend[ed] . . . public Ministrations rather than make any alteration."[12] When George Washington's successful counterattack at Trenton and Princeton made a swift return to British rule less certain, Odell realized that he might suffer the same fate as his imprisoned patron Governor Franklin and fled Burlington, without his family, to safety in British-controlled New York City.

Most Burlington Quakers confronted Revolutionary change less directly than the bombastic Anglican priest, even though most shared his sense that the war would be disastrous. Margaret Hill Morris (fig. 13), an independent Quaker widow, recorded her experiences in war-torn Burlington in a detailed journal that provides a rich view of the struggle's local impact. Morris lived in a large house, previously owned by Governor Franklin, among the handsome riverside residences on "Green Bank" just below the town center. As British forces marched across New Jersey and were rumored to be sailing up the Delaware in early December 1776, most town residents fled to the countryside, making "our little bank look lonesome."[13] Morris remained in town with her sister, Sarah Dillwyn, who lived with Morris during the frequent absences of her husband, the distinguished Quaker Public Friend George Dillwyn.[14]

Morris recorded myriad visits to the town by advancing and retreating British and American troops, and while these local skirmishes had no strategic impact on the course of the war, they shaped local life in lasting ways. The varied military forces that townspeople faced made negotiation and self-presentation crucial. At midmorning on December 11, 1776, the first group of nonlocal fighting men, a party of sixty rebel Pennsylvanians, retreated through Burlington. As they passed through the town, they warned of the impending arrival of Hessian troops and crossed the Delaware River to Bristol, where they made their defense.[15]

As the Pennsylvania soldiers crossed the river, word reached the town center that several hundred Hessians had arrived on the town's northern boundary. Jonathan Lawrence and other leading men went to ensure "the safety of the town" by meeting with the troops. First, however, they sent word to Captain Moore, who commanded the patriot galley ships patrolling the river, to explain their pacific purpose. With Moore's approval, Lawrence engaged in stilted negotiations because neither the town nor the troops could supply a bilingual translator. Nevertheless, the soldiers agreed to halt their advance on Broad Street before reaching the town center. Moore received word of the terms and agreed that an acceptable truce had been established. Because Burlington would not be attacked, he sailed downriver to confirm the arrangement with Commodore Seymour, who headed the patriot river forces.[16] Lawrence invited the Hessian commander and his officers to his house for a meal, and included Jonathan Odell, whose French language skills proved useful in sealing the accord. Although at the heart of the potential battlefield, negotiation had apparently saved the town from attack.

Meanwhile, Commodore Seymour had sent several boats upriver with orders to fire on any group of Hessians or loyalists. Unsuspectingly, Lawrence and two others went down to the wharf to greet the boats, thinking that Captain Moore's men had returned. The trio waved their hats, the agreed-upon sign that the galleys were to come ashore peaceably, which instead triggered hostile fire. To Morris the two sides behaved quite differently. While the Hessian commander had the appearance of "generosity and humanity," cannonading by patriots through the night marked "a cruel as well as unprovoked piece of treachery."

The troops that passed through, lodged, and fired upon Burlington in December 1776 marked the start of a seven-month period during which Hessian and British troops, Jersey and Pennsylvania militia, Continental soldiers, and naval forces on both sides harried town residents. Just two weeks later, more than fifteen hundred Pennsylvania militia crossed the river from Bristol and quartered themselves in Burlington. Patriot boats raided, destroyed property, and even carried off local men suspected of being tories. When the British finally gained control of the river in summer 1777, Morris felt relief, "I really think they have made an end of the [rebel] gondolas; I hope never to see another."[17]

Patriot setbacks elicited hope from Morris, while British advances received her approbation. She cheered British victories and even invoked satanic designs to explain patriot behavior. To her, the very "spirit of the devil . . . rove through the town in the shape of tory-hunters." Similarly, when Pennsylvania militia quartered themselves in Burlington after a successful battle, she countered their boasting by speculating that their easy

gains came as part of a divine plan that would soon lead to "the chastisement . . . reserved for them."[18] Nevertheless, local sensibilities and friend-
ships held sway even as the war threatened to rip them apart. Morris's
neighbor Colonel Cox served in the militia, but still trusted her with the
keys to his house. As a cordial neighbor, she handed them over to Pennsylvania militiamen on December 28 when they "civilly asked for the keys"
to pass the night. But Morris went even further in hosting the guests of her
absent neighbor, even though she herself had secretly harbored the loyalist Jonathan Odell. The militiaman William Young recorded in his own
journal the next day that "the good woman next door sent us two mince
pies last night, which I took very kind. May God bless all our friends and
benefactors."[19]

As a Quaker caregiver, Morris was appalled by the impoverishment and
the loss of life caused by the war. While nursing wounded and sick soldiers,
her "heart was melted to see such a number of my fellow-creatures, lying
like swine on the floor . . . many of them without even a blanket."[20] War
dehumanized people, and, like other members of the Society of Friends
who remained true to their pacifistic tenets, Morris decried the suffering
war wrought and actively assisted the needy regardless of their political allegiances. Though loyal to the Crown and critical of patriot violence, Morris, like most members of the Society of Friends, attempted to act as a
genuine neutral, a critical stance adopted by one of the Delaware Valley's
most influential groups that has not received careful study.[21] Friends
widely opposed the war, as required by the Philadelphia Yearly Meeting. As
the resistance movement radicalized in 1775, the Yearly Meeting adopted
a sharp position blaming the rebels for the "increased contention" that
"produced great discord and confusion."[22] When war came to the
Delaware Valley, the Society renewed their resolve. "Let not the fear of suffering, either in person or property, prevail on any to join with or promote
any work or preparation for war. Our profession and principles are
founded on that Spirit which is contrary to, and will in time put an end to
all wars."[23] The Society of Friends officially rejected the rebels as the principle instigators of martial mayhem.

Such a clear public stance led to widespread abuse of Friends throughout the Delaware Valley. Burlington Monthly Meeting member John Hunt
described the fear of harassment and impressments among local Quakers
who "were afraid of taking the great Roads because of the Soldiers" who
had jailed six men "because they would not sign or associate with [the
rebels]. Some others did sign and so were sent home. . . . This was a very
sore trying time."[24]

The strong Quaker presence throughout West Jersey made it suspect in
patriot eyes. The New Jersey state legislature, for example, expected
Burlington County to fill two regiments of the Continental Army from its
more than 2,600 men of military age, but so many Quakers were disquali-

fied from service that those eligible dropped to merely six hundred.[25] In the face of compulsory military service, Quaker men still widely refused to serve in the armed forces, which exacerbated anti-Quaker feelings and reprisals. Abuse continued even when the main theater of war moved to the southern colonies. Patriot soldiers destroyed Quaker meetinghouse property in August 1779 and occupied the building twice in 1782, a year after the war had supposedly ended at Yorktown.[26] When Quaker men contemplated joining the army, they often faced enormous family pressure not to do so. When one of Margaret Hill Morris's nephews considered going to war, he received a letter from seven family members explaining military service's "inconsistency with the religious principles of thy education" and that such a course would violate their "tenderest advice and most serious cautions."[27]

The abuse of Quakers during the war was central to Delaware Valley loyalists' sense of rebel misrule. One poem in the *Pennsylvania Ledger*, for example, unfavorably compared the Revolutionary legislature to their Quaker predecessors in the colonial assembly.

Blunderers go on: despise the Quakers—
You never shall their heighth attain.

The wisdom of their gentle ruling
Can bear the retrospective view;
And this, with all your boasted schooling,
Is more than will be said of you.[28]

Partisans on both sides of the civil war searched for clear and consistent ways to identify friends and foes, but the messiness of the conflict that divided groups, neighbors, and even families meant that individuals found themselves on all sides of the issue. While most Quakers maintained the discipline of the Society as neutrals, and thus became patriot pariahs, exceptions certainly existed. John Hunt noted that the resolve of some local Friends broke under coercive threats, while others rejected impartiality from conviction.[29] Most famously, the Burlington Quaker Isaac Collins printed an important patriot newspaper, *The New Jersey Gazette*, starting in December 1777, with direct support from Governor William Livingston and the state legislature.[30]

The Society of Friends' disciplinary process that assessed members' behavior and enforced group unity became especially important in these trying times. The Burlington Monthly Meeting carefully investigated members who were accused of wayward actions. Thomas Rogers, for example, remained a member in good standing despite swearing an oath to the Revolutionary government, owning a gun, hiring a man to serve in his place in the patriot army, and accepting compensation for an apprentice who enlisted. Although Rogers had done everything short of actual military service, when judged to have earnestly repented, he was readmitted to the Society. Such permissiveness was exceptional, however, as only five of the forty men brought up on disownment charges in Burlington remained Quakers. Langston Carlisle, who "assented to learn the art of war" and became a captain of Burlington County's first regiment, was disowned and never sought readmission to the Society.[31] Falling somewhere between the examples of Rogers and Carlisle, the patriot printer Isaac Collins would be disowned five months after starting his newspaper, but would be readmitted after confessing his errors a decade later.

Because only men had formal political and martial responsibilities, Quaker women such as Margaret Hill Morris discovered that gender facilitated their ability to maintain the peace testimony. The narrow compass of women's rights in early America allowed nonrebel women greater latitude for independent action than their male counterparts, who could not be universal caregivers, nor act as true neutrals, without transgressing the bounds of permissible masculine behavior. In patriot eyes, male neutrality indicated weakness and femininity or marked the man a traitor. Tom Paine, for example, played on a thoroughly gendered framework when he goaded his (male) reader to join the patriot cause and "not put *off* the true character of a man."[32]

The crisis of being Quaker during the Revolution challenged every dimension of Friends' lives, and that duress furthered a remarkable group revitalization that refused to retreat from the world despite being abused. The leaders of the Philadelphia Yearly Meeting strenuously worked to purify the Society through a renewed commitment to Quaker simplicity and truth during its severe wartime tribulations. Having prohibited its members from holding public office in 1776, the Yearly Meeting advised all monthly meetings that "our speech, Behavior, Apparel, and Household Furniture . . . should be more conformable to the Plainness of our Profession" the next year.

Remaking the Society centered upon aspects of everyday life that primarily concerned women and was taken up by Burlington's Monthly Meeting for Women.[33] Tellingly, the local women chosen by their meeting to carry out this reform all led independent female households. Grace Buchanan lived by herself, Elizabeth Haines's household had an unnamed dependent, and Elizabeth Barker's included two other adult women. These three were weighty Friends; Buchanan and Haines often served as representatives to Quarterly Meeting, while Barker was the long-term clerk of the Burlington Women's Monthly Meeting.[34] The plainness reforms may have targeted domestic concerns, but the single women who led local implementation were not standard-bearers of the "private sphere."

Quaker spirituality infused the world so thoroughly that no sharp line separating their public and private realms can be easily delineated, especially during the reformist ferment among Delaware Valley Quakers in the late eighteenth century. As many critics have warned, a male/public versus female/private dichotomy can easily be overstated.[35] Burlington Friends responded to the Revolutionary crisis by revitalizing their sense of being Quaker. When the Society of Friends prohibited participation in formal politics and rejected slaveholding in 1775 and 1776, it voided two of the most important avenues to power in early America. In some senses the Society dedicated itself more fully to concerns often assumed to lie within a feminine private sphere, but such a conclusion mistakenly explains this development from the vantage point of later categories. Delaware Valley Quakers had long placed family maintenance at the center of their group consciousness and collective strategy. As the Society's rules of discipline had long stated, the goal of simplicity meant that all members "should be of one mind and become one family."[36]

The gendered construction of war meant that it touched men and women in profoundly different ways. Margaret Hill Morris described several cases where she benefited from acting as a nonpartisan dispenser of charity. After she healed several patriots and their wives of "itch fever," one of them offered to guide her across British lines into patriot-controlled Philadelphia. Morris knew that the journey would be treacherous, but set off the next day with her friend Ann Odell, a former Quaker who had been disowned when she married the town's Anglican minister. Their return to Burlington proved especially arduous when the male guide failed to return to bring them home. Troubled by accounts of skirmishes and armed parties rounding up everyone they found, Morris and Odell made a quick departure, driving their horse so relentlessly, its harness broke, forcing the riders to jump from the carriage to safety. Eventually they fixed the broken part with the help of a local man and upon their return to Burlington told a daring tale over "a good dish of tea."[37]

Morris's description of the covert journey revels in risk-taking empowerment. When she and Odell were told never again to attempt such a "perilous undertaking," the women retorted that they would do it again, but next time would "look out for a stronger horse and chair, and be our own guide." In fact, Morris judged that "our late expedition, so far from being a discouragement, was like a whet to an hungry man, which gave him a better appetite for his dinner."

Morris's transformation appears especially striking by comparing her self-descriptions at the beginning and end of her account of the war. She opened in panicked desperation, "quite sick" and "ready to faint" at facing the conflict without a husband. She felt like one "forsaken" and only had "tranquility . . . restored" through the consolation afforded by "acquiescence to the Divine will."[38] Providence remained central to Morris, but she gradually asserted herself more forcefully. Part of this new sensibility arose from the advantages she enjoyed as the head of a female household. For example, she was exempted from quartering troops because "we rank ourselves among the [feeble and defenseless], having no man with us in the house."[39] While one could stress the negative female dependence here, Morris exploited the image of the defenseless widow with children to good advantage. By the end of her account, when she had become her own best guide, Morris had transcended socially prescribed behavior for single women.[40] By not remarrying in the half-century that she survived after her husband's death in 1766, Morris made plain that she valued the autonomy of *feme sole* status more than she feared the consequences of life without a husband.[41]

The Revolution caused turmoil, but it also created new possibilities, especially for elite women such as Morris who enjoyed the ironic reversals of war. After the Anglican minister Jonathan Odell had fled to New York from his windowless hiding spot in Morris's house, she relished the memory of his temporary debasement and dependence upon her. Confident of British victory, Morris expected that Odell would soon return to his leading local role and go on to even greater prominence as the likely first Anglican bishop in British North America. Morris mused that she now had something to hold over the head of her "refugee" and commented cheekily, but perhaps with bitterness as well, that after the war "he will then think himself too *big* to creep into his old auger hole—but I shall remind him of the place, if I live to see him created first B[isho]p of B[urlingto]n."[42] The Revolutionary opportunities seized by Margaret Hill Morris remained circumscribed and did not extend to all women in the period. Nevertheless, her Quaker spirituality, economic independence, and widowed autonomy combined with wartime events to reshape her sense of self in important ways.

The remarkable political gains of propertied white women in Revolutionary New Jersey exemplify the period's widespread social experimentation. Female religious leadership and women's administrative autonomy in the Society of Friends may have informed the gender-inclusive laws in the first New Jersey state constitution. Arguably the state's only notable contribution to the constitutional history of the early republic, the 1776 New Jersey constitution granted the franchise to any person assessed with wealth greater than £50. For the first time in U.S. history, propertied women were acknowledged to possess the necessary independence to vote. This opening was not caused merely by sloppy language or hasty constitution drafting, for a 1790 electoral reform law clarified that the property requirement could be met by "he or she," a right preserved until 1807. When the New Jersey Provincial Congress voted in Burlington to approve the constitution on July 2, 1776, local Quaker customs and Burlington's traditionally weighty role in New Jersey's political life might have helped to produce this remarkable definition of voting rights. At the same time, the constitution maintained property requirements for suffrage and thus represented a conservative decision by the New Jersey legislature that explicitly refused to enfranchise all taxpayers.[43]

The republican political ideology that has been the central focus of the most influential recent Revolutionary scholarship does not come close to explaining the meaning of the war in Burlington, where neutrality and loyalism had great influence. Nevertheless, significant social changes did occur there during the war, and some of its residents were among the most radical reformers of the period. Not only were they not inspired by republican ideology, but they also were not even patriots. While the American antislavery movement that began in the late eighteenth century is often yoked to patriot commitments, its strongest leaders in the Delaware Valley were Quakers, who, on the whole, opposed the rebel cause and its resort to violence. Tellingly, the Burlington Quaker John Hunt linked the upsurge in reform activity to the war years, but *not* to patriots. He reported that the Yearly Meeting that met in British-occupied Philadelphia in 1777 experienced "a most precious favoured quiet" where a "Concern of Reformation took its Rise . . . & was very lively Several years but all Dies away as soon as peace is Proclaimed."[44] To Hunt, wartime trials triggered the upsurge in wide-ranging Quaker reform activities.

Burlington resident Samuel Allinson (fig. 12) possessed one of the strongest voices for Quaker reform and worked tirelessly within a dedicated network of antislavery activists including Anthony Benezet and Granville Sharp. Allinson's sensitivity to the hypocrisy of patriot rhetoric led him to write Patrick Henry, whom he did not know personally, about the audacity of the resistance movement in rejecting the "limited Slavery" of colonial dependence, but still "by our practice declar[ing], that *absolute Slavery* is not unjust to a race of fellow Men because they are black."[45] To Allinson, independence threatened moral disaster because slavery possessed far greater legal and social support in America than it did in Great Britain. Whereas the Somerset decision had outlawed slavery in England in 1772, Allinson doubted that an American court, in the supposed "land of *Liberty*," would have passed the same proper judgment.[46] Like Jonathan Odell, Allinson knew that patriot claims to champion liberty were fundamentally flawed.

The American Revolution thoroughly dismantled the colonial order in Burlington. Odell would never return, and the Anglican Church faced a trying institutional redefinition in a republic that prohibited government influence on religion. But Quakers felt the brunt of Revolutionary change even more intensely, for the Society of Friends had directly instructed its members to stand apart from the patriot movement. Both religious groups would remain locally influential well into the nineteenth century, but their terms of engagement with national society would be stripped of their colonial privileges.

When Quakers found themselves persecuted by patriot conscription laws and loyalty oaths, the Burlington reformer Samuel Allinson explained to New Jersey's first postcolonial governor that protecting the rights of Friends would support "the ends of political harmony & union" far more than "measure[s] which, tho popular, may be more inflammatory & violent, & thereby cannot endure." Allinson's legal training ably prepared him to confront leading republicans like Governor William Livingston about how opposition whig values should be interpreted and implemented in the new republic. To Allinson, discriminatory anti-Quaker laws were "inconsistent with true Liberty" and "injudicious, hurtful, & therefore extremely impolitick."[47] Being a conscientious Quaker reformer by no means blinded Allinson to Anglo-American republican values; indeed, if fear of the abuse of power lay at the heart of that tradition, Quakers understood opposition ideology better than many patriots.

Governor Livingston's careful reply to Allinson tellingly reveals the tightly bound relationships among group identity, social order, and popular sovereignty in the new republic. Where Allinson feared that individual and group rights would be threatened by popular measures, the governor offered precisely the opposite view. To Livingston, the strength of the republic was that "whenever the people find any law inconvenient, & petition their Representatives for its repeal, it will, of course, be abolished." Beyond his confidence in majoritarian rule, Livingston further believed that legal exemptions for Quakers would harm the government and "tend to its dissolution." Because republican government was supposed to benefit everyone equally, a republic required "an equal partiscipation [sic] of what is manifestly necessary to the continuance of its existence."[48] During the Revolution, as in much recent debate about multiculturalism, many believed that making exceptions to general rules to accommodate diverse local circumstances would subvert the public good.

Livingston cast his refusal to protect Quakers in an otherwise cordial letter and accepted Friends as truly principled in their pacifist objections to war. His manner of explaining his warm feelings toward the Society fascinatingly invokes the ongoing challenges posed by the integration and exclusion of distinctive groups in a multicultural society. Livingston boasted, "I think myself as remote from bigotry as I am from Popery." As a prominent Presbyterian, from which position he had long championed the rights of religious dissenters against an Anglican establishment in New York, Livingston perceived Protestant unity as essential to the stability of the fragile republican experiment. In this religious struggle for truth, Livingston readily acknowledged that Quakers had done a great deal to challenge and expose the corruptions of Catholicism. In fact, he valued Quaker practices so highly as to exclaim, "*I am more than half a Quaker myself.*"[49] Although a high degree of sympathy informed the extended correspondence between Allinson and Livingston, their strong differences on fundamental issues never waned. Their sustained dialogue reminds us that our assessment of the American Revolution needs to examine how cultural forces based in religion, race, and ethnicity influenced Revolutionary experience.

Revolutionary Polarization in New Castle

Political opinion in New Castle divided sharply during the Revolution, but patriots gradually achieved dominance there as radical Presbyterians pushed more cautious Anglicans to support independence. This local development occurred in a state where Revolutionary allegiance followed a striking geographic pattern. Patriots in New Castle County spearheaded the Revolution in Delaware, well ahead of the state's two southerly and more conservative counties.[50] This partisan geography largely followed distinctive colonial immigration and settlement patterns. Northernmost New Castle County received strong Scots Irish immigration in the eighteenth century, and this group played an important role, pushing the Revolution forward against the wishes of many in the more Anglo southernmost counties with their stronger Anglican and Methodist presence. As one Delaware loyalist exclaimed, he preferred "a tyrannical king [to] a tyrannical commonwealth, especially if the d—d Presbyterians had the control of it."[51] The Revolutionary trajectory in the town of New Castle fits this statewide pattern. Although a divided community with loyalists and many conservative patriots, radicals gradually carried the day there, especially under the local leadership of Thomas McKean (later to achieve greater fame as governor of Pennsylvania) and the Presbyterian minister Joseph Montgomery.

Thomas McKean helped organize the resistance movement in New Castle starting in the 1760s and as an early influential radical leader had no counterpart in either Burlington or Easton. He was the son of Scots Irish immigrants and attended Francis Allison's New London Academy, overseen by the Presbyterian Synod, with several other future patriot leaders. McKean moved to New Castle in 1758 to study law with his cousin David Finney and within a decade was the busiest attorney in town. McKean soon entered politics and was elected to the assembly in 1762 at only twenty-eight years of age. Three years later he would be a delegate to the Stamp Act Congress and carried such a strong grudge against two delegates from Burlington who refused to sign the agreement that he traveled to their hometown to challenge them to duels.[52] Popular opinion in New Castle seems to have matched McKean's aggressive style, for crowds turned out there to create the growing protest movement. In 1765 stamps could not be unloaded across its docks for fear that they would be destroyed.

Delaware's unusual political status under the loose supervision of the proprietary governor of Pennsylvania meant that the colony had few recipients of direct British patronage and certainly none prominent enough to lead loyalist opposition against the cautiously whiggish assembly when McKean became the speaker in 1773, and especially after June 1774 when McKean organized a mass meeting to decry the punishment of Boston for its tea tax protests. He gave a stirring speech before an audience of more than five hundred, and his colleague, George Read Sr., the leader of conservative patriots in New Castle, observed, "not a sign of dissent appeared" in the whole crowd.[53] Quite unlike the cautious neutrality of Burlington, New Castle seized a leading place in its colony's protest movement. Nine men from the town (six of them from the top decile of taxpayers) were named to a thirteen-person committee to urge the assembly to send delegates to the Continental Congress. A month later, Delaware's key trio of Revolutionary leaders—Read and McKean of New Castle and Caesar Rodney of Dover—was sent to the Congress in Philadelphia.

The opposition now had a clear political infrastructure in place locally and continentally, but only the outbreak of war in Massachusetts in April 1775 decisively shifted the conflict from formal protest and sporadic resistance to sustained mobilization. Joseph Montgomery, the Presbyterian pastor at New Castle, observed the Continental Congress' day of fasting on July 20, 1775, with a sermon to the local militia company commanded by Samuel Patterson. Montgomery began by stressing the powerful communal nature of the fast day with some "two millions of intelligent Beings . . . engaged in the same public acts of religious worship," a "grand assembly of the inhabitants of the continent . . . by order of the Congress."[54] Participation in the religious ritual built local solidarity and reinforced the more abstract union of Americans throughout the colonies. Montgomery's long discourse emphasized that historical and biblical evidence not only legitimated but demanded armed resistance. The ease with which he shifted from congressional quotes to scriptural parallels demonstrates how a Calvinistic perspective helped encourage the popular movement toward war.[55] Whereas Jonathan Odell, the Anglican minister in Burlington, found his religious mission at odds with the illegal Continental Congress, New Castle's Presbyterian minister inspired men to rebel, a call that Quakers throughout the Delaware Valley abhorred.

The heart of Montgomery's sermon proclaimed the need for united action and fused religious and political inspiration. After reading from the long proclamation of the Continental Congress, he interjected, "My God, how important the day! . . . When the inhabitants of a whole country are forced, by a wanton exercise of arbitrary power, to fly to the *Lord God of Hosts.*"[56] The biblical exegesis that formed the body of the sermon examined the history of the Israelites from Abraham to Moses, closing with the injunction that success rested upon keeping their covenant with the Lord. In order to make the biblical text "suitable for our present solemnity," Montgomery allowed that "it may be necessary for us to take a short review of our political state . . . and then see, whether the words of my text wont apply to us, and whether I may not with propriety address you in the words of Moses."[57] The relationship between biblical example and the present situation may not have been entirely self-evident, but he carefully explained the parallel to push his audience to action.

Montgomery told the militia that the "the fatal day . . . is come, when our connection with the parent state must be dissolved."[58] Although colonists never primarily identified themselves as American at any point in the colonial period, Montgomery argued that the central experience justifying independence lay in the social development of Americans as a unique people. Violent contact with Indians caused American divergence from its Anglo origins. Colonists "conquered" Indians to "make room" for themselves when denied access to Native Americans' land. Because no "foreign aid appear[ed] to protect . . . [the colonists in] their infant state," a process of independent Americanization had begun that distinguished colonists from both Native Americans and Europeans.[59] Although Revolutionary allusions to Indians were historical and metaphorical in New Castle, we shall see that Native Americans remained a pressing Revolutionary reality in Easton.

As we have seen in Burlington, many Delaware Valley residents enjoyed the fruits of empire, and most Quakers remained committed pacifists even after the start of the war, so it is not surprising that Montgomery lampooned Quaker pacifism as unmanly. Americans would either "submit our necks to the yoke" of slavery or "stand up in our own defense, resolved to live free-men."[60] Because "common sense, and the feelings of mankind, have long since reprobated the absurd doctrine of passive obedience and non-resistance," he refused to consider any non-martial alternative. When "the dogs of war are let loose in our borders," men had to act because "the eyes of our aged fathers, our ancient matrons, the eyes of our wives, our maidens and children, will all look up to you for protection."[61] Montgomery put his case starkly: militiamen either fought or ignored their masculine responsibilities as sons, husbands, fathers, and free men. The mainspring of popular Revolutionary ideology here was biblical example, opposition to Indians, and manliness that together demanded military action. Ironically, Montgomery's passion for the cause soon deprived New Castle of an ardent radical. He lived up to his own rhetoric by becoming a brigade chaplain to the Delaware regiment of the Continental Army in 1776 and never returned to the town where he had been the Presbyterian pastor since 1769.[62] The lure of patriot leadership also led Thomas McKean away from New Castle as a Delaware delegate to the Continental Congress, and by 1775 he had moved permanently to Philadelphia with its larger stage for action.

On the same day of rest when Montgomery delivered his militia sermon, Alexander Porter, the wealthiest man in town, was censured by the New Castle County Committee of Inspection for working his slaves. While admitting that his actions were "apparently contrary" to the resolves of Congress, Porter insisted that his actions marked no opposition to the movement "to free our countrymen in America from a compleat system of slavery," for "work of necessity" deserved dispensation from the day of rest. Although his slaves had already been cutting wheat for two weeks, "owing to the scarcity of men to be hired in harvest," his grain was becoming too ripe to let stand any longer. As a result, Porter ordered his slaves to process the crop before it spoiled. Porter even claimed to have worked them from "an apprehension prevailing in the neighborhood of the Negroes rising, and destroying the white people." By keeping his slaves busy all day, he "prevent[ed] them running through the country, putting good people in fear."[63]

Porter's defense strikingly juxtaposed two dramatically different understandings of slavery. While he feared that white colonists might be enslaved, his own mastery prevented slave rebellion. Like most other slaveholders in the mid-1770s, Porter saw no contradiction in the seemingly paradoxical manner that slavery shaped his world, precisely the patriot hypocrisy that the Burlington Quaker Samuel Allinson denounced. Porter feared falling under a system of slavery and was committed to independence, yet his reliance on slave labor required that he break the patriot call for a universal day of rest.

Porter's fears about controlling slaves during the Revolution were well founded. Enslaved people continually fled masters whenever the opportunity presented itself, as it frequently did along Delaware's long coast where British naval ships provided slaves with a ready means to escape bondage. The pattern William Adair reported for the small port of Lewes in southern Delaware held true in New Castle as well: "English Men of War [landed]--·-Negroes gone aboard."[64] When provided with a reasonable opportunity for success, slaves liberated themselves.

Samuel Patterson, New Castle's militia captain, was among those unable to control his slaves during the Revolution. When his friend James Booth prepared to visit British-controlled New York City under a flag of truce, Patterson granted him power of attorney to recover his property, which included a "Negro man named Richmond, formerly my Body Servant," as well as another black man, aged sixty, named Port Royal.[65] The apparent inconsistency of patriots fighting enslavement while holding slaves created no impediment to Revolutionary participation for leading patriots like Patterson and Porter, but the Revolution nevertheless politicized racial identity for both whites and blacks and made slavery a public "problem" as never before.[66]

The clash between the ideals of the Revolution and the necessities of wartime exposed numerous contradictions in the patriot movement.[67] This conflict was especially apparent when African Americans fled bondage from slavery-decrying patriots. A New Castle slave named Jim was one of many who exploited the tremor in his master's control during the Revolution. Porter had rented Jim to Thomas Montgomery, a man of modest means, who hoped to increase the value of his small estate by putting Jim to work as an agricultural laborer. However, Montgomery soon discovered that this rented bondsman had no intention of complying. The temporary master wrote to Porter in a rough hand that Jim "says he wants to drive a wagon and is not willing to do anything else." Even more extraordinarily, Jim had found a more suitable position for himself during his truancy. Although he would not be allowed to make his own work arrangements, Montgomery's resolve to force the slave to do fieldwork had been broken. The renter offered to pay Porter for "what cloes and mony you think is reasonable for what time I have had him" since "he is not willing to stay with me."[68] The rhetoric employed by patriots and the disruption of everyday life during the war strengthened the limited ability of enslaved people to successfully challenge their unfree condition. Even so, enslaved people's quest for freedom fell outside the scope of what patriots judged legitimate political action.

Most moderate whigs, such as George Read Sr., hoped that resistance would cause little social change and sought reconciliation with Britain into the summer of 1776. The New Castle delegates at the Second Continental Congress, McKean and Read, sharply disagreed about the crucial vote for independence. Like his close friend Jonathan Dickinson, Read opposed severing ties to Britain, which necessitated Caesar Rodney's famed ride from Dover to Philadelphia to cast the deciding vote in favor of independence. Read later changed his position and signed the document after it had become a fait accompli.[69] When the Declaration of Independence was publicly presented in New Castle on July 24, a large crowd "gave three Huzzas—and immediately tooke the King's arms" out of the courthouse and "burnt them with the Constable's Stave &c."[70] Enoch Anderson, a member of the state militia remembered the day's events similarly, though as part of an organized military effort rather than a spontaneous crowd action. Anderson had marched with his troop from nearby Wilmington to New Castle, where "we took out of the Court-House all the insignias of Monarchy,—all the baubles of Royalty, and made a pile of them before the Court House" and "burnt them to ashes. This was our first jubilee on the fourth of July '76, and a merry day we made of it."[71] Outright rebellion in New Castle had begun by destroying the chief symbols of monarchy and English law to the cheers of a large crowd.

Although McKean and especially Rodney are remembered today as Delaware's heroes at the Continental Congress, both radicals would lose their seats there after the fall 1776 elections, while Read would be re-elected along with other conservatives. McKean remained friendly with Read, but judged that election a major setback. As he explained, "the situation of Delaware gives me constant anxiety; the choice of Representatives in October 1776, and *their* choice of officers have occasioned all its misfortunes."[72] As McKean suggested, Delaware troops performed poorly in the field. By September 1776, the former militia captain Samuel Patterson had become the colonel of Delaware's Flying Camp sent to aid the Continental Army at New York City. However, as Patterson explained to Read, the condition of the troops was dire. Even without having faced the enemy, his battalion suffered major internal dissent, with five companies "almost lay[ing] down their arms" upon learning that Pennsylvanians received a bounty for their service. Meanwhile, another entire company deserted in the night. Patterson blamed lower officers chosen by their own men, which "Sacrife Liberty to licentiousness. . . . [H]ad I known the men in general I would never [have] went with them."[73] Caesar Rodney was even more outraged by "the scandalous behaviour of our troops" who ran from their lines in "a most dastardly manner."[74]

The news from Patterson's Flying Camp was dismal, but their slow movement to New York saved them from suffering the terrible patriot losses at the Battle of Long Island on August 27. Gunning Bedford, a wealthy New Castle resident who had married Read's sister, did see action there and reported it "a hard campaign and a discouraging one." One month later, though, just prior to another major patriot loss at Fort Washington, Bedford became despondent. Badly outnumbered and fearing attack, he wrote his brother-in law, "I mean to decline serving any longer if you think well of it. I believe too many of our officers will also as they talk generally of it . . . for my part am tired of the service."[75]

The British advance from New York to the Delaware River that emboldened Burlington's Jonathan Odell to lash out against rebel assaults upon his liberty had a chilling effect upon patriots. When the term of the Flying Camp expired in early December, Read bemoaned that they "have left the General in whole brigades . . . tho ever more wanted in the field."[76] Meanwhile, John McKinley, the president of Delaware and a timid whig, wrote Read regularly about assertive militia demands about their term of service and "by whom they would be paid."[77] Patriot ideals of an egalitarian and volunteer fighting force fell short of the hierarchy and discipline needed in an effective army.

The patriot cause had reached low ebb by December 1776, though Washington's daring counterattack at Trenton and Princeton brought desperately needed hope. Even as ardent a patriot as Caesar Rodney, writing from Trenton in the aftermath of victory, recognized the grave cost of the attack that had taken the life of Delaware's Colonel John Haslett. "Good God—What Havock they have made. He that hath not seen it can have no Idea. . . . Thus Ends a History which perhaps will afford you much more trouble than Real Satisfaction."[78] If as staunch a patriot as Rodney recoiled from the carnage of the victorious battlefield, the bloodshed and suffering surely heightened the pacifistic tenets of Burlington Quakers.

Rodney's somber tone in the face of victory was well placed, especially for New Castle residents, because the war's next phase brought British forces to their immediate locale. The main British advance upon Philadelphia in the summer of 1777 came up the Chesapeake Bay and landed at the head of the Elk River, across the narrow Delmarva Peninsula from New Castle. Militia captain John Clark, a wealthy man in the top decile of New Castle taxpayers, summoned his company to march and meet the British. Their response reveals the shallow patriot support in a dark hour. The opinions of the sixty-four men in Clark's company ranged from steadfast commitment to "damn'd if I'll march." All together, 42 percent of the men were prepared to march, while 23 percent adamantly refused. Over half of the company can be located in the New Castle tax list for 1776, allowing a measure of the relationship between social status and political allegiance. Strikingly, three-fourths of those who refused to march were local taxpayers. But economic status did not decisively shape willingness to fight. Among the six wealthiest militiamen, two were ready to serve, two refused, and two had more ambiguous positions (one reported sick, and another hired a substitute). Meanwhile, the poorest twelve men were nearly equally divided, although slightly more willing to march: seven ready, four opposed, and one excused with a "family in distress."[79] Similarly, their religious affiliations showed no decisive difference between Presbyterian and Anglican willingness to meet the enemy.

The British advance clarified the vulnerability of New Castle's exposed river location, and the town's leading role in Delaware's formal political life was about to end. Although the new state constitution would be drafted there, fear of British naval attack and desire for a more centrally located capital led the state government to relocate to Dover. The move proved a wise step, as one Hessian soldier reported seeing 150 British ships anchored off New Castle in November 1777.[80] Attack from the river remained a constant local fear throughout the war, and Caesar Rodney reported being "Constantly Alarmed in this Place by the Enemy" because "seldom a day passes but Some man in this and the Neighboring Counties is taken off by these Villains." The British presence cooled the ardor of potential patriots, and Rodney knew many coastal residents "hearty in the cause, [who] dare neither act nor Speak lest they should be taken away and their houses plundered."[81]

While patriots cast such actions as villainous, the British presence encouraged neutrals and loyalists to hold their ground and offered profitable trading opportunities. Despite patriot strength in New Castle, a notable pocket of disaffected people lived in the town. Patriot courts regularly charged local people with illegally trading with the British. Jacob Vandegrift offered a typical admission that he had traded with British vessels "in the cove of New Castle and thare did deal with the crew on board and gave them a parcel of poultry and vegetables in satisfaction for a barrel of salt." In his appeal for a pardon, Vandegrift explained that he did so only from "fear of being distressed by ye English" who "were often a Shore . . . and threatened many that did not deal so I went and got a little salt as the rest of my neighbors did."[82] The New Castle taxpayer Charles Bryson embraced loyalism with unusual force, admitting to patriot authorities "he had dealt with the Enemy & would do it again and that he had taken Protection Under the Crown & would Defend it."[83] New Castle was a divided community in which political allegiance could not be taken for granted.

New Castle residents faced regular attack from the river for six full years, but local patriots must have been most fearful during the British occupation of Philadelphia from September 1777 to June 1778. When Ambrose Serle, Lord Admiral Howe's personal secretary, landed at New Castle in October 1777, he found it "utterly abandoned by the Inhabitants on account of their Concern in the Rebellion." After a brief meeting with Richard McWilliams, a wealthy New Castle man whose son was a lieutenant in the Continental Army, Serle judged "most of the people in the neighborhood, of Ireland" as participants in the rebellion and "tainted with its Principles." In contrast to the Irish, Serle viewed Methodists and Quakers as "generally loyal."[84]

Serle's perceptions of the rebellion were much like those of Jonathan Odell; both valued the stable order provided by an Anglican hierarchy crowned by the king. Thus Serle saw the conflict as "very much a religious war; and every one looks to the Establishment of his own Party upon the Issue of it."[85] Serle confirmed his views about the religious foundations of Revolutionary allegiance while visiting New Castle. A week after meeting McWilliams, he attended a service at New Castle's Anglican church while under the protection of the British fleet in the harbor. Independence altered the terms under which Anglican churches operated more than any other nonpolitical institution in the colonies, especially the patriot demand that the liturgy drop its traditional prayers for the king. Aeneas Ross, the Anglican minister in New Castle, however, did not halt services completely. When Serle attended Ross's church, he witnessed "an odd motley Service of religion. . . . The Parson, one Ross, read the Liturgy, garbled of the Prayers for the King and Royal Family; after w[hic]h, one of Mr. Wesley's [Methodist] Preachers mounted the Pulpit, and gave us a long & full Prayer for the King & a Blessing on his Arms, which, the author being evidently illiterate, was for the matter & manner curious enough."[86] Although Methodists are sometimes portrayed as ardent evangelical patriots, this mistakenly conflates two popular movements that mostly had opposite goals in the 1770s. As Serle observed, Methodists in New Castle, and Delaware more broadly, tended toward staunch loyalism. Methodism remained a movement *within* the Anglican Church until 1784, and its leader, John Wesley, clearly counseled loyalism. Meanwhile, Francis

Asbury, the postwar leader of independent Methodism in America, hid under the protection of a loyalist patron in southern Delaware for most of the war.[87]

The strong Methodist loyalism that Serle observed in New Castle was not fully shared by the Anglican rector Ross, who conformed to patriot laws by mumbling prayers for the Crown, yet permitted a loyalist sermon by a nonresident minister who could avoid punishment should patriots regain the town. Perhaps long family service prompted Ross to keep the church open throughout the war; his father had been the founding missionary of the church in 1705, and Aeneas had inherited the pastorate from him in 1758. At least when the British navy anchored offshore, an itinerant minister could preach openly in support of the king, although Ross himself avoided such a stand and may have been the most pro-patriot Anglican minister in Delaware.[88]

Numerous examples of loyalist activity around New Castle suggest that some people there strongly opposed the Revolution, but this evidence often resulted from the high level of patriot surveillance in the town. William Haslett, who told Captain Clark that he would "never march" in the militia in July 1777, was identified by a British undercover agent as an ally willing "to point out some inveterate rebels if an officer would call at his house"; however, without such assistance, "he is afraid to appear as they have threatened him."[89] Haslett had learned to disguise his political opinions because he had been brought into court earlier for referring "in a laughing manner" to the appointment of "the old miller," Samuel Patterson, as brigadier general in the militia.[90]

Openly loyalist New Castle residents faced abuse for expressing opinions considered moderate in the southern part of the state where armed loyalist bands rose to counter the rebellion. In New Castle, by contrast, retribution against loyalists came swiftly. John Watson reported that "he made all the opposition he could to the Rebellion & was therefore mobbed and insulted by the People of the Town." Watson even tried to organize an "Association of the Loyalists of New Castle for the purpose of assisting and supporting his Majesty's Government." However, when the British army left the area, his plans were "overset."[91] Loyal beliefs and actions forced Watson, the innkeeper John Drake, and their families to flee New Castle permanently. Drake's wife "received a wound from a Musket Ball in the back of her neck" when the militia fired at her and Mrs. Watson as they fled to a British vessel moored offshore New Castle.[92] Even in the face of a strong British military presence, the militia could act boldly, and Ambrose Serle almost suffered capture while wandering around New Castle when "60 of the Rebel militia, who had secreted themselves in an adjacent Wood for a Day and a night" seized the seamen who manned his transport.[93]

The determination of Watson and Drake to uphold British rule differed markedly from the path of the town's wealthiest loyalist, Theodore Maurice, who left New Castle peaceably in June 1778. His cordial stay in war-torn New Castle made the Loyalist Claims Commission suspicious about his political allegiance. He explained this by noting that the rebel "leaders were his Friends and very moderate People" who accepted him as "under Parole in point of honor not to act against them." The leading Pennsylvania loyalist Joseph Galloway offered Maurice supporting testimony—one "could remain there quietly without trimming—as they were moderate People in the Delaware Government."[94] Galloway even believed that a majority in the Delaware assembly favored retaining colonial status, but as a small state could not do so safely. The moderation of Delaware leaders, which so infuriated radicals such as Thomas McKean, allowed passive loyalists such as Maurice to remain in New Castle without harassment.

The mixed allegiance of local people in New Castle, as well as the relative lenience of the Delaware government, is showcased in the "Act of Free Pardon and Oblivion" that the assembly issued on June 26, 1778, as the British withdrew from Philadelphia. As the main theater of war shifted away from the Delaware Valley, the legislature sought to strengthen patriot unity by offering an olive branch to those disaffected from the cause. In order "to mitigate [rather] than to increase the horrors of war," the act promised that those who had previously abetted the British would be "fully, freely and absolutely pardoned," though barred from voting or holding civil or military office, upon swearing or affirming their support for the new state.[95] The act also cast forty-six especially offensive individuals into oblivion by barring them from the pardon. Twenty of these were from New Castle County, and the town of New Castle had the highest incidence of unforgivable loyalism, with seven men denied the pardon. Although New Castle was a patriot town, a strong undercurrent of loyalism thrived there.

The fracturing of political allegiance in wartime New Castle not only divided patriots and loyalists but also bitterly split radical and conservative patriots, an animosity that would shape local and state politics for decades to come. The war disrupted how local people understood one another, especially when religious and ethnic associations reinforced political allegiance. Presbyterians tended to be radical patriots, as suggested by Reverend Montgomery's early militia sermon and the leadership of Thomas McKean, while Anglicans were more likely to be conservative whigs like George Read Sr., or even loyalists, as suggested by sermons delivered at New Castle's Anglican church.

The general composition of the town's Anglican and Presbyterian congregations in the late eighteenth century gives an indication of their changing fortunes as religion became politicized in Revolutionary New Castle. Anglicans dominated in 1776, with 29 percent of all taxpayers and

82 percent of those with known religious affiliation. Although town residents at all economic levels belonged to Immanuel Church, Anglican influence was especially striking among the most affluent quintile of taxpayers, 42 percent of whom were Anglicans versus just 9 percent of whom were Presbyterians. However, the relationship between these two leading local religious groups changed dramatically by 1798. The refashioned Episcopal church basically held steady, with 28 percent among all New Castle taxpayers, but lost significant support among wealthy people, who increasingly joined the Presbyterian church. Presbyterians in the top tax quintile more than trebled from 1776 to 1798, while Anglicans in the wealthiest group plummeted by half. By 1798 New Castle's Episcopal church drew its strongest membership from the bottom three quintiles of the tax structure. Although additional factors need to be explored to fully explain the changing face of religious affiliation in New Castle, patriot success buoyed local support for Presbyterianism among economic elites and drove them away from Anglicanism.[96]

Many years later when Thomas McKean explained the basic cleavages of the Revolution in the Delaware Valley to John Adams, his close ally at the Continental Congress, he emphasized the intertwining of religion and politics. To McKean, the patriot movement in the region arose to contest a corrupt political system that gave Quakers unrepresentative political power. He further believed that loyalism in Delaware arose from Anglican missionaries who explained the rebellion as a "plan of Presbyterians to get their religion established." In short, McKean believed that "the opposition consisted chiefly of the Friends or Quakers, the Menonists [i.e., the Mennonites, a German pacifist sect], the Protestant Episcopalians, . . . and from the officers of the crown and proprietors."[97] A fuller sense of McKean's own family, however, reminds us of the permeability of culture and the necessity of assessing it from within the logic of local circumstances. McKean descended from Ulster immigrants and attended Joseph Montgomery's Presbyterian church in New Castle, but his wife was a pious Anglican, and his brother Robert (with whom Thomas was quite close) was an Anglican missionary and a strong supporter of an American episcopate.

The point in recovering the importance of religion for the Revolutionary transformation of the Delaware Valley is not to insist that all members of a particular congregation had common political views. Rather, religion offered a way of thinking and a set of beliefs and practices that people used to assess themselves and their society. Because the Revolutionary War inaugurated a sustained period of rapid social change, it heightened awareness about how cultural diversity shaped the fabric of everyday life in the Delaware Valley. To create a stable postcolonial society, however, the local passions that had been central to the wartime mobilization would need to cool, yet the conflation of religion and political allegiance that pitted radical Presbyterians against conservative Anglicans would continue in Delaware's vitriolic postwar struggles.

Forging American Unity in Easton

Residents of colonial capitals like Burlington and New Castle on the coastal plain mostly assessed the independence movement and its military struggle in relationship to Britain. The opportunities that had once been available to them as small ports in the imperial Atlantic world now became liabilities, as patriot galleys, British naval ships, and loyalist raiders all enjoyed easy access to places on the lower Delaware River. People in Easton, further upriver and near the frontier, still actively engaged Native Americans and settled what they believed to be "new" land. The Revolution politicized local identities in Easton, as it did in the other towns, but the logic of local circumstances took different shape here. While conservative neutrality had majority support in Burlington, and patriotism gradually won control in New Castle, Easton completes the spectrum of Revolutionary allegiance with a relatively unified embrace of the patriot movement. This unity was forged in an unfamiliar way, as the local Pennsylvania German majority overthrew a small Scots Irish colonial elite and solidified patriot solidarity in a backcountry war against Indians.

While the Scots Irish in New Castle were among its most ardent patriots, this did not hold true in Easton and surrounding Northampton County. The correlation of ethno-religious identity with political allegiance grows out of daily life, not from a biologically determined orientation to the world or fixed philosophical outlook. In the midst of massive Pennsylvania German settlement in and around Easton, the Scots Irish were colonial insiders, which tended to dampen their Revolutionary ardor. In fact, Mt. Bethel Township, just north of Easton, had the highest rate of seized loyalist property in Northampton County and was a predominantly Scots Irish and Presbyterian settlement.[98] The local conditions that encouraged this group to become patriots in New Castle did not exist around Easton. Similarly, while most (never all, as we will see) Pennsylvania Germans in Northampton County supported the patriots, this was hardly the case everywhere, as German-speaking settlers in the Carolina backcountry and in New York's Mohawk Valley were ardent loyalists.[99] The political salience of ethnic and religious identity must be explained with an understanding of local circumstances.

The place of the Scots Irish atop the colonial order in Northampton County begins with the prominent proprietary leader William Allen, Pennsylvania's chief justice, and perhaps the colony's wealthiest and most powerful individual. His son James Allen regularly visited his country estate of Trout Hall in Northampton Town (later Allentown), up the Lehigh River from Easton, and was elected to the assembly from the county in May 1776.[100] Although the

Allens participated in the early resistance movement, they never accepted independence. James feared the militia's emergence as a political force in the summer of 1775 because it knew "no subordination" and chose to become an officer in hopes that "discreet people . . . may keep them in order." He thought himself "very obnoxious to the independents" in the assembly and, after less than a month there, retired from public life in Philadelphia to the relative safety of Northampton County. Anglicized Scots Irish elites like the Allens chose loyalty in a rebellion that created two classes of men, "those that plunder and those that are plundered." To James Allen, the Revolution empowered a "wretched set" in a "convulsion" that "brought the dregs to the top."[101]

Lewis Gordon offers the best example of an Anglo-Scot elite in Easton during the Revolution, a local version of the powerful Allens on the reduced scale of the modest county seat. As a charter member of the St. Andrew's Society, a Scottish immigration association founded in Philadelphia in 1749, Gordon maintained a strong ethnic sense of self.[102] Nevertheless, he simultaneously moved in leading English social circles and married in Philadelphia's grand Anglican Christ Church. Gordon's ties to proprietary power appear in his appointment as a justice of the peace and prothonotary in Northampton County.[103] Two grand jury instructions that Gordon delivered at the Easton courthouse reveal the importance of Englishness to his sense of proper order. One explained to the jury that "amongst all the various and different forms and models of Laws and Constitutions which have obtained amongst mankind, none exceeds or affords greater blessings than those of the English." The other similarly lauded the distinctive benefits of English law and traditions: "The Liberty which English subjects claim as their indefensible inheritance and Birth-right is not such a freedom from all restraint . . . as would leave every man his own avenger. . . . For nothing is more consistent than Law and Liberty; nay there cannot be political Liberty without Law."[104] Such an understanding of the Anglo basis of legal rights was widespread in colonial America, but in the context of a predominantly Pennsylvania German local population, Gordon's views could spark local resentment.[105] Ethnic identity undergirded assumptions about the operation of the legal system in Easton, for when the justices there attempted to block an appeal by Nathaniel Vernon on a technicality, he insisted that "[although] I am not a lawyer; I am an Englishman and think myself intitled to the Benefit of the Law."[106] His outburst may well have stemmed from not wanting to be treated like a German colonist, who might readily suffer intimidation and discrimination in an English-speaking court.

Pennsylvania Germans certainly participated in the colonial court at Easton as plaintiffs, defendants, and jurors in the eighteenth century, but they rarely occupied the most powerful positions of magistrates or attorneys.[107] Most lawyers who practiced in eighteenth-century Easton were sojourners from Philadelphia. Indeed, only three Easton residents, all of them of British descent, were admitted to the bar before 1800: Lewis Gordon, Robert Traill, and Samuel Sitgreaves (who moved there from Philadelphia in 1786).[108] Similarly, formal politics allowed little local influence because Northampton voters, like those from other non-Anglo backcountry counties, sent only one representative each to the assembly until the eve of independence. Proprietary and Quaker political opponents cooperated to ensure that English areas retained electoral strength and dominated political and legal power in colonial Pennsylvania.

The Continental Congress' presence in Philadelphia created a political institution that challenged the legitimacy of proprietary power and the conservative popular assembly. When Northampton County created a committee of observation and inspection in December 1774 to enforce the boycott established by the Congress, an essential local institution began that empowered local people and eventually assumed all government responsibilities. Nobody could have foreseen such an audacious expansion of the county committee's authority, as its founders were leading local men rather than a radical vanguard. Five of the most active seven individuals who formed its standing committee and clerk were from Easton, or its immediate area, and represented wealthy and traditionally influential men, chief among them Lewis Gordon, who would chair the committee for the next two years.[109]

The slide toward war in New England and the committee's regular correspondence with others in the resistance movement gradually led Easton residents to accept and even embrace radical action. In the wake of the violence at Lexington and Concord, an Easton mass meeting unanimously resolved, "the British Ministry are fully determined and bent upon the total Extinction and utter destruction of American Liberty." Participants swore to join together to avert "being reduced to so abject a degree of slavery," a pledge which circulated in German and English newspapers. Eighty-seven Easton men, an easy majority of the town's taxpaying households, joined the militia under Captain Peter Kachlein Sr.[110]

Raising the volunteer military force dominated the attention of the Northampton Committee in the summer of 1775. If extralegal political institutions marked one crucial step toward ending colonial rule, the creation of the Revolutionary militia was an essential second one. As a locally based grassroots organization, the militia played an even larger role bringing the Revolution to ordinary people. The Northampton Committee chose Abraham Miller as the recruiting officer for the county militia to join the Continental Army at Cambridge, Massachusetts, and asked Miller if he would also serve as its captain. Colonial authorities in Philadelphia opposed this selection and advised the county committee that Thomas Craig was a more "proper person" to command the new company. Unwilling to dismiss a leading local Pennsylvania German in whom they had confidence, the committee only agreed to appoint Craig should Miller resign. When the militia itself voted for Miller to be their captain the following month, a pattern of local militia autonomy, often in defiance of Philadelphia authorities (whether the conservative colonial assembly or subsequent patriot leaders) emerged that would be maintained throughout the Revolution.[111]

Sustained armed conflict recast the local resistance movement. Lewis Gordon, who had chaired most local committee meetings and had been named as a delegate to most Philadelphia meetings (though these he declined to attend), suddenly found himself "indisposed" when the Northampton Committee met on May 30, 1776, to consider "establishing a new government under the Authority of the People" as directed by the Continental Congress. Abraham Berlin replaced Gordon as Easton's representative on the Northampton Committee of Inspection and joined Gordon on the influential standing committee that held real power. The transition of local leadership from Gordon to Berlin, like Abraham Miller's advancement over Thomas Craig to head the militia, marked a key shift as local Pennsylvania Germans increasingly took leadership positions, often against the wishes of centralized authority in Philadelphia. Craig and Gordon both were elite Scots with proprietary connections, whereas Miller and Berlin came from the county's Pennsylvania German majority. Berlin had been among Easton's founders in 1752 and as a talented blacksmith and gunsmith was taxed in the town's top quintile in 1774. Perhaps even more significant than his status as a long-term resident and skilled artisan, however, was his prominence in both local German churches. He served on leading Lutheran committees, yet baptized his children in the local Reformed church. Such mixed religious affiliation with active participation in both congregations occurred regularly among Easton's Pennsylvania Germans in the late eighteenth century and markedly contrasted with religious patterns in New Castle and Burlington. Indeed, in the early 1770s, more Easton taxpayers participated in both the Reformed and Lutheran congregations than solely as Lutherans.[112] The replacement of Anglo-American colonial leaders with Pennsylvania Germans such as Miller and Berlin brought Easton and Northampton County to the brink of Revolution. With patriot confidence booming in midsummer 1776, popular opinion surged beyond the control of Easton's colonial leaders. Lewis Gordon became the focus of patriot hostility when the Northampton Committee's moderation was denounced and its members accused of being "Tories and disaffected to the Common Cause of American Liberty." Gordon suffered direct attack when he was "openly and publickly called . . . a Scotch Bugger."[113]

The announcement of formal independence received symbolic community approval in Easton with a military procession complete with music and a new national flag flying at its head on July 8, 1776.[114] Peter Kachlein

Sr. and John Arndt marched in the parade as officers in the Revolutionary armed forces and help us to understand the composition of Easton's patriot leadership. Both possessed considerable property, were members of the local Reformed church, and strongly supported independence. Kachlein had emigrated from Germany and seems to have traveled with considerable resources—upon arriving in Easton he had built the town's first gristmill. When elected to the colonial assembly in 1774, he was the town's wealthiest taxpayer. John Arndt's father, Jacob, had immigrated and enjoyed success carving a farm from the Northampton wilderness, a livelihood that also prompted his service as an officer in the anti-Indian militia during the Seven Years' War. Jacob Arndt became active in civil politics during the Revolution and served in several capacities, including as a delegate at the state constitutional convention and as Northampton County's representative on the Council of Safety. In 1776, twenty-eight-year-old John Arndt followed in his father's martial footsteps by becoming a captain in Northampton's Flying Camp, serving under Colonel Peter Kachlein Sr.[115]

The encouragement of local leaders like Kachlein and Arndt, along with a three-pound bounty, stimulated a rush of enlistments in Easton the day following the Declaration of Independence parade. The *rage militaire* of war's opening moment appeared in full flower as relatives and friends joined together to fight. Kachlein's son served as the second lieutenant in Arndt's company, which itself included three other Arndt kin. A muster roll for John Arndt's company survives, allowing a close consideration of the social background of those who responded to the initial call to arms. Ten of the company can be located in Easton tax lists from the 1770s, and at first glance it seems that even at this opening stage of the war, military service mostly appealed to those at the low end of the economic scale, with seven men from the lowest two tax quintiles. Many more must have been too young or too poor to be taxed, but one should not rush to declare this a poor man's army, especially at the opening stage of the conflict. Many men in the company, like their captain who lived just across the town boundary, were taxed in other townships, and several young men in the company, like Peter Kachlein Jr., who was taxed in the fourth quintile, were sons from wealthy families. Interestingly, Sergeant Andrew Herster and Corporal Peter Richter attained leadership positions despite coming from the town's lowest tax quintile. Overall, age played a larger role than mere economic status in determining military participation.

The religious affiliations of fourteen men in the company reinforce the sense that these early volunteers had well-established local ties and were not mere drifters with limited options. Two striking anomalies appear when comparing the company's religious affiliation with that of the town's overall taxed population in 1772 and 1774. First, German Reformed adherents were dramatically overrepresented, at 54 percent of the company, versus 26 percent of the town. Furthermore, while the company's officers came from most economic ranks, five of them were Reformed church members (six, if we add battalion colonel Peter Kachlein Sr.). As we saw with Presbyterians in New Castle, it seems that Calvinists were more active patriots, though in Easton the Calvinists were German Reformed. Because only a single officer had unknown religious affiliation, the main underrepresented religious group in Arndt's company was the one that did not belong to any local congregation—23 percent of the company versus 36 percent in the overall taxed population. When the war began, those with weak ties to local institutions were also least likely to join the Flying Camp.

On the whole, Easton men responded enthusiastically to the patriot call, in notable contrast to the dissent that Samuel Patterson reported about the New Castle men who joined Delaware's Flying Camp. Such gusto meant little in the face of British military superiority, however, and Easton men soon participated in two of the worst patriot defeats of the early war. Colonel Kachlein's battalion stood at the point of attack in the successful British advance at the Battle of Long Island in late August 1776 that routed the patriot army. The battalion's ragged retreat and reorganization three months later at Fort Washington meant that they were among the large group that surrendered to the British there in November. Four months after its organization, more than two-thirds of Captain Arndt's 101–man company had been captured or killed. Colonel Peter Kachlein Sr. died while captive on a prison ship in New York harbor, and Captain John Arndt lost the use of his left arm from a battle wound.[116]

The patriot military failure around New York, which initiated the gradual British advance on Philadelphia, had a powerful impact in Easton, whose young men bore the heavy cost of defeat. Never again would the town rally so fully to face the British enemy, and the severe losses encouraged dissent on the home front similar to what occurred in New Castle. British military dominance in the Mid-Atlantic, starting in August 1776 and lasting through at least July 1778, produced sharp local conflict. The British advance across New Jersey in the fall of 1776 finally pushed Lewis Gordon off the Northampton Committee. After British general Howe announced an amnesty, Gordon refused to serve in any capacity, and the committee chose Abraham Berlin as their new chair. Thus Berlin completed his rise to local political prominence, which had begun when he replaced Gordon as Easton's representative on the committee seven months earlier.[117]

The changing fortunes of war encouraged complaints, especially from those who rejected the Northampton Committee's assumption of power. Patriot leaders frequently suffered angry chastisement, as when a group of local men "damn[ed] the Congress, Convention & Committee—saying that they were all a parcel of Dammed Rascals and were Selling the peoples liberties."[118] Disaffected local people often accused the patriot elite of peddling the peoples' liberties rather than protecting them. The most powerful rejection of local Revolutionary authorities built upon a sharp populist grievance. Michael and Jacob Messinger attacked the local committee as "the [Villains?] at Easton" and condemned its "leading men" as "Whigs for sake of Gains." The Messingers accused the movement's leaders of seeking personal profit and insisted that legitimate authority could only be based on majority support. Recalling the horrible causalities of war, they pointed out "many a thousand men we have lost by you Whigs already." Rather than follow such miserable leaders, they advised "that the people had better Rise and Hang" the rebels.[119] Although patriots maintained firmer control in Easton than in Burlington or New Castle, even here the Revolutionary struggle sparked divisive conflict over who should rule at home.

Popular sovereignty's wide-ranging implications could certainly be employed to condemn the Revolutionary government. The Messingers adamantly protested that they "had no right to be subject to . . . Laws of men that were not chosen by the majority of the people." As far as they were concerned, "the Council of Safety were robbers and them that put their laws in force were the same."[120] The elite loyalist James Allen, now captive in his Northampton estate and regularly harassed by the county militia, agreed that patriots had usurped proper representative government. Allen, after all, had been elected to the colonial assembly in May 1776 by a vote of 853 to 14, whereas the fall elections in 1777 only attracted 154 voters in the entire county, with just 5 votes cast in Easton. To Allen and loyalists like him, the "ridiculous" state government had made a "mockery of Justice," and the local militia acted as "barbarians."[121]

Commitment to popular sovereignty in the eighteenth century did not require an egalitarian vision. The Test Act, which compelled all adult men to swear their allegiance to the state, was a particularly offensive instrument. The Messingers denounced it as "an unjust oath and the King would hang us all and he had a right to do it." They went on to castigate the "foolish people that hath took the Oath" because anyone "had as good a right to be against the cause as . . . for it."[122] As all loyalists and neutrals painfully understood, patriots prohibited freedom of political conscience, and Delaware Valley rebels employed especially punitive force as the war turned disastrous for them with British control of Philadelphia in 1777 and 1778.

Pennsylvania Germans found the Test Act especially threatening because it required immigrants from Germany to explicitly break a previous loyalty oath. In order to enter Pennsylvania, Germans were required to "solemnly promise and engage that we will be faithful and bear true allegiance" to the king and the proprietor and to "strictly observe and conform to the laws . . . to the utmost of our power and best of our understanding."[123] The rationale for requiring people to swear commitment to the Revolutionary government rested upon a belief that autonomous individuals could equally and independently declare such a position. But this failed to acknowledge that individuals belonging to particular groups would feel the burden of such demands quite differently. Like Burlington Quakers whose peace testimony required that they decline even affirming commitment to the Revolutionary government, Pennsylvania Germans had distinctive reasons for dissenting from demands for Revolutionary conformity.[124]

Local implementation of sweeping laws like the Test Act, of course, allowed considerable latitude for evasion. Although Lewis Gordon refused to swear an oath to the new government and was supposed to have had his ferry seized as a result, he maintained the profitable privilege by leasing his boat and ferry rights to Peter Ealer, the county jailer, and to Jacob Abel, a tavern keeper. Gordon relied on a local social web that persisted despite intensified patriot-loyalist conflict. Notwithstanding such evasions, a new mark of public identity had been established that carried serious social consequences. Measuring individual allegiance through required oaths effectively reshaped the Delaware Valley's political culture.[125] When the constable John Batt attempted to bring two men before the court in August 1777, they threatened him with "a plaguey licking" because the constable "had not taken the Test according to the late Act of the Assembly." Another person confirmed the threat and added that had Batt attempted to serve him with a warrant, he would have "taken a stick and knocked [him] down."[126] The Test Act quickly became a required badge of commitment to the cause. In the limited social circles of the small town Delaware Valley, people knew where their neighbors stood. Those who refused to swear in places such as Easton and New Castle suffered harassment and verbal abuse at the very least.

Easton residents gradually offered broad general support to the patriot movement despite such rancor. Partly this happened because the county committee and militia systematically punished anyone who spoke out against the cause. Yet the growing patriot unity in Easton cannot be fully explained by brute punishment. As British attention turned to the southern campaign after the summer of 1778, local people increasingly viewed the armed conflict as a struggle against Native American enemies to the north and west. When local men marched to New York City to join the Flying Camp in early August 1776, preparations had also commenced to ensure "the safety of the County against the Incursions of the Indians." Arms were collected at Easton to repel the anticipated invasion from Indian country, and the militia would never be sent out of state (indeed, they protested leaving the county) for fear of Indian attack.[127] Even as the British army remained a direct threat in the Delaware Valley, the local militia refused orders to march for fear that "the Indians would be down upon their Families immediately."[128]

Before both sides descended into bloody violence, a final major attempt to salvage Indian-American relations took place in Easton. The conference held there from January 30 to February 6, 1777 was a faint coda to the town's weighty treaty meetings from 1755 to 1761. While significant changes had occurred over a decade and a half, a deep pattern of colonial-Indian relations reasserted itself as a council fire was lit one last time at the confluence of the Delaware and Lehigh rivers. The American rebellion portended dramatic new relationships, and at the start of the war British and American diplomats both rushed to ensure good relations with Indians, whose decisive action might decide the Revolution's outcome.

Easton occupied especially important ground for the varied Indian nations that had been forced from the Delaware Valley, first to the upper Susquehanna River Valley and now into the Ohio country. Symbolized above all by the Delaware leader Teedyuscung, who had defiantly challenged both proprietary and Iroquois power in the mid-1750s, and who had been murdered in his burned Wyoming home in 1763, the native groups that came to Easton in early 1777 still mostly sought an independent voice from centralized Iroquois control. Like proprietary and royal authorities before them, the Continental Congress hoped to limit its Indian diplomacy to negotiations with the Iroquois alone. The movement of "certain tribes of Indians living in the backparts of the country, near the waters of the Susquehanna" and their expectation of a conference at Easton forced the issue. Although the Congress deemed it improper "to kindle a council fire at that place, as they have already done the same at Albany," it ultimately agreed to the Easton meeting, though it viewed the western groups as "under the protection of the Six Nations."[129] The Pennsylvania and Continental governments in Philadelphia continued the colonial strategy of attempting to forge exclusive agreements between Iroquois and American elites who each would enforce compliance from wayward groups on their own side of the racial divide.

In late January some seventy Indian men, as well as women and children who traveled with them, arrived in Easton. Local preparations proceeded smoothly, as might be expected, as the town had hosted many such events since its founding only twenty-five years earlier. Indian access to liquor was restricted, and the militia provided a guard of three sergeants and thirty privates with a drummer and fifer to commemorate the event.[130] The meeting was held in Easton's largest building, the recently constructed union church shared by the German Reformed and Lutheran congregations, which had the additional advantage of an organ to enhance the proceedings. The conference began in the traditional manner, with shaking hands, exchanging belts, and drinking toasts while the organ played. A Seneca spokesperson, Captain Johnston, opened with a lengthy speech that ominously invoked the memory of Teedyuscung's death at Wyoming and insisted upon the end of land sales and new western settlement as established by the Treaty of Stanwix in 1768.

Johnston proved encouraging, however, on the Americans' most coveted issue and presented several belts and strings to clarify his commitment to peace and neutrality. He promised to prevent any parties from using Indian territory for military purposes and encouraged the Americans to "look to the Sea shore from whence all your troubles cometh." To Johnston, "the Quarrel is with you that are all one Colour and we have nothing to do with it."[131] Pleased by such sentiments, one Pennsylvania negotiator reported to state authorities that "with respect to the Present Dispute . . . they mean to be Neuter, we have already Learnt their good intentions and Great Expectations in Receiving Presents."[132] The cordial meeting continued with meals, dancing, and little hint of disturbance, although the American clerk Tom Paine refused to record Delaware and Munsee speeches that attempted to create independent places for themselves at the conference.

For their part, the American commissioners presented themselves on behalf of "the great Congress of the thirteen United States" and expressed pleasure "that you are come to Easton to keep alive the old council fire." They explained the American grievances against the British and reviewed the course of the war, emphasizing, of course, that British losses in New Jersey had the redcoats "running to their Canoes like frightened frogs." The commissioners worked to establish common ground by presenting belts and strings to encourage Indian neutrality that might become the basis for ongoing cooperation between Americans and native nations. Summarizing their main point in closing, they explained, "We have often told you in this talk that 'we have no other brothers but you' and in this Belt you will see that your English White Brothers are a going away and that you and we only remain to keep Up the old fire and shake hands together. A Belt."[133] Although traditional forms shaped this final Easton conference, most native people probably realized that American independence would terminate the fragile imperial restraints on white settlers' continued invasion of the continent. Overriding evidence of patriot lawlessness must have raised Native American doubts about future good relations with independent Americans.

The severe terms of postcolonial Indian relations became immediately apparent when the Continental Congress refused to recognize the agreement reached at Easton. Its Committee of Indian Affairs dismissed the negotiated truce, claiming "no Powers did exist in either of the Partys to enable them to engage in such a Treaty."[134] Easton would never again host an Indian treaty meeting that aspired to any sort of accommodation.

Hope for peace in the backcountry would be shattered the following summer. Many native groups, most famously the Mohawks led by Joseph Brant, judged their best prospects to lie with a decisive British victory, and significant bands of independent and integrated Indian, British, and loyalist forces operated throughout the Pennsylvania and New York interiors. This triple threat became the principle focus of the war for people in Easton and helped forge strong patriot unity. Native Americans came to Easton to light a council fire at the start of 1777, but two years later so many Indians were imprisoned there that they overflowed the jail and had to be held in militia colonel Isaac Sidman's stone house.[135]

After their terrible military losses to the British around New York in 1776, Easton men overwhelmingly sought positions in the anti-Indian militia, which allowed less onerous military service closer to home than the Continental Army. As a militia petition pointedly explained, "We have already done more than our duty." Rather than march south to neighboring Bucks County, the petitioners insisted upon staying in Northampton County, where "every three or four weeks murders [are] committed by them [the savage enemy] on said Frontiers."[136] The militia remained the preferred alternative for military service—as a home guard battling a demonized Indian enemy. Abraham Horn, for example, served as a sergeant in the Pennsylvania Line, but when discharged joined the militia "on the said frontier [of Northampton County] against the Indians" where he served for the duration of the war.[137] Others were drafted: Daniel Labar was only sixteen when conscripted into the militia at Easton "to repel the incursions of the Savages, which were then and at that neighborhood frequent and daring." His service as "minute man, or Indian Spy or Scout" lasted nearly two years.[138] Indian and loyalist attacks from the interior continued even after the American victory at Yorktown, and the Indian threat created a lasting Revolutionary memory in the area. Isaac Sidman's daughter Henrietta recalled in 1845 that "the old men living in Easton were in the habit of conversing" about "the incursions of the Indians" during the Revolution.[139]

After years of local appeals for a coordinated Continental Army invasion of Indian country, such a campaign finally took shape in the summer of 1779, with Easton as its main launching point. General George Washington's detailed directive to Major General John Sullivan left no question about the kind of war that was to be waged. "The immediate object is their *total destruction* and devastation, and the capture of as many persons of every age and sex as possible. It will be essential to ruin their crops now in the ground, and prevent their planting more. . . . [D]o it in the most effectual manner, that the country may not be *merely overrun, but* DESTROYED."[140] Washington required a ferocious effort of unabated destruction, since "our future security will be in . . . the distance to which they are driven, and in the terror . . . they will receive."[141]

The earlier peace efforts at Easton had been forgotten after two years of war. Sullivan tallied his troops' work with considerable pride. Forty towns razed, 160,000 bushels of corn destroyed, and "a vast quantity of vegetables of every kind" burned. While boasting that not a single town remained in Iroquois country, and that his army had "not suffered the loss of forty men," Sullivan noted that "few troops have experienced a more fatiguing campaign."[142] Sullivan's campaign used a brutality reserved for Indians who were considered to lie beyond the pale of civilization. Similar orders of total destruction were never issued against the British army or upon Euro-American settlements. Indeed, the violence central to Sullivan's campaign led some to recoil. Nicholas Fish, a regiment commander, commented that the expedition aimed at "an undistinguished destruction and carnage."[143]

Loyalists around Easton who allied with nearby Indians faced perilous consequences if discovered by patriots. Thomas Hughes, a British prisoner at Easton, witnessed the execution of Robert Morden, a "very old man" who was hanged there "for piloting some people through the back woods, to the Indians," one of only four civilians killed by the Pennsylvania government for treason during the Revolution.[144] Morden was a woodsman with working relationships with Delaware and Iroquois people and had helped the loyalist Robert Land escape Easton's jail. When discovered crossing the mountains north of town, Land successfully fled, but Morden chose to stay, faced trial, and suffered death by hanging on November 25, 1780.

The British and loyalist alliance with Indians solidified Easton residents' commitment as patriots, which by the end of the war helped to create a new understanding of their relationship to distant government authority. When the Treaty of Paris established clear protections for former loyalists who chose to return home, a mass meeting at Easton protested the reappearance of local men who had joined with Indians during the war. The meeting sent "instructions" to the state assembly to overturn the treaty. Easton residents' Revolutionary mobilization led to more direct participation in government and a new sense of themselves as Americans, a unity that rested on a racialized foundation. The instructions to the assembly explained that those returning to the patriot community "had joined the Indians" and "not only committed every species of devastation that attends the progress of such savage enemies, but had . . . their hands in the blood of our unprotected countrymen."[145] The fundamental mark of difference in Revolutionary Easton had become one that separated civilized Americans from savages who could be loyalists as well as Native Americans. An Indian presence helped to solidify what otherwise might have been diverse and unintegrated bands of European settlers and their descendants. The long-standing Anglo-American prejudice against Pennsylvania Germans as outsiders to their dominant law and culture certainly persisted, but with Englishness itself centrally challenged by the war, Pennsylvania Germans in Revolutionary Easton made major strides to achieve equality as white citizens of the new nation.

The viciousness of patriot-Indian encounters throughout the Revolution often seems to suggest that the enormous chasm separating the two groups could never be bridged. Although that divide increased dramatically during the war, the white versus Indian demarcation could still be transgressed as it had been during the colonial period. Even the journals of soldiers in Sullivan's campaign reveal more than a simple racial conceptualization of the world. The Continental soldiers who camped at Easton for two months in 1779 noted deep ethnic and religious divisions that challenged patriot unity and American nationalism. Samuel M. Shute saw in Easton a miserable town of about 150 houses with only "three elegant buildings in it, and about as many inhabitants that are any ways agreeable. Take them in general they are a very inhospitable set—all High Dutch & Jew." Daniel Livermore shared a similar opinion; to him, Easton residents were "chiefly Low Dutch, and . . . worship wholly in that way."[146]

James McMichael expressed the sharpest hostility toward Pennsylvania Germans around Easton. In marching through Northampton County's three principal towns, he encountered only a single person who spoke English, a linguistic divide that loomed large to him. "I was looked upon as a barbarian by the inhabitants, and they appeared to me like so many human beings scarcely endowed with the qualifications equal to that of the brute species." By contrast, McMichael found the residents of nearby Morristown, New Jersey, "very hospitable" because they were "all professors of the Presbyterian religion, which renders them to me very agreeable."[147] The New England soldier Joseph Plumb Martin offered a similar assessment of "middle states" troops as a "caravan of wild beasts." He continued, "they 'beggared all description'; their dialect too was as confused as their bodily appearance was odd and disgusting. There was the Scotch and Irish brogue, murdered English, flat insipid Dutch, and some lingoes which would puzzle a philosopher to tell whether they belonged to this or some 'undiscovered country.'"[148]

Even though a treaty among white belligerents would be delayed until 1783, and the war against Native Americans would last into the 1790s, active fighting with the British in the Delaware Valley had mostly come to a close by 1779. By the time General Sullivan's army returned to Easton that fall, a postcolonial settlement had begun to take shape in which a Christian framework proved especially important. In a sermon delivered at Easton's union church, the military chaplain Israel Evans commended the troops for opening "a passage into the wilderness, where the Gospel has never yet been received." The soldiers' holy work meant that a region inhabited only by "wild beasts, and men as wild as they" would now be open to Christianity. "For it cannot be supposed, that so large a part of the continent shall forever continue a haunt of savages, and the dreary abodes of superstition and idolatry."[149] This vision of America's Christian destiny to spread west could not explain what was wrong with the British Empire or why independence was necessary; however, it would play an increasingly significant role as the United States emerged from the war.

Identity and Revolution

The welter of changes wrought by the Revolutionary War in Burlington, New Castle, and Easton might initially seem only to reinforce what distinguished these places from one another. Unquestionably, the varied ethnoreligious character of each town and their different engagements with the war itself made for distinct experiences that need to be explained through the logic of local circumstances. In Burlington, religious and ethnic identity encouraged Quakers and Anglicans to remain neutral, if not loyal, and to view the havoc of war as a tremendously misguided vehicle for social change. In New Castle, Presbyterians and Anglicans divided over the Revolution, sometimes as whigs and loyalists, but often, and nearly as bitterly, as radical and conservative patriots. Coursing beneath those divisions, slavery and the control of African Americans became public problems there as never before. Finally, Pennsylvania Germans in Easton had mixed allegiances that might lead toward patriotism or loyalism in the intensely divisive politics of Revolutionary Pennsylvania, but, ultimately, the prominent Indian threat led most local whites to ignore their differences and forge bonds as independent Americans.

The particular issues differed in the three river towns, but in all of them the insertion of a powerful new public identity—patriot or loyalist—intensified, disrupted, and altered the balance of long-standing local relationships whose stability had been essential to maintaining the colonial status quo. Thus the wartime mobilization in these places reveals more than just divergent forces in their endless local variety. The Revolution unfolded here by inflaming awareness of the consequences of diverse local identities. Yet the reconfiguration of group relationships at the center of this Revolutionary identity politics did not end with the war. To properly understand these changes, we must continue to follow the logic of local circumstances as the people in these towns sought to make sense of their new situation in the postwar Revolutionary nation.

Chapter 3

Local Struggles and National Order in the Postwar Period

The vitality of the Delaware Valley's Revolutionary identity politics is evident in the intense conflicts that infused its public life in the two decades following the war. These struggles include formal political contests, such as early postwar elections, Constitutional ratification, and the Jeffersonian presidential triumph of 1800, which open and close this chapter. Careful analysis of electoral politics reveals that heightened local understandings of group identity from the Revolutionary War influenced political allegiances and fundamentally shaped early national consciousness in the Delaware Valley as Quakers in Burlington, African Americans in New Castle, and Pennsylvania Germans in Easton each negotiated distinct relationships with the emerging national order. Notwithstanding their distinctiveness from one another, these groups contributed to the creation of the nation in similar ways. All three were "outsiders" that sought a more central place in national society, although the outcomes of their efforts would be quite varied. Burlington Quakers remained marginalized for having failed to embrace the patriot cause, yet this ongoing persecution helped some Friends to become champions of radical reform. Most African Americans in New Castle experienced a swift transition from slavery to freedom after the war and attempted to achieve public recognition as respectable citizens. Pennsylvania Germans around Easton also battled to ensure that their Revolutionary achievements were not reversed in the 1790s, and they secured the most complete success of these three groups. Their varied struggles encompassed many aspects of daily life that had important political meanings beyond the confines of elections and statecraft. This politics of everyday life grew from material circumstances in each town, and in order to understand its points of contact with an emerging national society, we need to focus our attention on the logic of local circumstances in each place.

The analytical categories "localist" and "cosmopolitan" are often used to explain how individuals' economic status informed their positions in formal politics and can help us to situate our particular subjects in their broader context.[1] In general terms, the mobilization for war had empowered people to establish independence with a strong commitment to popular sovereignty and local autonomy, yet their actions also spurred cosmopolitan efforts in directing the war and stabilizing the nation thereafter. The egalitarian ideals of Revolutionary politics and the accelerating economic inequality of the postwar years created a fundamental tension in the new nation. The economic downturn of the 1780s, as well as growing material differences driven by the so-called consumer and market revolutions in the wake of the war, played counterpoint to Revolutionary ideals that touted the equality of all citizens. Leading local men who benefited from economic growth after the war played difficult roles that could seem inappropriate in a polity based on popular sovereignty. Men of high status and broad personal and social interests, that is "cosmopolitans," remained atop early republican society in spite of the "localist" upsurge central to successful wartime mobilization. Moreover, those with cosmopolitan perspectives often shared an Anglo style whose association with Englishness had illegitimate connotations stemming from two decades of anti-British resistance and war. Informing our understanding of these sometimes unwieldy two labels with local evidence can reveal the crosscutting influence of varied forces on particular human relationships. When these broad labels are refined to include awareness of religious, racial, and ethnic influences, they become especially useful for helping us to see how postwar developments in the public life of each town were central to larger collective processes of making the nation and giving it meaning.

No groups in these towns exclusively articulated cosmopolitan or localist perspectives. Indeed, individual commitments could vary according to the specific situation that they faced. For example, a localist ethnic understanding centrally inspired the Fries Rebellion near Easton, the explosive highpoint of Revolutionary identity politics examined here, yet some cosmopolitan Pennsylvania German leaders in Easton opposed the rebels. A cosmopolitan perspective was far from transcendent or dominant to people in these river towns in the postwar period; rather, it represented yet another local force attempting to define the consequences of the Revolution. A cosmopolitan orientation here implies neither a strict partisan association nor a steadfast ethnic or religious commitment, nor is it meant to denigrate self-serving elitists who opposed genuine Revolutionary change. By the same measure, the localist impulse should not be stereotyped as the ideal standard-bearer of the Revolution, for localism often rested upon the threat of coercive majoritarian violence to punish those perceived as outsiders. Quakers and African Americans both had good reasons to doubt and even fear the claims and actions of passionate localists. To understand the rich ways that Revolutionary identity politics shaped postwar life we need to hold simplistic judgments at bay while we investigate evidence from each river town. The key point to keep in mind is that the varied alliances in each place arose from the logic of local circumstances and not from some sort of normative imperative derived from the supposed essence of any single kind of identity.

Electoral Politics in the 1780s

The struggle for order in the postwar period tested the delicate balance among local, state, and national authorities, relationships that had also proved controversial during the war. As we saw in the previous chapter, patriots in Easton expressed disgust at the lenient terms accepted by national elites in the Treaty of Paris that allowed loyalists to return to their old communities without penalty. In Burlington, where loyalism and neutrality had much greater local support, the elections of 1782–1784 pitted "whig" and "disaffected" candidates against one another. These closely contested races indicate ongoing wartime tensions. Whigs claimed that they lost the 1782 election because those who refused to swear a loyalty oath to the state had been permitted to vote. The following year the militia mustered at the polls, claiming that it was "as necessary in Peace to guard against the private, as it was in War against the declared, Enemies of Our Country."[2] Aggressive militia actions, which included destroying their opponents' publicly posted tickets, helped to create a whig assembly victory by a mere twenty votes in 1783. When the "disaffected" candidates won a return to the assembly in 1784, Whigs protested that they had been blocked from opening the polls at their stronghold of Bordentown. As we might expect given local reservations about the Revolutionary War in Burlington, the implementation of popular sovereignty as a local political practice proved difficult. Indeed, these elections were only as close as they were because many local Quakers did not vote both from their own choice and due to intimidation by active militia bands.

The ongoing influence of wartime divisions was particularly acute in Quaker Burlington, but similar conflicts shaped the gradual demilitarization of the 1780s in the other towns as well. The story of Peter Jaquett, an ordinary soldier from New Castle, illustrates the angry polarization of postwar politics in Delaware. Jaquett served in the Delaware regiment of the Continental Army continuously from January 1776 until he returned home in 1783 from a three-year tour in the Carolinas. Once back in New Castle, Jaquett and his comrades-in-arms faced civil penalties for their military service. Ironically, while the militia in Burlington attempted to disenfranchise "tory" voters, here conservative Whigs tried to block radical soldiers from the polls. When the troops went to vote in the fall election, Jaquett claimed that George Read Sr., the state's most effective political leader from the Revolution to his death in 1798, refused to allow the soldiers to vote because their lengthy out-of-state service meant that they "had becam Aliens and that in law and Justice we had not a Right to Voat." Captain Jaquett, his men, and many others in New Castle were shocked by this claim. Jaquett wondered if "I should again be obliged to Apart by force a right for which I had contended for more the[n] seven years in the feald." The election judges were unsure of how to act, the mood of the election-day crowd turned angry, and as night began to fall Read grew "anxious for the Personal Safety of himself and friends" and at last permitted the soldiers to vote.[3]

Jaquett contemplated violence and later lamented that his "Greatest Sins of Omition" allowed conservatives like Read "to have Seen the morning light." To Jaquett, bold action in 1783 could have saved Delaware from "the reproache of being Governed by torys," and he condemned George Read Sr. as "the Greatest curs[e] to this State that Heaven ever suffered to live." Read had refused to vote for independence as a delegate to the Continental Congress in 1776 and led the state legislature in repealing the antiloyalist Test Act in 1783. To Peter Jaquett, and radicals like him, Read had "persicuted every Man that was Active in Securing the Independence of this Country" because they had "wrest[ed] it from the Power of his Much loved King."[4]

The most detailed assessment of Delaware politics penned in the 1780s shared Jaquett's hostility and used a blistering religious framework to explain the state's postwar political culture. James Tilton, the pseudonymous "Timoleon," condemned Read and dubbed him "the tyrant of Delaware" for leading a resurgent Anglican elite to roll back the gains achieved by Presbyterians. Tilton charged conservatives like Read with "the cultivation of religious prejudice as the main anchor of hope" for their success. "A new and extraordinary cry was therefore raised against Presbyterians" by reactionary gentlemen who "counsel[ed] their weaker brethren, to be guarded against the violence of Presbyterians." Tilton charged Anglicans with stirring up "ignorant pimps and bullies" by letting a "roar out in the streets against *Presbyterians* and *Calvinists*." Although such attacks probably never occurred in New Castle County, where Presbyterians had their strongest presence in the state, Tilton offered a scandalous example of a conservative judge on election day who "flourish[ing] his walking stick denominated it John Wesley's staff, with which he intended to break Jack Calvin's head." Tilton warned that Anglicans and their allies—Methodism was still a movement within the Anglican Church—championed an anti-Revolutionary program that linked the supposed "violence of republicanism, and the danger of presbyteriansim." Because conservatives failed to block independence in 1776 and had lost the war, they now used religious prejudice as their "main spring of action."[5] Jaquett embraced Timoleon's attack on Read and agreed that the "tories" aimed to turn back the gains secured by true whigs in the Revolution. By the mid-1790s, Jaquett and Tilton would both be active in new political societies that attacked conservatives and their federal policies.

Tilton's wildly outspoken expression of the radical Presbyterian and conservative Anglican split in Revolutionary Delaware was widely shared by political leaders and ordinary people. Radical leaders in Delaware like Thomas Rodney worried that the strident views of Timoleon and similar "rigid Presbyterians" would alienate moderates and Anglicans who had supported the patriot cause. However, when the legislature chose Read and Richard Bassett as the state's first U.S. senators in 1788, Rodney denounced them as "Enemies to the Revolution in this State" who excelled at the "fauning and cringing Arts" that "foment and increase the disunion of the Revolutionists."[6] Although independence had been secured, political passions remained red hot in postwar Delaware.

George Read Sr.'s political views and actions fanned the flames. As a delegate at the federal Constitutional Convention, Read favored a powerful executive with full veto power and life terms for U.S. senators. Although often portrayed as an advocate of small state sovereignty, his ultranationalism even led him to argue in favor of abolishing all state governments. Such views probably contributed to Read's defeat as a New Castle County delegate to the state ratification convention in November 1787, but the two local men who were elected hint at Read's looming influence and the interlocking familial nature of the Delaware elite.[7] Gunning Bedford Sr. had married Read's sister, while Kensey Johns trained at law with him; both strongly favored ratification and would be Federalist Party leaders by the mid-1790s. Timoleon would surely have stressed that all three were Anglicans and in the top decile of New Castle taxpayers.

Because the federal Constitution dominates the political history of the postwar era, our sense of the ongoing Revolutionary turmoil in Delaware has been eclipsed by its status as the first state to ratify the Constitution. Swift ratification, however, did not indicate any social consensus and certainly no political harmony. As the editors of the authoritative documentary history of ratification have noted, the "animosity among political leaders" in Delaware and its violence on election days "were probably unmatched in any other state" in the nation.[8] From the perspective of tiny Delaware, the strong central government that privileged state sovereignty in the Senate and electoral college could help to protect it from powerful neighboring states. Clearly, George Read Sr.'s political position was enhanced by the proposed Constitution, but it represented such a victory for small state residents that even Read's hyperbolic opponent, James Tilton, strongly supported it.

The easy course of ratification in Delaware was not repeated in Pennsylvania, where controversy abounded. Among the early states rushing to ratify, sharp opposition emerged only here. The state assembly's use of force to compel a quorum to initiate the ratification process shocked even many who favored the Constitution. When twenty-three delegates to the state convention published a nearly unanimous dissent, when anti-Federalists rioted at Carlisle, Pennsylvania, and as a campaign mobilized to reverse the state convention's ratification decision, it became clear that the proposed Constitution could be questioned and even defeated.[9]

In Northampton County, where Revolutionary committees and the militia had often been at odds with leading patriot authorities in Philadelphia during the war, the ground seemed ripe for conflict. Instead, ratification moved ahead swiftly there as Northampton Federalists carefully controlled the local process. The meeting to nominate delegates to the state ratifying convention, held at Moravian-dominated Bethlehem rather than patriot Easton, *required* all candidates to favor the Constitution. Obviously, no opponent to the proposed Constitution could emerge from this ratification process. The four elected delegates, including Easton resident John Arndt, never wavered in their support for the Constitution, which the state convention ratified on December 12, 1787. When an Easton meeting was finally held to discuss the Constitution on December 20, the delegates somberly explained the benefits of a strengthened central government and its anticipated economic rewards.[10]

Majority opinion in Pennsylvania seemed uncertain when Northampton provided 230 signatures among the more than 6,000 collected from six backcountry counties that called on the assembly to reverse the state's approval of the Constitution.[11] In a series of leading anti-Federalist newspaper articles, one salvo specifically denounced the machinations of a "despicable few" in Northampton County who claimed to express the will of the people.[12] How to ensure the proper representation of "the people" plagued postwar political life.

The ability of elections to accurately represent popular sovereignty also caused controversy in New Jersey. While ratification there mirrored the swift process in Delaware, with local antagonists unanimously supporting a stronger central government, New Jersey's remarkable first U.S. House of Representatives election in 1789 was a stark struggle for power waged with stunning chicanery. The combination of extreme campaign rhetoric, election fraud, and a disorganized opposition gave the conservatives a handsome reward. Their four candidates won handily, while of their thirty-nine opponents only Jonathan Dayton and Abraham Clark were viable statewide. The conservatives particularly succeeded by building massive turnout in places like Burlington, which saw a tenfold increase in congressional voter turnout over that for the state assembly election three months earlier.[13]

Crucial to the victory was a daring strategy crafted by a group of New Jersey leaders known as the "Junto," which included several prominent Burlington men whose profile suggests some qualities that unified their faction. Joshua Maddox Wallace, a leading Anglican layman in the top decile of Burlington taxpayers, had spearheaded local ratification efforts in 1787. Now he scolded other members of the Junto for not working hard enough on the campaign. Warning them against playing the part of disinterested gentlemen, he noted, "my strengths are fixed on but one subject and that is the *Election*."[14] Wartime experience compromised many Burlington Junto members as postwar political leaders. John Lawrence had been charged as a tory and had fled to British protection in New York City; Thomas Hewlings had left the United States during the war and had only recently returned from Nova Scotia; Daniel Ellis had signed an anti-independence petition in 1775 and was arrested by state officials in May 1777; and James Kinsey had fallen under suspicion as a wartime tory and refused to swear the 1777 oath of allegiance to the state. Although Kinsey was prohibited from practicing law during the war, he recovered nicely afterward, serving as chief justice of the New Jersey Supreme Court for over a decade.[15] In sum, eight of the Junto activists in Burlington can be traced in local religious records and divide equally into Quakers and Anglicans (two of whom helped lead the Episcopal reorganization of the church). Of the five whose Revolutionary partisanship can be identified, two were ardent loyalists, and three were disaffected to the patriot cause.

The leading Friend James Kinsey (fig. 15) exemplified cosmopolitan persistence in Revolutionary Burlington. Kinsey had been forced from office during the war, but rebounded afterward to play important roles in formal politics until his death in 1803, helping to legitimize the new republican order. Yet the return of some prominent Quakers to public leadership did not mark any kind of restoration of the former colonial status quo. Kinsey—nor any other Quaker in the postwar Delaware Valley— would ever match his father's towering role as a leader of the popular Quaker Party in the assembly and as clerk of the Philadelphia Yearly Meeting.[16]

Patriots had pushed most Quakers out of formal politics, but, so too, did several waves of reform within the Society of Friends, which increasingly viewed formal political leadership as a source of moral contamination. Kinsey's experience fits a familiar narrative of postwar retrenchment in several ways, but that assessment remains incomplete without considering his religious and local context. Because Burlington was a neutral stronghold in the war, Kinsey's return to public life validated local opinion rather than transgressed it, as would have been the case had he hailed from a staunch patriot place. Although radicals may have dissented, to members of the Society of Friends, having a fellow Quaker as chief justice from 1789 to 1803 must have powerfully symbolized the relaxation of wartime hostilities toward their members.

Kinsey descended from as prominent a Quaker family as existed in the Delaware Valley, but that hardly made his religious identity impregnable, especially as the rules for being a Quaker tightened in the 1770s and 1780s. The departure from Quakerism by James Kinsey's children emphasizes how Quaker discipline no longer centrally shaped the household of this worldly Friend. In November 1799, his eldest daughter, Ann, married

Charles Henry Wharton, Burlington's Episcopal minister. By June the Burlington Monthly Meeting disowned Ann and two sisters for disunity; and, ultimately, at least five of James and Hannah Kinsey's eight children were disowned by the Society, all within a few years of Ann leading the way.[17] James and Hannah's deaths marked the end of the Kinsey Quaker line in Burlington that had begun with a town founder in 1677. Nineteenth-century Burlington Kinseys were active in the Episcopal Church. If sketched in terms of theological doctrine, this move from Quakerism to Episcopalianism seems enormous, and yet long-standing ties connected these two leading local traditions. By marrying Ann Kinsey, Reverend Wharton followed the path of his predecessor, Jonathan Odell, whose Quaker wife, Ann Decou, had been disowned by the Society in 1772.[18]

James Kinsey's ties to the large Quaker population in West Jersey marked a crucial component of the Junto's electoral strategy, with its deep roots in Burlington, while Junto opponents in the town were poorly organized and less well-known. Joseph Bloomfield, who moved there only in 1781, was a wealthy Presbyterian who worshipped in Burlington's Anglican church and had been a Continental Army general, where he worked closely with Jonathan Dayton, the best-known non-Junto candidate for Congress. The distance that separates the Junto's frequent Revolutionary loyalism from their opponent's military service is underscored by the surprising fact that none of the local Junto men enrolled in the compulsory state militia, where Bloomfield served as brigadier general.[19] As we saw in New Castle, conservative postwar leaders in the Delaware Valley often faced their strongest opposition from military men who drew political legitimacy from their self-sacrifice in the war. Yet claims to martial privilege could trigger more suspicion than popular support in a neutral and anti-war place such as Burlington.

The Junto's careful campaign strategy included the circulation of a printed ballot to advance their four candidates in a crowded field. In addition to this united front, the Junto counted on overwhelming support from West Jersey, and its Quaker voters in particular, who were hostile to the 1783 Test Act that required voters to swear their loyalty to the state. The Burlington Junto leader, John Lawrence, believed his opponents had weakened their position by "pushing the Test [Act] against The Quakers," which he expected "will bring forward many here who perhaps otherwise would have staid at home."[20]

More than just exhibiting uncommon effort and shrewd political tactics, the Junto's manipulation of the polls made New Jersey's first congressional election scandalous. Because the Constitution empowered each state to establish its own election rules, and because conservatives had won control of the New Jersey legislature in October 1788, the fact that polls remained open for long periods in some areas but not others was technically legal. All Jersey polls opened on February 11, 1789, but no unified closing date had been established. Most eastern and northern counties with more radical sentiments had closed the polls by February 23, while most counties in West Jersey, where the Junto ran strongest, remained open until March 12. Meanwhile, in eastern Essex County, where the opposition was especially strong, the polls essentially never closed as Governor William Livingston and his council awarded the election to the Junto candidates on March 18 without having received a single vote from Essex![21]

This bold move surprised the opposition. Bloomfield did not know when the Burlington polls would close, nor did he realize that they would be moved repeatedly throughout the county to maximize conservative turnout. Bloomfield was even more distressed by the Junto's linking of religion and politics. When facing "rigid Quaqers," whose religious conscience prevented them from voting, Junto supporters had warned Friends, " 'You will loose Your freedom, Your Liberty and Your Property,—nay more, Your Religion, if you do not [vote];—we Church People see very clearly these Presbyters. Want to rule—and, then—there will be no other Religion suffered in this Country, but Presbyterianism, the most arbitrary and tyrannic of all Religions.' " The Junto reportedly cast their opponents as Presbyterians who "want another War" and the "opportunity to distrain Your goods for pretended Militia-duty." Bloomfield also warned that the Junto cast the leading opposition candidates—Jonathan Dayton and Abraham Clark—as bloodthirsty warmongers who planned "to hang all the Quaqers" as they had the Quaker loyalist Abraham Carlisle during the war.[22]

Ongoing wartime divisions, with their explosive politicization of ethnicity and religion, marked the formal politics of all three Delaware Valley states in the 1780s. In Pennsylvania's first federal elections, the authors of the standard documentary history conclude that "the German vote" was decisive.[23] The partisan fault line here stemmed from the state constitution of 1776 and pitted radical "Constitutionalists" against conservative "Republicans."[24] Both sides carefully selected U.S. House of Representative candidates at statewide conventions that produced two official tickets. The radical Constitutionalists met at Harrisburg and crafted a very strong slate, while the one forged by conservative Republicans at Lancaster suffered immediate criticism. As a Philadelphia newspaper reported, the conservative slate was pro-British and had "no Representatives from the German counties, viz., Lancaster, York, Berks, and Northampton."[25]

Partisan newspapers, of course, would say anything to condemn their opponents, but Easton's John Arndt, a staunch Pennsylvania German conservative and a delegate to the Lancaster conference, also disliked his experience there. He found that his every "request or representation" was treated as "absurd in the highest degree," and his central concern stemmed from an ethnic perspective. "My fear is that the ticket will not meet the approbation of the Federalists in general, and the Germans in particular. Should this be the case, the consequences may be disagreeable."[26] Arndt's private observation coincided with an influential broadside and newspaper article, circulating in English and German, which warned of the "degrading" way that Pennsylvania Germans had been represented on both tickets: "If this is the proceeding at the first election, what will be the consequence in the new government, when the English believe they can gain their point without the Germans, then they will be totally excluded, and the German nation in Pennsylvania, will be, and remain the hewers of wood and the carriers of water."[27] Benjamin Rush, now a conservative in state politics, probably penned that German call-to-arms, which appeared two months before his well-known "Account of the Manners of the German Inhabitants of Pennsylvania." Rush's powerful sense of the interlocking nature of politics, ethnicity, and religion in Revolutionary Pennsylvania is, unfortunately, not widely known. Like John Arndt, Rush complained that his call for "German representation" at the Lancaster conference met "indignation and contempt," a response that horrified Rush, who believed that "the happiness of Pennsylvania can only be established upon the basis of a union between the Quakers, Germans, and the virtuous part of the Irish."[28] The early national coalition that Rush envisioned built upon colonial alliances, where Pennsylvania Germans had played an important role in electoral politics since at least the 1750s.

A resolution to the crisis posed by weak Pennsylvania German representation on both original tickets appeared when newspapers circulated mixed tickets that combined the two Pennsylvania Germans from the Harrisburg slate and the one from the Lancaster slate. Statewide voters favored the mixed ticket and elected all three Pennsylvania Germans to the first U.S. House: F. A. Muhlenberg, J. P. Muhlenberg (sons of the Lutheran patriarch H. M. Muhlenberg), and Daniel Hiester, the top vote recipient in Northampton County, who ran especially well there as a local man from neighboring Berks County.

Northampton County's vote in the first U.S. congressional election suggests two notable political developments. First, Pennsylvania German ethnicity proved more important to voters in German areas than partisan identity. Although originally on different tickets, the three Pennsylvania Germans were the top three vote recipients in Northampton County, which allowed two men from the radical Constitutionalist ticket to displace the lowest running Republicans. Moreover, as the most popular candidate in the state, F. A. Muhlenberg became the first speaker of the U.S. House of Representatives, then meeting in the national capital of Philadelphia. Excluding the Pennsylvania German candidates from consideration, however, indicates that Northampton County voters gave stronger support to conservative candidates than their statewide averages. While ethnic solidarity overcame strict partisanship in the first federal congressional election, strongly Pennsylvania German Northampton County favored conservative candidates in the 1780s.[29]

The seeming unity of conservative statewide outcomes on the key federal issues of the late 1780s masked much more contentious state and local situations. The skulduggery of the New Jersey election—with its key politicization of Quakerism—may have been the most spectacular example of political vitriol in the Delaware Valley's formal politics of 1787–89, but radical dissent from conservative dominance in Delaware, where religion was also politicized, and the emergence of Pennsylvania Germans as a key group in Pennsylvania elections bespoke the ongoing significance of Revolutionary identity politics in the postwar Delaware Valley. The war itself may have left the region a decade earlier, but the public implications of group identity remained contested, and the electoral struggle for national power posed as many challenges as it resolved. In a region where religious, racial, and ethnic identities all had been infused with new public meanings during the war, national consciousness only gradually cohered and did so in relationship to categories of individual and collective self-understanding that need to be reconstructed from a local perspective.

Quakers and the New Nation

The turmoil of war, swift changes in political authority, and a shifting sense of group identity all weighed heavily on Quakers, especially leaders in Burlington who had long played a major role in the region's public life. If one looks only at formal politics and the ways that patriots had pushed Quakers from power, it is easy to discount Friends' ongoing influence in the Revolutionary Delaware Valley. Despite rejecting patriot demands to conform, Burlington Monthly Meeting grew steadily during the war and its aftermath. In response to increasing local membership, Mount Holly Monthly Meeting separated from Burlington in October 1776, Upper Springfield Monthly Meeting followed suit in March 1783, and the Burlington meetinghouse still needed extra benches (not just new ones) in 1804.[30] Linking tax records and religious affiliation reveals a consistent Quaker presence in Revolutionary Burlington: 40 percent of the taxed population in 1774, 35 percent in 1796, and 37 percent in 1814.[31] Meanwhile, the raw number of identifiable Quakers in these tax lists increased from 63 individuals to 89 and 145, respectively. Quakerism underwent a crisis in the Revolutionary period, but Burlington Friends did not wither away.

Quakers are generally assumed to have enjoyed unusual economic success in the Delaware Valley and throughout the early modern Atlantic world, a view that is borne out by their overrepresentation in the top rank of Burlington taxpayers in 1774. Although 40 percent of Burlington's taxed population was Quaker, they made up 57 percent of the top decile of taxpayers. The most striking finding about the relationship between Quakerism and economic status is that they became a wealthier group over time during the broad Revolutionary period, a growing affluence that is likely related to the aging of the local Quaker community.[32]

The experience of Samuel Allinson (fig. 12), a leading Burlington Friend, helps us to understand the creative adaptations that Quakers fashioned during the Revolutionary transformation of the Delaware Valley. As an ardent reformer who seized the opportunity to purify Quaker practices, Allinson's demands for sweeping change often stimulated controversy even among fellow Friends. His pacifism and his anti-tax-paying activism built directly upon issues confronted during the Revolutionary War. Because Friends who were active patriots had been disowned from the Society by 1780, opposition to war no longer stirred controversy among Quakers when Allinson penned his pacifist masterpiece "Reasons against War, and paying Taxes for its support." However, not paying taxes to the new government, with its broad implications about Friends' relationship to civil authority, was controversial. Allinson principally built his case for tax resistance upon scriptural authority. His sense of being Quaker derived urgency from biblical imperatives. He reminded his readers of Romans 12:2: "be not conformed to this World but be transformed by renewing your mind."[33]

Persuading Friends not to pay taxes due to their intended use had at least two major obstacles. First, Christ's example of rendering taxes unto Caesar established clearly the scriptural legitimacy of tax paying.[34] Second, Quakers had historically paid taxes, and on occasion supported martial efforts (short of bearing arms), without suffering reproof by the Society. While scriptural exegesis infused Allinson's argument, his historical understanding of Quakerism provides the most novel and compelling part of his argument. He fully acknowledged that his call for tax resistance broke with long-held practices among the weightiest Friends, including George Fox. Conscious of having departed from "our predecessors in the Truth," Allinson explained, "I desire to be understood with tenderness; I write with caution & great deference."[35]

Like the towering figure of John Woolman who had preceded him as a voice of conscience among Burlington Friends, Allinson feared that Quakers enjoyed "the smiles of Power" too much and had become dependent upon the "arm of flesh" in their worldly lives. "It is sorrowfully evident that our connection with offices of Government, and mixing with the World in their human consultations, manner, and policies, hath been a loss to many, and a general departure from the purity of our Principles hath been too prevalent amongst us." The worldliness that disturbed Allinson also targeted "the acquisition of much Wealth, which need[s] the arm of power to secure."[36] Like Woolman, Allinson feared that the "spirit of the world" and the "wrong spirit" were nearly interchangeable.[37]

In many respects Allinson represents an archetypal late eighteenth-century Quaker reformer campaigning to distance the Society from worldly contamination. Again drawing from scripture, Allinson hoped that Quakers would push themselves to become "a *peculiar* people zealous of good works."[38] Yet Allinson's Quakerism was deeply socially engaged, and Revolutionary events spurred his activism, for "it is clear that there never was a time in all respects similar to this." Conditions were so novel that our "worthy ancestors" who had accepted paying many kinds of war taxes would "differ from themselves if now living."[39] Far from maintaining a static vision of Quaker identity crafted solely from scriptural inspiration and the example of weighty predecessors, Allinson argued that Friends needed to respond creatively to current circumstances. "Knowledge is progressive," he explained, "every reform had its beginning," and the current moment demanded that the "Prophecy of Peace & Love *must go forward and be perfected.*"[40]

Heralded for its eloquence and careful explanation of an ardent reform position, Allinson's essay circulated widely in manuscript but has never been published. The Society's overseers of the press probably felt that it probed explosive issues too deeply in a time already beset by divisiveness.[41] While the Yearly Meeting never endorsed Allinson's position, many Quakers in Burlington County shared his ardent commitment. Two months after Allinson penned his manifesto, a Burlington militia officer complained that he could raise only seven out of seventy men needed for his battalion and believed he suffered "the Worst Situation of Any in the State." As he explained to the governor, the problem was not just local men's refusal to serve but also that a great number were "Conscience Bound against paying money for hiring men."[42]

How Quaker meetings approached such controversial issues gets to the heart of group-boundary maintenance among Friends in the Revolutionary period. Allinson's cousin, James Whitall, desired that a tone of "brotherly unity" prevail and complained to Allinson that acrimonious arguments consumed the meeting and "let self get uppermost & be rising up & up."[43] Whitall believed that Friends such as his cousin who advocated a stronger antitax stand pushed the meeting too far and that such individual assertions threatened to sunder Quaker community.

Not surprisingly, Allinson perceived things differently and thought the unresolved disputes brought a beneficial "weight & solidity over the meeting." As for his own role, Allinson insisted that he "cheerfully" left matters to the meeting once he had spoken, but that when his expressions were misrepresented, he had a duty to reply so that "the Truth may not be covered or tarnished in the Minds of the Hearers, by a supposition that what is thus said is unanswerable." He believed that his lengthy disquisitions were not expressions of self, but stemmed from "the consciousness of my own obedience to advance the great cause of Righteousness," and thus was "noways uneasy what others may think or say of me." Allinson believed his reform work to be guided by divine force. Ultimately he hoped that difficult conversations would lead others to question, "if they have too hastily left the Christian Path of Suffering for the sake of Popularity, of Profit, or of a false Rest."[44]

Allinson consistently argued that unique Revolutionary conditions required Quakers to take new action: "The World now knows our Principles, they did not then, and many not of us, approve them & see their rectitude, who do not fully embrace them & walk by our rule because they see & say we do not fully walk by it ourselves; the world is now more ripe for such a Testimony, and let none of us oppose Faithfulness in any."[45] To Allinson, Quaker values now required a fuller commitment. Quaker beliefs had become well-known as the result of ongoing patriot persecution, but as long as Friends failed to fully live by those ideals, they could be dismissed as self-serving hypocrites. The postwar period would be crucial to members of the Society of Friends, as they sought to reestablish themselves as public leaders in a new political context created by a war that they had officially opposed.

As Allinson's disagreements with his kinsman make plain, individual Quakers responded to the Revolutionary transformation in a variety of ways. James Craft offers another example of the dynamism of Quaker identity in this period and departs almost entirely from the route of Allinson. The Craft household fell in the fourth quintile of Burlington taxpayers in 1774, and they owned no identified taxable property. His four-person household in the Burlington meeting for worship was the third generation of Burlington residents in his family, all of them Quaker by his report, yet no vital statistics for them appear in the Burlington Monthly Meeting records.[46] His marriage with Sarah Cathrall received the Society's sanction, but she was relatively new to the area. Only one of Craft's four children remained Quakers, two would be disowned, and another never appears in the monthly meeting records. Because wealth was imperative to finding a Quaker marriage partner in the eighteenth-century Delaware Valley, poverty seems a likely reason for the next generation's departure from the Society.[47]

Recovering how nonaffluent people like James Craft thought about group identity and its intersection with public life is often limited by a lack of evidence, thus his surviving journal offers unusual insight into Quakerism during the Revolutionary crisis. It displays a strongly Quaker style, both in its dating system and in its disparaging comments about the Anglican Church and the use of hierarchical titles. Remaining neutral in the Revolution, as required by the peace testimony, caused Craft to be abused by patriot authorities who suspected him of loyalism. As a result, he was "dragged by Force" with a number of others as "Prisoners to [neighboring] Borden Town," where he suffered loss of health and property.[48]

So far, Craft's story follows a plot that might be anticipated: Quaker shoemaker of modest social standing adopted a neutral position in the war and suffered punishment for failing to support the rebels who attacked royal government. However, when Craft subscribed to the Test Act and affirmed his loyalty to the independent New Jersey state government in September 1779, and four months later became a master mason, he ran afoul of Quaker behavioral rules. As a result of these actions, Craft reported, "my Person was disowned by the Friends. No, not my deeds."[49] Craft's way of walking in the world had broached the stricter standards for group membership that reformers like Allinson helped to create in the late eighteenth century. Although Craft believed that his deeds remained true to the mandates of Quakerism, he was disowned and never regained membership.

The American Revolution helped to revitalize the Society of Friends by prompting a new commitment to idealistic social reform, but as James Craft plaintively testifies, the reformation included disturbing overtones as well. The Society's disciplinary functions increased and became more efficient as a result of the war. In 1782, for example, Burlington Monthly Meeting called on overseers and "active concerned members . . . to promote greater diligence and care in seasonably treating with offenders," an exhortation that increased committee visits to inspect disorderly households.[50] Rigorous attention to members' behavior, from slaveholding to alcohol consumption, became an increasingly central feature of group boundary maintenance.

By the 1780s the Society of Friends had identified a core set of public concerns that still centrally trouble American life.[51] More remarkably, this agenda had been fashioned in a relatively short period as Quakers removed themselves from (and often were forcibly denied access to) formal political power in the new nation. Because the issues that Friends made their own starting in the 1770s remain salient today, Quakers should not be dismissed as a peculiar people apart from the world. When Friends narrowed their sense of who should be acknowledged as members of their Society, as they undoubtedly did in the latter half of the eighteenth century, they did not sever a deep engagement with American society. Friends called for sweeping reforms on a host of issues, from race and poverty to nonviolence and gender equality, and did so from a self-conscious position outside Revolutionary leadership, and thus stand as a prime example of how outsiders have influenced American society by critiquing the dominant culture.[52]

What sets the Society of Friends apart from most other outsider traditions in American history is that Quakers had once been a dominant group.[53] Although Quaker demographic and formal political significance in the Delaware Valley had each waned in turn, Friends' influence was too deeply entrenched to be swept aside even by a decade of patriot harassment. Moreover, not all Quakers maintained vigorous spiritual scrupulousness. As with all the cultural groups discussed here, there was not simply one way to be Quaker, and the pointed animosity that Friends suffered during the long Revolutionary period spurred a variety of responses. While reforming Friends like the Allinsons redoubled their efforts to achieve distinctive Quaker ideals, others like the Junto member and state supreme court justice James Kinsey strove to maintain an older Quaker practice of formal leadership in the region's public affairs. Although harder yet to trace, we also must preserve a place in our historical memory for Quakers of ordinary means such as James Craft, who suffered persecution for his Quaker pacifism yet would still be expelled from the Society of Friends as it became more rigorous in defining group membership in the last decades of the eighteenth century.

National Order and Black Freedom

The decennial federal census provided the most comprehensive framework to explain the nation during the early republic. Established to measure rationally "the people" in order to determine proper congressional representation, the census provided a basic structure to order the new polity by accounting for diverse localities across a huge space in a single tabulation. This powerful defining role was central to the Constitutional creation of the census, which attempted to resolve a fundamental problem of the new national order. How would the local forces mobilized during the Revolution be contained within a single nation? The census fixed political representation by privileging particular aspects of individual identity and organizing them in a uniform way that when calculated together would palpably demonstrate something that had never been tangible in the colonial era—an American nation as the natural grouping of a unified people. Among the most important categories that the census counted, and thus helped to validate, was racial identity. By carefully enumerating whites, blacks, and Indians—and especially by conflating free and enslaved African Americans—the census helped solidify a white consensus about the meaning of blackness in the nation.[54]

The census attempted to smooth over local differences while making ordinary citizens the basis for national authority. To do this, it enshrined certain intertwined personal characteristics—race, age, gender, and free/unfree status—while eschewing other potential qualities such as religion, ethnicity, or economic status. The census' nationalizing technology made certain forms of self-understanding in the Revolutionary period more difficult for us to recover than others.[55] More than just a tool for the demographic reconstruction of certain features of local life, the census shaped key components of national order.

Among the most closely argued points at the Philadelphia convention that drafted the Constitution concerned how best to calculate each state's representation in the House of Representatives and its contribution to potential direct federal taxes. The crucial formula—now often referred to as the three-fifths clause—stated that the figure would be fixed by "adding to the whole number of free Persons, including those bound to Service for a

Term of Years, and excluding Indians not taxed, three fifths of all other Persons."[56] This legislation established three key categories. All free men and women, regardless of their indentured status, were to be counted as full members of the national polity. Indians were set beyond the embrace of nation. Slaves, the third category, were to be counted as three-fifths of a free person for national purposes. Gender and economic status had no relevance, while racial identity was awkwardly employed to define gradations of relationship to national society. Native Americans were excluded, enslaved African Americans had perverse partial entry, while free African Americans, at least technically, were included. This marked a critical first step toward the legal establishment of national race-based criteria.

The fragility of free black identity in the national imaginary was laid bare in the organization of the census. Shifting attention from the theoretical plane of the Constitution to its practical implementation in the census exposes a fundamental difference in how race operated in relationship to slavery in each setting. While the framers of the Constitution refrained from explicitly using the word *slave*, elusively referring to "other persons," the first three federal censuses adopted a different race-related reluctance by obfuscating the presence of free African Americans in the country. From 1790 to 1810, enslaved individuals were readily counted and tabulated in columns marked "slave," while free blacks appeared covertly as "all other free persons." Where the Constitution disguised slavery, the census disguised free African Americans.

Note the significant difference of delicacy here: the Constitution signaled its anxiety by avoiding the term *slave*, while the census avoided explicit acknowledgment of free blacks in the new nation. It elaborated on this anxiety by counting what it called "other free persons" (i.e., free blacks) within the broader age categories used for slaves rather than the more specific ones established for white men and women. The ages of slaves and free blacks were not assessed in the census until 1820, and even then four age categories were used for blacks instead of the five to identify whites. Although 95 percent of the African Americans in the towns examined here would be free in 1830, the way that they were categorized by the census identified them more like slaves than like whites.

By fixing race as a fundamental census category, the varied statistical contours of the black community in these river towns can be reconstructed with some precision. The earliest surviving census data for each town reveals that 23 percent of New Castle residents were African American versus just 9 and 4 percent in Burlington and Easton, respectively. By the end of this study in 1830, the black presence in New Castle had grown to 29 percent of its population, while declining slightly in the others to 8 percent in Burlington and 3 percent in Easton.[57]

The gradual emancipation of enslaved African Americans is probably the most poignant place where group identity intersected with public life in the Revolutionary Delaware Valley. Every state in the nation north of Delaware outlawed slavery during the early republic, beginning with Pennsylvania in 1780 and concluding with New Jersey in 1804.[58] Although slavery remained legal in Delaware, there too the majority of African Americans in New Castle County were free by 1800. These laws inaugurated slow and cautious change that nevertheless marked a profound transition in local experience and U.S. history. While non-whites were for all intents and purposes still excluded from participating in the region's electoral politics, legal and social changes for African Americans meant that the public meaning of blackness would be central to the region's Revolutionary identity politics. Moreover, the conflicts about the place of free blacks in the nation had ramifications for other groups, such as Quakers, who were closely associated with gradual emancipation.

Burlington residents carried the emancipation banner highest among whites in these three river towns. Quakers in Burlington Monthly Meeting reported in 1782, "there is now none remaining amongst us in bondage."[59] Quakers spearheaded the movement among whites throughout the Delaware Valley, and wealthy non-Quakers in Burlington often followed suit.[60] By 1796 only two men in town, both prominent Episcopalians, including the Federalist leader Joshua M. Wallace, remained slave masters. The slow-moving state emancipation law passed in 1804 had little consequence in Burlington, which had never been a major slaveholding area, and in 1830, just as in 1796, only two slave masters resided there.

Quakers played a leading role in the Delaware Valley's early abolition campaigns. The New Jersey Society for Promoting the Abolition of Slavery met annually in Burlington starting in 1793, and three of its five officers were Burlington taxpayers. Legal decisions by the state Supreme Court's chief justice, the prominent Burlington Friend James Kinsey, supported the "benevolent Design" of masters who posthumously emancipated slaves in their wills against the wishes of surviving family members who sought to retain control of human property via inheritance.[61] Burlington Federalist William Griffith was president of the New Jersey abolition society when the state passed its emancipation law, and his address to the organization that year highlights both its benevolent ideals and its racist context. Griffith's address presented a positive sense of the humanity and moral capability of African Americans by praising the "general good conduct and dispositions of this degraded people, and their capacity for higher usefulness." Even in the face of "complicated difficulties" that "physical, political, and local causes present, this people are advanced in the scale of intellectual and social existence." African American families, religious societies, and free black schools all exemplified the group's "progress" for Griffith, especially their goal to "assimilate, more and more to their superiors."[62] The question of black capacity for assimilation to white social norms would be an explosive issue for Revolutionary identity politics.

Conservatives in formal politics led much of the early gradual emancipation movement, a role that deserves attention, as it can help to balance
the Jeffersonian perspective that often still informs scholarly assessments
of the era.[63] The *Trenton Federalist* combined "reason and religion," in Griffith's words, to condemn slavery when it reprinted an account of a Quaker
who freed his thirty-seven inherited slaves and explained to one of them,
"Like our white brethren you ought to have been freed at twenty one. Religion and humanity enjoin me to give thee thy liberty."[64] Nevertheless,
emancipation leaders such as Griffith foresaw only a narrow space for free
blacks in the new nation. He favored a century-long time frame for slavery's eradication in the United States, and one of the chief benefits of the
campaign would be to reduce the political influence of southern states in
the House of Representatives. For Griffith, the end of slavery would terminate the three-fifths clause of the Constitution and would not be replaced
by full political representation for free blacks. Similarly, Griffith championed the cause of black education, and especially the training of black
teachers, because even with massive funding "*white* schools" could not be
expected to enroll black children.[65] This complex amalgam of antislavery
and racialist thought was at the vanguard of white efforts to address racial
inequality in Revolutionary America.

The strong Quaker cast of gradual abolition in West Jersey and Pennsylvania also appeared in northern Delaware. Here, however, the effort was
less successful, due partly to its less influential Quaker presence. The
Wilmington-based Abolition Society of Delaware was an extension of the
Friends' Quarterly Meeting.[66] Like other abolition societies in this period,
it concentrated on legal strategies to protect the rights of individuals who
had been promised their freedom yet would still remain unfree for several
years. The frightening ambiguity of life as a slave under these conditions
was especially striking in borderland Delaware, where slave masters were
prohibited from transporting human property out of state, yet slavery
would remain legal there until the end of the Civil War.

When Wilmington Friends called for gradual emancipation, their opponents condemned Quakers as un-American for failing to support the patriot cause. One newspaper attacked them for having "used all the
[in]terest they dared, to destroy the liberties of the country, and establish
tyranny." Another lampooned a major Quaker text and implied that the
faith was un-Christian by noting, "I know not how it is written in Mr.
Barkely, but in my Bible I find" scriptural support for slavery.[67] Proslavery
writers consistently degraded calls for emancipation because of their
tainted association with Quakers. "What can be their views" now that they
have "relinquished their favorite theme, dependence on Great
Britain? . . . [M]en who would crouch down under the rod of a tyrant, and
submit to the grossest indignities, are become the warm advocates for the
priviledges of freedom, to a race who have not a single qualification."[68]

In addition to campaigning against slavery, Quakers in the postwar period carefully reconsidered their terms of group membership and explicitly decided for the first time in 1796 that "convinced persons" should be admitted to the Society "without respect to nation or colour."[69] In a period of swift changes in the meaning of religious, racial, and ethnic identities, the Philadelphia Yearly Meeting committed itself to racial and ethnic inclusiveness. Here again we see that despite being outside the patriot coalition, Quakers pushed forward some of the most important changes in the region's Revolutionary identity politics.

Gradual emancipation and its profound implications for black identity even influenced life in places like Easton with few slaves and no Quakers. Pennsylvania's gradual emancipation law required slave owners to register their human property, which led to the recording of fifty-six slaves at the Northampton County Courthouse in 1780. A quarter of the slaves in the county lived in Easton, most of them owned by two families. George Taylor, Easton's signer of the Declaration of Independence, registered Tom and Sam, both age thirty. The shopkeeper Myer Hart owned five slaves, three of them younger than seven, while his son Michael, also a storeowner, registered an eighteen-year-old woman named Phillis.[70]

Slavery's formal end in Pennsylvania and the legal mechanisms put in place to monitor its termination offered one woman in Easton an avenue to protest one of its worst abuses. The slave Phillis, who had been registered by Michael Hart in 1780, appeared in court three years later to accuse her master of rape. Phillis explained how Hart would call her to the stable and "promise her ribbons and blow out the candle & make her stay with him[,] . . . made her lie down[,] . . . pull[ed] up her clothes, and put into her his [scratched out] and had carnal knowledge of her body." At other times these sexual assaults occurred on the kitchen floor or in the bedroom when Hart's wife was out of town. When Phillis "at last found herself to be pregnant," she went to court to testify against him.[71] Surveillance by new groups such as the Pennsylvania Abolition Society allowed some access to protection against such attacks. Unfortunately, however, the outcome of Phillis's charges remains unknown. Michael Hart owned no slaves in 1800, but a free black of unknown age and gender was enumerated in his household that year in the census.

Gradual emancipation's legal assault on slavery boldly departed from the near universal white acceptance of slavery a short time earlier. However, it was too cautious and narrow an approach to effect widespread change quickly enough for many African Americans, as the experience of Molly Evans shows. When Evans's owner died in late 1793, the administrators of the estate thought they sold her for a term of eight years to a New Castle man. As one of the administrators recalled, the purchaser claimed to be a member of the Abolition Society with "the cause of the blacks at heart." Evans and her four children—three of whom had been born after her sale—appeared as slaves in Samuel P. Moore's New Castle household in the 1800 census. However, when her legal enslavement expired in 1802, Moore produced a bill of sale that claimed the purchase had been made for life. Although the administers of the estate (the widow and brother of Evans's deceased master) and several other local whites insisted that she had only been sold for a term of years, the Abolition Society of Delaware dropped her case after nine months of careful work, when they gave up hope of finding any contradictory paper evidence.[72] Even with the support of white allies, African Americans could reasonably judge slavery's postwar decline to be fragile and incomplete.

The looming specter of black freedom that emancipation invoked for many whites produced a venomous public debate. Almost all the letters to the *Delaware Gazette* in the fall of 1789 that had attacked Quaker abolitionists as un-American also insisted upon the fundamental difference between whites and blacks and warned that chaos would ensue from encouraging black freedom in a nation based on popular sovereignty. As one writer concisely explained, "There are confessedly different grades in the human species. . . . [W]e would not wish to see them [negroes] share in our councils, marry in our families, and be exalted to rule over us." Indeed, the writer claimed to know a free black man of property who had voted in a recent Wilmington election and had been "shook by the hand as a clever fellow, for espousing a particular party, in order to gain an election in their favor."[73]

In some ways black freedom extended the loftiest ideals of patriots, who had made liberty and resistance to enslavement the most cherished values of the Revolution.[74] The New Jersey Abolition Society, for example, used the famous opening lines of the Declaration of Independence as the epigram to its constitution.[75] Ultimately, however, the consequences of black freedom in a republican polity made ending slavery *more* threatening to most whites. As another newspaper writer explained, Revolutionary values and republican political culture argued *against* black freedom. For this writer, slavery needed to be maintained because "if you free them, you must tax them, and from that they must have the vote by your own principles. They will control politics from Pennsylvania to Georgia." Even this awful political consequence fell short of the grossest fears expressed by proslavery advocates:

Can you expect to assimilate and become one people—what give your daughters in marriage to their sons, and choose the partners in your beds . . . from among their daughters? No, my fellow citizens nature has marked the lines of distinction too strong to be erased, and though it were possible you could consent to such a degradation of your nature, they would never accord with it, the idea of a mixture is as disagreeable to them, as you, and though particular instances may be adduced of this sort of—I had almost said bestiality, yet the general abhorrence on both sides, would under all circumstances, tend to keep us separate and distinct races.

To this writer, race mixture subverted the natural order of human distinction. While "some philosophers have almost exhausted the powers of language to prove them descendents of the same pair with us—contrary to the evidence of our senses that black was white! Yet we may be very confident, that the order of nature will not be reversed." Because "subordination and dependence are the main pillars of society," whites must retain their natural dominance over blacks. To do otherwise would destroy rational order and lead to chaos. "The negro govern the white man, as well might the caffrarian govern the negro, the ourang outang govern the caffrarian, the baboon or ape govern him, and the monkey govern the whole."[76] Such fears and hostility among increasingly race-conscious Americans all but terminated any meaningful black engagement with formal politics in the new United States.

Growing black freedom did more than just generate a hostile theoretical newspaper debate. Whites in New Castle demanded new laws to limit black rights in a town with a large, growing, and mostly free African American presence after 1800. Petitions to the state legislature from New Castle complained that racial mixing among the lower sort disrupted local life. One objected to peddlers who exchanged goods indiscriminately with apprentices, servants, and slaves, while another targeted the "frequent riotous assemblages of disorderly people, particularly negroes," in the town's "Tippling Houses." An unusually popular petition, signed by more than a quarter of the town's taxpaying whites, complained that "the assembly of free negroes, mulatoes, and slaves within the limits of the town of New Castle" demanded more laws "to regulate and to prevent such disorderly meetings."[77] With greater public visibility, African Americans in New Castle suffered greater social coercion; discipline that had once been the responsibility of masters was increasingly expected from the state.

While the petitioners might have believed all local African Americans to be troublemaking rabble, the state taxed African Americans and carefully recorded black taxpayers after 1776. Although no African American paid taxes in New Castle Hundred in 1776 (or at least nobody was identified as black in the surviving records), 5 percent of its taxables were African Americans in 1798, a figure that climbed to 11 percent in 1815 and 1826. Though concentrated at the low end of the tax structure in 1798, their economic position improved by 1815. By that year New Castle's black community demonstrated some economic diversity, with the two most affluent African Americans now in the second highest quintile of taxpayers, nearly 20 percent of black taxpayers in the middle bracket, with the remaining three-fourths still at the bottom of the general population. While still overrepresented among the town's poorest, free African Americans had achieved some economic success there by 1815.

Two petitions calling for further restrictions on blacks in New Castle were drafted in 1816 just as local blacks achieved their best economic accomplishments of the period, for the modest economic improvement among African Americans from 1798 to 1815 collapsed by 1826. None of the six men who had risen above the bottom half of taxpayers in 1815 persisted as taxpayers in 1826, and only two of twenty-three free blacks had property valued above the bottom half of the general population in 1826. The number of African Americans who had climbed out of the bottom of the taxed social structure dropped from just over a quarter in 1815 to less than 10 percent in 1826. The growing antiblack legislation and antiblack violence of the 1820s had an economic impact on African Americans in New Castle, yet the persistence of black taxpayers demonstrated a commitment to local public life and a sure sign that they had left slavery behind.

Because the boundaries defining blackness were often sweeping and coercive, it is particularly important to develop a nuanced sense of how black group identity shaped the contours of everyday life. Due to the race consciousness of official record keepers of the time, whether in tax, census, or church documents, we can recover some significant local patterns. New Castle's strong black presence and the persistence of legal slavery in Delaware distinguish it from the other river towns, but even in New Castle slavery underwent unmistakable decline, as free African Americans increased from 58 percent of the local black population in 1800 to 71 percent in 1810, 75 percent in 1820, and 91 percent in 1830.[78] New Castle Town was an especially important locus for free African Americans in the first decade of the century, as the transition to freedom came more slowly in rural New Castle Hundred that surrounded the town, where the percentage of blacks held in bondage declined more slowly.

New Castle Town included twenty-one independent black households in 1800 in which neither slaves nor whites resided. Although these pioneering households represent only 7 percent of the town's domestic units, they forcefully expressed the rapid local transition that closed the eighteenth century. This relatively small number of households accounts for nearly a third (29 percent) of New Castle's entire black population. Although one generally assumes that the largest concentration of blacks in a slave state like Delaware would occur in the households of wealthy slave masters, only William Stidham's twelve slaves rivaled the scale of the largest free black households in New Castle. Interestingly, three of the five largest free black households were businesses: Double Dick Steel & Company, with nineteen free black residents; S. Davis & Company, with eleven; and Robert Vonjoy & Company, with ten. Although these might have been boardinghouses for laborers in white-owned companies, two of the three black heads of households in the 1800 census also appear in New Castle's 1798 tax list. The wealthiest of them, Samuel Davis, placed in the third quintile of taxpayers, the midpoint of the local economic structure. Similarly, the local tax assessor judged Robert Vanjoy's property in the fourth quintile, and his economic success continued so that by 1815 he ranked in the second quintile. Fascinatingly, the tax collector failed to identify Vanjoy as "colored" that year, though he did so for twenty-one less affluent African American taxpayers.[79] Whether consciously or accidentally, Robert Vanjoy's economic ascent seems to have allowed his black racial status to disappear from the tax record.

Free blacks' economic marginality was not mirrored by a corresponding lack of churchgoing. All seven black taxpayers in 1798 appeared in local church records, a surprising fact because nearly 40 percent of all taxpayers that year had no known religious affiliation. Moreover, if we isolate the taxpayers with no known religious affiliation in the bottom three quintiles of the tax structure, where all the black taxpayers appeared in 1798, the racial contrast in religiosity is even more striking. The 100 percent known religious affiliation for African Americans far outpaced just 51 percent for their white economic counterparts. All the black taxpayers married in the Episcopal church, and two of them (both taxed in the fourth quintile in 1798) would later rent pews in the Presbyterian church. The practical need to document marital unions among free blacks probably encouraged black taxpayers in New Castle to make their marriages a matter of public record via the Episcopal ritual. Beyond such pragmatic impulses, black participation in organized religion arose from additional important sources. For some religious practice was a route to social respectability and a central commitment of black cosmopolitanism, while for others religious devotion stemmed from a localist evangelical populism. Moreover, the cosmopolitan and localist dimensions of African American spirituality intertwined in compelling ways as free blacks made a central contribution to the Delaware Valley's Revolutionary identity politics.

The growth of black freedom, followed by some material improvement, and then collapse in the 1820s, was an important trajectory for African Americans in New Castle. It also characterized the general experience of blacks in the broader Delaware Valley and can usefully be compared with the experiences of Quakers and Pennsylvania Germans. Analyzing the particular patterns of distinct groups in the broad Revolutionary period is necessary to understand their differences from one another as well as to grasp how they responded to similar conditions in forging the meaning of the nation in this region.

Cosmopolitans, Pennsylvania Germans, and the Fries Rebellion

Samuel Sitgreaves (fig. 17) was a cosmopolitan figure in provincial Pennsylvania German Easton. Whereas James Kinsey in Burlington enjoyed long-lasting leadership in his appointed position as chief justice, Sitgreaves's aspiration to be a gentleman in the Revolutionary nation was frustrated by the rapid transformation of political culture that outran his willingness to adapt to the times. Sitgreaves moved to Easton as a young man in 1786 when forced to flee creditors in Philadelphia. As he explained to his bookseller there, he lived in the country "by a rigid Economy," yet still had not discharged his debts and found himself "reduced by the increasing Poverty of the Times to the mortifying necessity of throwing myself on the generosity of my creditors."[80] Even prominent local men such as Sitgreaves found it difficult to attain the lofty standards established by leading men in Philadelphia.

Like all the river towns studied here, Easton mediated between the trends of Philadelphia and its large rural hinterland. As the most recently settled of our three towns, and at the greatest distance from the metropolis, Easton remained more closely connected to its rural surroundings than the other two. The majority of its residents before 1800, and especially the mass of country people who regularly came to town to take advantage of its centralized market and legal services, shared an understanding of everyday life largely at odds with the values of newcomers like Sitgreaves. He may have wanted to convince his creditors that he lived economically in the country, but most local people found him ostentatious. Sitgreaves headed one of only four Easton households taxed for owning silver plate in 1798, and he always ranked in the top decile of local taxpayers, even becoming the second wealthiest person in town by 1814.

Sitgreaves trumpeted his cosmopolitanism by choosing to build a brick house in 1792. By shunning local limestone, the preferred building material for substantial structures in the area, he committed himself to a non-local style. Despite the extravagance of raising the first brick building in Easton, he soon found it too small and undertook the construction of an even grander house dubbed "Sitgreaves's folly" in local popular memory.[81] This house displayed a cosmopolitan sensibility that distinguished its occupants from the majority of town residents. It symbolized more than just socioeconomic gentility by also making a related ethnic, religious, and political statement. Sitgreaves's Episcopalianism marked him as a decidedly Anglo figure in an overwhelmingly Pennsylvania German place. Moreover, he was a staunch conservative and the most important Federalist leader in the area.

It may seem surprising that Pennsylvania Germans from Northampton County would elect a relative newcomer like Sitgreaves to represent them, but they did so more than once. In the 1794 U.S. congressional race, organized by district rather than at-large in the state as later, Sitgreaves won handily and did so on an even more massive scale when reelected in 1796. Deference had only been partly dismantled during the Revolutionary War, which allowed a wealthy Anglo like Sitgreaves to succeed in popular politics into the mid-1790s. His wealth, education, connections to Philadelphia, and ability to claim access to the first rank of Anglo-American society—in short, his cosmopolitan qualities—encouraged local voters to defer to his talent and ability. As a visitor to town commented in 1794, a position in the U.S. Congress required a man of high status, and, besides Sitgreaves, "there was no other to do credit to the county."[82] Given the concentration of government power by the federal Constitution and the sweeping privileges granted to the Pennsylvania governor by the new state constitution in 1790, deferential politics made a renewed bid for acceptance in the closing decade of the century.[83]

Sitgreaves helped lead the postwar resurgence of deference in Pennsylvania and received the most votes of any Northampton County delegate to the convention that revised the state constitution. At the convention he played a leading conservative role, especially by arguing that representation in the new upper house of the assembly should be based on population and wealth. Sitgreaves acknowledged that this position led some to view him as a "Disciple of Aristocracy," but he insisted that property-based safeguards were essential for rational and stable republican government.[84] Such aggressive conservatism appeared to many local people to break with the egalitarian thrust of the Revolution and helped to trigger a major partisan realignment in Northampton County in the late 1790s.

The growing tension between elite Anglo cosmopolitanism with strong Philadelphia ties and an increasingly assertive Pennsylvania German localism based in small town and rural culture shaped everyday life throughout postwar Northampton County. Although only sometimes erupting into formal politics, oral traditions highlight the gender and class dimensions of cosmopolitan and local conflict. In the early nineteenth-century an elderly Easton resident recalled a significant event from the 1770s when the town's "inhabitants were mostly . . . sturdy Germans" with an "inveterate attachment to the old order of things." Pennsylvania German women, the "good *fraus*" who maintained local customs, conveyed such values in their "antiquated quilted caps," "homespun gowns," and "pockets in the shape of saddle bags."[85] Pennsylvania German women were key markers of ethnic community.[86]

Controversy erupted when an affluent non-German newcomer arrived in town and set up house in its best neighborhood. She distinguished herself from long-term residents in a number of ways, such as by purchasing kitchen furniture that needed to be delivered from Philadelphia. She apparently drew upon considerable financial resources and had taste that could not be met by local craftsmen. Her economic status and cosmopolitan style reinforced an Anglo-American identity that distinguished her from the majority of local people.

These differences became public in an explosive manner through her clothing. Rather than wearing the "short stuffed petticoats in vogue among the German," the newcomer preferred "a long flowing skirt [that] set off to advantage a figure of remarkable grace." The traditional calf-length skirt was well suited to agricultural and household work, while a long dress demonstrated a conspicuous consumption of fabric and disassociated its wearer from manual labor. As the account stressed that the dress accentuated the newcomer's body, presumably an Empire gown that accentuated her bosom, her clothing projected a flirtatious sexuality. Such an understanding of her self-presentation made her the target of communal violence. One evening after midnight a "large band of prominent women" broke into the outsider's house, gagged her, dragged her to a pond, and dunked her repeatedly. While the punishment was kept secret, the story reportedly circulated for many years thereafter "as a warning to give point to the lessons of careful mothers."[87] The divide separating cosmopolitan and local styles in Easton could cause dramatic conflict and shaped public memory there. This social rupture where ethnic, status, gender, and sexual identities meaningfully expressed themselves through clothing reveals key qualities about everyday life in Easton that remain obscure in traditional historical sources.

A growing sense of ethnic divergence from Anglo-American norms occurred throughout the Pennsylvania German region surrounding Philadelphia during the early republic. The carpenter and folk artist Lewis Miller recorded a similar cultural clash in an 1806 depiction of residents in the county seat of York, Pennsylvania. Miller's domestic drama depicted a Pennsylvania German country woman in traditional petticoat and short-gown on the left, balanced by two women in long, sexualized dresses of the Anglo-American cosmopolitan style on the right, with a country man awkwardly standing between them (fig. 18). Fortunately, Miller added some text, mostly in Pennsylvania German dialect, that enriches our understanding of the scene. His caption identified the person on the left as the old Grethel who scolds her husband Joseph with a raised index finger and switch clasped behind her back. Below the two women in long dresses, Miller added the English title, "A Strumpet." As in the Easton memory, Anglo culture was embodied by promiscuous women who required repression in Pennsylvania German areas.[88] In sexualizing the cosmopolitan style and portraying Pennsylvania German localism as dominant and able to mobilize appropriate communal violence against outsiders, evidence from Easton and York points to a widespread postwar crisis in the Pennsylvania German heartland, where varied local identities coalesced to contest the imposition of cosmopolitan values.

Pennsylvania German ethnicity underwent significant changes stemming from the political rupture of independence, the popular mobilization and social turmoil of war, the decline of slavery in the region, and the increasing proportion of American-born Pennsylvania Germans in the period.[89] Ethnic stereotyping of French radicalism and Irish crudeness were widespread in the early republic, as was the sense that Pennsylvania German norms in foodways, clothing, spirituality, popular culture, and, especially, language and dialect were significantly different from Anglo-American ones.[90] These sometimes buried forms of cultural difference burst into public view in the Fries Rebellion. Although less well-known than the Shays and Whiskey rebellions of the postwar period, the Fries Rebellion was inspired by a similar continuation of Revolutionary ideals of liberty, popular sovereignty, and local autonomy with the important addition that it occurred in an area dominated by Pennsylvania Germans fewer than one hundred miles north of the national capital of Philadelphia.

The Fries Rebellion arose in the Easton area in opposition to federal policies of the late 1790s that limited the rights of aliens, attacked free speech, and imposed a novel federal direct tax on domestic property.[91] Pennsylvania German identity provided a powerful sense of solidarity that helped mobilize and unify people in scores of local actions in 1798 and 1799 and marked the most violent antinational movement in the postwar Delaware Valley. The explosive intersection of ethnicity and national politics at the rebellion's center make it critical for understanding the region's postwar Revolutionary identity politics.

The transformation of Pennsylvania Germans from colonial outsiders to full-fledged Americans was initiated by their martial service in the war, recourse to armed resistance that continued to defend local practices against distant external authorities in the late 1790s. The multifaceted motives that inspired widespread resistance in Northampton, Berks, Bucks, and Montgomery counties require a multicausal explanation that goes beyond singular political, economic, or ethnic factors that are still too often posed as exclusive explanations. The economic and ethnic dimensions of the conflict were powerful by themselves but only became explosive through their interaction with one another and the still-urgent ideals and experiences of the Revolutionary War. Like other backcountry resistance movements that erupted from Maine to the Carolinas after the war, Fries Rebellion activists were inspired by localist strains of Revolutionary ideology that rejected the Thermidorean cast of Federalist leadership.[92]

The formal politics of the 1790s had been driven to chaotic heights by the increasing violence of the French Revolution, the broadening war in Europe, and a rabid sense of domestic political instability. National politicians responded to the decade's wide-ranging crises by passing several controversial laws in the summer of 1798. Together, the federal tax to fund war preparations, prohibitions on the rights of aliens, and curtailing newspaper criticism of the government heralded a decisive shift in national politics that aimed to strengthen the state and the Federalists who held power. Although this legislation caused controversy in the late 1790s and is mostly remembered disparagingly today, the intensification of national authority received strong support from many at the time. As "A Whig of '76" explained his support for the Alien and Sedition Acts, foreigners could come to the United States to work but should not involve themselves in politics. "We made our constitution and government ourselves . . . and woe is me, if any foreigner among them all, friend or foe, shall ever touch them, while I can wield a sword or pull a trigger." In conservative West Jersey, strong nativist appeals aimed to block "Irish patriots and Gallic Africans [i.e., Haitian revolutionaries]" from having the political rights "for which our ancestors toiled, and for which many of us have struggled at the risk of health, fame, and fortune."[93] Such views led the U.S. congressmen representing all three river towns to support the laws that expanded national power. Easton's congressman, Samuel Sitgreaves, even played a lead role drafting the Alien and Sedition Acts.[94] While the laws' main targets may have been radical French and Irish émigrés, the legislation carried distinct repercussions for Pennsylvania Germans, who formed a majority among Sitgreaves's constituents.

Popular opinion in Northampton County opposed the laws passed by the Federalist Congress, and neither of the area's incumbent House members, Sitgreaves and the Quaker John Chapman, would be returned to office in the October 1798 election. Sitgreaves had resigned to accept appointment as a commissioner of the controversial Jay's Treaty, whereas Chapman suffered a landslide defeat to two Revolutionary War officers, the Lutheran J. P. Muhlenberg and the Scots Irish Presbyterian Robert Brown. Voters in the county decisively rejected Federalists in the fall of 1798, which paralleled a significant statewide shift, as the Federalists' opponents achieved a 10-to-3 advantage in Pennsylvania's congressional delegation.

Notwithstanding the apparent rebuke offered by Pennsylvania voters in the fall election, implementation of the federal direct tax went forward at the end of October. Even more shocking to popular sentiment in Northampton County was the appointment of Jacob Eyerley, a conservative Moravian from Bethlehem, as the local tax commissioner. Not only was Eyerley's allegiance in the Revolution questioned, but he had also run for Congress on the Federalist ticket in Sitgreaves's place and lost badly. Now he was rewarded by distant elites as the top local man to oversee the unpopular tax. Not surprisingly, Eyerley had enormous trouble finding local people willing to serve as assessors. As one man who refused to accept the office explained, the "people were very much opposed to the law, and he did not well understand it himself."[95]

The numerous public meetings, local associations, and liberty poles raised to resist the new tax levied by the national government drew on still-smoldering Revolutionary experiences. Assessors were widely accused of being "tory rascals," while others were warned, "none were friends to the present government except tories."[96] One Easton man reported that John Fries explained to the crowd at the largest direct action of the rebellion, "all those People who were Tories in the last war mean to be the Leaders. They mean to get us quite under. They mean to make us slaves."[97] The direct tax reminded many of British actions that ultimately had led to the

Revolution. Acting within the Revolutionary traditions of local popular mobilization to protect their liberties, Pennsylvania Germans north of Philadelphia refused to allow their property to be assessed by federal officials.

Revolutionary memory, social unrest, and ethno-religious affiliation reinforced one another in dramatic ways that starkly polarized the public. Swift implementation of the tax despite the opposition's victory seemed to many to deny popular sovereignty and demanded a forceful response. Many local people even believed that the federal Constitution sanctioned resistance to the laws passed in the summer of 1798. As a Northampton County petition explained, the concentration of executive power in the Alien and Sedition Acts was "directly opposed to the spirit and even the letter of the constitution." The newly elected congressman Robert Brown presented similar petitions when he arrived in the House of Representatives in early 1799.[98] Local meetings called for the repeal of all the offensive laws, and militia captains helped circulate petitions. Popular associations used strategic violence to block tax enforcement and refused to elect their own local assessors. As one group explained, if we elect local officials, "we at once acknowledge that we will submit to the laws, and that we wont do."[99] Local assemblies and militia enforcement of popular opinion had been central to the Revolutionary mobilization in Northampton County, and now such actions challenged the national government.

The local movement—like that which began the Revolutionary War—extended beyond an orderly assessment of legal rights and ordinary political expression via elections. Federally appointed assessors faced enormous hostility when attempting to enforce the law. The threat they faced survives in a brutal letter written in Pennsylvania German dialect, and signed with a drawing of a pistol and broadsword that warned, "these are the weapons for your slaughter." The letter accused the tax officers and their allies of being in league with the Devil and threatened to "burn your house and barn and will shoot you and your brother dead. . . . [Y]ou are never safe in your house." While the German-language threats would not have carried meaning to English readers, the drawings successfully communicated its menacing violence (fig. 19).[100]

The linguistic and ethnic distinctiveness of most rebels added an essential element to their movement and to the federal government's response. Anglo Federalists viewed Pennsylvania Germans as ignorant, lawless, and requiring strong disciplinary action. As a result U.S. District Court Judge Richard Peters issued warrants that required the accused to stand trial in a federal court in Philadelphia.[101] The heavy-handed Federalist response to the resistance stimulated the conflict and elevated it from a local event to one with national implications.

The federal marshal's arrival in the region and his imprisonment of local men in Bethlehem en route to Philadelphia triggered the rebellion's climax when several armed bands converged on the Moravian town to liberate their colleagues. To those who already felt that the 1798 laws subverted Revolutionary principles and the express protections of the Constitution, the denial of a local jury demanded immediate action. Armed rebels successfully freed the marshal's prisoners on March 7, 1799, and insisted that the prisoners "should be tried at Easton and should not be taken to Philadelphia."[102]

Tensions ran high and the threat of violence appeared everywhere, but no blows were levied, nor did blood flow that day. The popular action mobilized as a communitarian effort that shielded leaders from being singled out for exceptional punishment. When a member of the marshal's posse asked to speak with the crowd's leader, he was told, "they were all commanders," while an insurgent noted that no leader was necessary because the people "seemed to be all of one mind."[103] Although the prosecution would later identify a main leader to blame, the rebellion centered on the traditional ideal of popular mobilization on behalf of the entire community. As had also occurred in the Revolutionary War, mass communal violence was sanctioned by support of "the people."

Sentiment in Easton, however, was somewhat more mixed. The U.S. marshal's posse of fewer than twenty men included six from Easton. John Barnett and his brother William served, but they had trouble "find[ing] any more good persons for that business."[104] The Easton members of the posse, along with Samuel Sitgreaves, are the only known townspeople to have opposed the resistance. Yet popular opinion in the region so overwhelmingly supported the rebels that even this handful marked Easton as a conservative place to some. As a letter in a Philadelphia Federalist newspaper cautiously explained in the wake of the successful liberation, most insurgents believed that "everybody thinks as we do, except a few d[amne]d tories in Easton."[105]

Although Sitgreaves may have been the lightning rod for this characterization of Easton, the Barnett brothers, wealthy tanners and Lutherans, were key figures who bridged the Anglo-German fault line. They were especially important for the marshal's posse because their bilingualism allowed them to communicate with the rebels who marched on Bethlehem. The judge, William Henry, reported that all the rebels' threats "were spoken in German," and at the trial William Barnett carefully described John Fries's Pennsylvania German orders to the mob. When Fries entered the tavern to negotiate with the marshal, he told his men to hold their fire unless he was shot, and then "they must strike and stab and do as well as they could. *Seblaget, steebet, und macht so gut als ibr konnet.*" By contrast, Easton posse member John Mulhallon was mystified by the rebels, for "they generally spoke in German or broken English, which I could not understand. . . . There was a great deal said, but none of them spoke to me in English."[106]

Just as Mulhallon's limited language ability circumscribed his understanding, Pennsylvania Germans who did not speak English also suffered
the limits of monolingualism. A Northampton attorney and "noted high
toned Federalist" described passing a liberty pole erected outside Easton
with a flag "inscribed in large letters [with] the motto Liberty, Equality,
and Independence." When asked to translate the banner into German by
a crowd in front of the tavern who sympathized with the rebellion, he
seized the opportunity to degrade them. Readying his horse for a swift escape, he turned a clever pun. Instead of offering a proper translation,
"*Freyheit, Gleichheit, & Unabhaenigheit,*" he told them it read, "*Frechheit, Gei-
theit, und Unverschaesntheit*"—meaning in English, "Insolence, Lewdness,
and Impudence."[107]

News of the successful resistance spread quickly, and within a week the
usually taciturn Burlington resident James Craft noted, "bad news from
Northampton County" where "a set of Disorganizers, Friends to the
French" had taken bold action. This "conduct I very highly disapprove—
despise—Hate." The rebellion loomed large in local discussions throughout the Delaware Valley. Craft returned to the subject repeatedly in the
next two weeks and even commented, "if I was King—I would make them
rue it." On the last day of March he crossed the river to Bristol, Pennsylvania, to see the federal troops off to Northampton and worried that the
rebels "muster very strong [and] are armed and well provided—what sor-
rowful news—worse and worse."[108]

Craft misjudged the ability of the resistance to repel federal troops, and
the insurgents' fortunes spiraled downward after the liberation at Bethlehem. Local attorneys and judges in Northampton County—men such as
Sitgreaves and William Henry—soon met with the army and U.S. District
Court Judge Peters to coordinate action to snuff the rebels.[109] Armed repression, however, could not terminate all local resistance. For example,
Peters's nephew, Tom Smith (whose Republican opinions set him at odds
with his Federalist uncle), jokingly offered the judge a dollar as he prepared to depart with the army. Smith contributed to the cause, he explained, "with all my heart, for . . . it is the best contrivance to turn
Dutchmen into Democrats."[110] He clearly understood that military force
would intensify the ethnic basis of partisan politics and push Pennsylvania
Germans solidly into the opposition.

The army rounded up thirty-one insurgents in their sweep of the area
and charged fifteen men with treason and sixteen with lesser crimes.[111]
Only three would subsequently be indicted in the district court, chief
among them John Fries. The trial record provides the richest evidence
about the movement and highlighted the ethnic identity of the rebels. As
a concession to the accused being tried outside their local courts, the jury
was divided between city and country residents, two of whom from
Northampton County spoke only German. These jurors were assigned an

official translator, and it was noted that "they would understand many of the witnesses better . . . several of those being Germans also, and could not speak English."[112]

The court drama began with the charge from Judge James Iredell, who felt no need to shield his antagonism toward the accused. He pointed out that they had been grossly misled by the "awful example" of Revolutionary France and misjudged the intentions of the federal government, for nobody suffered "oppression" in America. Nevertheless, he acknowledged that certain recent laws had been received with "great discontent," and because some Pennsylvania legislators "have publicly pronounced them to be in violation of the Constitution of the United States," he devoted the rest of his remarks to explaining their legality. Iredell recognized that the Naturalization, Alien, and Sedition Acts provided the key context for resistance to the direct tax.[113] The main ground for doubting the Alien Acts' legality stemmed from the Constitution's ambiguous language to protect the transatlantic slave trade. By declaring that the federal government had no right to legislate about "the migration or importation of such persons as any of the states . . . admit until 1808," the law seemed to address newcomers, whether white or black, free or enslaved. Iredell accepted this as a technical possibility, but he assured the courtroom that the Constitutional prohibition aimed solely at the slave trade.[114]

Judge Iredell closed apocalyptically by warning the jury that the rebels' actions threatened the future of the republic. He explained, "if you suffer this government to be destroyed, what chance have you for any other? A scene of the most dreadful confusion must ensue. Anarchy will ride triumphant and all the lovers of order, decency, truth, and justice be trampled under foot."[115] The U.S. attorney William Rawle, a Quaker who had fled the Delaware Valley for British protection in New York City during the Revolutionary War, rose next to indict the accused as "moved and seduced by the instigation of the devil." He charged Fries and more than one hundred associates for assembling with "guns, swords, clubs, staves, and other warlike weapons . . . to raise and levy war, insurrection, and rebellion against the said United States."[116] The defendants were accused of heinous acts to destroy the nation.

Samuel Sitgreaves played a substantial role in the prosecution's opening argument and examination of witnesses. As he commented at the close of the trial, its outcome held special personal interest for him because "my lot is cast in that part of Pennsylvania where this unfortunate event occurred." As a result, he felt "particularly for the good order, peace, and prosperity of that part of the state, but I have unhappily seen it in such a situation that all the harmony of the society was destroyed."[117] Sitgreaves had known of the intense local resistance for some time, as federal tax assessors had turned to him for protection six months earlier. His Federalist politics, cosmopolitan Anglo style, Episcopalian religious beliefs, and commitment to strong national order perfectly suited his role as a prosecutor in what seemed to be a decisive Federalist triumph. As an optimistic conservative wrote to an ally in Easton at the close of the trial, the hanging of the rebels and the election of a Federalist governor in the fall of 1799 "will make this a Federalist state."[118]

At the end of the long courtroom drama in Philadelphia, which included a second trial, three defendants were convicted of treason and sentenced to hang. Ignoring the advice of hardliners in his cabinet, which fully exposed the growing schism among leading Federalists, President Adams pardoned the men on June 21, 1800. Adams later explained his humane decision not on overarching legal, political, or philosophical grounds, but by excusing the behavior of "miserable Germans" who were "ignorant of our language . . . [and] our laws."[119]

The Fries insurgents and their opponents both understood ethnic distinctiveness to have been central to the resistance, and memories of the conflict persisted in the collective consciousness of local residents well into the nineteenth century.[120] The rebellion dramatically exposed a major clash that built upon ethnicity, politics, Revolutionary localism, and the economic travails of the postwar period. As the bitter Federalist Alexander Graydon later recalled, "the great Germanic body of the people" had been stirred up by the "friends of the people" to oppose federal laws, climaxing with the Fries Rebellion and the elections of Governor McKean and President Jefferson.[121] This combination of forces began to shift partisan allegiance in the area, as the overwhelming majority of Pennsylvania Germans in Northampton County would never again support Federalists as they had earlier in the decade.

Electoral Politics at the Close of the Century

The Fries Rebellion demonstrated that the increasingly hostile character of American society could move beyond angry language to physical violence in direct popular actions and state repression. In this explosive context, the 1800 presidential contest was rife with importance for the nation's future. Although Thomas Jefferson would win the national election, John Adams held a 17–8 majority from electors in the Delaware Valley. Because state legislatures would choose all the presidential electors from the region in 1800 (as they did in eleven of the nation's sixteen states that year), the state context of presidential politics is obviously important. Moreover, based on the popular vote in the region's 1800 congressional elections, with its 15–4 Republican advantage, Jefferson probably should have carried the region as well as the nation, but, as we have seen previously, the rules of the game matter a great deal in determining electoral victory and demand that we examine presidential politics from local and state perspectives in addition to the national one.

The Pennsylvania gubernatorial contest in 1799, which barred the non-partisan incumbent Thomas Mifflin due to term limits, was the most pivotal postwar election in the region. It pitted the Federalist James Ross of Pittsburgh against the Republican Thomas McKean, who had begun his political career as a radical whig in New Castle, Delaware, and now headed the Pennsylvania Supreme Court. The governor's race stimulated enormous interest and brought more than seventy thousand voters to the polls, nearly trebling turnout from the 1796 direct vote for presidential electors. Everyone understood that this bellwether contest would forecast Pennsylvania's weighty position in the upcoming presidential election.

The hard-fought governor's race stimulated an expansion of newspapers across Pennsylvania, including the founding of the *American Eagle* in Easton. The English-language paper declared itself "impartial," but almost immediately supported Federalist policies and James Ross. The paper also issued German-language supplements to woo ethnic voters. The first of these defended the Alien and Sedition Acts and announced support for Ross. Eighteen men signed the supplement, sixteen of whom can be found in the Easton tax list for 1796. Almost all these local Federalist leaders were of German descent, and the handful that was not had strong local ties to the Pennsylvania German community. Not surprisingly, they were quite wealthy, half from the top economic quintile, while those with more modest economic standing tended to be young and just beginning their careers. The religious profile of these local Federalists indicates stronger Lutheran and mixed Lutheran-Reformed allegiance than among taxpayers at large, but the twelve signers with known religious affiliations represented a balanced spectrum of local religious life.

Statewide voting in the governor's race was quite close, with the Republican McKean winning 54 percent of the statewide vote. The Pennsylvania German area to the north of Philadelphia proved critical to his election because places like Northampton County gave him 80 percent of its votes, providing the margin of victory in an otherwise close contest. Even in supposedly conservative Easton, with its Federalist newspaper, 81 percent of local voters chose McKean over Ross.[122] McKean clearly benefited here from his strong opposition to the Alien and Sedition Acts, popular repugnance with the Fries repression, and his modest role as a defense attorney at the rebels' trial. Although local conservatives organized more diligently than ever with a partisan newspaper, majority opinion among Pennsylvania Germans had turned decisively against Federalists.

The Republican victory in Pennsylvania cannot be properly explained as a statewide realignment of Pennsylvania Germans from Federalism to Republicanism. McKean ran very poorly in heavily German Lancaster County where Ross received his largest vote in the entire state. Even as Federalists retained their strength in Lancaster in 1800, where they held all six assembly seats, they decided not even to field a ticket for the assembly in

Northampton. In short, the political significance of ethnicity must be explained in conjunction with local circumstances.

Pennsylvania Germans spearheaded the Republican emergence in Northampton County, but some of them, of course, remained devoted Federalists. The family history of Easton resident John Arndt, whose military leadership in the war and active partisanship thereafter have been discussed earlier, provides a detailed view of how German inheritance influenced a committed conservative. Arndt penned an account of his family's key experiences for the benefit of his descendants in the blank pages of a lavish family Bible. This carefully wrought narrative highlighted certain aspects of his self-understanding. His German ancestors were mostly "poor humble mechanics" and consequently "lived in obscurity unnoticed by the bulk of Mankind."[123] Arndt never personally experienced the Old World, and even his father had left Baumholder, in southwestern Germany, at six years of age when the family emigrated in 1731. Nevertheless, he drew upon family "traditions" and "some written documents" to record aspects of life in Germany that furthered his celebration of America.

The manumission document that permitted Arndt's grandmother to depart her natal village figured prominently. He explained that she was bound there under terms of "vassalage," which he described as "something similar to the fate of a Virginia Slave or Negro, who is transferred with the soil which his Master owns when he chooses to sell the same." Leaving Germany meant escaping bondage, reserved in America only for Africans and their descendants. Arndt viewed his grandmother's experience and the looming role of state authority in Germany as "very singular to a free born American Citizen," and he hoped to "stimulate my Posterity ever to give a rational support to Legal Liberty." Arndt and the vast majority of eighteenth-century central European immigrants understood America as a place where they could more readily achieve personal independence.[124]

The 1799 election's most bitterly fought contest in Northampton County was not the governor's race, but that for another open seat whose occupant had an even more direct impact on everyday life. This sheriff's race highlights the vitriol of local politics around Easton as well as the rapid refashioning of partisanship in the volatile 1790s. Term limits prevented the incumbent, Henry Spering, from running again, and he threw his support to Abraham Horn, who had been elected to the state assembly in 1798 and had helped spread anti-direct tax sentiment in public meetings preceding the Fries Rebellion. The key local person opposing him was John Mulhallon, a member of the anti-Fries posse who testified at the rebels' trial in Philadelphia.[125]

Horn may or may not have participated in the March 7, 1799 events at Bethlehem that climaxed the Fries Rebellion, but he was well known as an anti-administration agitator who labored to connect local dissent with electoral politics at the state and national level. He had denounced the military mobilization against the insurgents as "merely a [Federalist] Electioneering Scheme" at a Philadelphia tavern and was also accused of stirring up local trouble by stating to a large group "that the President had sold the States and that the People should oppose the Laws."[126] Not surprisingly when Horn denounced Mulhallon in the sheriff's race, conservatives retorted by demanding to know the "pretensions" by which Horn "set himself up as the standard of political purity."[127] Horn went on to demolish Mulhallon among Easton voters but would finish a distant second to another candidate in the countywide race, while Mulhallon finished sixth in the ten-candidate field.[128]

Federalism's sudden collapse in Northampton County made control of the Republican nominating procedure critical to electoral success there. The next year a newspaper writer dubbed "Minority" protested how the party "decreed and dictated" whom the voters should select and named his own slate that included the dissident Abraham Horn.[129] Once again Horn handily won his hometown of Easton, but he finished a distant fifth in a countywide race that seated the top four candidates. Without the backing of the Republican organization, even a former office holder like Horn with clear pro-Fries credentials could not carry his county. Republican hegemony arrived early in Northampton County, but this hardly meant that formal politics would be complacent there. Dissidents regularly denounced the dominant Republican machine in Easton and Northampton County as partisan politics became an ever stronger feature of political life in the early nineteenth century.

Federalists had lost influence across Pennsylvania in the late 1790s, but they still retained a 13-to-11 majority in the state senate in 1800 and used that advantage to deny Jefferson the state's full fifteen electoral votes. The long stalemate between the Republican assembly and the Federalist senate even threatened to deny Pennsylvania participation in the presidential election until a last-minute compromise gave Jefferson an 8-to-7 electoral college majority in the state. The legislative negotiation meant that no popular vote occurred for the presidency that year and undoubtedly inflated Federalist strength in Pennsylvania.

Pennsylvania Germans around Easton provide an especially dramatic example of how ethno-religious identity intertwined with formal politics, yet other areas of the Delaware Valley also experienced similar developments whose local context has not been carefully studied. Federalist newspapers in conservative West Jersey, for example, viewed the Fries Rebellion with horror and hyperbolically warned of its close connections to Jacobinism and the Shays Rebellion. Moreover, the paper called on Quakers to reengage electoral politics. Failing to go to the polls when our tranquility "is disturbed by insurrections and domestic broils" meant "no small portion of the guilt must attach to you" as "unwilling to cooperate with the friends of peace and good order."[130] This Federalist paper insisted that the Society of Friends had an essential role to play in postwar politics.

Burlington County Federalists dominated its formal politics, but partisanship at the statewide level in New Jersey was very evenly matched in the late 1790s. Just as we saw in its first congressional elections at the start of this chapter, political boundaries were critical because district versus statewide races could produce strikingly different results. Republicans enjoyed a statewide popular majority in 1798, but because the congressional race that year occurred in five separate districts, two of its five congressmen were Federalists. Conservatives ran best in West Jersey districts, with their strong Quaker presence, and Burlington County voters once again demonstrated their lopsided partisanship by casting 84 percent of their votes for Federalists.

Although New Jersey Republicans tried to end legislative selection of presidential electors for 1800, a one-seat Federalist assembly majority prevented this change.[131] Thus, the county-level popular election of state legislators in October 1800 would decide New Jersey's vote in the presidential contest and stimulated the rapid development of its party organizations. The partisan struggle sparked an elaborate pamphlet and newspaper exchange that produced a more carefully documented local election than ever before. Republicans organized at the county level throughout the state and even challenged Federalists in their Burlington County stronghold. Joseph Bloomfield, who had led anti-Junto efforts in the first congressional election, remained the most substantial opposition figure in Burlington and initiated modern party politics there by holding political meetings, organizing local and county committees, and publishing their results.[132]

The earliest Republican efforts in Burlington County targeted Quakers by stressing Republican dedication to peace and a restrained national government. Jefferson, and by extension his party, deserved Quaker support as the author of the Declaration of Independence and for having led the fight against the established Anglican Church in Virginia, which supposedly indicated his support for Friends' silent worship. Bloomfield also denounced Federalist leaders as too fond of Britain to guide the young republic. Republicans made plain that they favored popular politics, opposed legislative control of the presidential election, and condemned those calling for changes to the state constitution of 1776. They charged constitutional reformers as "lawyers and justices" who expect "implicit obedience to their influence" and had an "abhorrence of all popular influence," barbs that targeted Burlington resident William Griffith, one of the most active Federalists in the state.[133]

Burlington Federalists responded to such attacks with their own partisan meetings and publications. Both parties courted local Quakers, many of whom had not returned to the polls after their formal disenfranchisement during the war and the intimidation that they continued to suffer in the postwar period. Federalists insisted that Adams was the true peace candidate, whose party had "set our feet in the rock of ORDER" and condemned Jefferson as a harbinger of bloodshed and civil war.[134] Most importantly, Federalists praised the Adams administration for having put down Pennsylvania's "two *rebellions*, excited by *foreigners*." Since then, Pennsylvania had fallen into discord under Republican governor McKean, and its legislative deadlock between Republicans and Federalists had supposedly "suspended" government there. New Jersey Federalists warned that such chaos would only be repeated on a larger scale should Republicans win the presidency.[135] Burlington Federalists levied repeated nativist charges and warned that Republicans would "gratify foreign emigrants and satiate the unfortunate resentments of a few passionate Americans."[136] They similarly warned of a growing alliance of large states, a "French faction," and a "class of aliens" who aimed to reduce federal power. Fear of immigrants and large-state machinations fused to lead small states like New Jersey to insist upon the preservation of the national status quo.[137]

William Griffith's calls for state constitutional reform also highlighted the electoral threat posed by aliens and immigrants. Griffith's opposition to female suffrage under the 1776 state constitution chiefly emphasized the law's ambiguity that allowed "many an electioneering trick." He was prepared to accept women voters but insisted that the law needed consistency. By contrast, the "inundation of foreigners . . . of every description of character" that had come to the polls was an unalloyed evil. Griffith opposed slavery and tolerated women's voting rights, positions that derived unusual popularity in a Quaker area, but he strongly opposed immigrant voting as a threat to the republic.[138]

Federalists easily won in Burlington in part because Republican invocations of the Revolution failed to understand its ambivalence for many Quakers. Eighty percent of Burlington Township voters picked the Federal ticket for the state legislature over an opposition that was dubbed "anti-Federal" and "Jacobin" by their opponents.[139] Federalists ran stronger in Burlington County than anywhere else in New Jersey, yet they also did well statewide, again winning control of the state legislature. By the start of November all seven of the state's electors were secure for Adams, among them William Griffith.

Despite this key Federalist victory in the legislature, the statewide contest for five U.S. congressional seats two months later revealed New Jersey's closely balanced partisanship. Federalist newspapers warned Burlington voters not to be complacent, as a low turnout there might allow Republicans to capture the state based on large majorities in places such as populous Essex County, the Republican stronghold in East Jersey that acted as a mirror opposite Burlington. Both parties presented a five-candidate ticket to voters who showed remarkable discipline in supporting the entire slate. Not only did nearly 99 percent of voters choose the full ticket, but they also turned out in higher numbers than they had for the legislative race. Whereas only 169 Burlington people cast votes in their safe countywide election in October, a stunning 3,352 voted in December's uncertain statewide congressional contest. Burlington voters once again overwhelmingly supported Federalists (79 percent), and their large turnout was important in an incredibly close statewide race where only 370 votes separated the bottom of the victorious Republican ticket from the top of the defeated Federalist one. New Jersey may have given all its electoral votes to Adams in 1800, but it simultaneously sent all Republicans to the U.S. House of Representatives, the first time that the "opposition" party had swept the state.

New Jersey's 1800 congressional election marked a critical transition in the state's formal politics. Republicans would win control of the state legislature the following year, which allowed them to elect Burlington Republican Joseph Bloomfield to the largely symbolic position of governor. Unlike Pennsylvania where the popularly elected governor wielded considerable power under the revised frame of the 1790 constitution, the legislature remained the dominant force in New Jersey politics. A legislative stalemate would deny Bloomfield the governor's seat in 1802, but thereafter Republicans enjoyed relatively easy control of the legislature until the wartime crisis in 1812. Burlington Federalists confronted an unfavorable climate in a remarkably stable partisan pattern for the next two decades. Despite overwhelming Federalist sentiment in Burlington County, Republicans dominated the state, which exacerbated local people's sense of the illegitimacy of electoral politics. In the 1803 countywide legislative race, for example, nearly four thousand Burlington people voted, whereas in the statewide congressional contest two months later fewer than one thousand bothered to go to the polls. The statewide party system, with its coordinated nomination process and united support for a set ticket of candidates, was a remarkable Republican achievement that in a sense disenfranchised people in places such as Burlington.

New Castle offers an important third route for Delaware Valley partisan formation at the close of the century. Leaders of both parties resided in the former colonial capital, while surrounding New Castle County, with Wilmington as its main urban center, soon became the Republican stronghold in an otherwise staunchly Federalist state. After 1800, Federalists in Pennsylvania had local influence at best, and in New Jersey they could not win at the state level, yet in Delaware, unlike anywhere else in the nation, robust competition between Federalists and Republicans extended without interruption from the mid-1790s through the 1820s, and Federalists enjoyed almost uninterrupted success.

The town of New Castle offers a useful microcosm of statewide partisanship. About 13 percent of local taxpayers (19 individuals out of 147 records) played a known role in formal politics, with Republicans outnumbering Federalists 12 to 7. The economic backgrounds of these party activists reveal that while the entire group was affluent, Republicans were less so. Their most frequent place in the town's economic structure in 1798 was in the second tax quintile, while Federalists were mostly in the top decile. These party leaders belonged to all local white religious groups, but Republicans were more likely to be Presbyterians, and Federalists had stronger standing in the Episcopal church. James McCullough, a Presbyterian trustee and the president of the Patriotic Society of New Castle County, who placed in the second tax quintile, serves as a representative Republican leader from New Castle in this period, while Kensey Johns, a wealthy attorney who had trained with George Read Sr. and the arch-Federalist justice Samuel Chase, stands as a representative Federalist leader.

Kensey Johns attempted to disrupt the formation of the Patriotic Society of New Castle when he insisted on recording who voted in favor of the new organization's constitution in 1794. The Patriotic Society was among the many democratic societies founded throughout the United States in the mid-1790s, along lines similar to Jacobin clubs in Revolutionary France. Burlington was too conservative a place to host such organizations, while the longstanding anti-French sentiment among Pennsylvania Germans in Easton inhibited such a group being created there. However, New Castle County, with its large number of postwar Irish immigrants, was more attune to radical developments in the Atlantic world, and this largely Presbyterian group played a major role in the opposition to Federalist dominance in Delaware. Formal political allegiances in New Castle often followed a pattern of Anglo Episcopalian dominance and Scots Irish Presbyterian exclusion from privilege.

The idea of a nontreasonous opposition to the government was still widely unsettling in the 1790s. In the face of such suspicions, the Patriotic Society took pains to declare its staunch support for the state and federal constitutions and insisted that "the PEOPLE have the inherent right and power" to criticize, make, and alter their government. Meeting at New Castle four times a year, the group labored to hold back "the Storm of British Tyranny" that had been weathered during the war but that now seemed resurgent.[140] When Federalists condemned democratic clubs as illegal organizations, the Patriotic Society of New Castle countered that similar bodies devoted to "freedom of opinion" had once been condemned by King George and had "brought about the revolution."[141]

The ongoing polarization from the Revolutionary War helped to give another new political organization in Delaware an unusual political orientation. As a fraternal organization of Continental Army officers, the Society of the Cincinnati was usually a leading conservative force in postwar politics, but not here. Its first president was James Tilton, who wrote the scandalous attack on the conservative patriot George Read Sr. The Society's early officers were all Presbyterians, and by the late 1790s its members would also be leading Jeffersonians.[142] Just as we saw in Burlington, military service, even as officers, often led to a radical position in postwar Delaware Valley politics. By 1795 the Delaware Society of the Cincinnati and the Patriotic Society of New Castle had largely overlapping memberships and together spearheaded the state's anti-Adams movement. Peter Jaquett, who had denounced George Read Sr. for trying to prohibit Continental troops from voting in New Castle, was now the vice president of the Cincinnati and condemned John Jay to purgatory for the treaty that bore his name. In a July 4, 1795, toast before the Patriotic Society, its president, New Castle resident Archibald Alexander, called for the British people to "shortly experience a revolution in the administration of their government."[143] Such sentiments helped Alexander become the opposition's standard-bearer when he ran for governor in the fall.

The governor's power in Delaware had been increased by the new state constitution of 1792, which also made the popularly elected three-year post (without possibility of renewal) the most important and vigorously contested election in the state. The Federalist Joshua Clayton had won in 1792 over a divided opposition vote, but in 1795 a clear two-man race pitted sharply differing New Castle residents against one another. Gunning Bedford Sr., who had married George Read Sr.'s sister, championed the Federalist side, while Alexander, a relative newcomer from Virginia with martial credentials, led the opposition. Bedford was among the very wealthiest men in New Castle Hundred (ranking eighth out of 398 taxables in 1796), while Alexander's wealth placed him in the middle of the second quintile. Bedford won the contest, but by only 210 votes—2 percent of those cast in the statewide race. Only 38 percent of New Castle County voters had favored the victorious Bedford, but with the lowest turnout among the state's three counties that year, Alexander's strength there could not overcome Bedford's downstate popularity.

Longstanding geographic patterns of religious, ethnic, and political differences persisted in Delaware even as its formal politics took new shape in the 1790s. As a Federalist newspaper advised its readers in 1794, "let the people be no longer amused with the idle and useless distinctions of Whig and Tory, court party and country party, presbyterian and church, aristocrat and democrat; they neither apply to time nor place; but let them take up the only true and useful distinction, of federal and anti-federal, of friends to their country and enemies to it."[144] Delaware Federalists had good reason to avoid the wartime labels, as they were strongest in areas that had been loyalist strongholds.

Two years after Alexander's loss in the governor's race, he ran for the U.S. Congress, another statewide office, but lost once more, this time to

James A. Bayard, a moderate Federalist from Wilmington, who would serve in the U.S. House and Senate from 1797 to 1813. The Federalist strategy of running a New Castle County candidate for statewide office was particularly effective because a native son could cut into the opposition's popularity there. This was especially true for a popular centrist like Bayard, who ran so well in the northern part of the state that Alexander only won New Castle County by three votes and thus suffered a lopsided defeat statewide. Even more telling of Delaware Federalists' strength, New Castle resident Nicholas Van Dyke Jr. (fig. 16) won the countywide race for state assembly in 1798. Like Bayard, Van Dyke was a moderate Federalist and had sometimes differed openly with party leaders. Van Dyke, for example, had joined the Patriotic Society of New Castle in calling for free public education and, as a person active in both the local Presbyterian and Episcopal churches, offered an atypical religious affiliation for a Federalist leader in Delaware.[145]

As elsewhere, the 1800 elections stimulated intense partisan activity in Delaware. A new Republican paper in Wilmington stirred the opposition in the state and attacked Congressman Bayard for supporting the controversial Federalist policies of the late 1790s. *The Mirror of the Times* especially denounced the direct tax as "the masterpiece of all your policy—for this produced the [Fries] *insurrection . . .* which afforded a good pretext for the army" and additional federal power. In the midst of such familiar attacks, the paper also charged Bayard with false pietism, which he supposedly exhibited for fear of "the defection of the Methodists." Religious affiliation always lurked beneath the surface of politics in Revolutionary Delaware, and Methodists, with their strong presence in the southern part of the state, were essential to the Federalist coalition, the most prominent of whom was Federalist governor Richard Bassett, incidentally, Bayard's father-in-law. When Republicans warned of the desperate actions of "anglo-Federalism in the agonies of death," the emphasis on Federalist Englishness was not just ethnic and political but alluded to Methodist and Episcopal affiliations as well.[146]

The Mirror of the Times' strenuous anti-Federalism led to scrutiny under the Sedition Act, an investigation controversially headed from the bench by the federal district judge Samuel Chase. When the court met at New Castle in June 1800 at the onset of the election season, Chase held the grand jury in extended session and demanded an investigation of local political speech. Witnesses later disagreed about Chase's precise instructions, but George Read Jr., the U.S. district attorney in Delaware, provided the most damaging account at Chase's impeachment trial before the U.S. Senate. Read recalled that Chase had said in court that "a highly seditious temper had manifested itself in the state of Delaware, among a certain class of people, especially in New Castle County" and that papers of "a most seditious printer" needed to be examined by the grand jury.[147] Even

Judge Chase's local supporters felt that he acted rashly. As Gunning Bedford warned him after court that day, "I believe you know not where you are; the people of this county are very much opposed to the sedition law, and will not be pleased with what you said."[148]

George Read Jr. offers a particularly interesting case of the dilemmas faced by cosmopolitan leaders in the postwar period. As the eldest son of the conservative patriot George Read Sr., he could certainly claim the mantle of traditional leadership in New Castle. He enjoyed the benefits of high social status, served as the U.S. district attorney in Delaware from 1789 to 1815, held several town offices, and always appeared in the top decile of New Castle taxpayers. Nevertheless, a mediocre reputation as an attorney, aggressive social striving, and the impossible standard set by his father combined to make him a frustrated cosmopolitan. Read's quintessential effort to project himself as a gentleman centered on an elaborate house-building project that rejected local talent and materials in favor of work by Philadelphia craftsmen who shipped goods downriver to New Castle from the metropolis. Even more than his cosmopolitan counterpart in Easton, Samuel Sitgreaves, Read risked everything to raise his mansion (fig. 14). He was constantly in arrears to his workers on the multiyear project and even faced the possibility of a duel over his financial misdealings. Yet, when it was finally completed, at least one traveler judged the large Georgian riverfront house "in bad taste."[149] Such costly extravagance was an important part of Read's presentation of self in postwar consumer society, where material possessions helped him to express his high status. Similarly, he was the most generous donor to the 1822 building project that added an elegant clock tower to his Episcopal church, transforming it from a squat early eighteenth-century building into something much more refined.[150] This architectural legacy continues to speak to us today, for his house still stands in New Castle and helps to center an affluent Federalist sense of place in contemporary popular memory. Visitors to the house today can gaze across the broad Delaware River through its expertly crafted Palladian window, an act that usually stirs fantasies of cosmopolitan respectability, rather than memories of the conflict, poorly compensated work, and laborers' skill that the house also represents.

Read had a cosmopolitan bearing that underlay a new national culture of authority in the postwar Delaware Valley, but he broke with the political faith of his father by becoming a Republican in the 1790s. While the coterie of leading families in the town of New Castle mostly maintained an ardent Federalism in the face of growing Republican popularity in New Castle County, Read tested the uncharted waters of Jeffersonianism. He accurately assessed the future of national politics in this commitment, but this decision limited his influence in Delaware, where Federalism remained dominant into the 1820s.

The structure of legislative politics in Delaware gave equal weight in its assembly to each of the state's three counties. Even as Republicans came to dominate New Castle County, they could not win a majority in the state's two southern counties, and thus Federalists usually triumphed in statewide elections. Close attention to Federalist Delaware in the midst of the Jeffersonian revolution of 1800 might seem a prime example of the myopic nature of local history. However, when the electoral college failed to produce a president, tiny Delaware and its lone congressional representative ended up deciding the election. As Bayard explained in a letter to his father-in-law, Governor Bassett, upon arriving in the new capital of Washington, D.C., Delaware alone could choose the next president, and Bayard intended to "remain *inflexibly* silent" so as to gain the best favor for "little Delaware."[151]

Before the electoral college crisis Bayard had plainly expressed his dislike of extremist New England Federalists and condemned President Adams whose "gusts of passion little short of frenzy" had "palsied the sinews of the party."[152] At this point, however, victory was to be decided between the tied candidates on the Republican slate—Thomas Jefferson and Aaron Burr. Although Bayard initially favored Burr, when the New Yorker "acted a miserable paultry part," Bayard ultimately decided in favor of Jefferson. When the Delaware congressman announced his decision to Federalist colleagues, it "produced a great clamour and the violent spirits of the Party denounced me as a Deserter," but on the thirtieth ballot in the House of Representatives Jefferson won the presidency with the support of ten states.[153]

Jefferson's election was a complicated affair from any perspective, particularly in the Delaware Valley where overall electoral college support strongly favored Adams. This regional outcome, however, largely reflected Federalists' ability to define advantageously the rules of the election. Although Federalists would remain influential in Delaware and in western New Jersey, Republicans would control the future of electoral politics in the region and the nation.

The top-down political perspective of the presidential synthesis has dominated our understanding of the early republic for too long. Jefferson's election was a critical turning point in U.S. politics, but to understand its significance fully we must look beyond national elites and electoral college tabulations to assess how his victory intertwined with the everyday politics of the street. This more inclusive approach allows us to gauge how national politics gradually gained potent meaning through its integration with local life. The local celebrations of Jefferson's election in our three towns in March 1801, and the very different contours of each fête, shows us how national politics increasingly intertwined with local politics.[154] Not surprisingly, the most forthright Jeffersonian celebration occurred in Easton, where music played from the cupola of the courthouse in the center of town. That building had symbolized proprietary power and Anglo influences since its construction fifty years earlier, but now a newspaper explained that the music marked the end of "Anglo-Federalism."[155] The election led to a reimagining of local space and the renaming of a prominent limestone hill as Mount Jefferson, which became a principal site for July 4th celebrations. Jefferson's victory became even more clearly part of the Revolution's antiproprietary thrust in Easton when an agent for the proprietors came to town to attempt to collect ground rents that had gone unpaid to the Penn family since at least 1776. As an early nineteenth-century account explained, "the demand raised the ire of many of the inhabitants," and an effigy of the agent was paraded around town, taken to the top of Mount Jefferson and "amidst many ceremonies publicly burnt."[156] Jefferson's election celebration in Easton was consistent with its Revolutionary tradition of collective violence against an external enemy. The demise of Anglo-Federalism, like the assault on the proprietors, resonated with ethnic meaning in this Pennsylvania German place.

Local opinion about Jefferson's election, like the Revolutionary mobilization itself, was more mixed in the other two towns. Burlington overwhelmingly supported Federalists, but local Republicans such as Joseph Bloomfield still marked Jefferson's victory in classic fashion by firing guns and reading the Declaration of Independence followed by a procession to the inn of a leading local Republican where some two hundred persons enjoyed a dinner. The repast included a huge number of toasts that emphasized the Revolutionary and antiaristocratic nature of Jefferson's triumph. The partisan toasts promoted aspects of the Revolution that made Quakers, in particular, uneasy. For example, a "well trained and well armed" militia was heralded as "the Terror of Tyrants, and [the] impregnable rock of the Republic." Like their fellow partisans in Easton, Burlington Republicans touted "the election of the man of the People" and the failure of "the pretended friends of government" as a shining moment of Revolutionary fulfillment.[157]

The 1800 election reminds us that the Revolutionary struggle included conflict among Americans and even among patriots. Jeffersonians felt that they had "restore[d] the nation to that purity of Republicanism, from which it has been so long perverted," while dismayed Federalists worried about coming chaos.[158] The coercive violence of Revolutionary abuse had long been obvious to Burlington Quakers, but now many Federalists shared similar concerns. In this transitional preparty era, one's political opponents were mostly understood as dire enemies of good government, a sensibility that informed the barbed title of the new Republican newspaper for western New Jersey. *The True American* made explicit that its political opponents were inauthentic Americans.

Republican dominance in places like Easton effectively limited the range of political debate there, but in conservative Burlington even the celebration of an elected president could be contested. The night before the local Jeffersonian fête, "the warm friends of Mr. Adams" removed the clapper of the bell atop the Episcopal church. Rather than allow the church bell to announce, sanction, and even consecrate the new head of state as, of course, Anglican churches had traditionally done, the building would stand mute on the Republican feast day. To local Republicans, such actions were to be expected from "Burlington County libelers."[159]

Republicans made little headway in Burlington County, given their over-arching self-characterization as true patriots and denunciation of Federalists as enemies of the Revolution. As the leading Republican newspaper in West Jersey explained, "In this manner have the Anglo-American tools been employed! During the revolutionary contest the world knew them by the well-known appellation of Tories. Let us see—what are they now? Why they are all, all good Federalists!"[160] Characterizing Federalists as conservatives with strong Anglo cultural affinities, even charging them with opposing the Revolution, did more to attach Burlington Quakers to the Federalist cause than to lead them elsewhere.

The local response to Jefferson's election in New Castle was even more divisive than in Burlington. Political disagreements emerged in all three towns, and none of them was homogeneous, but in New Castle partisan allegiance was most evenly divided, and Jefferson's election sparked a conflict linked to differences in social status. When the ships in New Castle's harbor were "dressed out in their best Coulers in Honour of the President," Federalist ship owner John Stockton "Angerly ordered the Coulers struck, and Dismissed the captain from his imploy for Daring to hoyst a flag in Honour of Mr. Jefferson's Election."[161] Here Jeffersonian men of the sea were pitted against a Federalist merchant from the top decile of the local social structure.

The battle over how Revolutionary values should shape postwar society was especially bitter in Delaware, where early partisanship, like allegiances in the war, was so evenly matched. Whereas the actual election of Jefferson was quite distant from local voters, the 1801 governor's race brought the momentous political questions of the day to the local level in dramatic ways. Two candidates from conservative southernmost Sussex County stood against one another. Republicans nominated David Hall, a Revolutionary War officer, while Federalists ran Nathaniel Mitchell, a prominent political figure who had served in the Continental Congress and had been accused of leading armed bands against Irish and Presbyterian voters in previous elections.[162] The contest proved remarkably close, and New Castle County provided Hall with the winning difference as its voters shifted their previous mild support of Federalist gubernatorial candidates to an overwhelming Republican commitment. Backed by 68 percent of the vote in New Castle County, Hall achieved an eighteen-vote victory out of nearly seven thousand cast statewide. Federalists still controlled the legislature due to safe margins in Kent and Sussex counties, but for the first time an opposition figure had captured the executive office in postwar Delaware. As a Republican paper crowed, Hall's election "rescue[d] the reins of government from the fangs of Old Tories and Apostate Whigs."[163]

Delaware Federalists considered challenging the validity of Hall's election, as they suspected that Irish aliens in New Castle County had voted for him in large numbers, recalling the nativist thrust of some Burlington Federalists. Congressman Bayard's reelection loss to Republican Caesar Augustus Rodney by fifteen votes the next year renewed the anti-Irish and anti-alien charges. A political meeting in Sussex County complained that "the irishmen of N[ew] C[astle] are to govern Kent & Sussex," while a Federalist newspaper blamed the loss on "the shameful transaction of naturalizing a large number of foreigners on the eve of an election, for the express purpose of making use of them as tools of party."[164] Like Pennsylvania German ethnicity in Easton, Irish ethnicity was fusing with Republican partisanship in ways that were both self-affirming and derogatory.

The Revolutionary War may have come to a formal close with the 1783 peace treaty, but its struggles continued in these river towns well into the nineteenth century. In one sense, the war had been the easiest phase of the Revolution, with clear external enemies in the British and Native Americans against whom violence was officially sanctioned. The implementation of the disparate ideals contained within the capacious concept of republican popular sovereignty would require enormous effort and innovation. From elections and formal politics to the bureaucratic rationale of the census, new impulses toward gradual emancipation, the explosive ethnic resistance of the Fries Rebellion, and the slow emergence of party organizations—not to mention the formal exclusion of white women and all African Americans from most of these arenas—the transformation of politics in the postwar Delaware Valley centered upon reformulating relationships among personal identities.

Figures 12 and 13. The American Revolution confronted Burlington Quakers Samuel Allinson (left) and Margaret Hill Morris (right) in profound ways, yet both drew strength from their noncompliance with the patriot movement. Both were active in the Burlington Monthly Meeting, but Allinson, along with his wife, Martha Cooper Allinson, was an exceptionally strong Quaker reformer who pushed the Society of Friends to live up to its radical values on a host of controversial issues, from opposing the payment of war taxes to antislavery. His silhouette is an especially fitting representation of the plain style of an ascetic Quaker reformer. Although Morris was no public activist, the Revolution also transformed her sense of self as an independent adult woman.

Figure 12: Samuel Allinson (1739–91), silhouette, collection 968, box 3. Courtesy of Quaker Collection, Haverford College Library, Haverford, Pennsylvania. Figure 13: Margaret Hill Morris (1737–1816), engraving (ca. 1816), collection 850. Courtesy of Quaker Collection, Haverford College Library, Haverford, Pennsylvania.

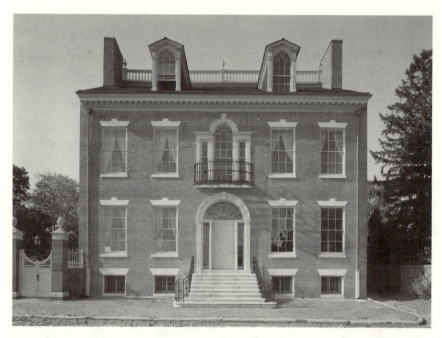

Figure 14. This magnificent 1801 Georgian mansion in New Castle can easily be invoked to recall an idealized past of Federalist Founding Fathers. Yet such uses are incomplete, at best, and in this case misleading. This building's owner struggled to live up to the achievements of his distinguished father, became a Jeffersonian Republican, and was ridiculed for building an opulent house (which he could not afford) on the town's working waterfront. George Read Jr.'s preservation of letters exchanged with the Philadelphia builders of the house grants unusual access to his cosmopolitan self-fashioning in the new nation.

George Read Jr. house façade, finished ca. 1801, New Castle. Photograph (1982), Historic American Buildings Survey, DEL, 2-NEWCA, 9-8, Library of Congress.

Figures 15, 16, and 17. The artist Charles B. J. F. de Saint-Memin's profile portraits are a classic visual representation of Federal America. His depictions of individuals from all three of our towns offer a measure of how fully each place participated in leading social circles of the post-war period: eight portraits of Burlington residents, three from New Castle, and just one from Easton. The three here show wealthy Federalists who held important public offices, but they are more than just traces of an elite pantheon. The Burlington Quaker James Kinsey (fig. 15, top) disagreed with his legal pupil Samuel Allinson's reforming ardor. Whereas Allinson (fig. 12) refused to practice law after the Revolutionary War, Kinsey would be the chief justice of the state supreme court, maintaining an older ideal of Quaker public leadership dating back to William Penn. Kinsey's short hair (in marked contrast to the prominent queues in the other portraits) reveals how he maintained Quaker simplicity and distinctiveness. Nicholas Van Dyke Jr. (fig. 16, center) was an elder in New Castle's Presbyterian church, where his ancestors had donated the communion silver, exemplifying the successful Dutch Calvinist assimilation to a new order over several generations. If Kinsey and Van Dyke both represent socially ascendant combinations of public prominence and local ethno-religious traditions, Samuel Sitgreaves (fig. 17, bottom) was an oppositional figure whose Federalist, Anglo, Episcopalian, and moral reform commitments set him at odds with the majority of Pennsylvania Germans in Easton.

Figure 15: James Kinsey (1731–1803), engraving (folio 36R) by Charles Balthazar Julien Fevret de Saint-Memin (1807). Courtesy of Corcoran Gallery of Art, Washington, D.C. Gift of William Wilson Corcoran. Figure 16: Nicholas Van Dyke Jr. (1770–1826), engraving (folio 23L) by Charles Balthazar Julien Fevret de Saint-Memin (1802). Courtesy of Corcoran Gallery of Art, Washington, D.C. Gift of William Wilson Corcoran. Figure 17: Samuel Sitgreaves (1764–1827), drawing by Charles Balthazar Julien Fevret de Saint-Memin (1798). Courtesy of Sitgreaves Library, Washington National Cathedral, Washington, D.C.

Figures 18 and 19. These images with their Pennsylvania German texts add to our understanding of the broadly expressed Anglo-German cultural divide in the early national period. In the domestic scene by the Lutheran carpenter and folk artist Lewis Miller (fig. 18, top), a housewife in Pennsylvania German clothing scolds "her Joseph," with his back to two women in Anglo-American empire gowns, one of whom is denounced as "A Strumpet." If the violence in this ethnic clash is largely implied, the conflict explodes in the threatening letter from the Fries Rebellion (fig. 19, bottom), which explained in dialect to a federal tax collector that the broadsword and pistol "are the weapons for your slaughter."

Figures 20 and 21. These paired images of African Christians in Philadelphia demonstrate the highly politicized nature of black Protestantism in the Revolutionary era and deepens our understanding of the conflicts faced by members of the Union Church of Africans in New Castle. The watercolor (fig. 20, top) by an outsider to evangelicalism condemns the chaotic scene and even depicts sexual misconduct; note that the central female figure on the ground with arms and legs spread wide has a naked chest. This hostile view of a religious orgy (which bears comparison with the anti-English sexualization in fig. 18) stands in complete contrast to the respectable African American congregants entering the genteel brick church whose marble tablet below the fan window announces that this is "The African Church" (fig. 21, bottom). The increasing racial violence of the 1820s would lead one free black benevolent society to call for a retreat from such public declarations of racial identity.

Figure 20: "Black Methodists Holding a Prayer Meeting," watercolor and pen and ink by Pavel Petrovich Svinin (1811). All rights reserved, The Metropolitan Museum of Art, Rogers Fund, 1942 (42.95.19). Figure 21: "A Sunday Morning View of the African Episcopal Church of St. Thomas in Philadelphia," drawn by William L. Breton, lithograph by Kennedy and Lucas (ca. 1829). Courtesy of Historical Society of Pennsylvania (Bb862 B756 #44).

Figures 22 and 23. The skilled work of the Easton schoolteacher Johannes Ernst Spangenberg contributed to the flourishing of Pennsylvania German *fraktur* (a text style based on a Gothic typeface) in the late eighteenth and early nineteenth century. These examples highlight the varied uses of such folk art: from the German and Latin frontispiece of the lavish Basel-printed Bible (fig. 22, top) given to the Reformed congregation in the late 1740s by the missionary Michael Schlatter, to the English-language cursive lettering used in the *taufschein* (birth and baptismal certificate) of Anne Andreas (fig. 23, bottom), with its plainly festive figures.

Figure 22: Schlatter Bible, *fraktur* title page, hand-drawn and colored by Johannes Ernst Spangenberg (after 1767). Photograph by author. Courtesy of First United Church of Christ, Easton, Pennsylvania.
Figure 23: Anne Andreas *taufschein*, hand-drawn and colored by Johannes Ernst Spangenberg (ca. 1783). Gift of Edgar William and Bernice Chrysler Garbisch. Image © 2006 Board of Trustees, National Gallery of Art, Washington, D.C.

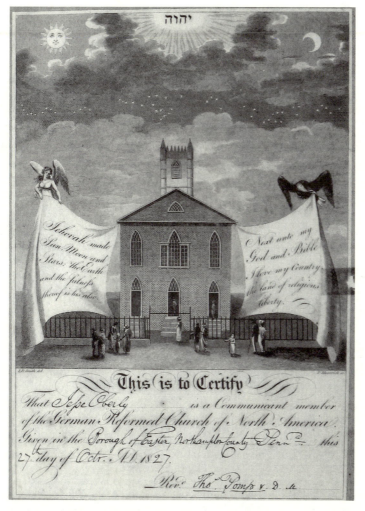

Figure 24. This 1827 religious certificate might seem purely American and proto-Victorian, as its mass-produced English-language form seems a sharp break from the colorful hand-drawn examples of the immediately recognizable Pennsylvania German style. Nevertheless, it is better understood as an extension and modification of the *fraktur* and *taufschein* traditions. The German Reformed Church of North America here shows its engagement with early national American society. The document insists that we not treat Pennsylvania Germans as backward rural people who will eventually fade away. As the text in the curtain held aloft by the eagle makes explicit, "Next unto my God and Bible I love my country, the land of religious liberty." Unlike African Christians who made a similar bid for respectable inclusion in the broad Revolutionary period (note the analogous presentation of church and congregants in fig. 21), Pennsylvania Germans largely succeeded in their effort to be American and to retain ethno-religious distinctiveness in the 1820s.

Jesse Oberly confirmation certificate (1827). Photograph by author. Courtesy of Rare Book Department, The Free Library of Philadelphia.

Figures 25. The dynamic union of popular religiosity and commercial production in Pennsylvania German religious certificates is nicely demonstrated by the *taufschein* here and in Figure 26. Blank *taufschein* forms were first printed commercially in the mid-1780s, and machine production stimulated the expression of ethno-religious identity on an amazing scale: more than twelve hundred printed variants have been identified, and a single rural artist purchased seven thousand forms from a press in the first decade of the nineteenth century. The German-born printer Christian J. Hutter produced many such forms in Easton in the 1820s, which were completed by adding individual information and color by hand. The form here for Maria Steiner was printed in Ephrata, Pennsylvania, around 1810.

Maria Steiner *taufschein*, watercolor and pen and ink by Francis D. Levan on printed form (ca. 1810). Photograph by author. Courtesy of Rare Book Department, The Free Library of Philadelphia.

Figure 26. This certificate for Christina Kerkendal commemorates her baptism, confirmation, and marriage by Easton's Reformed Reverend Thomas Pomp from 1818 to 1836. This entirely hand-drawn example clearly follows the model in the printed version that appears in Figure 25. Like the Oberly confirmation certificate (fig. 24), a comparison of these two *taufschein* shows the seamless interaction of ethno-religious identity and modern technology.

Christina Kerkendal *taufschein*, hand-drawn and colored by Jacob Hartzell (ca. 1820).

Photograph by author. Courtesy of Rare Book Department, The Free Library of Philadelphia.

Figure 27. The union church in Easton (fig. 7) served its German Reformed and Lutheran congregants well for nearly six decades. However, the two German church groups grew increasingly distant from one another in the early nineteenth century over issues such as English-language preaching. Their growing sense of difference from one another was reflected in the marked decline in rates of mixed religious affiliation among local Pennsylvania Germans over time. The Lutheran congregation raised this grand brick building in 1832 after it left the union church. The new church was the largest and most lavish place of worship in the three river towns and serves as a fitting final image that hints at some of the dramatic changes accomplished by Pennsylvania Germans in the Revolutionary period. Like the divergent ways that Allinson (fig. 12) and Kinsey (fig. 15) carried themselves as Quakers in the postwar period, Lutheran and German Reformed members in Easton accommodated new national norms at different rates, while still retaining a strong sense of self as Pennsylvania German citizens of the new nation.

St. John's Lutheran Church, originally built 1832, Easton. Photograph by author.

Chapter 4

Protestant Diversity in the New Nation

The postwar challenge to understand local, regional, and national life ranged far beyond the political arena examined in the previous chapter. Religion centrally shaped early national developments as inhabitants of these river towns negotiated a place for themselves in the new republic. As authority began to be reconstructed in the wake of the war, religious institutions and spiritual self-understanding increasingly became an arena of social contest. While distant debates and even unseen forces often determined political and economic trajectories, an intensely local struggle over the relationship between Christianity and Revolutionary ideals coursed through the Delaware Valley and the nation.

National independence reshaped the denominations in all three towns, especially as they swiftly asserted their autonomous authority to ordain ministers without European oversight. Although less true for American Presbyterians, whose eighteenth-century schism had centered on issues of ordination, Anglican, Reformed, and Lutheran traditions all operated in a radically altered postindependence context that destroyed Old World religious control. The Revolutionary transition was especially traumatic for the Anglican Church, of course, since it had been so fully bound to royal authority and English rule.[1] Lutheran and Reformed ministers in colonial British America had somewhat more freedom from European control, but all still needed to confirm most major decisions with transatlantic authorities. By 1782, the *Coetus* of the Reformed Church (its chief American governing body) took steps to resolve their relationship to such oversight by declaring its "right at all times to examine and ordain those who offer themselves as candidates for the ministry, without asking or waiting for permission . . . from the fathers in Holland." This decisive factor led it to separate from European control, a movement completed with the creation of the Synod of the Reformed German Church in the United States of America in 1793.[2] Pennsylvania Lutherans had made a similar change the previous year in drafting a constitution and renaming itself the German Evangelical Lutheran Ministerium in Pennsylvania and Adjacent States.[3] In both cases the termination of European authority included a key self-assertion as distinctively German. The Lutheran and Reformed churches fused ethnic, religious, and national claims in the wake of the Revolutionary War.

Evangelical Protestantism had an even more profound impact on American life in the first three decades of the nineteenth century than these institutional changes in organized religion. The broad and varied social movements grouped under the label *evangelicalism* had two basic thrusts in the early republic that contrasted sharply with each other even as they shared important spiritual values. On the one hand, populist evangelicalism inspired ordinary Americans to a deep new Christian engagement centered upon a direct relationship with God, especially through an emotional personal conversion experience. The camp meeting revival is the best known institutional vehicle for this dimension of evangelicalism. This populist, and perhaps even "democratizing," movement helped shape and in some cases evolved into a more conservative cosmopolitan evangelical project committed to moral reform. This second wing of early national evangelicalism sought to renew social order through an enormous range of pan-Christian benevolent action. While populist evangelicalism built upon and often exacerbated local differences, thus making a central contribution to the Delaware Valley's Revolutionary identity politics, conservative evangelicalism placed a contrasting priority on respectability, decorum, and Christian unity.[4]

The importance of local autonomy during the Revolutionary War helped to stimulate an intensification and proliferation of diverse religious traditions in the new republic. In New Castle African American Methodism burst forth as the most novel and challenging new expression of Protestant diversity. Grounded in a strong commitment to Africanness, its public visibility and institutionalization as the Union Church of Africans highlights the unanticipated directions that Revolutionary identity politics could lead. Members of the Society of Friends in Burlington faced ongoing political and social coercion after the war and also confronted strong pressure to conform to emerging evangelical sensibilities that threatened Friends' traditional ways. Quakers had long occupied the margin of Protestantism in the Anglo-American Atlantic world; now even their preeminence in the region was lost.

As Quakers were pushed from the center and blacks made a daring bid for public inclusion as African Christians, Pennsylvania Germans made steady gains from their former position as colonial outsiders. Yet this move to the center also caused new difficulties. Pennsylvania Germans in Easton had long cooperated closely in the *kirchenleute*'s shared "union church" (*gemeinschaftliche kirchen*) and burial ground. New public legitimacy gained by Pennsylvania Germans, partly as patriots in the war, gradually gave rise to stronger differences between the two confessions, especially over the use of English for religious worship. While Easton's Lutherans embraced English earlier and more fully, both Pennsylvania German groups retained a strong ethnic sensibility even as they assimilated at different rates and lost some of the intensely fused identity that they had shared at the onset of the Revolutionary War.

These diverse African, Quaker, and Pennsylvania German ethno-religious cultures threatened the vision of cosmopolitan religious leaders dedicated to an over-arching American Christianity that would support the new national social order. This conservative Christian view sought national solidarity through a common Protestantism. Such evangelical cosmopolitans were driven by the knowledge that the diverse religious traditions of people in their own towns and region posed a formidable hurdle to meaningful Christian unity. The struggle over religious authority in the nation, like the intertwined economic and political contests that it paralleled, did not merely pit distant elites against isolated local provincials. Representatives of both cosmopolitan and local traditions arose in all these river towns, and their struggles created a new understanding of the nation. The cosmopolitan evangelical effort will receive intensive examination in the next chapter, while here we principally consider the diverse local practices that made the people in these towns distinct from one another. Conservative religious leaders understood these local spiritual expressions to be components of a common threat that spurred their own cosmopolitan evangelical social movement as they wondered how differences among the Union Church of Africans, the Society of Friends, and German Reformed and Lutherans could possibly be reconciled in the Revolutionary nation.

Blackness and the Union Church of Africans

The conflict between populist and conservative evangelicals manifested itself in their diametrically opposed devotional behavior.[5] The former centered on physical testimony by lay members of the congregation, while conservatives like New Castle's Presbyterian minister John Latta demanded the "perfect order" of silent reflection on a minister's sermon. Latta's opposition to any excitement among the faithful led him to caution ministers against the false popularity of a dramatic preaching style. We "must not watch for the applause or commendation of [our] hearers. Here we are particularly exposed to danger."[6] As populist evangelicalism grew and encroached on Latta's pastorate, his descriptions of religious enthusiasm became more lurid and even hinted at the particular abuses of black spirituality. One sermon contrasted the goodness of scriptural light versus being "in a state of *darkness, gross darkness.*" For Latta, evil religious practices consisted of "all kinds of confusion, disorder and extravagance, [and] in leaping, dancing and shouting." Such worship reveled in "drunkenness, lewdness, and debauchery," all of which starkly opposed the good light of proper Christian order. He sweepingly condemned "the dark places of the earth" as "*full of the habitations of cruelty.*"[7] Although such color-based metaphors of good and evil have deep roots in Western civilization, to understand Latta's particular vision we need to attend more closely to New Castle's local religious landscape.

Latta attacked pagan idolaters generally, but the area where he preached and the language he employed suggests that he feared black evangelicalism in particular. The increasing African American presence around New Castle stimulated his hostility to enthusiastic religion and probably contributed to his negative black imagery. Surely Latta noticed the dramatic shift in black status in New Castle during his pastorship, as the local free black population doubled from 1800 to 1830, while the white population declined by 7 percent. By 1830, African Americans made up 29 percent of the local population, and 91 percent of them were free. The growing prominence of African Americans also occurred at the county level where they rose from 16 to 22 percent of the population in these decades.[8]

An extraordinary account of an African American Methodist service in New Castle further suggests that Latta's opposition to religious enthusiasm targeted local black evangelicalism and that his fears were widely shared among white leaders. One summer Sunday in 1806, the traveler Benjamin Latrobe found himself stranded in the town because the coach could not operate on the Sabbath. A few years previously, while surveying the town and designing a proposed canal, Latrobe had met "an old negro . . . methodist preacher in this place" and now decided to attend his services with a ship captain and a sailor named Jamieson. Latrobe recorded a wonderfully detailed description of the event in his journal:

The poor enthusiast began his harangue in the usual style, uttering an immensity of incoherent nonsense. As he rose in his exertions, Jamieson began to groan most piteously . . . and he fell flat on the floor. The preacher came down to his assistance, and prayed over him most fervently and outrageously. . . . He at last threw himself upon the sailor, and vociferously called him to life. Jamieson, who seemed much incommoded by weight and heat opened his eyes:

He is converted from sin, exclaimed the negro, say brother what has you seen, glory, glory, glory, what has you seen.

Nothing answered Jamieson, but a damned big black b——gg——r, who is going to stifle me, if I do not right myself.

Have mercy on his damn'd sinful soul said the parson. No man can serve two masters, you want to serve God and the devil. . . .

That's a damn lie said Jamieson, I serve God, the Captain, and the mate, and that's three, and if I don't do my duty they give me a hell of a walloping.[9]

In closing the scene, Latrobe gratifyingly noted, "an irresistible and universal laugh sent the congregation home." He judged this a dismal Christian service. Clearly no "perfect order" existed here, with just the leaping and shouting that John Latta railed against as expressions of "gross darkness."

In all likelihood the English-born and Moravian-educated Latrobe was stunned by this religious service. To make sense of it in his journal, where he regularly recorded the pettiness of provincial habits from his cosmopolitan perspective, he resorted to stereotypes. Like Pavel Svinin's contemporaneous watercolor of an African Methodist service in Philadelphia (fig. 20), Latrobe focused on the importance of bodily movement, direct personal revelation, and the lack of separation between preacher and congregation, all features of African American spirituality. In his own journal, Svinin, a Russian diplomat in Philadelphia, described African Methodism as hellish. The church's doorkeeper looked "very much like Cerberus," and the minister was "a black terrifying skeleton." As the preacher "ignited the imagination of the listeners with his terrible images and body movements," Svinin worried that the building would collapse "with each strike of the agonized demon-possessed, who jumped and threw themselves about in all directions and who fell to the ground beating it with their arms and legs, and gnashed their teeth to show that all the evil spirits were leaving them."[10] Evangelical abandonment was satanic and animalistic to this outside observer.

Svinin's painting further placed black Christianity in a lurid context by conflating it with sexual promiscuity. Three figures form a triangle in the center of the image: a man dancing on the left with arms to the sky, a female partner matching him with one hand to heaven and the other to her breast, and the preacher directing activity from the church doorway. An orgy occurs between the couple, where they will presumably collapse when overcome. A woman sprawled on the ground with her arms high, legs spread, and dress pulled up to expose her knees and thighs appears at the center of the image. The standing male dances between her legs with his toe pointing suggestively up her dress. Incredibly, the recumbent woman's checked blouse covers only her arms, exposing a naked chest, while another man drapes himself over her torso. This man hugs another woman sprawled in the foreground of the image, with yet another woman leaning against his buttocks. Svinin's watercolor dramatized aspects of African Methodism that many whites believed to be central to black religious enthusiasm but deemed too delicate to describe in writing. As an antievangelical pamphlet queried, "do those who are delighted with such things, consider what delights them? Some times . . . they are from such impure sources, as I am actually ashamed to name in this place."[11] Latrobe demonstrated similar reserve by muffling Jamieson's charge of sodomy by not spelling out *bugger* in his journal, yet his repulsion clearly stemmed from a deep sense of physical impropriety.

These detailed accounts suffer as observations by outsiders. However, a careful reading of Latrobe's description can yield an alternative interpretation to what he intended. Not all whites, for instance, were outsiders to black Christianity. Evangelicalism provided an important site for black and white interaction and solidarity in early America. Furthermore, as a small port town, New Castle was filled with common sailors like Jamieson. Jack Tar's working world brought whites and blacks together in close quarters that sometimes allowed them to share similar perspectives as common laborers and men of the sea.[12] Finally, the Scots Irish associations of Jamieson's name suggest another possible tie between low-status white ethnics and African Americans.

Returning to the discussion of the New Castle service with the awareness that some whites participated in black religious culture leads to a reassessment where Jamieson's performance is critical. By presenting the sailor as mocking African Methodism, Latrobe implied an alliance between them as whites, but Jamieson may have been a penitential participant. He certainly was more likely to be one than either Latrobe or the sea captain. Thus, when Jamieson fell to the floor during what Latrobe understood as the minister's "harangue . . . of incoherent nonsense," the sailor possibly experienced genuine inspiration. The minister regarded his actions as appropriate, calling on him as a brother and asking, "what has you seen, glory, glory, glory, what has you seen." Latrobe recorded that Jamieson said he saw nothing but "a damned big black b——gg——r, who is going to stifle me, if I do not right myself." On first reading it seems that he insulted the preacher, but he may have been witnessing to an inner confrontation with the Devil. Postmodern calisthenics are not required to read across Latrobe's version to see that Jamieson may have acknowledged the religious authority of the black minister. Jamieson's intention in wanting to "right myself" is ambiguous. Did he need to physically stand up and get the preacher off of him? Did he need to right himself spiritually before the Lord? Or was he a trickster who recognized the opportunity to play to both a white and a black audience and simultaneously lampoon each to the other?

We need not resolve Jamieson's inner motivations. The black minister probably understood the sailor's comments in a metaphoric sense, as would have been appropriate in this evangelical context. The preacher attempted to help the sailor win the struggle for his soul, calling out, "no man can serve two masters, you want to serve God and the devil."[13] Jamieson agreed and expanded that he had to serve three masters (God, the captain, and the first mate), highlighting how worldly hierarchies ignored the essential matter of salvation. Latrobe and the captain—the outsiders at the service—were probably the targets of Jamieson's joke. Latrobe's closing comment that "an irresistible and universal laugh sent the congregation home" bolsters the likelihood of this reassessment, for the entire congregation obviously did not suddenly find humor in being made fools. They more likely understood the sailor to ridicule those whose place atop the social order transgressed the spiritual equality of all Christians. Role-reversing humor is a major tool of cultural resistance among oppressed groups and most likely triggered the laughter that swept the black congregation.[14] Here white elites were out of place and temporarily unable to exert control or authority. When Latrobe observed that the farcical event was "too degrading to human nature to be called ridiculous," he revealed his distance from it, a disclaimer that may even indicate an unconscious recognition that these black Christians laughed at him.

This example demonstrates how black and white identities were shaped in performances that intertwined ethno-racial identity, socioeconomic status, and spirituality. Because populist evangelicalism had the potential to cross varied social boundaries, it threatened a social order already undergoing fundamental changes in the Revolutionary Delaware Valley. The creation of state-sanctioned African churches was one of the unanticipated revolutionary social changes that occurred in the postcolonial transformation of the region. Conservative Delaware legislators, who regained power after the war, sought laws protecting religious freedom from fears that radical Presbyterians would target Anglican elites, who were often conservative whigs, if not loyalists, for punishment. To ensure safe public space for religious differences, the legislature allowed all Christian groups to appoint trustees and incorporate their congregations. State power to incorporate had previously been a royal prerogative, but with sovereignty now vested in the citizens through their representative legislatures access to this privilege opened dramatically.[15] State legislators in 1787 hardly suspected that African Americans in northern Delaware would use this law to establish an independent black denomination in 1813.

The city of Wilmington and the town of New Castle, just five miles apart, were the most significant urban areas in New Castle County and the birthplace of the Union Church of Africans.[16] The creation of this black denomination outside the white-controlled Methodist Episcopal Conference arose gradually from the social changes of the postwar period. American Methodism had only separated from the Church of England in 1784, and the presence of two black preachers, Richard Allen and Harry Hoosier, at the "Christmas conference" that founded the Methodist Episcopal Church, suggests the importance of African Americans to the new denomination. The first Methodist Episcopal church in Wilmington was a biracial institution whose congregation was nearly a third African American at its 1789 founding. Thirteen years later its 117 black members comprised just under half the congregation, but they lacked access to its leadership positions. As the black presence in the congregation grew, African Americans faced increasing discrimination from white members. Blacks were required to sit in the gallery, prohibited them from taking communion, and African American lay preachers were denied full ordination. The catalyst for the first separation in Wilmington's Methodist congregation occurred in 1805 when whites instructed their black brethren to hold class meetings in the gallery even when the church was otherwise empty.[17]

The terms under which Wilmington's black Methodists formed the Ezion Methodist Episcopal Church reveals a steady move toward racial autonomy. This separate, but not yet independent, black congregation conceded that a white minister "for the time being is to have the directions and management of . . . [our] spiritual concerns." This minister visited occasionally to perform the sacraments, while black leaders led regular worship, and the new congregation also permitted preaching by those who "appear to have gifts and grace proper to appear in public." Furthermore, only "persons of colour" were "empowered" to control its "Temporal revenues." In addition to financial matters, black trustees controlled membership and maintained exclusive disciplinary authority over those who "walked disorderly."[18]

The commingling of spiritual and temporal authority among whites and blacks in the Ezion church collapsed with the permanent assignment of a white preacher in 1813. Nearly three-fourths of the African American Methodists in Wilmington terminated their connection to the biracial institution.[19] Although the Methodist Episcopal Church was probably the most racially progressive denomination in the country at this time, the majority of its black members in Wilmington rejected its oppressive terms for worship to found their own denomination.

In September 1813, thirty-four men and six women signed the Articles of Association forming the Union Church of Africans and elected seven male trustees.[20] The Union Church of Africans (UCA) clearly made racial autonomy central to their denominational consciousness. The UCA was explicitly founded upon a shared African identity, and its articles required that "no person shall have any vote, say, or rule in, or be elected a Trustee . . . but Africans and the descendants of the African Race."[21] By taking such a boldly Africanist position in their organization, UCA members made a radical claim to legitimacy in a state where slavery remained legal. Running parallel to better-known developments in Philadelphia, where Richard Allen would found the African Methodist Episcopal (AME) denomination in 1816, free African Americans in Wilmington formed the first black church in the United States that stood independent of white denominational authority and received legal recognition by a state government.

The UCA stressed local control in their new institution. Financial decisions required a two-thirds vote by church members, and the congregation also determined who could preach or exhort before them. In vesting such power with rank-and-file members, the UCA broke decisively with the Methodist Episcopal Church and selected a less leader-centered structure than the AME would adopt in Philadelphia.[22] Part of the UCA decision to place greater authority at the local level may have stemmed from their loss of Ezion congregational property when some black trustees chose not to separate from biracial Methodism. Of the seven Ezion trustees in 1805, only three signed the UCA's founding articles eight years later.

The majority of blacks in the biracial church left it to create an African denomination. In the year before the UCA founding, the 178 black Methodists in Wilmington outnumbered their white brethren, the only part of the entire Philadelphia Conference with a black majority. Clearly they were ready for black autonomy, and only forty-six African Americans remained within biracial Methodism the next year.[23] This sudden departure from mainstream Methodism is especially striking because most blacks must have had white landlords and employers whom they risked offending by leaving the white-dominated denomination. The decision by some blacks to remain within biracial Methodism nevertheless indicated that the decline of slavery and separation from white-controlled institutions could accelerate divisions among African Americans.

The UCA was just one example in a broad movement demanding public respectability for African Christians in the new nation.[24] An 1810 anti-slavery tract written by Daniel Coker, an African Methodist minister in Baltimore, reveals the movement's intensity and breadth. Coker's searing black consciousness highlighted the radical thrust of the African church movement in self-identifying as a "descendent of Africa" and dedicating the book to "People of Colour in the United States of America." There can be little doubt that those who organized black churches demanded public recognition as Africans. His book also listed fifteen African churches from four denominational traditions from Baptist to Presbyterian.[25] These dispersed African churches, which thrived where members were mostly free, had a clear geographic center in the urban belt from Baltimore to New York City. The six churches in the Delaware Valley—three in Philadelphia and three more just south of the city (in West Chester, Pennsylvania; Salem, New Jersey; and Wilmington, Delaware)—made it the geographic center of the new African Christian movement. African Americans made their strongest bid for autonomy and equality in the Revolutionary nation through such independent black denominations. Thirty-one congregations eventually established a connection to the UCA from Maryland, Delaware, Pennsylvania, and New York. At the same time that it maintained independence from white Methodism, it also refused overtures from Richard Allen to join with the AME and remains an independent denomination to the present day.[26]

African Americans in New Castle formalized their long-term participation in black religious and social life in nearby Wilmington when seven men legally registered their congregation as the African Union Church of the Town of New Castle in October 1817 and five months later purchased a lot for building their church.[27] This congregation's affiliation with the UCA marked the public emergence of underground black Methodism that had been growing there for many years, and it surely continued the group that Benjamin Latrobe had observed there a decade earlier. Unfortunately, only one local member can be identified with certainty, the trustee Anthony Hays, who signed its property deed. He was assessed in the town's lowest tax bracket in 1815 and 1826 and appeared as the head of a five-person household in the 1830 census. By that time he and the eldest woman in the household, presumably his wife, had both passed fifty years and had three young people living with them, one still younger than ten. Household conversations must have discussed the rapid changes in black life witnessed by the adults, from the collapse of local slavery to the establishment of an independent black church where they could worship as full members with an African American minister.

In an era when slavery no longer completely dominated African American experience in the region, black church leaders developed heightened concerns about the behavior of their flock. Maintaining authority posed an especially delicate concern for leaders of churches with an enthusiastic evangelical ethos. Like all denominations of the era, the UCA crafted precise mechanisms for expelling those who failed to carry themselves in an "orderly and sober manner."[28] African ministers especially strove to manage proper righteousness.

A single surviving copy of a UCA hymnal allows essential access to some dimensions of its religious practices and hints at differences between its leaders and lay members. The hymnal opens with a comment by three black ministers, who published it in response to popular demand. "Since it has pleased the Lord to revise his work of grace among us in such a wonderful manner, the cry of our members continually is that they want Hymn Books, which they wish us to supply them with."[29] These leaders also hoped to steer their members toward greater respectability. They observed, "as we all know [that] singing is a part of divine worship, there needs not much to be said on the subject," yet they called for a particular performance style—"sing with the spirit and with the understanding also." As African churches sought public acceptance, some leaders hoped to restrain congregational enthusiasm. These ministers continued, unless "you set the Lord before you . . . all our singing and praying is in vain. Therefore when you sing, sing to the Lord; and when you pray, pray to the Lord." UCA leaders worried that evangelical enthusiasm, particularly in communal singing, could become dangerous if "spirit" lacked the counterbalancing influence of "understanding."

St. Thomas's African Episcopal Church in Philadelphia made the greatest effort of any black church in the region to be a respectable and cosmopolitan institution. Absalom Jones, its first minister and a former Delaware slave, was known for his personal restraint and seems to have shied away from the populist evangelicalism embraced by most African churches in this period. By the 1830s, the average wealth of its members was more than six times greater than the nearby African Methodist Episcopal church, and later in the century it would have an even greater association with the black professional elite in Philadelphia. The respectability of this church is wonderfully displayed in an engraving of members entering its doors for a Sunday service in 1829 (fig. 21). The handsome brick building in Georgian style with elegant windows, and the dignified clothing and composure of the family groups who entered it, all testified against those who attacked black Christianity. This bid for social inclusion as African Christians was not one that attempted to "pass" as white. Black churches all promoted African American autonomy in their institutional rules, and, as we can see, the marble tablet at the top of St. Thomas's façade proclaimed to all that this was "The African Church."[30]

Black ministers were especially sensitive to white scrutiny of their churches, which sometimes led them to encourage restraint among their flock. As the UCA ministers explained in closing the introduction to their hymnal, if the congregation demonstrated proper devotion, "then may be said, 'they that were not a people have become the people of God,'—and we shall rejoice."[31] These remarks expose a fundamental dilemma of being African and Christian in the early republic. UCA leaders acknowledged that their own forebears had not been "a people" without an awareness of Jesus Christ and even suggested that only by overcoming a non-Christian past could African Americans become a legitimate people and claim public space in the nation.

The hymns in this collection offer access to broader dimensions of Afro-Christian identity among UCA members. Because it was compiled in response to popular demand, its 132 songs were likely chosen from congregational favorites. In most respects they fall within the canon of Anglo-American Christianity, especially Methodism. A sample of UCA hymns checked against several indexes reveals that well over half were from Anglo-Christian sources, with compositions by John and Charles Wesley and Isaac Watts predominating.[32] Yet this seeming Anglo traditionalism can be misleading, for popular black evangelicalism could transform old songs and give them new meanings.

One Philadelphia critic attacked the new religious music of the early nineteenth century as "a growing evil," where "*merry* airs, adopted from old *songs*" became widely popular despite being "miserable as poetry, and senseless as matter." Worse yet, these songs were "most frequently composed and first sung by illiterate *blacks* of the society [i.e., Methodists]."[33] The threat of the new performance style lay largely in its African American origins, which then spread rapidly among evangelical whites. Just as Latta, Latrobe, and Svinin had reported, disturbing body movements accompanied such singing, which this critic judged "consonant [with] animal spirits." Following his description of black religious dancing, often cited as an example of the survival of the West African ring dance, he concluded, who "can countenance or tolerate such gross perversions of true religion! But the evil is only occasionally condemned, and the example has already visibly effected the manner of some whites."[34] African Christianity threatened conservative whites who feared that its movement across racial boundaries would transform white religious practices.

Attempting to understand how congregational singing may have sounded in the early nineteenth century is a complex undertaking. Although reliance on recent recordings of early hymn-singing styles can further muddy analysis by imposing present-day musical and performance standards, it provides a necessary place to begin to think about music as lived experience. Fortunately, an excellent Smithsonian recording has taken great care to re-create early African American singing styles and includes three hymns from the repertoire of Philadelphia's AME church.[35] The Richard Allen Singers' performance of the Isaac Watts hymn "Am I a Soldier of the Cross?" suggests how the UCA congregation may have sounded. This traditional English hymn is performed in a "lined out" style where the leader raises the tune and the congregation then takes it up. A call-and-response style was customary in both English and African singing traditions; however, the African American approach drew out each line for a long period with a complex and layered audience response, while Anglo-American technique generally responded in unison. In the recorded example of the Watts hymn, the congregation responded to the leader's introduction with a dirge-like mass of sound that broke sharply from Anglo-American congregational singing conventions.[36]

The songs in the UCA hymnal reflect particular choices within Christian traditions and reveal a distinctive African American theology stressing a mission to social outcasts. This tone began with the epigram from Isaiah on the title page, which concluded, "for the Lord has comforted his people, and will have mercy upon his afflicted." This emphasis was crucial to a church whose leading members were drawn from the lower ranks of society. Out of the forty founding UCA members in 1813, only four were able to sign their own names, all of whom were chosen as trustees. Literacy may have added to the distance separating church leaders from members, but even the church elite ranked low in the general social order. Of the six trustees who can be located in a Wilmington city directory, four were identified as laborers and two as blacksmiths.[37] Given this background, the UCA not surprisingly prayed to a God who judged the lowly most deserving. One hymn declared,

He fills the poor with good,
He gives the sufferers rest;
The Lord hath judgments for the proud;
And justice for the oppress'd.[38]

UCA hymns often testified about a sinful world where Africans were subjected to singularly severe punishment. When the congregation called on their Savior to "unloose the bonds of wickedness, and let the captives go," surely they referred to slavery and protested the corrupt world that allowed such injustice.[39] Another traditional Anglo-American hymn rang with obvious resonance for UCA members:

We will be slaves no more,
Since Christ hath made us free,
Has nail'd our tyrants to his cross,
And bought our liberty.[40]

Such hymns encouraged resistance and make plain why white leaders in the South closed African churches in the wake of planned black rebellions with links to Afro-Christianity.[41]

To discuss only the hymns that embrace such sentiments would be misleading, however, for the hymnal also counseled patience and passivity in a sinful world. Many songs emphasized a more just future to come with salvation. Hymns such as "When Rising from the Bed of Death" and "Happy Soul Thy Days Are Ended" emphasized that a better life waited in the next world.[42] Taken as a whole, these songs reveal a complex spiritual life that helped UCA members to negotiate their new group identity as free African Christians.

The single most startling hymn in the UCA collection unites several often-conflicting themes by explicitly addressing the relationship among African, free, slave, American, and Christian identities. Individual church members negotiated these multiple roles successfully in their daily life by stressing one over the other as befit particular social circumstances, but significant potential for tension existed among them, especially as these interrelated identities changed dramatically during the Revolutionary period. "On Afric's land our fathers roamed" acknowledged the African origins of the congregation, clearly departing from traditional Anglo-American hymnody. The next line suggested a divided assessment of the African inheritance, as the fathers were "a free but savage race." The positive value of freedom was countered by a savage state where "no word of light their minds inform'd, of God's recovering grace." African and Christian could stand opposed, even as members of early black churches struggled to balance them. One route to reconciliation explained the origins of the slave trade as divinely ordained. In the terms of this hymn, God "let us o'er the Atlantic flood, that we might learn his ways."[43] This was not, however, a self-hating hymn such as might have been employed by whites hoping to use Christianity to buttress slavery. The hymn sharpened its view of the relationship between race and Christianity when it explained:

Yet colour is no mark that shows,
The inward state of mind;
Thro' white and black corruption flows
Infecting all mankind.[44]

The hymn suggests that UCA members fused an understanding of the African past that lacked the saving grace of Christianity with an equally strong sense that white Christians deserved no special status. The free black embrace of Christianity to distance themselves from Africa may seem a startling aspect of Afro-Christian identity; however, it was precisely as African Christians that free blacks most boldly challenged the assumptions of mainstream white America.

The Union Church of Africans used traditional Christian forms to testify against the corruption of the world, and its members drew on diverse cultural inheritances in their assertions of self. What they recognized—and what is perhaps still too easily forgotten—is that Christianity was far from exclusively "white" in the early republic. Surviving evidence from black churches allows some of our best access to voices of people of color in this period and reveals a dynamic free black experience with considerable internal diversity. Black churches produced some of the most urgent nationalist expressions in the period, but they could also be profoundly conservative institutions that encouraged members to conform to emerging middle-class standards.[45] Analysis of black culture too often becomes locked in an all-or-nothing debate about the relative weight of European or African cultural inheritances. The Union Church of Africans offers a rich example of self-conscious Africans combining selective Anglo-American Christian elements in a syncretic American institution. Such a doubled identity was not maintained without tension, but that fusion of diverse elements made Afro-Christianity a powerful source of creativity, expression, and change in the new nation.[46]

African American identity in the New World drew upon European and African traditions but remained distinct from both. At the broadest level this group identity united people of color throughout the Atlantic world, but such breadth relied upon a loose imaginary consensus ultimately bound together by the oppression of slavery. Of course, individuals always maintained multiple identities even under slavery, but slavery's effectiveness depended in significant ways upon manufacturing a homogeneous image of blackness that allowed little recognition of individual variation among the enslaved. By contrast, the Union Church of Africans claimed blackness as a functioning free identity while still facing slavery as a living and legal force. African Christianity, however, was just one variant of the widening religious expression in the Revolutionary Delaware Valley that gave public voice to its multicultural inhabitants.

The Evangelical Challenge, Quakers, and Female Public Friends

The famed American Methodist leader Francis Asbury can lead us from New Castle to Burlington. Asbury personified the intense itinerancy of evangelical preachers and visited both towns repeatedly from 1771 to

1815, meeting success and failure in both places. His preaching might draw large or small crowds on any given day according to the skill of his advance men and the quality of his competition, for in addition to its spiritual dimension, religion also contributed to local life as entertainment. Thus he drew poorly in Burlington when its residents attended a local fair instead, while in New Castle he once complained about poor turnout because "Satan was there, diverting people by a play."[47]

Given the popularity of Methodism among African Americans, and especially its great strength on the Delmarva Peninsula, one might expect Asbury to favor New Castle over the Quaker and Episcopal stronghold of Burlington. Asbury's most sustained ministry in New Castle occurred from 1772 to 1774, and though it met with some success, he refused to preach during his final visit when the faithful were "out of order."[48] Asbury never seems to have reached black Christians during his visits there; perhaps the dominance of slavery until the 1790s meant that African American Christianity remained largely covert until the turn of the century.

Asbury found Burlington more hospitable, and by 1789 a Methodist meetinghouse had been raised there with the help of a leading local Presbyterian. While Asbury successfully awakened souls in the West Jersey town, he and his followers still could suffer significant local hostility. Methodism appeared to take off in Burlington during a four-day revival meeting in 1791 that inaugurated a "searching season." The next evening, "we had a shout," but "then came the bulls of Basham and broke our windows. It was well my head escaped the violence of these wicked sinners." Despite the attack, the multiday service continued and built to a spiritual climax with "a love feast" at which "a genuine, sweet melting ran through the house." Success arose from a carefully crafted ritual for bringing people to public conversion and from advance work by local preachers who gained "six hundred souls" through "professed conversion" in the six months leading up to the revival. This evangelical upsurge proved mercurial, however, and when Asbury returned in 1800, he disliked what he found, commenting curtly, "this is an awful place."[49]

The daybook of the disowned Quaker James Craft allows us to assess some of the changes in Burlington's postwar religious landscape. He had been expelled from the Society of Friends in 1780, but maintained an intense religiosity; indeed, his wide-ranging spiritual curiosity may have hastened his expulsion from the Society. Craft attended local services by Episcopal and Baptist ministers as well as occasional services offered by Methodist itinerants. His terse diary entries rarely run beyond a dozen words, but he kept careful religious records. For example, when he attended Episcopal and Baptist services on the same day, he noted the preacher's name, the scriptural text on which he spoke, and any hymns or psalms that were sung.[50] When he attended what Asbury called his "awful" service in 1800, Craft offered a rare flicker of emotion by noting, "Bishop, so called, Asbury on 1 Cor.: 7, 29, 30, 31, Hymn 8 & 9th."[51] The former Quaker apparently disliked Asbury's inflated title.

The brief ascendance of Baptists around Burlington probably sapped Methodism's local popularity. Craft increasingly attended Baptist services in early 1800. Previously he had steadily attended services by the Episcopal rector Charles H. Wharton, but gradually he came to favor sermons by the Baptist William Staughton. In recording forty-five public events in Burlington over eight months in 1800, Craft attended twenty-nine Baptist sermons versus just eleven Episcopal ones, while the three nonreligious events he recorded (two political speeches and the appearance of a "Learned Pig"!) outnumbered the two Methodist ones.

William Staughton had settled in Burlington sometime during 1798, and in the seven years until he accepted a call from a Philadelphia Baptist church, he attracted a notable local following as his congregation grew from just fourteen to ninety-three members.[52] His success with a traditional religious style must have contributed to Asbury's rather sudden dislike for Burlington. By 1800, local popular religious culture shifted away from the brief enthusiastic opening of 1791, that itself had triggered oppositional violence, to revert to a more restrained religious expression. Staughton's "Calvinistic" preaching style was "mighty in scripture," an approach also evident in his surviving sermons printed by the local Baptist Stephen Ustick. A family memoir elaborated that Staughton "abhor[ed] the idea of prevailing upon men, at public meetings, to commit themselves by a show of being on the Lord's side, under excitement of momentary feeling."[53] The public conversion at the center of Asbury's revival meetings clearly was quite different from Staughton's approach, which was more in keeping with the restrained spiritual life of most Burlington residents.

Although all but unknown today, Staughton seriously rivaled Asbury as a leader of rising religious groups in the postwar Delaware Valley. Staughton not only appears with great regularity in James Craft's daybook but also had a significant impact on the religious views of Elizabeth Booth, a New Castle resident, who felt her first religious stirring when she heard the "popular Baptist minister" in Philadelphia in 1809. "The first sermon I heard from him was on the immortality of the soul," she recounted; "it made a deep impression on my mind." This initial step toward awakening was completed seven years later, when after "weekly meetings for prayer and exhortation" she "united in communion with the Presbyterian Church under the pastoral care of Rev. John E. Latta."[54] Booth's Baptist-initiated awakening that led her to join the Presbyterian congregation in New Castle seems especially notable because she withdrew from its Episcopal church where her uncle, Robert Clay, was rector. The malleability of her spiritual identity in no way indicated superficiality, for her awakening inaugurated a life marked by extraordinary religious devotion. Elizabeth Booth never married and would serve as the secretary of the Female Bible Society of New Castle from 1822 until her death in 1884.

Disowned Quakers, like James Craft, may have found succor in Staughton's sermons, but the Society of Friends remained the largest religious group in Burlington and maintained a vital religious life precisely because it expelled latitudinarians such as Craft. While Quakerism is often described as a gentle alternative to more patriarchal Christian traditions, its interlocking meeting structure also produced a high degree of surveillance that demanded strict behavior from members in good standing. When individuals acted contrary to the discipline of the Society, a committee named by their local meeting would approach them, and if the transgressor could not offer a convincing explanation or apology, he or she would be expelled. This strong commitment to group purity had intensified during the trials of the Revolutionary War, which moved Quaker practice in an opposite direction from the ecumenical impulse that inspired both populist and conservative evangelicalism that based themselves upon spiritual experience rather than strict rules or dogma.

Despite their significance as the charter group in founding the Anglo Delaware Valley, Quaker religious practice was located on the margin of early American religious life.[55] The spiritual distance of Friends from other American Christian groups was probably most clear in their commitment to silent worship. This religious practice not only did away with a set liturgy and sermon, it also meant that Quaker services never required a minister. The local religious leaders, who were essential to functioning Christianity in all other American religious groups at the time, were dismissively termed "hireling priests" in the parlance of Quaker discourse and meeting records. If Christian conservatives were worried by the rise of evangelical preachers who had not received advanced theological education, what were they to think of the Society of Friends, who rejected the ministerial profession altogether?

Quakers were often called upon to justify their wayward interpretation of early modern Christianity. Thomas Colley's An Apology for Silent Waiting Upon God became the classic defense of Quaker spirituality and would be reprinted in Burlington in 1805. While the title suggests a defensive tone, Colley sharply criticized professional ministers for abusive sermonizing, prepared sermons, and rote prayers that might be received or uttered, "whether the mind be influenced with the spirit of prayer or not." For Quakers, creedal statements and such essential rites as the Lord's Prayer were marks of spiritual contamination, because "formality in . . . outward forms" distanced the individual from truly engaging Christian principles. Quakers' silent worship circumvented these errors, as one emerged from silence with increased "ardor and fervor of the soul in proportion as it comes under the spirit of Christ." Quaker religious practice fundamentally relied on an unmediated relationship to divine light that should not be artificially stimulated by a minister. There can be little wonder, as Colley noted, that silent worship was "little understood and much despised by professors of religion."[56]

George Withy explained Friends' distinctive practices in similar ways after attending a meeting for worship in Burlington in 1822. He was moved to speak extemporaneously by being brought "very low" by the need to defend Quakerism. Key to him was that "*profession* is one thing, and *possession* is another." "Outward observations," like baptism, could be attained by "great strangers to the life of God in the soul." Just as he dismissed the significance of traditional Christian sacraments, Withy also disparaged seminaries and theological degrees. For Quakers, true spiritual leadership was not "the product of study or man's wisdom" but a "living gift in the ministry of the Gospel of Christ Jesus."[57]

A radical egalitarian potential flowed from Friends' central tenet that "there is that of God in everyone." This belief led to the early development of a significant role for female autonomy within the Society and to the emergence of a significant number of female Public Friends, the title given to those with a special calling to voice their inner light.[58] An examination of Burlington Monthly Meeting minutes from 1788 to 1802 reveals that five women there felt the call to become Public Friends, while only two men were so moved. Lydia Hoskins stands out among this group for embarking on trips to Canada, New England, and Georgia in these years.

Not surprisingly, non-Quakers found such behavior, which was sanctioned and regulated by the Society, to be aberrant. Richard Bisset, for example, teased his sixty-five-year-old aunt, the Quaker Margaret Morris, whom we met earlier, in mildly ribald fashion that he wanted her to send "some pretty, enthusiastic preacher to come over here" and "make a convert of [him]." Bisset emphasized that female religious authority and independent travel betrayed proper behavior for women, which should center on physically attracting men like himself. As to women Quakers, he could not "recollect to have seen any of your preachers that were pretty, tho' many very pretty without being preachers. Your good nature, my dear aunt, will pardon my joking a little."[59] Apparently to the non-Friend Bisset, only ugly women chose to become Public Friends, or perhaps attractive ones were made more masculine by attempting something beyond their proper sphere. Although far more restrained than the charges of sexual license cast upon black evangelicals, once again we find that condemnation of religious distinctiveness emphasized physical transgression.

While female religious authority and personal independence may have offended most early Americans, it was not so unusual in Quaker areas like Burlington where the rate of female-headed households strikingly exceeded that of comparable Delaware Valley towns. The 1774 Burlington tax list yields 19 independent women (8 percent) out of 233 total taxpayers. In heavily Pennsylvania German Easton, only a single independent woman appears among 102 taxables, and she was identified as a widow. Easton's status as a frontier town in the mid-1770s might suggest that the incidence of female independence would be low there, but long-settled New Castle had an even lower incidence, with just a single taxed woman there out of 263 records.

The 8 percent of taxed women in Burlington is a striking anomaly, and Quaker influence offers a likely explanation. Burlington's independent women taxpayers were more likely to be Quaker than the town's overall taxed population. In Burlington, twelve of the nineteen taxed women were Quakers, or from known Quaker families, yielding a 63 percent rate of Quakerism among women taxpayers, far exceeding the 40 percent Quaker affiliation in the total taxed population. A strong correlation existed between female independence and Quakerism in Burlington. Moreover, the prominence of independent women among Burlington Quakers must have influenced non-Quakers as well.

Quakerism buttressed female autonomy in a society that increasingly viewed adult women property holders as problematic in the postwar republic. The high rate of women taxpayers in Burlington directly counters the trend in Philadelphia, where the female presence in tax lists decreased from 8 percent in 1756 to 5 percent in 1774.[60] Burlington, by contrast, maintained a civic culture that acknowledged independent propertied women in an era when such women were increasingly excluded from the public role of paying taxes. In fact, the rate of women taxables in Burlington increased from 8 percent in 1774 to 9 percent in 1796, and 14 percent in 1814. Not surprisingly, these independent women with property were more predominantly Quaker than the overall taxpaying population.[61]

The meaning of Quaker female independence can best be seen in the qualitative records left by Public Friends, who built social networks during their religious travels. One indication of the unusual autonomy of Quaker women can be teased out of the close relationship between Martha Barker and Grace Buchanan, who both enjoyed some degree of economic independence. Buchanan never married, but Barker did and had six children before her husband died in 1745.[62] Apparently she had sufficient resources to avoid having to remarry, for she appears as an independent householder and shopkeeper of middling status in 1774. By 1796 she had prospered and appeared in the second highest tax quintile. Almost all her assessed wealth derived from a house lot valued at £16, a house so fine that only 43 individuals among the 388 taxed had more valuable houses. After living most of her life in households as a servant, Grace Buchanan also appears in the 1796 tax list as the owner of a house lot valued at £5, her entire taxable estate, but sufficient to place her in the middle of the second lowest quintile of taxpayers that year.

A 1781 letter between the two Public Friends suggests their extraordinary bond. Buchanan had apparently been in Philadelphia for some time, and Barker wrote to assure her that she was remembered fondly across the river in Burlington: "many waters cannot Quench Love, neither can floods drown it, much less such a distance cause us to forget the sweetening seasons as well as the trying ones we have had together . . . this is the way for us to be as epistles written in one anothers Hearts by the power of Love."[63] This intimate expression makes plain that Quaker spirituality added a profound richness to these women's lives. Quakerism allowed more women in Burlington than in the other towns to participate in a wide degree of public activity as Public Friends, as independent property holders, and even as letter writers. The sheer quantity of surviving manuscript material for Quaker women—letters written by women, between women, and, most strikingly, between women of modest economic status—all indicate that the Society of Friends helped these women to move outside the narrow compass usually proscribed for them in early American society.

Quaker women not only enjoyed notable economic and spiritual independence but also had greater administrative responsibilities than women in most other Protestant groups in early America. The Society institutionalized female competency and autonomy by creating separate meetings for women. Burlington women Friends held management positions in their local religious organizations in numbers that exceeded their male counterparts from 1808 to 1839. While the Society of Friends permitted women unusual latitude to exert themselves as autonomous individuals, this freedom should not be overstated. The Women's Preparative Meeting in Burlington performed circumscribed duties that mostly consisted of appointing women to sit among children during meetings for worship to keep them in good order. Its other main responsibilities were to clean the meetinghouse and to raise money for firewood. As if these were not meager enough areas of control, a Men's Preparatory Meeting committee decided in 1802 on the "propriety of . . . relieving Women friends from the business of collecting money . . . and taking care of the Meeting House and c."[64]

While Margaret Morris's Revolutionary War experiences, examined in Chapter 2, led her to a stronger assertion of her own autonomy, the range of public options even for Quaker women remained modest by present-day standards. Morris's sense of women's proper behavior as wives plainly appeared in her advice to a granddaughter about how best to behave toward her fiancé. Morris instructed, "do not trouble thyself to dispute with him on trivial matters; rather give up thine own will than provoke him to make harsh replies . . . be not only condescending, but obedient; it is the duty of a wife so to be."[65] Morris's understanding of a wife's dependent duty may have been what encouraged her to choose to remain single for fifty years after the death of her sole husband. Whatever her personal circumstances, Morris's caution to her granddaughter, and the actual duties of women's meetings, require acknowledging that the opportunities enjoyed by Quaker women remained quite circumscribed.

If we are to assess Quakers within the context of the early national period, however, it remains plain that most Americans saw them as peculiar and even subversive. Most Protestants found Friends' central religious practices not just odd but fundamentally objectionable. As one opponent noted about silent worship, Quakers "mistake meditation for inspiration; for, it is impossible for a man who directs all his thoughts toward one single point, aided by silence, without any distraction to avoid working himself up to a point of giving birth to some rambling maxims and phrases."[66] Most American Christians believed Quakerism to be a seedbed for misleading beliefs. When such spiritual peculiarities extended to encourage female religious authority and to prohibit masculine martial activity, Friends clearly encouraged behavior that most Americans dismissed as bizarre.

Samuel Hanson Cox, an ex-Quaker turned Presbyterian minister, published an especially severe attack titled "Quakerism not Christianity" that among other charges expressed deep disdain for Quakers' "feminine vendors." The extended defense mounted by the Quaker journal *The Friend* hinged on the issue of group identity. Cox had charged Quakers with being so distinctive and exclusionary as to insist upon Quakerism as "the identity itself," that is, as the sole legitimate expression of Christianity. The Quaker response rejected this claim and asserted that Calvinists were the ones who thought of their sect as the only true example of Christianity. *The Friend* offered a classic statement of early national American Christianity when it declared, "The sacred system of Christianity is a divine unit, supremely above everything else, and infinitely beyond every other 'identity' in the universe of God."[67] This ideal of a cosmopolitan ecumenical Christianity was widely shared; however, a chasm separated such abstract beliefs about Christian unity from the pragmatic reality of religious expression in everyday life.

The evangelical transformation of early national American religion directly threatened the Society of Friends. Enthusiastic evangelicalism, with its charismatic preachers and boisterous demands for public conversion intruded on one front, while cosmopolitan evangelicals broadened their efforts to unite all Christians in new types of conservative reform organizations intruded on another. Many Quakers clung to their distinctive religious traditions and opposed both these efforts to reformulate American Christianity as a broadly unifying force. This new context for early national religion ultimately led to a major schism among American Quakers, with those in the Orthodox wing more prepared to participate in conservative cosmopolitan evangelicalism, while the Hicksite wing clung to a more traditional (and simultaneously more radical) sense of Quaker exceptionalism. This Quaker separation of the late 1820s gets ahead of our story, for in feeling threatened by evangelicalism, Burlington Friends shared a great deal with two other distinctive Protestant groups in our third Delaware River town.

Solidarity and Discord among Pennsylvania Germans

Easton's religious culture arose from a demonstrably ethnic landscape. When the popular travel writer Anne Royall identified the owner of an Easton tavern where she lodged as an "English-man," she explained to her readers that in this area that meant any native-born person who was not German or of German descent.[68] This local idiom tellingly indicates how different everyday life was in Easton from the other two river towns, where the term would have referred more specifically to someone born in England and probably a foreign visitor. Pennsylvania German distinctiveness sets Easton apart in some ways, but this difference is best understood within a comparative multicultural framework. Just as religion provided a powerful vehicle for distinctive public expression by Burlington Quakers and by Union Church of African members in New Castle, so too religion cannot be disentangled from Pennsylvania German ethnicity.

The Lutheran and German Reformed churches that dominated formal religious life in Easton each had counterparts among Anglo-American denominations, with the high church forms of Lutheranism paralleling Anglicanism and the Calvinistic core of the German Reformed tradition placing it close to the Old Side strain of Presbyterianism. The theological and organizational parallels among these groups, however, never came close to matching the deep local engagement between Lutheran and German Reformed people. The theological distance separating Lutheran and Reformed practices could be important, but more often their common language, cultural inheritance, and status as outsiders to Anglo-dominated society led these congregations to align themselves closely throughout Pennsylvania. Ethnic cooperation trumped strict theological consistency, and this was not purely a New World development. Lutheran and Reformed churches in the multiethnic polities of southwest Germany often shared worldly burdens by holding separate meetings for worship in a common union church. The two German "church" groups (*kirchenleute*) drew even closer together in Northampton County for a variety of reasons including their mutual antipathy toward German "sect" traditions (*sektenleute*) such as those of nearby Moravians with settlements at Bethlehem and Nazareth.[69]

The high rate of "mixed" religious affiliation in 1770s Easton is the most striking feature of its general religious profile. On the eve of the Revolutionary War, 21 percent of town taxpayers played active roles in both local congregations. Such a high degree of mixed affiliation had no parallel in Burlington, where Quaker insistence upon spiritual purity limited the

Spangenberg's artistry was decidedly Pennsylvania German and did not confine itself to German. His English-language baptismal certificate for Anne Andreas in 1783 even eschewed gothic letters in favor of cursive script, while retaining the essential visual tone of the form (fig. 23). As in his Schlatter Bible work where a portly trumpeter played out in Latin "Glory to God in the Highest" and in German "To God Alone Give Honor," trumpeters and violinists celebrated the baptism. Religious music infused Lutheran and Reformed religious practice, and as a schoolmaster, Spangenberg's responsibilities included religious instruction through hymn singing. But the musical celebration in the Andreas *taufschein* has a strong festive quality. Piety may have moved these musicians, but their serenade for three prominently drinking couples on the bottom border underscores that sacred rituals also permitted revelry. Spangenberg's bilingual *fraktur*-work demonstrates his importance as a cultural go-between for local Pennsylvania Germans, a role that also informed his work as a teacher and scrivener who drafted English-language wills for German-speaking clients.[104]

Although Spangenberg was clearly bilingual, his English was somewhat stilted, and the majority of his work used German, as in his more typical Elizabeth Wagner *taufschein* of her baptism by the Lutheran pastor Christian Endress.[105] While examples survive for members of both Easton's Pennsylvania German congregations, the Reformed ones are more numerous, even though slightly more Lutherans can be located in Easton's tax lists. Beyond the vagaries of the survival and collection process, several factors shaped the Reformed predominance in local *taufschein*. Reverend Pomp's long service in Easton meant that his congregation faced few leadership transitions, and parents may have preferred to have a child baptized by a man they knew well. Both local congregations drew members from the rural countryside and surrounding towns, and the Reformed congregation may have had a stronger rural component that valued *taufschein* more highly. Moreover, Endress's English-language preaching and greater Anglo-American acculturation, features of his leadership continued by his successor John Peter Hecht, may have decreased local Lutheran attachments to such cultural markers. All of these likely shaped the greater number of Reformed *taufschein* that survive today, but this may have arisen simply because Reverend Pomp gave them as gifts to those he baptized, as has been documented for other pastors.[106]

Whatever the cause of the more frequent preservation of Reformed *taufschein* from Easton, a closer look reveals their rich integration with contemporary currents in American society. These objects did not mark a more traditional German tendency within Pomp's congregation. Maria Schneider's baptism by Pomp was recorded in a *taufschein* by the prolific itinerant known as the *Ehre Vater* Artist, whose work highlights two significant aspects of Pennsylvania German popular culture in the period.[107]

First, the extraordinary geographic range of this craftsman whose examples survive from North Carolina to Ontario dazzlingly demonstrates the sweep of this tradition from its core in southeastern Pennsylvania. Although our attention is grounded in the experiences of residents in three river towns, American society was on the move in this period for Pennsylvania Germans as much as for other groups. For example, a Virginia *taufschein* by the *Ehre Vater* Artist in 1789 recorded a baptism performed by Christian Streit, who had been the Lutheran minister in Easton for seven years before becoming a chaplain in the Continental Army and then settling among Pennsylvania Germans in Virginia.[108] The constant movement of people in the broadening zone of Pennsylvania German influence meant that the group interacted with the full range of forces reshaping American society in the early national period.

The second notable quality of Maria Schneider's *taufschein* is its emphasis not just on baptism as a religious event but also on the child's birth itself. This document carefully noted the date of November 18, 1808, the time at two in the morning, and her astrological sign of Sagittarius. That she was baptized two months later seems almost incidental. Many *taufschein* give greater emphasis to the date of birth than the baptism and are, perhaps, more appropriately identified as *geburts und taufschein*, birth and baptismal certificates.[109] This emphasis reminds us that a complex medley of beliefs shaped popular religiosity that extended beyond doctrinal and confessional statements. Popular belief in astrology was especially strong among Pennsylvania Germans.[110]

While these certificates often stand as markers of a distinct ethnic culture, some examples, particularly ones later in the period under study, demonstrate a rich interaction with Anglo America. The most striking example of an Anglicized religious certificate in Easton commemorated Jesse Oberly's confirmation by Thomas Pomp in 1827 (fig. 24). Technically speaking, this certificate fell outside the specifications of *taufschein* and *fraktur* work as it was printed in English cursive script and did not document a baptism. Furthermore, the standard visual codes of the genre do not appear here. Instead, a church building dominates the center of the back-and-white engraved certificate, with an angel to the left and a religious inscription and an eagle on the right, with a banner stating "Next unto my God and Bible I love my Country, the land of religious liberty."[111] The overtly nationalist elements, the use of English, and the lack of any readily identifiable Pennsylvania German imagery might suggest this as a sign of wholehearted assimilation. However, it actually struck a balance that engaged certain impulses of an increasingly common American Christianity while still retaining an important degree of ethnic distinctiveness. Because the printed form had been commissioned by the German Reformed Church of North America, whose denominational name appeared in large cursive script across the second line of text, it exemplified an effective confessional embrace of modern technology and national style. Moreover, an essential localist focus remains in the form's blank spaces for entering the name of the individual, congregation, minister, and date.

This confirmation certificate suggests one way that Pennsylvania Germans arrived as full members of American society without leaving a distinctive ethno-religious consciousness behind.[112] While still fully steeped in essential local circumstances, religious identity permitted German Reformed and Lutheran church members in Easton to participate in national developments. Jesse Oberly's confirmation certificate announced denominational and national commitments, while the stars, sun, and quarter moon framing the upper half of the image hinted at the persistence of Pennsylvania German popular religiosity. Who knows whether this young man still saw astrological significance in the twinkling stars in the night sky on his certificate, thus continuing the spiritual values documented in more traditional *taufschein*.

The mechanical mass production of Pennsylvania German folk art in this 1827 certificate culminated a development of several decades. The earliest known Easton example of a printed *taufschein* filled in with hand-drawn decorations dates to the start of such forms in 1781, and by the mid-1780s the Ephrata cloister in Lancaster County had begun its commercial production (fig. 25).[113] The demand for printed forms was so great that one press printed nearly seven thousand of them for a single rural artist from 1801 to 1813.[114] Such demand encouraged technical innovation but also helped to narrow the form's range of conventions. As an important early scholarly assessment of *fraktur* noted, "it cannot be emphasized too strongly how homogeneous and standardized the various local types became."[115] This standardization was especially true of the baptismal hymn texts that reappeared in later *fraktur* with great frequency.

The union of commerce and popular religiosity occurred in Pennsylvania German areas just as it did throughout the country. The Easton newspaper offices of Christian Jacob Hutter had begun selling printed *taufschein* as early as 1807, a year after his relocation to Easton from Lancaster, and numerous examples by his press survive from the 1820s.[116] Machine production of a traditionally handcrafted genre helped ethno-religious self-understanding to express itself with great vigor in the new nation and contributed to the intricate web of ethnic, religious, and social interaction that created and maintained group identities in the Revolutionary Delaware Valley.

Christina Kerkendal's *taufschein* strikingly demonstrates the dynamism of the period's Pennsylvania German folk art (fig. 26). This freehand certificate closely follows the model in a printed version from Ephrata.[117] This example reveals a social experience where technological innovation furthered the clarity and force of Pennsylvania German expression, which perpetuated *fraktur* as a popular form into the twentieth century. The Kerkendal *taufschein* reviewed key moments in her spiritual life: baptism by Thomas Pomp in 1818, confirmation by him in 1834, and marriage two years later. We also learn that she was born at midnight in the sign of Pisces.

Verses inside two hearts in the certificate's bottom corners emphasized her sacramental salvation through baptism. These classic texts appeared in the same locations on the printed form and derived from the baptismal hymn in Johann F. Starck's widespread devotional book, first printed in America in 1726 but not issued in English until 1855. The hymn appeared with extraordinary frequency in *taufschein* from all periods and regions and expressed an important religious belief:

I am baptized! And though I perish,
O grave, where is thy victory!
My patrimony is in heaven,
And it shall never fall from me.
When death arrives, I shall receive
Far purer joys than those I leave.[118]

The explicit point here was implied in all *taufschein*. Infant baptism was an essential means to salvation. This widespread belief departed from growing evangelical calls for a new birth in adult conversion and parted ways with conservative Presbyterian and Congregational traditions that emphasized human deprivation and limited salvation.[119]

Pennsylvania Germans in Easton experienced rapid changes in the postwar period as its Lutheran and German Reformed congregations began to loosen some of the bonds that had connected them in the colonial period. Nevertheless, their union church persisted, and they remained the dominant local religious organizations into at least the 1830s. Whether facing popular evangelicalism, conservative evangelicalism, or traditional "English" churches, there can be little question that a shared Pennsylvania German identity shaped their self-assessments and their engagement with early national society.

Protestant Diversity and the Elusive Quest for Christian Unity

The leading ministers of the traditional Christian denominations in these towns enjoyed long terms of service in the postwar period. Charles H. Wharton was the Episcopal rector in Burlington from 1798 to 1833 and previously served in New Castle from 1784 to 1788. John E. Latta was the Presbyterian pastor in New Castle from 1800 to 1824, and his Episcopalian counterpart, Robert Clay, led his church from 1788 to 1824. In Easton, Thomas Pomp held the German Reformed pastorate from 1796 to 1852, and Christian F. L. Endress led the Lutheran one from 1801 to 1815.

These men all served until death, save Endress, whose replacement, John P. Hecht, had an even longer pastorate, from 1815 to 1845. Despite their seeming permanence, these spiritual leaders served at the discretion of their congregations. Such durable leadership marked significant personal and institutional stability through sustained local relationships. Yet these church leaders shared a cosmopolitan commitment to reconcile local religious diversity that sometimes set them apart from members of their own congregations.

Conservative ministers in New Castle and Burlington made especially strenuous efforts to forge pan-Christian alliances in the early republic. Reverends Latta and Wharton cast religious diversity among Protestants as a hazard for the nation and sought a broad Christian unity to undergird the republican social order. Their uneasy hopes for religious harmony shared similarities, especially in deriding enthusiastic evangelicalism as a threat to the order that they favored. In many respects the traditional denominations that these men represented experienced decline in this period, but to portray only fast-rising popular evangelicalism as dominating early republican religious life oversimplifies a gradual and highly contested process. Men such as Latta, Wharton, Pomp, and Endress effectively countered populist evangelicalism in their towns.

Charles H. Wharton's commitment to forge a united American Christianity partly stemmed from his own mixed religious background. Born in 1748 to a prominent Roman Catholic family in Maryland, he began attending the English Jesuits' College in France at the age of twelve. He later served as the Roman Catholic chaplain in Worcester, England, but had a conversion experience during the American Revolution, left Catholicism, and returned to America in 1783. His intriguing personal transformation of intertwined political and religious changes helped prompt him to become the leading anti-Catholic writer of the early American republic.[120]

Wharton's first public statement after his conversion presented the motives for his change as springing from a careful "rational investigation" that required rejecting Catholicism's "discriminating doctrines," especially "the absurdity and uncharitableness of believing . . . that the members of no Christian church, but your own be saved." This "master-error" forced him out of the faith. Wharton believed that the new nation's best hope lay in Christian unity. "I look forward with rapture to that auspicious day, when Protestants opening their eyes upon their mutual agreement in all essentials of belief, will forget past animosities, and cease to regard each other as of different communions." In the spirit of rational amicability, Wharton even extended his vision to Catholics, suggesting that at the time of Protestant union, perhaps they too might "awake from their prejudices" and "throw off the galling yoke of old European prepossessions."[121] Like many other religious leaders in the postwar period, Wharton argued that the country's highest calling lay in overcoming the corrupt religious divisions of the Old World. For him, the promise of nationhood lay in its potential as a united Christian polity.

Wharton's ecumenical hopes, however, often seem mostly rhetorical. While speculating about a future Protestant-Catholic union, he averred that Catholicism had fallen so far from scriptural truth that "with equal merit might [a Catholic] be a jew, muselman, or an idolater, as each of these grounds his principles on authority, whose decrees he deems sacred, whilst he neglects to examine them." Wharton was too much the fervent recent convert to be an effective religious unifier, yet his crucial conflation of Protestantism and Christianity—"I now belong . . . to the *christian catholic church*"—that excluded Catholics was shared by most Americans.[122]

If Wharton's hopes to unite with Catholics were clearly fanciful, what of his insistence upon Protestant unity? It seems unlikely that he would compromise his own denominational commitments. Because Anglicanism had long seen itself as offering a middle route between Calvinist and Catholic extremes, an Episcopal minister could comfortably champion holistic Protestant reform, and several prominent Burlington Presbyterians were regular members of his church. But could Wharton's Christian unity embrace Quakers, German Reformed believers, and black evangelicals? Probably not, for he maintained that only men "in *my circumstances*" should practice searching rational inquiry, while "the lower sort of people" who lacked "education," "abilities," and "leisure . . . must rely principally on the authority of their teachers."[123] To cast order aside by encouraging common men, much less women, to engage in religious inquiry was far from what he sought.

Wharton yearned for an organic unity in American life and believed that religious diversity imperiled the young republic. The scriptural example of the church of Corinth, which suffered from "a divided state with reference to its pastors," offered a pointed example to him. Some there had "stiled themselves of Paul, others of Apollos, others of Cephas or Peter." In the face of this diversity, the apostle endeavored "to convince them, that it is unbecoming a Christian, who belongs solely to God, to glory in men."[124] Interestingly, Wharton found himself vulnerable to Catholic counterattacks on this point that charged him as the schismatic. Was not Protestantism to blame for the dangerous divisions within Christendom? So argued a Baltimore priest who called on Wharton to return to his natal faith before death and damnation, "for among all the Protestant sects, what choice can be made, one opinion being as good as another, whether it be Luther's, or Calvin's, Fox's, Wesley's, Socinus's, Priestly's, or any other non-descript society?"[125] This effectively targeted a key dilemma for Wharton as a seeker of Christian unity who represented a particular faith. Ultimately, religious diversity, even among Protestants, threatened the dependence that Wharton and fellow conservatives expected from ordinary people. Social order in the new nation could be ensured only through religious solidarity, and "a society thus united . . . in the bonds of true Christian charity" would defeat "the efforts of every adversary."[126]

John E. Latta, New Castle's Presbyterian minister, similarly strove to lead a united American Christianity for the good of the nation. He worked especially hard to counter enthusiastic evangelicalism that distracted people from respectable Christianity. Presbyterianism had long been influential in his northern Delaware charge, but Methodism grew at a stunning rate on the Delmarva Peninsula below New Castle, memorably described by one scholar as the "Garden of American Methodism."[127] After a missionary tour of the southern peninsula, Latta reported wretched spiritual conditions in the backwater area, yet also noted that "several persons attached to the Methodist Church . . . are truly Calvinistic in their principles." To Latta, like Wharton, better leadership could counter evangelical success. Latta believed that the "low ebb at which the taste for preaching appears" stemmed from a lack of proper guidance and had no doubt that Methodist converts "would join the Presbyterians if they started preaching."[128]

Latta repeatedly cited examples of the redeeming power of traditional religious leadership. When he preached to a large Methodist congregation, he noted that "order, decorum, silence and solemnity, much greater than ordinary, prevailed." When a man dropped to "his knees at the door of the church" in the middle of his sermon "and began to pray with a voice audible throughout the assembly," Latta immediately stopped, and "no sooner had [I] done this than one of the Methodist society went, and laid his hand on the shoulder of the person praying, and requested him to desist. The request was forthwith acquiesced in and perfect order restored."[129] Latta clearly felt a strong attachment to Old Side Presbyterian Calvinism. As one fourteen-year-old who attended his school complained to a friend, Latta "has not yet been able to get over the prejudices of the old school" and "continues to tire us with his long Saturday prayers."[130]

Latta's opposition to the chaos of popular evangelicalism led him to become an astute cosmopolitan evangelical organizer. His success as a conservative activist derived from several sources, including his willingness to circulate his beliefs broadly through published sermons, but above all, it was driven by his deep conviction "to bury sectual names and prejudices and unite in a Christian harmony."[131] Even as he condemned Methodists and believed Calvinism to be the most valid expression of Christianity, Latta labored to create a united American Christianity that would restrain religious partisanship. Latta understood religious and political diversity as similar threats to a stable nation. "Party spirit in church and state is very common. In both, within certain limits, it may be useful. When, however, it becomes excessive, it is extremely dangerous."[132] It is hard to imagine how the UCA, Quakers, or even Pennsylvania German church members could have been included in Latta's vision of Christian harmony other than through a deadening silence of homogenizing assimilation. While earnest in his commitments, Latta's universalizing language was highly selective.

Transforming American religious diversity into Christian unity was extremely challenging. For example, the Pennsylvania German embrace of baptismal salvation, with its positive implications about children, broke from the view promulgated by conservative Presbyterians like Latta. His "Short Catechism for Children" concluded with two questions where the terror of dying without experiencing conscious conversion figured centrally.

Q. 46. Do you know how soon you may die?
A.   No: I have not a moment to call my own. Children, much younger than I, have died.

Q. 47. Should you not then endeavour always to be ready to die?
A.   Yes.

For Latta, the mere outward form of baptism was insufficient to ensure salvation that demanded sustained religious education, prayer, and the personal commitment of a conversion experience. The Isaac Watts "Hymn for a Child" that concluded Latta's catechism underscores the divergence of popular Pennsylvania German spirituality from most Protestant religious traditions in the new nation. The final verses of the hymn asked,

Can such a wretch as I
Escape this cursed end?
And may I hope whe e'er I die,
I shall to heav'n ascend.

Then I will read and pray,
While I have life and breath;
Lest I should be cut off to-day,
And sent to 'ternal death.[133]

Such a severe view also informed much of the material in the Union Church of Africans' hymnal, whereas most members of the Society of Friends, whose belief in the inner light encouraged a very positive view of children, maintained an attitude closer to Pennsylvania Germans, though Quakers, of course, rejected the sacred power of sacraments altogether. In short, the coursing spiritual diversity of the Delaware Valley provoked those striving to forge a united American Christianity as a bulwark for the nation.

The variety of lived religious experience in these towns strained the potential for broad Christian unity even as that diversity spurred unification efforts. Despite all being descendents of the Reformation, the wide-ranging expressions of African American Methodists, Quakers, German Reformed, and Lutherans overwhelmed any easy religious assimilation. Each group's ability to resist conformist demands gained strength from how spirituality intertwined with other forms of personal identity such as race and ethnicity that found few other avenues for legitimate public presentation in the early republic.

The quest for Christian unity inspired many segments of early national society, including people in all of the towns studied here. Ministers in local pulpits with an obvious devotion to their own denominations ultimately had limited roles to play in forging extensive Christian coalitions. Instead, new corporate organizations led by laypeople on a national scale proved far more effective in building this new American Christianity. These institutions took advantage of an emerging national print culture and enormous grassroots participation in a dramatic campaign for national unity. The Bible societies that spearheaded this effort faced a stunning range of local challenges in New Castle, Burlington, and Easton, where, race, radical theology, and ethnicity, respectively, exacerbated the "sectual names and prejudices" that John Latta feared and that never would be fully overcome.[134]

Chapter 5

The Campaign for Christian Unity

The vitality of local diversity that had been stimulated by the Revolutionary War and continued to assert itself in the new nation led conservative evangelicals in the Delaware Valley to attempt to assimilate those differences into a common American Christianity that they believed essential for national stability and prosperity. As the Bible Society of Delaware optimistically proclaimed in its first annual report, "We behold Christians widely separated from each other, by countries, forms, and names, daily approximating, and coalescing into one spiritual body."[1] By insisting upon the fundamental unity of Americans as Christians, evangelical reformers strove to transcend the multiplicity of local identities with their clashing oppositional interests that increasingly seemed central to national life with permanent conflict between political parties in the nineteenth century. Religion and politics faced similar challenges as they took shape within and informed the increasingly national context of public life. As two Bible society missionaries reported of their organizing efforts in the west, a broad denominational base was crucial, for the perception of Presbyterian control led many to decide that "they could not unite" with the movement. Expressing a central opinion of cosmopolitan evangelicalism, these reformers found it "peculiarly injurious to the cause of religion, that party spirit or sectarian zeal should ever keep good men from uniting heart and hand, in a cause of the purest benevolence."[2] Conservative evangelicals sought to reduce diversity in American life, yet their work often stimulated even greater difference.

Evangelical activists demonstrated enormous energy and creativity in their moral reform efforts, especially via sophisticated use of print culture to communicate their common values that they implemented through numerous interlocking organizations. Although never totally successful, conservative evangelicals made major contributions to the new national culture created in the Delaware Valley, and in many other parts of the country, in the 1810s and 1820s. The dramatic increase of Christianity's ideological and institutional presence in the new nation also bred resistance from individuals who feared the implications of uniform Christianity. Those who found its conformist demands overly burdensome reasserted local traditions against conservative reformers, who in turn modified their

movement to accommodate certain aspects of local resistance. This negotiation helped moral reform to draw strength from populist evangelicalism with substantial local support. In the towns studied here, respectable
women, some Pennsylvania Germans, and Presbyterians, above all, played
important roles in cosmopolitan reform. For people in these groups, at
least, the American Christianity of the early national period expanded to
embrace difference in a newly inclusive manner.

Bible societies contributed centrally to the Benevolent Empire of overlapping local, state, and national reform organizations created in the early
nineteenth century. The Bible movement aimed to instill a common sense
of Protestant national purpose and peoplehood throughout the United
States. Residents of Burlington, New Castle, and Easton founded local
Bible societies and female auxiliaries from 1809 to 1822 that brought a
cosmopolitan national vision to each place as never before. Led by Elias
Boudinot, non-Quakers in Burlington played an especially influential role
in the country's earliest Bible societies, not just locally and in New Jersey
but across the region and the nation. Although somewhat slower to be established, the Delaware Bible Society would draw on wide-ranging support
from New Castle residents. John Latta, the town's Presbyterian minister,
was one of the guiding forces of the organization, and the Bible movement there encouraged especially dramatic social activism by respectable
local women who created the New Castle Female Bible Society. Easton was
the last of the towns to form a local Bible society, and while some Pennsylvania German leaders participated in the movement, local people there
showed greater indifference to it than in the other river towns. For Pennsylvania Germans and for Quakers, the Bible movement challenged familiar forms of religious life. Conservative evangelicals' success in crafting a
unified American Christianity arose from their ability to adjust their movement to accommodate the logic of local circumstances in places throughout the nation.

The Vision of a Christian Nation

Cosmopolitanism always had local representatives in these river towns who
drew inspiration from leaders and trends in larger and more sophisticated
cities. Philadelphia, of course, was the cosmopolitan center of the
Delaware Valley, and just as it was essential to the political, economic, and
social expression of this perspective in the region, and often the nation,
so too was it at the forefront of cosmopolitan evangelicalism. The Bible Society of Philadelphia (BSP) was founded in 1808 to dispense Bibles among
the poor and pioneered the movement in the United States. The distribution of Bibles "without notes," thus avoiding any scriptural interpretation,
was absolutely fundamental to the Bible movement that hoped "all denominations of Christians, without exception, may unite." From the start,

the BSP insisted upon a multidenominational effort to include all Christians—really, all Protestants. Moreover, it endeavored to provide Bibles "in the native speech of all who shall be disposed to read it; so that . . . it may not remain a sealed book." Linguistic diversity, a key expression of ethnic distinctiveness, was an obvious obstacle to be overcome. The new organization made significant efforts to distribute German-language Bibles as well as ones in French, Welsh, Gaelic, and Native American languages. Finally, the BSP distributed the Holy Scripture "without money and without price," because "it is to the poor chiefly that we have it in expectation to send the inspired and authentic records of that gospel."[3] This marked an extraordinary commitment to reach across denominational, ethnic, and economic boundaries to spread the Bible as widely as possible.

The new institution's founders considered two distinct systems "for rendering the contemplated charity extensively useful." Should they organize as a national association, or as one with a primary emphasis on their city, state, and region? The regional plan ultimately prevailed because they could not imagine a viable national organization. As the Episcopal bishop William White explained in his inaugural address as BSP president, they rejected plans for a national association because it "would never be conducted with vigour." By contrast, a regional organization "within its proper sphere" would prove "more efficient."[4] While committing itself to the state and region, the BSP called for similar societies to form and join in the glorious cause of spreading the Bible throughout the nation.

The first annual report of the BSP announced the new institution to the public by distributing unsolicited printed pamphlets, a technique of mass communication that built upon lessons learned in building a popular movement during the American Revolution. Such novel advertisements led BSP managers to apologize for intruding upon those who had not requested the pamphlet. The importance of the cause allowed them to think it "proper to invite the pious and benevolent, through the medium of public prints, to come forward and subscribe." They quickly "exhausted" their initial distribution of six hundred English and three hundred German texts and ordered a larger second purchase, but already they faced a stumbling block in bridging linguistic distinctiveness because it was "not practable to obtain a cheap edition of the German Bible in this country."[5]

The BSP's immediate success clearly tapped an issue with broad popular support and resonance. The organization primarily worked among the poor in Philadelphia, but it also had a prominent role throughout Pennsylvania and the Delaware Valley and would send Bibles to Easton, New Castle, and Burlington within the decade.[6] The BSP's regional breadth was matched by its inclusion of key Pennsylvania German religious leaders. Reverend J. H. C. Helmuth, the leading Lutheran minister in Philadelphia, successfully entered a motion with the governing body of his denomination to thank the BSP for the German-language New Testaments it had sent to the backcountry, and the ministerium directed its members to assist the new Bible organization as fully as possible in 1809.[7] Reformed and Lutheran church leaders in Philadelphia would soon be BSP leaders and served on its board of managers.

The Burlington resident Elias Boudinot was among the handful of BSP founders who established themselves as lifetime members with an initial donation of $50 in 1808. Two other Burlington residents joined him as founding members: the Episcopal rector Charles H. Wharton, in whose church the Presbyterian Boudinot worshipped, and the leading Episcopalian layman, Joshua M. Wallace. Boudinot played a towering role in the Bible movement as a founder of the BSP, the New Jersey Bible Society, and, most significantly, as the driving force behind the American Bible Society as an explicitly national organization.

Boudinot had retired from government service to Burlington in 1805 as a weary Federalist in a Republican world. He had performed a range of weighty public duties as a long-term member of the Continental Congress (and its president in 1782), a New Jersey representative to the U.S. Congress from 1789 to 1795, and as director of the U.S. Mint for a decade starting in 1795.[8] Deeply troubled by the revolutionary changes of the era, Boudinot sought to counter its worst abuses in 1801 by battling Thomas Paine in the realm of print. Boudinot's reactionary vision helps explain the milieu that gave rise to the Bible movement. His first publication refuted Paine's *Age of Reason*, objectionable due to its anti-Christian message, of course, but all the more so as "the subject of conversation in all ranks of society." Reaching a popular audience by being "generally plausible in his own language" made Paine dangerous. Even worse, the scandalous book sold for just "a cent and a half each, whereby children, servants, and the lowest people, had been tempted to purchase [it], from the novelty at buying a book at so low a rate."[9] Paine's accessibility to ordinary people threatened Boudinot and other conservative evangelicals committed to a fixed Christian social order. Boudinot's *Age of Revelation* aimed to "meet Mr. Paine . . . on his own ground, in a plain and simple manner," but in this Boudinot failed.[10] His contorted argument is difficult to follow, and nothing indicates that it enjoyed a broad audience.[11]

Boudinot's long dedication to Susan Bradford, his recently widowed daughter, stressed a social role for the Bible in the new republic. He feared that the trauma of widowhood might plunge his daughter into a "melancholy . . . spirit of infidelity" and expose her to the "extravagant and ludicrous ideas" of the "infidel author." Instead, Americans needed to rely on the Bible as "the Alpha and Omega of knowledge." The key to scripture required recognizing that "the Gospel revelation is a complete system of salvation," while criticisms by men like Paine only poked at "detached principles, separated from the system." While Boudinot conceded that "the world at large" presently put "little value" upon scripture, "the time . . . is not far off, when they will command a very different reception among the sons of the earth."[12] Evangelical reform's rapid rise in the next three decades bore out his prediction that the Bible would soon achieve a much more central place in American life.

Millenarianism fundamentally shaped Boudinot's public commitments as it did for most moral reform activists in the period. His next major publication argued that the second coming of Christ was close at hand, and by relying on a systematic reading of scripture, such as he had called for in opposing Paine, Boudinot interwove biblical prophecy and contemporary events to demonstrate the immediate proximity of Judgment Day. Napoleon played the role of "the antichrist foretold" in scripture, a fact that Boudinot believed obvious to anyone who compared the history of France since 1790 "with the language of holy writ." Boudinot was not a crackpot, but a leading figure of his day, and buttressed his views by citing learned scientific authorities such as Isaac Newton, who also observed that "scarce a prophecy in the Old Testament . . . doth not, in something or other, relate to his second coming."[13] Boudinot carefully distinguished his own cosmopolitan evangelicalism with its grounding in reason and science from the populist revivalism of his day. His careful Bible study departed from recent "enthusiasts" whose calls "have produced the greatest confusions in government." Whereas evangelical radicals encouraged "extravagance of conduct," Boudinot saw the Second Coming "as a rational and glorious expectation."[14]

As a standard-bearer of conservative evangelicalism, Boudinot aimed to overcome what he saw as the excesses of revolutionary change both at home and abroad. He believed that the United States was destined to play the central role in the coming millennial age by reconciling two outcast groups. According to his biblical exegesis, Jews and Native Americans figured decisively in the coming perfection of the profane world. Boudinot believed that Native Americans had originally inhabited the Holy Land and migrated from there to Asia and then to North America. As the main body of Jews on Earth, Indian conversion to Christianity was crucial to millennial regeneration. Although this "sinful and suffering people, once so dear to the God of all the earth" experienced miserable decline in their transformation from Jews to Indians, for Boudinot they remained a "standing and unanswerable monument and proof of the truth of prophecy to all nations."[15] Boudinot's vision has too often been dismissed as a shallow cover for American nationalism and a bizarre justification for Indian conversion.[16] It may have been those things too, but Boudinot's genuine commitment to Indian, and thus Jewish, conversion underscores an essential feature of cosmopolitan evangelicalism—only by overcoming human diversity could it transform the nation and the world.

Such a massive project required enormous effort, and Boudinot and others realized that it demanded more than simply writing books. The trio of Burlington men who helped found the BSP in 1808 carried their enthusiasm for Bible societies to their own state when they helped to establish the New Jersey Bible Society (NJBS) the following year. This organization began with a heavy Presbyterian influence, as its initial plans were drafted at an "assembly of ministers of the Presbytery of New Brunswick and other gentlemen," yet from the start Burlington residents played a large role in the state Bible society. Elias Boudinot served as its first president until his death in 1821, and he was joined on its first board of managers by Joseph Bloomfield, the governor of the state, and Reverend Charles H. Wharton, while Joshua M. Wallace was active in several roles including as its agent for Burlington County.[17] These Burlington men all worshiped in Wharton's Episcopal church, though Bloomfield and Boudinot were Presbyterians. The nineteen NJBS members who can be located in Burlington tax and census records reveal a clear local profile: overwhelmingly affluent (fourteen in the top quintile of taxpayers and eleven in the top decile) and predominantly Episcopalian (ten, conservatively, to whom we might add Boudinot and Bloomfield).

The pan-Christian ideal of cosmopolitan evangelicalism constantly foundered on the reality that the movement appealed to some religious groups more than others. By insisting on distributing scripture "without notes or comments," the Bible movement made nonsectarianism central to its work. Similarly, it tried to prevent religious prejudice from affecting who received its charity. The NJBS's first rule for Bible distribution required that they be given "without any regard to the sect or denomination to which the receivers may severally belong."[18]

Boudinot's inaugural presidential address to the NJBS was infused with idealism about their profound opportunity to "supply the word of life" to mankind. This goal demanded that "the lovers of truth and righteousness of all denominations" participate in the new organization, which modeled itself on the great examples of the British and Foreign Bible Society and the new BSP. These Bible groups cooperated closely with one another and shared a deep belief in the power of the Bible to transform the world. As Boudinot emphasized in quoting a British and Foreign Bible Society leader, "wherever the religion of the Bible has appeared and prevailed in its purity, there you have the best laws, the best government, liberty more perfect, property more secure, human nature in a higher degree of civilization and man more happy and respectable." Boudinot called his audience to perform their "benevolent work . . . by dispensing . . . what is the richest gift in our power to bestow, the Holy Scriptures." Participation in the Bible movement meant becoming "fellow workers with God."[19] Such stirring calls mobilized cosmopolitan evangelicals in a transcendent cause with divine sanction.

Of course, implementing inclusive Christianity and creating such organizations proved more difficult. State-level NJBS leaders had a strong Presbyterian cast, while Burlington members were disproportionately Episcopalian. The managerial board recognized the interdenominational challenge in their first annual report, which stressed that county agents must be "gentlemen of character and integrity, but of various religious denominations, where they can with propriety be obtained."[20] The tension was clear as character, integrity, and propriety might override the pan-Christian goal.

The Bible movement's commitment to broad denominational outreach stretched beyond mere rhetoric, as a closer look at Burlington's NJBS membership reveals. Two prominent local Quakers played an important role supporting the new organization. Samuel Emlen Jr., a weighty Friend who had many administrative responsibilities in Quaker meetings, joined two Episcopalians as the NJBS' first agents in Burlington County, and he was very effective in raising funds among his fellow Friends. Their collective contribution of $168 in 1811 made up more than half the local donations that year.[21] Isaac Collins was also an early Quaker NJBS supporter. Collins shared a strong professional affinity with the new organization as a printer who had produced a handsome Bible in 1789. Although Emlen and Collins both served as NJBS agents, neither seems to have become a member, and in many ways Collins's participation in it paralleled his controversial role as a patriot printer during the Revolutionary War. Once again he joined a broadly popular cause that made many Quakers uneasy.[22] Generally speaking, the involvement of Delaware Valley Friends in the Bible movement was unusual and helped spur the Hicksite separation of the Society in the late 1820s, which we shall turn to in the final chapter.

Delaware Valley Friends had increasingly committed themselves to exacting group standards that implicitly, at least, prohibited the kind of interdenominational work at the center of the Bible movement. As one Bible society missionary noted, Friends had a "general opposition" to the cause, and he reported little success in Quaker areas.[23] Such a sweeping group characterization, however, is extreme. Quakers did accept the divine sanction of scripture, and in places like Burlington some Friends played a substantial role in the broader Bible movement. Nevertheless, they tended to participate from a distinctive Quaker perspective and mostly focused their reform efforts within their own religious group. The Burlington Preparatory Meeting for Women, for example, clearly knew about NJBS efforts and sympathized with them, for it conducted a survey of Quaker households in the summer of 1812 to ascertain "how many copies of the Bible it will be necessary to procure" in order to supply poor members with one.[24] Susanna Emlen, Samuel's wife, who was an active Friend in her own right, was named to this Quaker women's Bible committee. Interestingly, this committee may have been formed outside the regular operation of the Preparatory Meeting, as it has an irregular entry in the minute book. While many Burlington Quakers supported the goals of the

NJBS, identifying the Bible as the most essential element of Christianity departed too far from Quaker traditions for most Friends to participate directly in the movement.

That a women's meeting made the first institutional response to the Bible movement among Burlington Friends is not surprising given the breadth of women's involvement in evangelical reform. The earliest NJBS membership list included four Burlington women, and the male organizers of the state Bible group had anticipated a role for female members by ensuring that "he or she" could become members with an initial contribution of $4. Interestingly, the NJBS adopted this gender-inclusive policy at its founding in 1809, just two years after such language was removed from the franchise clause of the state constitution. While female membership may seem rather modest—and no woman is ever mentioned as attending its annual meetings—female participation expanded with the creation of the Burlington Female Bible Association in 1814.[25] As discussed later, women were essential to the Bible movement and cosmopolitan evangelical reform as a whole.

The NJBS received unparalleled early support from Burlington residents. The town provided twenty founding members, headed the list of subscribers in the society's manuscript minutes, and donated a large share of the statewide organization's initial annual contributions.[26] Not surprisingly, Burlington County agents reported in 1814 that "the city of Burlington and its neighborhood need but few Bibles" and only "the remote parts of the county are in want of considerable supplies."[27] The affluence of the town and its status as a focal point for local religious services were surely important to this prominence, as was the leadership of Elias Boudinot. A Burlington meeting of the NJBS on August 31, 1814, announced the first plans to create a national Bible organization. This national aspiration may have arisen from a dwindling sense of local purpose. While leaders like Boudinot, Wallace, and Wharton remained key Bible movement leaders in the state, the lack of local demand and Quaker attention to their own group limited sustained fervor in Burlington.

When the Bible Society of Delaware (BSD) organized in November 1813, it was the last state-level group to organize in the country, and it took another three years before their first report, public address, and constitution were printed for public distribution. These publications effectively recap the main thrust of the Bible movement that had been building throughout the nation, especially in the northeast. Most importantly, as the first article of its constitution explained, "the Society is intended to embrace persons of every Christian denomination, and therefore the Bible distributed by them, shall be without notes."[28] Probably because of the persistent bitterness of ethno-religious conflict in Delaware's public life throughout the Revolutionary period, the group took special care to emphasize its interdenominationalism that operated "without the least encroachment upon outward distinctions, and without compelling a single individual, to desert his own church, and pass over to another."[29]

The BSD wanted to reach all Christians to counter serious religious decline in the state. It warned that "the people are very destitute of the Bible" and "religion consequently languishes."[30] As Elias Boudinot also stressed, the spiritual crisis of the times demanded bold action to fulfill the divine plan for global regeneration. As the BSD exhorted, since "Bible-work has prospered among the heathen," it would truly work wonders "among our slumbering brethren."[31] The Bible movement everywhere aimed to speed the Second Coming of Christ.

John Latta, the BSD's first president, promised that the Bible's spiritual power could bridge all human divisions, and he addressed the relationship between religion and race directly. "What makes the difference between the Hottentot of Africa and the Christian of America? The Bible. This is the light which dispels the darkness, that covers the earth, and the gross darkness that overwhelms the people." In this formulation racial identity was extremely elastic, and Christian unity could embrace all those with access to the Bible. Indeed, Latta believed that the "most remarkable" work of the Bible movement was its "unparalleled and successful efforts . . . to translate the scriptures into different languages, and the uncommon zeal . . . to circulate them amongst all descriptions of people. Is not this the dawning of the future glory of Zion?"[32]

In addition to such promises, Latta also claimed that the Bible movement could heal more prosaic social divisions. The "union" in the movement "amongst the different denominations of Christians, is a powerful motive to encourage their establishment. Round the Bible, as a common standard, all Christians rally." The cause may have been explicitly spurred by a sense of religious crisis, but this dovetailed with the new fragmentation of partisan politics. By contrast, unity in the Bible movement would "bury party names and party creeds, and unite heart and hand for the promotion of the great common cause."[33]

Bible movement activists fused a pragmatic worldly plan with an idealistic spiritual vision as they furiously engaged their society. The American and French revolutions, with their rationalist and populist thrusts, as well as an increasing awareness of non-Christians in India, Asia, and Africa all provided evidence of the need for large-scale evangelical reform. As the BSD queried in its founding statement, "has any period of the world exhibited such wonderful testimonies of the concurrent progression of events, tending to the fulfillment of these promises?"[34] The key promise, of course, was that they might hasten the Second Coming of Christ. The union of everyday work with a transcendent goal shared some important impulses with the broad popular mobilization during the Revolutionary War, but Bible societies departed from that cause in significant ways. Most importantly, rather than collectively mobilizing all true Americans as patriots, the Bible movement, and cosmopolitan reform generally, organized around a basic divide that distinguished the dispensers of benevolence from the recipients of charity. As Elias Boudinot noted, "poor families" were to be sought out and assisted by those "in circumstances not merely of decent competency but of affluence."[35]

As the Bible movement engaged the world in unheralded ways, it could as easily alienate as assimilate. The book-centered Bible movement admitted only those with sufficient literacy to participate in the world of print culture and thus heightened social distinctions that separated respectable members of the new nation from a large group beneath them. Despite evidence of literacy rates among white men in the early republic as high as 85 percent, and white women's gradual increase from a rate of about 45 percent in 1790 to parity with white men by 1860, these figures are often based on overly technical definitions of literacy that overstate those with a sure command of reading.[36] While most individuals could sign their names on legal documents in the postwar era, this rough mark of literacy probably excludes the majority of Americans. Many recipients of Bible-movement charity would surely put the book to more talismanic uses than reformers intended, but printed texts had nevertheless become the crucial medium that connected the dispensers and recipients of evangelical moral reform.

All the U.S. Bible organizations owed a great deal to the shining example of the British and Foreign Bible Society (BFBS). The American Revolution had not completely severed transatlantic connections, and the movement shared a fundamental commitment to overcome diversity through respectable Christianity on both sides of the Atlantic. This sweeping cosmopolitan commitment to human improvement truly transcended provincial differences, even those of the emerging nation in the immediate postcolonial period. All the major Bible societies of this era coordinated their efforts and saw themselves as engaged in a common cause. Even in the midst of the War of 1812, the BSD contacted the British organization and described themselves as "a miniature likeness of yours." In response, the BFBS made a generous financial contribution to the Delaware group, as it also had done to the groups in Pennsylvania and New Jersey, and praised the cooperation of the movement "while the Nations of which they severally form a part were engaged in hostilities." Hopefully peace would bring "our Transatlantic brethren and ourselves closer to divine blessings and glory."[37]

Concerns with local diversity had also stimulated the formation of the BFBS. John Owen, its first secretary and historian, explained that its "primary creation" arose from "the scarcity of Welsh Bibles." As early as 1787, complaints had reached the Society for Promoting Christian Knowledge that non-English Bibles were too few and expensive, but the Anglican missionary body moved slowly, if at all, to respond to the need. By 1803 a group of evangelicals in the London-based Religious Tract Society began to act.

The personification of the Welsh Bible crisis lay in the probably apocryphal story of Mary Jones, which grew to mythic proportions as the origin legend of the BFBS. The little Welsh girl desired a Bible, and after saving enough money from her small earnings and walking a great distance to town to purchase a Bible in her native language, she discovered that none was available. Evangelicals in London sprang to action upon hearing of her dilemma. As one of the BFBS founders exclaimed, "Surely a Society might be formed for the purpose; and if . . . for Wales, why not also for the Empire and the world?"[38] An awareness of ethnic difference and how this isolated individuals from access to Bibles controlled by the Anglican establishment informed the creation of the first Anglo-American Bible society.[39]

BFBS founders also confronted the challenge of internal religious diversity from the outset. When three Quakers attended its first meeting, John Owen expressed surprise, as he believed that members of the Society of Friends "entertained only a qualified respect for the letter of Scripture; and that, consequently, the Bible was very little read and recommended among them." He soon learned better of his Quaker colleagues and noted that the BFBS encouraged the surmounting of religious prejudice through its inclusive Christian vision. From the start, the BFBS embraced Quakers and Germans as central to the movement. The Lutheran minister Reverend Steinkopf, who would become a significant early leader in the organization, addressed their first meeting about "the spiritual want of his German fellow-countrymen." Rather than encourage the separation of distinct religious groups along national, ethnic, linguistic, or theological lines, the evangelical BFBS was a "Catholic Institution" to "correct the errors into which Christians of every denomination have been betrayed in forming their judgment of each other."[40] The Bible movement in the United States shared the BFBS's inclusive strategy, and both were inspired by evangelical assimilation.

While British and American Bible societies shared many qualities, some differences set them apart from one another. When Owen dedicated his history to "the Right Honorable John, Lord Teignmouth," president of the BFBS, he signed himself "Your Lordship's Faithful servant." No acknowledgment of aristocratic preeminence would do in the postcolonial American republic. As an American Bible Society officer would explain to a leader of the movement in Delaware in comparing the British and American organizations, "The claims of rank and privilege are there admitted. Here you know they are not. We are all free and equal, and systems which are predicted upon a difference between classes in the community as higher and lower, rich and poor, are not palatable, if at all practicable."[41] Because the BFBS operated in a more structured and hierarchical society, its evangelical emphasis met opposition from traditional elites who saw its aims as fundamentally subversive. One Anglican critic of the BFBS charged in 1805 that it was the product of "the monster Jacobinism" that can be "detected lurking behind the cross."[42] Such an accusation would never be levied against U.S. Bible societies or their leaders. Rather than threatening to detract from the efforts of the established church, as in England, cosmopolitan evangelicalism in America built an institutional structure to bolster the nation.

American evangelicalism drew strength from the separation of religious and political authority in the new nation. As a result, moral reform in the United States operated outside government circles, unlike in Great Britain where they overlapped more regularly. Indeed, American reformers often accused government officials of opposing Christianity. As Elias Boudinot charged in his 1809 presidential address to the NJBS, "struggling for empire and panting after worldly dominion and fame" consumed political leaders who should have committed themselves to benevolent reform.[43] Bible societies offered participation in a more worthy project than base partisan politics. In a moving scriptural image that all the Bible societies regularly invoked, evangelicals were called upon to work toward an age when "the knowledge of the Lord shall cover the earth as the waters do the sea."[44]

The Bible movement proved enormously compelling for individuals who sought to purify a corrupt world by spreading Christianity and soon overflowed the boundaries of individual states. More than one hundred state and local Bible societies had been established by 1814 when Boudinot spearheaded a drive to establish a "General Association of the Bible Societies in the United States."[45] His circular letter to Bible societies throughout the country announced a Philadelphia meeting, yet the BSP rejected the call for a national society. Boudinot responded to William White's public objections by explaining that the overriding purpose of the general association was to avoid divisions and wasted effort among those laboring toward the same goal. To Boudinot, a national union would "destroy our little animosities and unite the prayers . . . of all Christians. Here we can all meet, forget our differences and recognize our common relation to the same divine master, and our common obligation to support his cause in our World."[46] Boudinot also employed a practical argument and had the towering example of the BFBS on his side. The British institution had originally encouraged the BSP to organize on a national basis and pledged financial support to assist such an undertaking. Furthermore, the expansive work of the BFBS included affiliates in Russia, Poland, and Germany. He chided the BSP managers that if the British had been able to rise "above these jealousies of rivalry," then surely Americans should not be held back "by the small consequences in the scale of states."[47]

Creating a national organization required expanding the BSP's commitment beyond the Delaware Valley. White condemned the national plan's proposed scope, and Boudinot took umbrage at White's disparaging use of the term "National Institution," deigning it a "slip of the pen" on the part of his opponent. After all, Boudinot argued, no "voluntary association, however enlarged their plan," could become a national institution "without being constituted by the government by charter." Boudinot drew on his long experience heading the U.S. Mint and knew from painful personal experience that a formal relationship to government would only taint the proposed Bible organization. He also charged that the BSP's objections were lawyerly and elitist, as they had only come from its managers and suspected that rank-and-file members supported the national vision.[48]

Pennsylvania Germans in the BSP leadership were especially steadfast in their opposition to the formation of a national Bible organization, whose scope they feared would undermine the mission to their ethnic brethren undertaken by the Philadelphia-based group. Between a fourth to a third of BSP annual reports were printed in German, and the organization carefully sought inexpensive German-language Bibles, usually from Halle in Saxony via the BFBS, as a central part of its efforts. When the BSP suffered financial difficulties in 1819, it reconsidered whether it should join the American Bible Society (ABS), and in the 9-to-5 vote to retain their independence, the Pennsylvania German bloc of two Lutheran and one German Reformed minister was key to rejecting affiliation with the national organization.[49] This wariness was quite prescient because the national organization would never appoint a Lutheran to its board of managers in the nineteenth century. As the historian Peter Wosh noted in his thoughtful assessment of the ABS, its managers shared "an aggressive Anglo-American consciousness."[50]

However pragmatic the BSP's opposition to the national movement may have been, it seemed provincial and backward looking to those championing the new organization. The American Bible Society's constitution proclaimed it as a novel undertaking that linked urgent nationalist and millennialist themes. Rather than attribute its origins to the worldly example of the BFBS, as the BSP had done eight years earlier, the ABS claimed birth from a particular crisis in American society as the "political world has undergone . . . stupendous" and "unexpected" changes that left "thoughtful men with the most boding anticipations." It condemned the horrid changes arising from "a period of philosophy, falsely so called," that had sprung up "under the imposing names of reason and liberality" that "attempt to seduce mankind from all which can bless." The ABS constitution unabashedly adopted a reactionary position against the creeping rationalism of the period. "We hail the re-action, as auspicious to whatever is exquisite in human enjoyment, or precious to human hope. We would fly to the aid of all that is holy, against all that is profane; of the purest interest of the community, the family, and the individual, against the conspiracy of darkness, disaster, and death—to help on the mighty work of Christian charity—to claim our place in the age of Bibles."[51] The ABS opposed the decline of religion that conservative evangelicals consistently identified as one of the grave unanticipated consequences of the American Revolution.

The organization justified its national scope as a means to overcome "local feelings, party prejudices, [and] sectarian jealousies [all of which] are excluded by its very nature." The breadth of the organization assured that such divisions "can find no avenue of admission." Just as Federalists in the late 1780s had argued for a stronger central government to limit local abuses by petty men, so the ABS sought religious harmony by organizing on a national scale. It posed the same rhetorical question that the BSP had asked years earlier: Should it organize as a "national Society, or by independent associations?" To ABS proponents the answer was obvious. "A national object unites national feeling and concurrence. Unity of a great system combines energy of effect with economy of means." Moreover, the national scheme allowed more direct access to an international arena for benevolence because "the Catholick efforts of a country, thus harmonized, give her a place in the moral convention of the world; and enable her to act directly on the universal plans of happiness which are now pervading the nations."[52]

The new institution believed it would help members to understand their place in the nation and in the course of global events. It called on members to look beyond the locality, mired in prejudice and small differences, to cast their actions with allied evangelicals throughout the country and the world. The rapid expansion of the ABS built effectively on this breathless vision of the benefits of the national organization. Stimulated by, and contributing to, the resurgent nationalism in the wake of the War of 1812, the ABS took off in dramatic fashion, swiftly adding auxiliaries throughout the country, particularly in the northeast, and distributing vast numbers of Bibles. Its early popularity was matched by impressive longevity, and it remains an active organization with an international scope to the present day.

The ABS helped make the contours of the nation more palpable, but it fundamentally relied on volunteer members in local and state auxiliaries. The ABS provided managerial guidance, technical expertise, and printed texts from its headquarters in New York City, but these resources amounted to nothing without active local members seeking out the needy. The rhetoric of national purpose provided inspiration, yet the work relied on individual efforts organized by local groups. While the national evangelical effort insisted that all could access a common identity as Bible-based Christians, local members confronted persistent local differences that could not be eradicated by such claims. Bible society members were fundamentally aware of the diversity of local life where they labored, even as their national priorities stressed American unity. The NJBS celebrated the formation of the new ABS in just such terms. It proved that "the nation is awakening from its slumbers" and would promote "the union of rank and talent, [and] of sex and age" by "promoting an institution whose noble aim is to *give* that valuable treasure, the BIBLE, to the destitute."[53]

The Bible movement's core goal of overcoming local diversity through the power of the Holy Book inspired widespread local activism. As one NJBS report explained, the Bible was the " 'sword of the spirit' . . . adapted to every age and nation—to every class and condition of man."[54] Because of its divine origins, the Bible could speak to all inhabitants of the United States regardless of their worldly differences, and Bible societies' annual reports helped establish this fact by cataloguing how the gift of the Bible united people distinguished by class, race, and gender. The ABS was founded as a reaction against the discord of early national society and culture. As Peter Wosh has aptly observed, in contrast to this surging Revolutionary diversity, the early Bible movement hoped to restore a "unified consensual society" by creating a "national culture, based on the Book."[55]

To understand the Bible movement's achievements and limitations, we need to look beyond an institutional perspective and the ideals of its leaders to understand what local Bible activists actually did and how they perceived their cause. Rather than labor to get new members to join, local reformers sought people to receive transformative charity. While the Bible movement, and moral reform generally, sought to overcome diversity through Christian unity, the very practice of seeking out people in need of benevolence helped to make the gulf separating the two groups apparent. The scholar Paul Gutjahr has similarly observed that the ABS's mass production of Bibles was supposed to bring the nation together around a single text, yet their work "greatly amplified the fragmentation of the American bible market."[56] If the cause of unity produced greater diversity in book production, the cultural difference that it also stimulated threatened the movement even more fundamentally.

The poor were, of course, the group most in need of Bible-based reform. Common seamen and African Americans were the most frequent representatives of the poor in Bible society annual reports. The NJBS celebrated its successful outreach to both groups and found mariners "not swearing, intoxicated, or disorderly, as is too frequently the case with this class of persons—but with decorum—*every man with a Bible under his arm.*" A similar transformation marked the "happy influence which the diffusion of scriptures has had on people of colour in the United States." The NJBS presented the Bible as working in tandem with slavery to civilize and Christianize a barbarous people. In slavery they had "learnt to be contented with their lot . . . and more faithful," and now as free people the Bible was even more essential, as they might lose their way without the positive structure supposedly provided by bondage and a master's Christian guidance. "Where [blacks] have been in enjoyment of freedom, the influence of the

Bible has kept them from degrading vices and profligate companions, and has made them more estimable in domestic life—and more useful as members of Society."[57] The behavior of working seamen, slaves, and free blacks challenged Christian unity, but conservative evangelicals reported major advances as the Bible restrained, and even overcame, these differences.

The Bible Movement and Pennsylvania Germans

Racial and economic difference would prove more difficult to reconcile in a united American Christianity than such optimistic reports claimed, and other challenges troubled evangelical reformers as well. The increasingly national orientation of the Bible movement under ABS leadership included a strong Anglo-American cast to its Christian sensibility. The ABS embrace of British evangelicals as "of one blood with the most of ourselves" is particularly striking in the immediate aftermath of the War of 1812.[58] Unlike the inaugural statements of the BFBS, BSP, or NJBS, the new national organization did not initially emphasize a commitment to distribute Bibles in languages other than English. Such an organization could make little headway in places such as Easton where Pennsylvania Germans predominated.

The BSP retained its independence from the ABS, and the creation of the new national organization spurred the Philadelphia-based group to strengthen its auxiliaries throughout the state. As it moved into Pennsylvania German areas surrounding the metropolis, the BSP faced increasing tension between an older Episcopal leadership, epitomized by its president, Bishop William White, and the religious cultures of inhabitants in more rural places. The gulf separating Pennsylvania Germans and cosmopolitan Anglo-American reformers did not only appear over language differences but also reflected fundamentally different ways of understanding the Bible movement's place in history. The annual reports of most Bible societies included considerable praise for international efforts in the cause. This global dimension encouraged praise for the czar's support for Bible societies in Petersburg and Moscow and descriptions of ships carrying Bibles to Canton, which were repeatedly announced in the annual publications of all the societies.

The place of Bible societies in Germany, however, raised a potentially unsettling, if not controversial, issue, because they threatened to push Anglo-American institutions into a secondary role in the millennial drama. In 1818, the BSP dutifully reported that it had received pamphlets from eleven Bible societies in German cities, "all of which appear to be in successful operation" but that otherwise provided "no information of a very interesting nature." Nevertheless, the BSP noted that the Bible Institute at Halle, Saxony, had a standing press that had been issuing Protestant imprints since 1712—more than two million Bibles and nearly one million New Testaments.[59] The leading role played by German-speaking people in the Reformation and their initiation of vernacular Bibles were all the more evident in 1817 with the celebration of the tercentenary of Martin Luther's launching of the Reformation. The scant attention that the BSP granted to the Halle Bible Institute is especially notable because the Pennsylvania group relied on Halle for its German texts.[60] Despite this reliance and the early foundation of Halle, the BSP still trumpeted the BFBS as "the acknowledged parent of all similar institutions in every quarter of the earth."[61]

The BSP sponsored a missionary tour in 1819 by the Episcopal reverend Samuel Bacon to establish auxiliary Bible societies in places such as Northampton County where none yet existed. During his sixty-nine-day journey he preached seventy-four times and covered one thousand miles.[62] His account highlights the challenges the Philadelphia-centered institution faced as it organized in the Pennsylvania German hinterland. Bacon stressed that many rural people doubted the ability of human action to bring about the millennial changes that the Bible movement promised. When Bacon preached about the need for a "universal extension" of the Bible to hasten the "final triumph of the *church* of Christ," many responded, "He will accomplish it in *His own time and manner.*" In short, the public Bacon encountered judged proselytizing to be "work for God alone," an attitude especially in keeping with Lutheran belief in justification by grace and not through good works.[63]

Bacon rejected such antievangelical views because "the gospel is to be disseminated by human instrumentality and that it is the work *chiefly of Protestant Christendom.*" To him the Bible served as "*the most effectual instrument of civilization*" and offered "*a remedy for all the diseases that affect the body politic.*" Proponents of the Bible movement like Bacon saw it as a weapon against the false philosophy of reason. To him, the Bible reached "the heart, to reform and purify" rather than as "a speculative notion for the head, to enlighten . . . and increase its ideas."[64] In seeing the Bible as the centerpiece of experience-based reform, Bacon stood closer to popular religious understanding than a figure like Boudinot, who, for all his significance as a national leader, never undertook missionary work himself.

As Bacon traveled across the countryside, he recognized that the Bible movement depended upon engaging a populist impulse based in experiential religion. Nevertheless, he clearly spoke from a position of authority and with a distinctive denominational perspective. Much like John Latta's preference for a Calvinist style, Bacon noted that his own "mode of worship peculiar to the Episcopal Church" opened other church doors "with alacrity." Furthermore, "the Bench and the Bar . . . patronized his mission" and provided his strongest support.[65] Bacon received his fullest aid from Episcopal, legal, and judicial leaders—standard-bearers of traditional authority.

Support from such quarters must have given Bacon a distinctly Anglo-

American quality when he visited Pennsylvania German areas. A comic oration printed in an Easton newspaper the same year as Bacon's tour underscores the challenges he faced in such places. The satire lampooned conservative evangelical goals by putting their moral and nationalist claims into the voice of Theophilus Drunkard, who argued that the "virtue of Drunkenness" would allow "our infant republic" to achieve greatness. The fulfillment of drunken "masculine virtue," however, was inhibited "by the study of biblical literature," which "enfeebled" the "native virtues" of "young men." Theophilus called "in the name of patriotism" for the Bible activists to desist and pay more attention to their own "ecclesiastical assemblies" that "demand the exercise of their talents."[66] This satire brilliantly subverted Bible movement themes to cast doubt on its legitimacy. That evangelicals should confine themselves to the spiritual sphere of their own denominations resonated among Pennsylvania Germans who were deeply suspicious of the intrusive claims made by Anglo-American moral reformers.

Two popular travel writers in the period praised the opposition to evangelical reform that they saw championed by people of German descent. J. K. Paulding complained about superstitious Americans who "believe in those delectable little tracts to be found in taverns and steamboats, in which children are converted at four years old, and special interpositions of Providence are quoted to supply [the populist Methodist itinerant] Lorenzo Dow with a pair of breeches. . . . Whatever may be the imaginary, the greater portion of the real denizens of this part of the country are mere matter-of-fact Germans; four square, solid, and deliberative smokers, as e'er put a pipe in mouth, or carried a tin tobacco box."[67] Anne Royall similarly celebrated the common sense of Pennsylvania Germans, which made their communities one of the few places in the nation where she could escape the "gripping fangs of these maruad[ing] . . . missionaries."[68]

Such one-sided depictions misrepresent the diversity of opinion among Pennsylvania Germans, and towns such as Easton were certainly far from homogeneous in the early nineteenth century. The Northampton Bible Society (NBS) was founded in Easton as an auxiliary of the BSP in 1820, perhaps as a result of Reverend Bacon's missionary visit the previous year. It began modestly with twenty-three English texts and six German ones distributed the first year and called on people of all Christian denominations throughout the county to join in "administer[ing] to the spiritual wants of immortal souls, [rather] than to the material necessities of perishing bodies." Also central to this initial public statement was a call for women to take a lead role because "the females of Northampton county, will not suffer themselves to be outdone in any exertion of Christian benevolence."[69] When the Female Bible Association of Easton was founded the next year, the county society explained that "the female heart, formed for benevolent and humane exertion" would play a central role in the movement.[70] Women's participation was a definitive feature of the Bible movement.

The creation of Easton's Bible societies owed a great deal to Samuel Sitgreaves (fig. 17). Like Elias Boudinot, the Federalist Sitgreaves had withdrawn from formal politics during the Jeffersonian era and turned to religious work.[71] His known participation in evangelical reform began with the formation of the town's Sunday school, which began receiving texts from the BSP in 1817. The school aimed to instruct poor children, "those little bands of triflers, who are the pest and annoyance of society on the Sabbath," and its enrollment more than doubled to two hundred students when it provided clothing as well as religious instruction to those who attended. By providing the "rising generation" with religious books to bring home, the school extended its efforts to include "reforming an impious father, or irresolute mother."[72]

Sitgreaves was also the driving force behind the formation of the Episcopal church in Easton. He served as its lay reader until an ordained minister was sent to the town in 1820, and the congregation met in a house that he owned until Sitgreaves donated the land and designed the Trinity Episcopal Church building. Almost every NBS report extracted in BSP records arrived from Sitgreaves, who announced in 1821 that "the Bible cause was gaining ground in Northampton County."[73]

Sitgreaves's public face often seems stern, but he revealed a playful side in letters to his daughter Susan, who often stayed with family in Philadelphia for extended periods. He supported her desire to spend time there and often made light of the narrow society in their hometown. When Susan had the opportunity to take the measure of Reverend John Rodney before he was sent to Easton as its first Episcopal minister, Sitgreaves wrote her to inquire

whether he is handsome, whether he is agreeable and sociable, whether he understands music, and some of us go so far as to enquire whether he is a good Preacher, that is to say whether he has good eyes and a good voice. If you can answer all these questions affirmatively, why then, we may hope to see the young Ladies at Church again. As to his Piety, his Orthodoxy, his Learning and such outlandish qualities, I cannot say that I have heard much Solicitude expressed about them, nor indeed is it a Matter of much Importance. If he can only *please* us, we will take care of our own *Improvement*. Indeed, we are all of us already so good, that we do not require mending. But we are sadly in want of *Entertainment*.[74]

While this letter certainly reveals Sitgreaves's wit and able pen, it also demonstrates his self-consciousness as a reformer who struggled against popular attitudes that he believed superficial if not irreligious.

The profile of NBS leaders in Easton highlights the narrow range of town residents who became moral reformers. Not surprisingly, almost every known member was affluent, with 50 percent from the top decile of taxpayers in 1830, while the poorest two (from the middling quintile) were both ministers. The religious affiliation of members is even more revealing, with 69 percent of members from Easton's new non-German churches. Despite the Episcopal commitments of Sitgreaves and Bacon, Presbyterians had the strongest NBS presence with 44 percent of its leaders. This may have resulted from annual meetings being held in the session room of Easton's Presbyterian church, but, whatever the cause, the NBS's call for "friends of the Society of whatever denomination" was not heeded.[75]

NBS members struggled to achieve the success that the Bible movement experienced elsewhere. As the group noted at its second annual meeting, "our publick journals are so replete with the triumphs of the cause," but local progress was disappointingly limited to Moravians and women. They declined "to add anything more" about their work because any claims "will be deemed but a reiteration of what we daily hear and read." Only a handful of individuals in Easton's Female Bible Association are known by name, but none was Pennsylvania German and most—including Susan Sitgreaves, S. C. P. Bishop (the widow of the town's first Presbyterian minister), and Lucy Hicks (the wife of Easton's second long-term Episcopal minister)—had close family ties to male evangelicals.

While the local Bible movement was primarily an Anglo-American phenomenon, Easton's Pennsylvania German ministers did play a role in it. The Lutheran pastor John Peter Hecht opened the annual meeting in 1821 with a sermon, and the Reformed pastor Thomas Pomp served as NBS president in 1831. Although some Pennsylvania Germans participated in the Bible movement, this represented a departure from the dominant ethno-religious pattern. For instance, the Lutheran Ministerium fumbled to explain the meaning of the word *tract* at its annual meeting in 1818.[76] Clearly, if the more cosmopolitan hierarchy of the church struggled to explain one of the central tools of evangelical reform, most ordinary Pennsylvania Germans viewed the movement as skeptical outsiders.

While the figures extracted from BSP annual reports give only a general sense of the Bible movement in Northampton County, the fact that the NBS ordered 264 German texts versus 189 English ones from 1817 to 1829 makes plain that local circumstances required that the Bible movement concentrate on Pennsylvania Germans here. Yet such outreach only mildly softened the Bible movement's Anglo-American style. Cosmopolitan evangelical inroads often prompted resistance fueled by ethno-religious imperatives that rejected the assimilating American Christianity sought by reformers.

The Bible Movement and Women's Activism

Unlike the somewhat intrusive situation of the NBS in Easton, with its limited appeal to Pennsylvania Germans, New Castle residents were members and leaders of the BSD in far greater numbers than their proportion in the overall population. This heady participation in the Bible movement also occurred among many Burlington residents who embraced the NJBS. The inhabitants of both former colonial capitals may have sought to reclaim something of their former public significance via the Bible movement, and in both places leading local men were the first presidents of their state organizations. The general profile of New Castle BSD members is particularly notable because only here did the movement draw people from most segments of white society in roughly equal numbers. While Burlington and Easton Bible reformers were disproportionately wealthy and political conservatives, the Bible movement in New Castle was much more balanced. Out of 159 founding members of the state society, 22 can be precisely identified in the New Castle tax list for 1815. The wealthiest men in town joined the BSD in the greatest numbers (45 percent of local members were from the top quintile of taxpayers), but others from all economic ranks joined too, with nearly a third from the middling quintile. Five known Democratic Republicans and three known Federalists were New Castle BSD members, roughly in keeping with the town's balanced partisanship. The Bible movement in Delaware clearly strove to be bipartisan, as suggested by its 1828 annual meeting where either the former Republican congressman, Willard Hall, or the current Federalist one, Kensey Johns Jr., would speak.[77]

The religious profile of New Castle Bible reformers tilted toward Presbyterianism, as it did in much of the national Bible movement and in the other river towns studied here. This orientation should be expected in New Castle where the Presbyterian church was especially active (unlike in Easton where they were a small minority of newcomers) and because its local minister, John Latta, was the organization's president. Roughly speaking, one-half of known BSD members in New Castle were Presbyterians, and the remainder divided evenly between Episcopalians and those who participated in both denominations. This high rate of mixed religious affiliation, more than double that of the overall taxed population, and the socioeconomic and partisan balance of New Castle BSD members suggest that the Bible movement here had begun to achieve the kind of unified American Christianity so important to the cause.[78]

Although Episcopal leaders often saw their institution as the most reasonable middle course for Christian unity, Presbyterianism was better suited to gain broad support in the new nation as a long-standing church that still embraced many aspects of the new nation's surging populist evangelicalism. Under the pastoral guidance of John Latta since 1800, New Castle's Presbyterian congregation grew in size as well as affluence. By 1815 Presbyterians were the largest religious group among the town's wealthiest taxpayers. Their 35 percent of the top taxpaying quintile that year marked a substantial change from a mere 9 percent in 1776, and this shift may even undercount the growing respectability of local Presbyterianism because many in the disproportionately wealthy mixed religious affiliation group had probably come to think of themselves as Presbyterians in the first two decades of the nineteenth century. Some of the radical connotations of Presbyterianism in New Castle during the Revolutionary War had begun to wane as this local religious group played a leading role in conservative evangelical reform.

Of all the ways that the BSD engaged a fuller range of American society than the other Bible groups considered here, none is as striking as the prominence of women in the Delaware movement. Almost one-fifth of BSD founding members were women, among them four from New Castle. The sudden emergence of a prominent role for women in early national moral reform was linked to the creation of modern American political culture and its relationship with economic, religious, ethnic, and racial formation in the new nation.[79] When Episcopal bishop William White addressed the newly formed Female Bible Society of Philadelphia in 1814, he predictably stressed the great advantages of the interdenominational Bible movement for "promoting unity of affection" among those otherwise divided by "irreconcilable differences of opinion." The unifying force of evangelical reform had initially emphasized denominational differences, but the drive toward union soon led to a more startling sense of who should participate in the movement. White reasoned that if forging unity from difference was one of the Bible movement's chief goals, "can any scruple be well founded, which would restrict the benefit to men?" He concluded, "I will not suffer myself to believe, that your sex, any more than ours, are debarred from promoting these blessed ends."[80] As an ABS official explained a few years later, he expected that "the most efficient conductors of the details of the Bible Society . . . will be females. The details of a beneficial distribution require a zeal, an assiduity and a patience and leisure and Condescention which females posses in a greater degree than men."[81] Such sentiments soon led to the widespread formation of female Bible organizations including ones in Burlington (1816), Easton (1821), and New Castle (1822). The extraordinary institutional presence of women in gender-specific reform organizations throughout the country made conservative evangelicalism a dynamic and lasting movement.

By working as evangelical reformers, respectable women demonstrated that they had a major public, and therefore political, role to play in the new nation. Women's place in the Bible movement was not as degenerate recipients of evangelical charity but as dispensers of light. This hierarchy of who dispensed benevolence and who needed reformation is an important indicator of who stood at the center of cosmopolitan evangelicalism and who fell at its margins. The mobilization of two state Bible organizations is instructive. The NJBS reached out to sailors, children, and blacks as needing aid, while the BSP made even broader efforts to Cherokees, Pennsylvania Germans, sailors, and new settlers in the west. Women were mentioned in such accounts only as the agents of reform, not as its ob-jects.[82] Respectable women crucially contributed to the Bible movement's effort to overcome local diversity by creating American Christianity.

A rich collection of New Castle Female Bible Society (NCFBS) material permits a close analysis of women's increasing role in the movement and how they used it to forge a central place for themselves in the nation. Founded in 1822 as a direct auxiliary to the ABS (thus bypassing the BSD), the group's first public announcement demonstrated the degree to which its members understood themselves to deserve full access to public space and attention. When they met in a public hall on the New Castle com-mons, they recorded their proceedings and printed two hundred copies of their constitution for public distribution. Such actions bespoke a new con-ception of women's ability and right to participate as responsible and in-dependent members of American society.

The legitimation of their work with a written constitution indicates one way that Revolutionary political culture had altered life for some women in the new nation. The constitution announced the names of its twenty-one initial members as an inducement for others to join. In a manner parallel to what members of the Union Church of Africans had accomplished, these women created an institution that demonstrated a fuller commitment to participate in national public life than they had during the colonial period.

Like other voluntary societies, the NCFBS elected officers at its next public meeting, yet in one significant way it altered the leadership style of most male-dominated organizations of the period. The NCFBS broadened its leadership corps to include a majority of its members. Sixty women at-tended the first meeting recorded in the minutes, among whom six were elected as officers and thirty elected to serve on the board of directors, producing more leaders than rank-and-file members.[83] Women in the NCFBS organized on more equal terms than their male counterparts, who maintained sharper status divisions within the movement.

The NCFBS's inclusive leadership partly arose from the exclusive nature of its membership that was predominantly from the upper range of the town's social structure. Three-fourths of the seventy-two members listed in the minutes from 1822 to 1830 came from families that can be located in local tax lists. Eighty-five percent of the known members came from the top two tax quintiles. As might be expected, the large leadership class was even wealthier. All seven of the officers whose families can be found in the tax lists came from the top two quintiles, six of them from the very richest families in town. Almost none of the members who belonged to families taxed in the bottom half of the social structure ever achieved leadership roles. The class differences within the NCFBS were quite sharp. Its leader-ship almost unanimously came from the upper half of the town's social structure, while fully a third of rank-and-file members (a relatively small group in this leadership-heavy institution) were from the bottom half.

NCFBS members were more affluent than BSD members for interlocking ideological and practical reasons. The female group broke new ground as an organization in which women contributed to the public good by working outside their own households. Female benevolent organizations made novel claims about the propriety of their collective action as women, and they drew members mostly from leading local residents whose economic status reinforced their claim to be dispensers of charity. A practical reason also explains the exclusive nature of the NCFBS. Because members had to pay two dollars to join and would be fined for missing meetings, they had to have sufficient wealth and leisure time to participate. Only those with a substantial degree of financial stability could devote the time and money necessary to join such an organization. Finally, the ideals and work of the Bible movement probably had more appeal for affluent women as they developed new social codes of Christian respectability as the most important mark of distinction in their community and nation.

Networks of leading families supplied the male and female activists who created the Benevolent Empire. Nine leading New Castle families played an essential role in evangelical reform there, sending twelve men to the BSD and eighteen women to the NCFBS. These key evangelical families were exclusively from the upper tier of the local social structure, with eight in the top quintile and one from the second. The women from these evangelical households contributed decisively to the leadership of the NCFBS, with sixteen of the eighteen serving as officers or directors, and they filled five of the nine most prominent leadership positions through 1830.[84]

Even New Castle's highest taxed business in 1826, the Union shipping line owned by Thomas and John Janvier, was associated with evangelical reform through the participation of its owners and three female family members. The Union Line also exemplifies how evangelical reformers harnessed technological progress to advance its cause, as it offered Bibles for passengers to read and also ferried Bibles from Philadelphia to New Castle for local distribution.[85] As the Union steamships helped draw New Castle closer to cosmopolitan Philadelphia by reducing travel time and freeing ships from dependence on wind and tides, evangelical reform also drew men and women close together in a shared campaign to improve their world.

The rare poor women in the NCFBS leadership appear to result from their relationship to the town's leading evangelical families. In one known case an NCFBS leader was a local resident too poor to be taxed. Miss Eliza Harvey was a founding member and served on the board of directors. Her ability to achieve such prominence likely arose from her service as a domestic servant in George Read Jr.'s household, one of the nine leading evangelical families in town.[86] Domestic servants such as Harvey and other

New Castle residents of ordinary means certainly participated in the popular evangelicalism of the early republic along with the leading families who championed cosmopolitan reform. Elizabeth Booth described her family nurse, Sally Meekimson, as a crucial figure in her own spiritual development. Meekimson decisively shaped Booth's upbringing, and she recalled that although her nurse "possessed no learning or worldly wisdom . . . she was 'made wise unto salvation.'"[87] Meekimson never joined the NCFBS, but she helped form Booth's spirituality, perhaps most directly in sharing a devotion to religious music, which her charge later formalized by compiling and publishing a collection of hymns.[88]

Booth used similar language to describe the religious devotion of the servant Meekimson and a slave that her family had freed. The former female slave was "one of the best and most exemplary Christians I ever knew, though she could neither read nor write. 'The law was written in her heart.'"[89] New Castle residents of modest economic standing, such as Meekimson and members of the Union Church of Africans, helped forge the religious culture of a town that largely welcomed moral reform, but only in rare instances did people with limited financial means become active in its institutions.

The actions of NCFBS members amounted to much more than an exertion of elite hegemony. From the start it organized a Committee of the Destitute, whose members operated in pairs to call at the houses of the poor to "ascertain their condition as to Bibles." The committee divided New Castle at Harmony Street, with one group to canvas the north end of town and the other the south. Two months later they presented their report to the Society. Unfortunately, the report has not been preserved, but it led the NCFBS to order four dozen inexpensive New Testaments at a cost of $.25 per copy and four large Bibles to be sold for $2.00.[90] The early days of the institution were heady times; as the NCFBS secretary explained to an ABS agent, "we are sorry to trouble you again so soon for another supply of Bibles." Additional money had been collected from subscriptions, and, more urgently, "there is still a demand for Bibles, or, more particularly for testaments." The order was filled in New York just two days later, bringing sixty-four texts for the spiritual care of the poor in New Castle.[91]

Two years later the NCFBS reported a "pleasing occurrence" that reveals their aspirations. Influenced by the circulation of moral tales in the popular religious tract literature of the period, and following the plot of the tale of the Welsh girl whose Bible crisis led to the formation of the BFBS, an account told of a little boy who resided several miles outside of New Castle. After saving money for a long period, he walked into town, located an NCFBS member, and explained to her that he had come to purchase a New Testament. When she asked if he would prefer to receive it as a gift, "he hesitated a moment, but soon replied, I had rather purchase it." Here was a pressing need that the NCFBS could fill. As the NCFBS secretary

Elizabeth Booth noted, if the boy's "anxiety to possess the word of God, proceeded from a real desire to read and practice it," then "the fruit may appear in future time, when this little incident shall have been long forgotten." This event especially suited women reformers, as Booth continued, "in this way, the retiring female, without stepping from her proper sphere, may send 'the gospel to every creature'; [and] spread the knowledge of Christ from sea to sea, and shore to shore."[92]

NCFBS members confronted the reality of local diversity in their daily work. The people they contacted defined precisely those groups that cosmopolitan reformers hoped to reshape as moral Christians. More than simply demonstrating that the poor and African Americans occupied important places in local life, the NCFBS encouraged new types of relationships between respectable women and those defined as needy. As these women went door to door to find destitute individuals, they encountered people strikingly different from themselves. They approached blacks and whites, men and women, a host of individuals identified by institutional locations in ships and in the county jail, and soldiers stationed in the town.

A quarter of the destitute people that these women reformers worked with from 1822 to 1830 were identified as "coloured," which roughly corresponds to the local proportion of African Americans. Given higher illiteracy among blacks just emerging from slavery, as well as their likely reticence to negotiate with white women calling at their doors, the NCFBS appears to have been quite successful in contacting black residents. The most detailed account of their fieldwork appears from the summer of 1825. A town survey discovered six destitute white families, one headed by a woman, and another seven "coloureds," five of whom had female heads. The NCFBS apparently found it easier to contact black women than black men. White and black Bible recipients also received different treatment from one another. The white families were judged destitute and received Bibles as gifts, while all seven African Americans purchased their Bibles. Their subscription terms required a $1 payment, probably half the total cost, before the book would be delivered.[93]

Perhaps the NCFBS discriminated against black clients by requiring partial payment before delivery; however, when the Bible recipients are located in local tax and census records, it appears that the black recipients may indeed have been more stable and better prepared to purchase the Bibles. Only two of the six white families can be identified in local records, and only a single white man, William Harrison, appears in both tax and census records. He headed a six-person household with a free white woman of his same age, between thirty and thirty-nine years, with four additional members of the household, all younger than fourteen, presumably their children. If William Harrison was the most stable white recipient of NCFBS largess in 1825, he still lacked long ties to the community, as he was one of only six unnaturalized aliens there in 1830.

Unlike the whites who mostly failed to appear in local records, five of the seven African Americans can be located, four of them in both tax and census records. As was the case with the two whites, all five tax-paying blacks were assessed at the lowest local rate. The NCFBS reached people at the bottom of the social structure. Family size reinforces our sense of the social distance separating NCFBS members from the households they visited. The ability to maintain a large household was closely related to wealth, and most households receiving Bibles consisted of just two persons, or included children still too young to be bound out for service. All the Bible recipients were quite young, with the exception of Susan Liston, a black woman older than fifty-five years of age, who appears in Emperor Liston's household in 1830. The relationship between household size and economic standing is best demonstrated in comparing the average size of varied households: leading evangelical households (10.5), average household size in New Castle (6), independent black households (4), and Bible recipients (3.5).

At its best, the evangelical impulse encouraged people to universalize their understanding of humanity and to recognize that individuals shared common interests and needs. Women in the NCFBS certainly reached out aggressively to economic and racial outsiders. While they committed themselves to focus on local residents, no town was sealed off from the outside world, especially an active seaport like New Castle with its many common sailors and their families. Given the prevailing sense of shipboard life as brutally laborious and inescapably masculine, it is surprising to discover that NCFBS members boarded ships. In August 1830 "some Ladies" of the society learned that the *Kensington*'s "crew were destitute of Bibles" while the ship was lying off New Castle. After confirming this situation, they granted the crew three Bibles and a dozen testaments. Lieutenant Hudson wrote that his "sensation" of appreciation to the Society was "doubly enhanced from the circumstances of our having left Philadelphia without a supply" of Bibles. Surely some of the crew were religiously inclined, but their spirituality seemingly did not require ready access to the Bible. As an earnest ally of respectable reform, Hudson assured the NCFBS benefactors that he would play his part "in the performance of so sacred a duty." The book alone might work miracles, but human action could spur salvation, and Hudson offered to "impress on those that receive them, the necessity of an attentive perusal and adherence to their sacred contents."[94] In reaching out to common seamen and African Americans, NCFBS members participated in a social movement that redefined their own place in the social order. By working in the streets, on the docks, and on ship decks, female Bible society members defined themselves in contrast to those deemed needy.

Female Bible societies were at the vanguard of shaping middle-class respectability. While early industrialization began to detract from the household as the primary center of work, and formal politics was becoming ever more boisterously a realm for democratic conflict among men, religion's traditional centrality to public authority helped respectable women to shape their rapidly changing world. For all the traditionalism of Christian authority, members of the NCFBS understood that their institution and their actions boldly departed from previous understandings of proper female behavior. By taking to the streets as social activists and legitimating their work in institutional form, women in the Bible movement asserted their right to rule over much more than just the parlor.

The minutes and letter book kept by Elizabeth Booth, the NCFBS's diligent corresponding secretary, help to reveal what motivated its members. Her fine hand and command of language attest that she was well educated, highly skilled, and perfectly suited to be the public voice of the organization, a role she filled from 1822 until her death in 1884. The Booths were among the most prominent evangelical families in New Castle. Her wealthy Federalist father, James Booth, was an officer in the BSD who would fail in his bid to be governor in 1822, while her mother, Ann, was the first president of the NCFBS. Whereas the parents were active in the local Episcopal church, under the spiritual guidance of Ann Booth's brother from 1788 to 1824, Elizabeth was a member of the local Presbyterian congregation.

Elizabeth Booth's first NCFBS letters went to ABS officials in New York City to announce their formation and intention to affiliate with the national society. In both letters she carefully justified why they had organized as a specifically female society, although each offered a somewhat different explanation. To Reverend Woodhull, the ABS secretary of domestic correspondence, she relied on scriptural justification. Drawing on a familiar biblical image widely invoked to describe women's work in the Bible movement, Booth noted, "we trust, that He who approved of the widow's mite when she cast into the treasury all she possessed, will not overlook our humble desire, and weak efforts, to aid in enriching the poor with the 'pearl of great price.'" Two days later she wrote John Nitchie, the ABS distribution agent, in a more businesslike manner that emphasized their social motivations. Along with $56 for their initial purchase of sixty texts, she explained that "the females of the town of New Castle" had organized "with a wish to emulate the good example set them by so many of their sex in different places."[95]

By choosing letters as their central means of communication, rather than printing annual reports like those of the male-dominated Bible societies considered here, the NCFBS utilized a more feminine means of public expression. Yet these letters still celebrated their contribution to the dawning of a millennial age made possible by print culture. The 1824 epistolary annual report penned by Booth admitted that they had "as yet been disappointed" in their local effort, but still deemed their work essential as it connected them to the Reformation's gradual effort to end the era when "the Bible was a treasure hid from the people, and accessible only to the clergy." "By means of the art of printing," the Bible spread into so many languages and nations that it "reminds us of the miraculous gift of tongues conferred on the Apostles, when 'every man heard in his own language the wonderful works of God.'" Bible movement participants took action because sacred and profane time seemed united in their own day. Booth continued, "the time has arrived, when everyone calling himself a Christian may possess a Bible," read and meditate on it daily, and thus "form his character on those pure and perfect precepts." Setbacks for the local organization hardly mattered given the global increase of the "knowledge of Revelation" that would inaugurate "the millennial season."[96]

NCFBS members had a strong sense of their distinctiveness as a female organization. Still frustrated by the limited success a few years later, Booth wrote despairingly, "Can a little band of females be instrumental in sending the gospel over the earth?" The rhetorical question prompted a resoundingly affirmative response: "Yes!—let not our zeal grow cold, let us go on joyfully, while we remember how much the gospel has done for us."[97] Such commitments to evangelical reform helped these women to refashion female identity in the early republic.

The striking emergence of female moral reform led to both praise and condemnation. One New Jersey newspaper cited it as a mark of national progress. Women who are "exhibited as the mere servile instrument of convenience or pleasure" were backward and un-Christian, while Bible women were "the equal, the companion, the help mate of man."[98] NCFBS members linked their Christian equality to national progress by comparing themselves with widows in India who were burned alive on funeral pyres. These heathen women, "degraded almost to the level of irrational animals," provided a foil for female Bible reformers and a compelling reason to spread the Bible cause throughout the world.[99]

The innovative quality of female reform also opened it to attack. The popular writer J. K. Paulding, for example, complained about his own aunt who belonged to "six-and-forty charitable societies" and still hungered to join more. In contrast to such foolish public activities, he praised Quaker women for their quiet good works within their own families. To him, "the exercise of benevolence" had spread too far; women had "duties to perform at home" and "ought to leave public charities to men." Much like Theophilus Drunkard's defense of masculine drinking from the onslaught of evangelical effeminacy, Paulding condemned women reformers for being "efficient members of some odd society for the propagation of—anything but the human species."[100] Once again sexuality proved a key terrain for condemning one's opponents as aberrant. A husband who shared Paulding's traditional sense of female domestic propriety would have been an unbearable partner for a woman reformer. Not surprisingly, the most active of them drew support from evangelical families who helped them to craft an impressive sense of female independence and autonomy and to institutionalize it within cosmopolitan evangelical reform.

The NCFBS helped build the Benevolent Empire by supporting other local reform groups. In addition to linking New Castle to the ABS headquarters in New York, the movement drew together five separate Bible societies in Delaware that all cooperated closely.[101] In addition, local Sunday schools organized for colored students and three separate categories of whites: male, female, and poor. Leaders of the New Castle Sabbath School Society, a merger of the three schools for white children, confirm that a handful of evangelical families institutionalized local benevolence. Out of the nine evangelical families with members in both the BSD and NCFBS, seven also participated in the local Sunday school.[102] More importantly, their evangelical outreach to children united white boys and girls and forgave tuition to poor whites, yet pointedly excluded free blacks. Moral reform furthered white racial solidarity, while downplaying economic difference, and thus reinforced central developments in national political culture.

The New Castle Sunday School Union made these connections explicit. The school's integrative purpose followed the political mandate of "our government—[that] all have equal rights. . . . In this country the children of all should occasionally associate together upon an equal footing. The rich and the poor derive great, perhaps equal benefit from this," as only "fatal delusions" arise from "associating with their own class exclusively." The organization's self-identification as a "union" society referred to its "various denominations of Christians—Episcopalians, Baptists, Methodists, Presbyterians, Congregational. There is no danger therefore to any denomination," because it only taught the "great, universal and undeniable truths of the Christian religion."[103] Although no Pennsylvania Germans are known to have lived in this area, it is striking that Quakers were not listed, and, of course, no African Americans, regardless of their denominational commitments, could attend the union Sunday school.

The nuanced calculus of inclusion and exclusion in evangelical reform attempted to transcend economic differences among whites and to include many Christian groups (though certainly not all). At the same time, it exhibited a growing wariness about the place of African Americans in the nation, especially as they became free and organized independent organizations such as the Union Church of Africans. Respectable women Bible reformers pioneered female public life in a variety of ways, especially by organizing themselves along lines of gender solidarity. Female Bible societies in these towns created new space for women's public action. Formal politics and law still left these women with narrowly circumscribed rights, and economic changes in the early nineteenth century probably encouraged greater female marginalization than the traditional world of shared household work. In opposition to these powerful forces of constraint, cosmopolitan evangelicals demanded and created a central place for respectable women in the new nation.

The National Campaign: "A Bible to Every Household"

Encounters between benevolent women and those destitute of Bibles occurred too infrequently for NCFBS members. As Elizabeth Booth lamented, "we have had but few calls for Bibles in our own neighborhood." Fortunately, the broader movement gave a larger sense of purpose as they "pour[ed] our contributions into the treasury of the Am[erican] Bible Society" and "rejoice[d] in the idea, that we send 'the best gift of heaven' where our feet have never trodden."[104] The larger cause gave their work meaning even when discouraged by local experience, and this national framework for action became ever more important in the 1820s.

The local limitations to evangelical reform faced by activists in all three towns spoke to a widespread problem as the ABS fundamentally depended on its local auxiliaries in this period. The ABS worried about a decline in the movement and called local groups to renewed action in the mid-1820s. ABS secretary John Nitchie sent warning letters to auxiliaries throughout the country about their flagging efforts. The overlapping connections among local, state, and national organizations in New Jersey caused confusion and competition among the groups, and he wrote to assure the treasurer of the NJBS that the "falling off" of local chapters to affiliate directly with the "parent Society" was not encouraged by the ABS. Nitchie promised to help "revive and invigorate their exertions" within the state organization. He also chided NJBS managers that the state organization needed to meet more frequently to "animate their hearts in the glorious work."[105] Similar letters went out to the NCFBS and warned "that our National Bible Society" in ten years of operation had not been able to distribute even as much as one-fourth of the scriptures needed by the destitute, "who are increasing at the rate of nearly half a million of accountable beings yearly." Nitchie closed with an urgent call: "what incentives to zeal and activity on the part of Christians do these facts disclose. Tell them to your associates, and let them act in the fear of God."[106]

Nitchie's letter exchange with the BSD secretary, Presbyterian reverend E. W. Gilbert, underscores that denominational differences threatened the demise of the movement in Delaware. Nitchie wrote about the "inactivity in so many of the Soc[ieties] of your state" and warned that "destitutes are increasing instead of decreasing in our land."[107] The situation remained unchanged the next year: "there is great need of exertion in this cause generally and I should suppose particularly in your state." When Gilbert suggested that the ABS include a stronger Presbyterian message in its publications, Nitchie admonished, "whatever we may *as Individuals* think of such combinations, yet as members of a Society embracing all religious denominations," we must "harmonize" and circulate the Bible without note or comment.[108]

Delaware's Bible movement lagged without the strong leadership of New Castle's Reverend John Latta. When he missed a BSD meeting in 1817, the managers adjourned because they didn't know what to do, and in 1823, as the aging Presbyterian minister faced death, the state organization recorded its weakest annual record of Bible distribution, a mere nineteen Bibles and forty-two New Testaments for the whole state.[109] Undeterred by Nitchie's admonishment two months earlier, Gilbert repeated that the cause faltered due to its overly ecumenical leadership. Gilbert described one as a "'high churchman' and rather cold in the cause," while another was "a sort of deistical Quaker" who was "not *deeply* interested in the inculcation of Bibles." According to Gilbert, the perilous religious situation in Delaware arose from Quakers in the northern part of the state "whose shyness of our associations you are probably acquainted with" and Methodists who predominated in the south and "are generally opposed to all Benevolent matters, except [those of] their own denomination."[110] Dating back to the origins of the BFBS in 1804, the Bible movement had organized as a nonsectarian force for Christian unity, but in places like the Delaware Valley, religious diversity among Protestants resisted homogenization and made such goals difficult to implement.

Probably in response to a growing sense of dullness in the cause, the BSD set a dramatic new goal for itself in the fall of 1824 when it decided to canvas every family in the state to inquire about how many Bibles they owned and if every person in the family could read. Even more remarkably, BSD managers expected this information to be collected by local tax assessors throughout the state. The Society failed to get forms to collect the information into tax officials' hands in time for the "comprehensive" survey, so redoubled its efforts the next year and also decided to distribute a Bible to every needy household in New Castle County. When BSD members met at New Castle's Presbyterian church the following year, they found relying on local government officials "discouraging" and decided to "employ Theological Students" instead in the effort.[111] Bible activists' expectations that the government would participate in evangelical reform met with disappointment, and the attempt to enlist fuller government participation in moral reform sparked widespread resistance among nonevangelicals. Bible activists, however, could not imagine that their increasingly public efforts could cause a backlash and undertook their boldest effort yet to remake the United States as a unified Christian nation in the late 1820s.

The BSD's comprehensive effort in Delaware was matched by similar state-based campaigns in New Jersey and Pennsylvania. Just as evangelical reformers in New Jersey had initiated the call for a national organization in 1816, so too that state led the way in planning a campaign that would literally reach everyone in the state who needed a Bible. Nitchie wrote to the NJBS secretary in 1827 to praise their statewide effort. "I have indeed heard of the noble improvements in your state towards placing the word of God in the bosom of every family and we have already filled many orders." As news of such efforts spread, other state societies rose to the challenge, and Nitchie reported that demand had doubled. By the end of the year, the ABS "Depository has been swept almost bare of Bibles."[112]

The BSP, still unaffiliated with the ABS, aimed for total coverage when it announced a three-year plan in 1827 "to supply every destitute family in the state with a copy of the Sacred Scriptures."[113] An address by its president placed the campaign directly within a national context. Based on census data, he estimated a need for 65,690 Bibles in Pennsylvania. The census not only set the statistical goal but also offered proof that such a massive undertaking could be accomplished. As he observed, "the visiting of all the families throughout the whole State, however arduous, has, we know, actually been effected, and that repeatedly, for the purpose of making a Census." If the federal government could measure the nation in "inquiries far more numerous and minute than any which we will need," then surely the BSP could reach every household in its sacred cause. A growing national consciousness encouraged reformers to adopt a more extended plan. President White, who was never identified by his title as an Episcopal bishop in BSP literature, added the "express injunction" not "to inculcate, or even suggest, any sectarian opinions. It is not to promote a sect, but to deliver a Bible, and to recommend its careful perusal, that every family is to be visited."[114]

The NBS was among the BSP auxiliaries that agreed to manage their part of the comprehensive campaign without the assistance of outside agents.[115] Success seemed close at hand in 1829—the work had been "vigorously sustained, and to a very considerable extent accomplished." Positive reports arrived from Jonathan Gray, the new Presbyterian minister in Easton, and another minister from the county reported "acceptable tidings relative to Northampton," where more than twelve hundred Bibles had been distributed.[116] The BSP adopted a self-congratulatory tone and even boasted that the effort marked a turning point in its relationship with the BFBS, which now began to plan its own comprehensive campaign.[117] But the effort in Northampton County probably did not unfold as smoothly as Bible reformers asserted. When the BSP sent a circular letter to establish exact needs, they warned of a scarcity of German Bibles, and Northampton was one of three Pennsylvania counties that made the heaviest requests for such texts. The BSP had known from the start that German-language Bibles would be the Achilles' heel of the effort, and White had estimated in his initial address that almost all of them would need to be imported from Europe.[118]

Comprehensive efforts were already underway in ten state Bible societies when the ABS committed to oversee a nationwide campaign in May 1829.[119] By October the NCFBS received a circular from the national organization announcing the "benevolent and noble undertaking of supplying every family in the United States with the Holy Scriptures in the space of two years."[120] This announcement arrived when state-led efforts were once again at low ebb, as "unforeseen difficulties and hindrances" frustrated the statewide effort in Delaware in 1829. Nevertheless, "the late noble resolution of the Parent Society to supply the whole United States" encouraged redoubled effort.[121]

The idea of placing a Bible in every household in the nation exemplifies the movement's simultaneously traditional and innovative approach to evangelical reform. Obviously, access to scripture marked a long-standing Protestant commitment. A traditional emphasis on Bible-based household religious order was now to embrace the whole nation, an expanded commitment that demanded aggressive action and the wholesale embrace of new technology. The national organization did more than simply exhort local societies to greater effort. The ABS had already begun to transform American publishing in the early 1820s. Its production of close to sixty thousand Bibles a year by 1821 shattered earlier average press runs of approximately two thousand volumes per edition, which remained the maximum standard output for most professional printers in the early republic. At the start of the national campaign, the ABS printed nearly 345,000 Bibles a year, all while cutting the cost of production almost in half to 11.6 cents per copy.[122] This print explosion relied on three major technical advances, which the ABS, along with other evangelical organizations, pioneered in the United States: the steam-powered press, the process of stereotyping, and the use of machine-made paper. As the scholar David Paul Nord has astutely emphasized, the effort of industrial evangelicalism to deliver the same printed message to everyone in the nation marked "the first genuine mass media in America."[123]

The ABS's national campaign to supply every household in the country with a Bible by 1831 was the defining effort of the organization's early years and of early evangelical reform more broadly. Made possible by integrating national leadership, mass production, and a vast network of auxiliaries, the local organizations played the essential distribution role in what was known as the "general supply effort." The opportunity to work locally in the national event inspired evangelical activists throughout the country. As the Female Bible Association of Easton explained, "our beloved country . . . appears to be destined to take a distinguished part . . . in the promotion of the 'latter-day glory'" by setting "an example to the nations of the world in systematically supplying the destitute with the Holy Bible."[124]

The pressure to successfully complete the national campaign with its plain millennial significance could stimulate self-doubt as well as nationalist celebration. For example, the BSD, already beset by internal disagreements, adopted a more punitive assessment of what it meant to be a committed Christian in this crucial period. Its 1829 annual report scolded those who "profess . . . that the less exaction religion makes upon them, the purer they deem its character," while those who "predicate the purity of their religious principles upon their opposition" to contributing to religious societies "are the advocates, in effect, of infidelity; and by hindering Christian energy, while they remain in the ranks of Christians, give to the enemy more efficient aid, than they could by open opposition."[125]

In the midst of the national campaign, the BSD proclaimed that only evangelically committed Christians merited full fellowship. "That Christian, who in this day, is not actively engaged in the service of God, incurs a dread responsibility. For this day is filled with institutions enabling all to exert to the best possible advantage whatever means they can spare."[126] The ABS adopted a similar view when it trumpeted "A Bible to Every Household, A Bible to Every Household—must be the motto of each Society, and must be sounded through all our borders, until every soul in the whole land has access to this fountain of life."[127] The stridency of the national campaign marked a new assertion of "Christian power in the American Republic," as the historian Jon Butler has described the stunning ascent of institutional Protestantism and denominational authority in this period.[128]

The national campaign ultimately failed in its lofty goal to provide every American household with a Bible. The effort was stunning in terms of book production, issuing some 1 million Bibles in three years for a country with three million families.[129] The greater challenge concerned distribution, and while the northeastern parts of the country were reasonably well canvassed, the southeast and west lagged farther behind. ABS managers in New York City predictably placed the blame on local auxiliaries' failure to overcome petty differences in the larger glorious cause. The sense that "local particularism" undermined the national campaign led the ABS to moderate its millennial ideals in the 1830s and to reorganize itself on the more centralized and businesslike model of a national corporation that principally relied on paid employees.[130]

The "general supply effort" of 1829 to 1831 fell short of its quixotic goal. Though discouraging, cosmopolitan evangelicals could still feel pleased by how much they had accomplished in the mere two decades since the Bible movement began in the United States. Cosmopolitan evangelicals had made organized religion more central to public life in the early national United States than it had been at the start of the American Revolution. Evangelical activists effectively presented American Christianity as a major unifying force for the country. Despite the success of this impressive reimagining of what mattered most in American public life, a vision that would persist and expand for many decades, those reformers were spurred

to action by awareness that many Americans did not share their evangelical passion about what the nation and its citizens needed to prosper. The
national Bible campaign coincided with a turning point in U.S. electoral
politics that drew much of its force from a sense that cosmopolitan evangelicalism betrayed what was supposed to have been central to the republic created by the American Revolution. The reformation of formal
politics in the Delaware Valley in the 1820s grew out of the region's Revolutionary identity politics, yet would transform it in ways that also left the
Revolution behind in fashioning a recognizably modern, and extraordinarily long lasting, bipartisan political system.

Chapter 6

The Campaign for Political Unity

Political parties drove the transformation and bridged the transition from early republican to early national politics in the first decades of the nineteenth century, and Jeffersonian Republicans went almost without challenge during the period. But even a passing familiarity with local and state politics in the Delaware Valley offers a strikingly different view of an era of supposed Republican dominance. Whereas New Castle, Delaware, was a mixed but Republican-leaning town in a Federalist state, Burlington, New Jersey, was an ardently Federalist place in a Republican state. Easton and Pennsylvania both were staunchly Republican, but the bitter controversies within that party in local and state contests easily matched, and probably exceeded, the two-party acrimony elsewhere. In short, these Delaware Valley towns demonstrate the complexity of representative politics in the first decades of the nineteenth century that can too easily be glossed over from national and presidential perspectives.

Although organized political competition had been a feature of colonial politics in the Delaware Valley, especially in Pennsylvania, the growing legitimacy and significance of political parties began to coalesce into a bipartisan structure by the 1820s that would be the hallmark of modern American politics. The two-party system's later dominance in American electoral politics, however, can lead to a basic misunderstanding of early U.S. political culture, when parties still suffered widespread suspicion as corrupt institutions likely to destroy a true republican society.[1]

Ethnic and religious dimensions of local experience that had been central to the Revolutionary mobilization in the Delaware Valley helped to shape the emergence of party organizations that hoped to exploit such identities for partisan purposes. A local perspective is required to see how people understood politics in their own day and shows that ethno-religious considerations shaped voter perception and action in fundamental ways. Yet identity politics never dominated electoral politics in a monolithic or all-controlling manner, and individual examples can always be given that counter broader group tendencies. Partisan politics cannot be convincingly explained with a single formula that links parties to religious and ethnic groups for the simple reason that successful parties needed to build broad coalitions. Nevertheless, ethno-religious identities intertwined with partisan politics in the Delaware Valley, and these influences deserve close examination to uncover the subtle ways that group consciousness informed political activity and allegiance.

Jacksonian Democracy once played a central part in historians' assessments of the early United States, and interpretations of that concept and era are as varied as the multiple groups in early national society. The rise of regular two-party competition that originated with the personalist contests between Andrew Jackson and John Quincy Adams in the 1820s has been most influentially explained in terms of oppositional economic classes, ethnic and religious group mobilization, and the professionalization of party leadership and machinery. Recently, broad socioeconomic differences arising from the Market Revolution have again emerged as the leading force explaining the politics of Jacksonian America.[2] While often contradictory, these standard explanations of the creation of a modern two-party political system generally share a top-down perspective on party formation that relies on presidential contests, the nation, and key state examples as the critical explanatory and evidentiary criteria. This approach usefully identifies broad patterns, yet reinforces one of the central consequences of the party system by obfuscating the richly varied local activities that often ran counter to larger trends. As most late eighteenth-century political actors keenly understood, a strengthened nation directly challenged the importance, influence, and diversity of local political expression.

The formation of the second party system closed the era when Revolutionary values directly shaped American politics. By the 1820s the generation that had participated in the Revolution was waning and no longer played the leading role in American life. The emerging society that Jackson symbolized culminated the broad Revolutionary era that had wrought enormous change not just by separating from the British Empire, but also by spurring particular internal developments in the postwar United States. Whether one sees the numerous changes of this era as heralding movement toward a more egalitarian polity or decries them as curbs placed upon a potentially more transformative Revolution, the electoral system created in the decades after the war would be the period's most durable and direct social change.[3]

Ethnicity, Religion, and Politics in the Republican Period

Delaware's persistent bipartisan competition was unique in the so-called first party system of the early republic.[4] This competitiveness arose from a distinct geographic pattern of party allegiance with clear connections to the Revolutionary War. New Castle County in the north was strongly Republican, while the state's other two counties, especially southernmost Sussex, were Federalist bastions. As a result, Federalists regularly controlled the state assembly (based on equal representation by county) with significant results for national politics because the Delaware legislature chose presidential electors and U.S. senators throughout the period under study. Federalists also held Delaware's popularly elected governorship for most of the early nineteenth century, narrowly losing the office only four times before 1830. As we saw in Chapter 3, occasional Republican gubernatorial victories came by the smallest of margins—just eighteen votes out of nearly seven thousand cast in 1801.[5]

As Federalist success at the national level declined after 1800, conservatives in Delaware prided themselves as the only state, along with Connecticut, that maintained "correct principles . . . when our country was overshadowed by the gloom of Democracy."[6] Delaware ran directly counter to national developments, as Federalists remained the state's strongest political force until the late 1820s. Delaware Federalism thrived, but Republicans organized effectively there as well. Local elections in New Castle generally produced Republican majorities, but the town's successful statewide politicians usually stood for office as Federalists. The town's conservative political elite may have failed to win most local contests, but support from downstate Federalists carried them to victory in statewide races.

Delaware's close partisan balance led to hard-fought elections because the manipulation of even a single polling district could alter statewide outcomes. In 1802, Federalists challenged voter qualifications in several New Castle County hundreds (the local voting district in Delaware), and Republicans claimed that "Federal Persecution" targeted the so-called "*Wild Irish.*" In contrast to Federalist prejudice that denied citizenship rights through fourteen-year residency requirements, Republicans embraced new immigrants as the "Generous Irish" who had "fought and bled for American Independence."[7]

The Republican press took great care to explain their solidarity with the Irish in New Castle County. The *American Watchman*, the party's leading newspaper in Delaware, reported on "HIBERNIAN PROCEEDINGS" where a "numerous and respectable meeting of the Sons of Erin of Christiana and New Castle Hundreds" endorsed the Republican ticket nominated by the county convention. Further, it warned that a false "Hibernian Hand-Bill and Ticket" had been circulated to defeat the cause. An even stronger ethnic appeal appeared in the next issue when "The Shade of Emmett" reminded the Sons of Erin that when "driven from your native land by the oppression of England," the Republicans welcomed you, while the Federalists have been "uniformly your enemies and oppressors."[8] A long list of Federalist antagonism toward Irishmen in America followed, from the Alien Law of 1798 to the attempt to bar Irishmen from U.S. Army service during the War of 1812.

At the same time, partisan papers on both sides were aware of the fluidity among ethnic, religious, and partisan commitments. The Republican *New Castle Argus* caustically explored the question of voter volition in a comic piece supposedly written by an Irish laborer. As "Wun uf the Well-Boarns" explained, he chose to become a Federalist because "we hav knot oanly got awl the tallents and lurning, but awl the vertu and ruligin."[9] Even Republican papers that courted Irish voters sometimes employed the period's caricature of ignorant and easily manipulated Irishmen. Although Federalists' claims to superiority had supposedly persuaded this uneducated laborer to join the more respectable party, Republicans lampooned this betrayal of proper partisanship by ridiculing the attempt to become an elite by voting Federalist. The social commentary of this comic piece had force because Anglos with ties to Episcopal and Methodist churches were leading Delaware Federalists whose dominant alliance was challenged by Republicans in New Castle County, who were often identified as a Presbyterian party with strong Irish and Scots Irish support.[10] The divisions of the Revolutionary War remained alive and bitterly contested in Delaware's first party system and beyond.

At first glance, Republican dominance in Pennsylvania seems to mirror the national-level trend of Federalist failure after 1800, from which Delaware so strikingly departed. However, the dizzying factions and hostile personal attacks that shaped Pennsylvania's partisan politics gives the lie to its supposed role as the "keystone" of Republican success.[11] Despite strong electoral support for Republican presidential candidates, the actual operation of Pennsylvania politics rested upon countless party schisms that resulted from and fueled remarkable local animosity. Republican success thinly veiled strong third-party and antiparty traditions in Easton, surrounding Northampton County, and many other areas of the state.

Easton's local politics offers a particularly effective vantage on the changing political culture of the early republic. First, strong antiparty beliefs persisted there even in the face of Republican victories. Second, local political differences often hinged on personality clashes that produced scandalous accusations. Third, Pennsylvania Germans were recognized as the crucial voting group in the area, and as a result ethnic identity centrally shaped the gradual transition to a modern party system there. At the same time, ethnicity was never monolithic at the local level. Despite the apparently staunch partisan commitment of Pennsylvania Germans that seems to be validated by county-level voting statistics, a closer look at specific campaigns, local newspapers, and individual politicians reveals a richer intersection of ethnicity and politics. Ethno-religious identity unquestionably contributed to partisan orientation and everyday political culture, but how it did so was more subtle and varied than party leaders wanted to acknowledge. Understanding the vital ways that local life and an emergent modern political culture shaped one another requires a closer look at specific individuals, places, and events.

As discussed in Chapter 3, the national Jeffersonian triumph in 1800 had been foreshadowed in Pennsylvania when Thomas McKean narrowly defeated the Federalist James Ross in the 1799 governor's race. Jefferson's subsequent victory there via the legislatively brokered electoral college vote seconded a long string of Republican electoral success at the highest levels of elected office in the state. Beneath this apparent dominance, however, extraordinary disagreements existed about how a political party should operate. The demand that individual voters follow party dictates remained controversial everywhere in the early republic, and in the inchoate political world of Pennsylvania, a fluid third party arose variously identified as Quid, Constitutional Republican, and Independent Republican. Although almost entirely forgotten in the rush to discover the origins of a modern two-party system, this shifting centrist group successfully contested elections in Pennsylvania for nearly two decades, winning the all-important governor's race in 1805, 1820, and 1835.[12] Although sometimes dismissed as a Federalist wolf in sheep's clothing, this misrepresents the fundamentally centrist and antiparty commitments of the Quids. For example, Samuel Sitgreaves, Easton's leading Federalist, sought no alliance with Christian Jacob Hutter, the local Quid newspaper editor, whom he described as a "slippery fellow." As he warned his fellow local conservative John Arndt, "our political adversaries, whether Democrats or Quids, should not be appraised of [our plans]. . . . I give you fair Warning, beware [Samuel D.] Ingham & the Quids."[13]

Republican unity may have overcome the state's Philadelphia-led Federalism in 1799–1800, but that solidarity quickly dissolved into countless internal factions. The 1805 gubernatorial contest found the incumbent Thomas McKean, a former state supreme court justice, notable Revolutionary leader (whose public career had begun in New Castle), and a supporter of the rebels at the Fries trials, rejected for renomination by the Republican-controlled assembly. Simon Snyder, a younger self-made Pennsylvania German businessman and the assembly's speaker, opposed him as the party's official candidate. Peter Muhlenberg and Joseph Hiester rallied their fellow Pennsylvania Germans to support McKean. A letter from Muhlenberg to Hiester circulated widely in English and German newspapers to persuade their ethnic kinsman not to vote for Snyder. Muhlenberg acknowledged that it was "very natural" that Pennsylvania Germans would want a German governor and that the office "should be once made out of their number." However—and here it seems likely that he had himself in mind—that person needed to be a man of the highest talents and not associated with the call of Philadelphia radicals to draft a new state constitution to limit the power of the judiciary. Following this line of thought, a brief appendix to Muhlenberg's letter in a German-language supplement of Easton's *American Eagle* newspaper warned that "good honest Germans in the region" were being told by Snyderites of the "honor it would be for us to have a German governor."[14] Not surprisingly, the conservative paper cast this as a shallow feint to avoid discussing Snyder's supposed call for a new constitutional convention. The ethnic appeal was decried as an illegitimate and sentimental ruse that avoided a rational focus on policy issues.

The Easton paper's regular English-language edition took a decidedly harsher stand in describing the attack on the state constitution by "needy foreigners."[15] In fact, Snyder was Pennsylvania born and did not support the constitutional convention proposed by radical Philadelphia Republicans, but his actual biography and political stance hardly mattered in the vitriolic newspaper battles of the day. The supposedly rational Muhlenberg, for example, denounced Snyder as simultaneously favoring a new radical constitution and consorting with "violent Federalists." Hostile and often unfair accusations against political enemies had been widespread in the colonial era, intensified during the Revolutionary War, and remained quotidian features of early national political life.

If stereotypes held true, one would expect Pennsylvania Germans in Easton and Northampton to rally to the cause of their fellow ethnic outsider, but this did not happen. Local voters remained committed to McKean as a towering Revolutionary figure. In a statewide race carried by fewer than 4,800 votes, Northampton County delivered the crucial support to secure McKean's reelection.[16] As a result of this outcome, Northampton County voters established the heavily Pennsylvania German area north of Philadelphia as essential for victory in close state elections.

Immediately after Snyder's defeat in the governor's race, Thomas J. Rogers moved to Easton to publish a reliable Republican newspaper. Over the next two decades, Rogers would become the area's most influential political figure, publishing several newspapers and serving in Congress from 1818 to 1824.[17] As a newcomer in 1805, however, he cautiously sought to change the antiparty and third-party sentiment in an area that had delivered key Quid support to McKean. Accordingly, the first issue of his *Northampton Farmer* committed itself to "strict impartiality" in partisan matters and drew upon a telling Jeffersonian quote as its motto—"Equal and exact justice to all men, of whatever persuasion, religious, or political."[18]

The *Northampton Farmer*'s position in its first election season, however, left no doubt about its searing partisanship. One active local Quid charged that "Rogers, was set up in Easton by the Snyderites and others" expressly to attack people like himself who had backed McKean, "and, if possible, to print us out of credit and confidence with the people."[19] Reporting on local and district Republican committee meetings, the paper supported the decision not to renominate Frederick Conrad to Congress because it seemed likely that Federalists would also nominate him. Conrad was a nonparty centrist who muddied sharp partisan lines. Although he was elected to Congress as a Republican in 1804, the likelihood of Federalist backing in 1806 led Republican loyalists such as Rogers to reject his candidacy. Moreover, Rogers's

paper rabidly denounced Governor McKean and all other Quids and Constitutional Republicans as no different than Federalists.[20]

Local people such as Abraham Horn, a Revolutionary soldier, anti-
House Tax leader, and local political candidate whom we met briefly earlier, dissented from the growing demand for party discipline made by
professional partisans like Rogers. In a remarkable bilingual broadside
(printed in English and German) Horn rejected the "unblushing false-
hoods" circulated about him by "time-serving politicians" who attacked his
political principles as well as the intelligence of Pennsylvania Germans
who were supposedly susceptible to manipulation because their "means of
information are limited." Horn contrasted his own steadfast values and
local roots against Rogers as an outsider and propagandist sent to Easton
to support the misguided national policies related to the widening war in
Europe. "I was opposed to raising a useless and burthensome army under
John Adams, and am equally opposed to raising one under Jefferson."
While Jefferson's embargo was supposed to have hurt external foes, in fact
it had brought "ruin to ourselves and a total stagnation of trade." In the
face of the embargo's devastating impact on the local wheat economy, "we
are told by the Snyderites that the embargo is a blessing!" Moreover, Republicans act as if "we have no right to question the wisdom of any measures of the government; and we have in Easton been abused for so
doing."[21] Just as Horn had opposed bad Federalist policies in the late
1790s, he called now for local people to reject bad Republican ones. He
closed by dismissing his political opponents' supposed "spirit of prophecy"
about the upcoming election and urged readers to vote for his attached
list of Quid candidates from the governor's office to the local coroner.[22]

Abraham Horn's political commitments merged with those of Christian
Jacob Hutter, who published the influential German-language *Northampton Correspondent* from nearby Allentown starting in 1806 and would expand his publishing business to include the English-language *Pennsylvania
Herald and Easton Intelligencer* just in time for the 1808 elections. Hutter's
papers in this period enthusiastically backed Quid candidates and produced a virulent and hyperbolic newspaper war with Rogers, who spearheaded Republican efforts in the area.[23] Indeed, though the *Pennsylvania
Herald* pledged to print material from all political perspectives, it
adamantly backed John Spayd for governor in 1808 as the proper Constitutional Republican candidate in the tradition of outgoing governor
McKean. Like Horn's broadside, the paper emphasized that the Republican political machine viewed Pennsylvania Germans condescendingly,
quoting one party leader as saying that "he could lead the stupid Dutchmen of Northampton county by the Nose." As was true for all political
newspapers of the period, the *Pennsylvania Herald* mostly spread invective.
In its view, the opposing editor, Rogers, was a madman headed for bedlam,
and the Republican candidate, Simon Snyder, a "king of ignorance" who

aimed to abolish the state constitution and create property requirements to disenfranchise the poor. The *Northampton Farmer*, by contrast, denounced Hutter as a mercenary hired by Quids in 1805 (when he backed McKean) and was now paid by Federalists to support Spayd.[24]

The two papers' extreme accusations shared a prominent tactic of accusing each other of Federalism and aristocracy. Because Rogers had purchased the type for his press from the defunct *American Eagle*, this supposedly revealed him as a Federalist puppet. Similarly, the *Pennsylvania Herald* mocked Snyderite claims to be the "Farmer's Party" by printing the occupations of its nominees to reveal an "Aristocratic Ticket." More surprisingly, Hutter's severe characterizations of Snyder would continue after he had won the race, which Hutter decried as the product of "political delusion and deception."[25] Two years later, Hutter's *Der Unabhangige Republikaner* described the governor as "drunk on dumbness" in a July 4th speech and suggested that his support for national failure to retaliate against the British resulted from the governor's tory advisers.[26]

The Quid editor Hutter invoked the American Revolution as a polestar in politics and warned that the "'damn' party system" broke from Revolutionary traditions and would destroy the republic. To him, parties "sow black hate" by making politics a cabal of office hunters seeking patronage. Instead, he called on all Americans to "bury the party flag and raise the one of freedom and independence anew . . . *Not before the party system is overthrown, will we be a truly happy and invincible nation!*"[27] Vehement antipartyism shaped Hutter's caustic opposition to the Republican Party and Governor Snyder.

Although both sides cast accusations of "aristocracy" against their political opponents, the profiles of Quid and Republican leaders in Easton drawn from committee lists published in party newspapers reveal little economic difference between them. Four of six Republicans who can be found in the 1814 tax list were in the top decile, while eight of ten Quid leaders also hailed from the top of the town's wealth structure. Because Easton lacked a Federalist newspaper, that party's local leadership is difficult to assess, but of known Federalists only one had modest taxable wealth, Thomas D. Dick, the young clerk at the Bank of Easton.

The vigorous local Republican and Quid newspaper war in this election can be misleading, for election returns reveal a healthier local Federalist Party than would otherwise be expected. In Easton, Snyder beat the Federalist James Ross by merely two votes (100 to 98), while only thirty-three voters favored the Quid John Spayd. At the county level, the numbers changed considerably, with Snyder winning easily and Spayd a distant second, just ahead of Ross. Meanwhile, in the state at large, Snyder won handily with 61 percent of the vote, while Spayd finished dismally, placing second only in the Pennsylvania German corner of the state from which he hailed (Northampton and neighboring Berks counties). Meanwhile,

Lancaster County, often considered the quintessential Pennsylvania German heartland, was one of only six counties that favored the Federalist James Ross. Local contexts varied considerably and shaped how Pennsylvania Germans cast their votes. Positive and negative ethnic assertions about them frequently appeared, but when three parties made statewide efforts and when two of the top candidates were Pennsylvania Germans, the political implications of ethno-religious identity remained labile and unpredictable.

Thomas J. Rogers worked hard to make his party a legitimate local institution and slowly came to dominate the Republican machine in Northampton County; nevertheless, this achievement rested atop seething local animosity. It is little wonder that when Robert Traill, the Germanized Anglo political leader and attorney discussed earlier, wrote an end-of-life advice letter to his wife and children, he warned them to steer clear of politics and its nasty conflicts. "Easton is a place of much discord, ill-will toward one another, and very much tattling."[28] When the clear partisan guide of presidential candidates disappeared in the 1820s, Rogers found himself unable to guide local Republicans toward the preferred candidate of party insiders such as himself. Instead, they would be forced to adapt to the unexpected popular dictates of a party system that they had labored to create.

Partisan political development in New Jersey seems to mirror Pennsylvania in many respects, for here too the Republican Party enjoyed statewide control almost immediately after the election of 1800. However, in dramatic contrast to the eventual Republican dominance around Easton, Burlington County consistently and decisively voted Federalist. From 1800 to 1823 it filled 120 seats in the legislature (4 lower and 1 upper seat each year) of which only 6 went to non-Federalists. Although the Republican *Newark Centinel* overstated the case when it charged Burlington County as "the only stronghold federalism has," the six New Jersey counties that sent Federalists to the legislature in 1808 had little influence in the face of a well-organized Republican majority.[29]

Not surprisingly, New Jersey Federalists felt that the electoral system misrepresented the true sentiments of the people. As one letter to a Federalist paper explained, Jefferson's reelection in 1804 by 162 to 14 electoral votes presented a misleading image of Republican dominance and insisted that a mere five thousand votes cast differently in key states could have changed the election's outcome. To Federalists the villainous Republican achievement lay in "forming combinations in every county, and claiming to be the people." Thus a small group had "delude[d] a large portion of their unsuspecting fellow citizens . . . and have, in fact, dictated to the people the persons they should choose" for office.[30] Fear of party leaders as "dictators" who manipulated the public to their own ends was a standard charge throughout the period. The silencing of a significant

Federalist presence in New Jersey through Republican legislative dominance exacerbated minority complaints there about the tyranny of majoritarian democracy.

Elias Boudinot, Burlington's archconservative and Bible movement
leader, spearheaded the local denunciation of democracy as "anarchy and
confusion." He felt that American politics had been corrupted by "the
fashionable principle, that our government is a Republican one. Although
this may be true in a strict sense, it is certainly not so in a popular or democratic idea of the term."[31] Charles H. Wharton, Burlington's Episcopal
minister, had a similarly lurid view of democracy in action. While visiting
the Republican stronghold of Newark, he wrote to Joshua M. Wallace, another Federalist in his vestry, decrying the disorderly street life of a city
"dedicated to riot and drunkenness by all the white and black negroes of
the place" with "misrule that . . . plainly bespoke it to be a Pandemonium
of democracy."[32] Wharton and Boudinot's debauched view of participa-
tory politics, which for Wharton also invoked racial contamination,
spurred their turn away from electoral politics and toward conservative
evangelical reform.

Boudinot and Wharton's democraphobia prevented them from being
central to New Jersey Federalism after 1800. Instead, Burlington residents
such as William Griffith and William Coxe Jr., who regularly served as its
elected Federalists, were the party leaders. Griffith accepted that postwar
political culture centered upon contested elections with universal voting
rights for white men. In his view, "the least privilege which the poor should
enjoy, is that of giving a solitary vote for their rulers."[33] Griffith and
Boudinot were political allies and friends; Griffith even married
Boudinot's niece, but their understandings of healthy American politics
were built on divergent premises.

As the historian David Hackett Fischer has noted, Boudinot was an "Old
Federalist" still committed to a hierarchical eighteenth-century deferential culture, while Griffith and Coxe were "Young Federalists" (not necessarily in age, but in ideological terms) whose conservatism accepted the
legitimacy of regularly contested elections with standing political parties.
The contrasting response of Coxe and Boudinot to Constitutional reforms
proposed by the Connecticut Federalist James Hillhouse illustrates this division. To Boudinot, Hillhouse's plan to weaken the executive and expand
legislative authority by linking it more directly to the popular vote "entirely subverted" the goal of the founders by creating "a really Democratic
government in the fullest and most popular sense of the word." By contrast, Coxe was sanguine about Federalist chances in a more open electoral framework and judged the proposals "replete with sound
principles."[34] More flexible conservatives aimed to compete and succeed
in an electoral system that favored direct voting, closer local representation, and universal white manhood suffrage. Effective New Jersey Federal-

ists such as Coxe and Griffith, like their much more successful counterparts in Delaware, clearly departed from extremists such as Boudinot.

The Society of Friends played a key part in making Burlington County the base of the state's Federalist Party. To conservative Quakers, the slaveholding regime of Republican presidents exemplified the great danger of popular politics with its unrestrained democratic majority. Quakers certainly understood suffering public abuse in the postwar period. As "A Voice in Behalf of the Oppressed" explained in the state's leading Federalist paper, Quakers "separated themselves from 'the world,' in dress and language, no less than many other particulars, 'for consciences sake,' or, in other words, because they feel it to be a solemn and unavoidable duty." Most Americans took offense at the "assumption of peculiar character," especially when they viewed it "as an affection of uncommon sanctity," but the writer believed that hostility toward Quakers derived from unfair assumptions that they were odd and haughty. Instead, he insisted that Quaker religious liberties needed to be safeguarded in the new nation. In an era when Revolutionary service remained a chief determinant of legitimate political leadership Quakers suffered widespread disapprobation. Members of the Society of Friends clearly preferred the Federalist Party. Even though local Quakers rarely sought political office, they were key voters, and Federalist newspapers explicitly appealed to them to come to the polls, while Republican ones pleaded with them to reconsider their Federalist commitments.[35]

The harassment Quakers suffered in the long Revolutionary period and the Society's internal reformation that called for a less intensive role in formal politics led Friends to view postwar electoral politics from a distance. David Allinson, for example, printed a nonpolitical paper in Burlington whose editorial stance reflected this withdrawal. To Allinson, the youngest son of the Quaker activists Samuel and Martha Cooper Allinson, the partisan press had destroyed "true patriotism" by focusing on "the conflicts of party." The "passions or the patronage of a party" caused the "public mind" to be "obscured and distorted through the agency of party newspapers."[36] Quakers widely shared Allinson's partisan disavowal, which, of course, also resonated strongly among Federalists, whose influence had been eclipsed by Republican dominance. Partisan organizations directly challenged important ideals of voter independence and political virtue by making "*party spirit* and not *moral conduct . . .* the only road to office and preferment."[37] Nevertheless, partisanship was essential to successful newspapers in this period. Allinson's *Rural Visitor* lasted only a single year, and the nonpolitical *Quarterly Theological Magazine*, edited by Reverend Wharton (and printed by the Allinson press in Burlington), also failed to reach a large audience and did not endure.

While Burlington Federalists usually had to content themselves with success in county-level elections, the War of 1812 prompted a Federalist surge that demonstrated their political savvy and tenacity. Burlington Federalists used a September 1812 nominating meeting to attack "the war measures, which a violent party in the Legislature have so steadily promoted." The Republican legislature expressed confidence in the congressional decision to go to war, and Burlington Federalists charged them with illegally converting the state militia into a national army. As a result, they observed "with alarm their fellow citizens lately dragged into the continental service . . . in open violation of their rights as freemen, and to their great peril and loss." Burlington County Federalists pledged themselves to follow Connecticut's policy of reserving its militia for state duty unless repelling an invasion.[38] Pacifist Quakers strongly supported this antiwar stance and provided overwhelming Federalist support throughout West Jersey.

Casting themselves as the "Peace Party" in advance of the October legislative election, Jersey Federalists supported three new congressional candidates, along with the three incumbent Republicans who had voted against the declaration of war. When Federalists won a majority in the state legislature, however, they swiftly altered the terms of the upcoming federal election in November. Because Federalists could win in some counties, but could not carry the state with at-large popular voting, they revised the electoral system. First, the new Federalist legislature decided that they would select the state's presidential electors, in place of a statewide popular vote, and cast the state's eight electoral votes for the opposition presidential candidate DeWitt Clinton. Second, the Federalist legislature dropped two of the three Republican incumbents from their peace ticket for Congress. Third, they changed congressional districting from six statewide seats to three districts with two representatives each. Finally, the date of the federal election was pushed back more than two months to mid-January. Naturally, all the new electoral rules favored Federalists. In a reversal of previous statewide elections when many Federalists chose not to vote and the party often even declined to name a slate of candidates who were foreordained to lose, Republicans now declined to contest the congressional race in the Burlington district. The new 1812 electoral rules meant that four of the state's six congressmen were Federalists, prominent among them William Coxe Jr., of Burlington.[39]

Republicans, of course, treated the election rule changes with great disdain, and older polemical historical accounts have also portrayed Federalists as crude manipulators of elite control.[40] Yet the commitment to district congressional elections, while unquestionably self-serving, also achieved a more accurate representation of West Jersey voters who opposed the war. William Coxe Jr., the persistent Federalist assemblymen from Burlington and the head of the state's Federalist congressional delegation in 1813, personified the dilemmas of a minority peace party in time of war, though he may have found Washington more congenial than Trenton. Republican control of Congress had slipped notably from 1811 to 1813, opening room for Coxe to receive a seat on the House Ways and Means Committee. Nevertheless, his genuine hopes to work for peace in Congress were frustrated. As he wrote to his son, most congressmen preferred a violent course: "Canada they say must be ours at any price of men or money."[41]

As they still do today, the rules of the political game could determine electoral outcomes. Although new districting allowed New Jersey to elect a predominantly Federalist delegation to Congress in 1812, the next congressional election occurred with Republicans back in control of the state legislature and seats for Congress again contested statewide. As a result, Jersey Federalists were swept from national office when Republicans carried the state with a 1,117-vote majority. Federalist majorities in five of the state's twelve counties (led by Burlington, which gave the Federalist peace candidates their largest majority of 1,550) were lost once more in the Republican triumph. Despite Federalist control of Burlington County and other places, New Jersey Federalists never enjoyed broad electoral success in the state again.

The Federalist Party as a national organization never recovered from the stigma attached to its New England leaders who were charged with contemplating secession at the Hartford Convention during the War of 1812. Strident antiwar actions were totally rejected by Federalists in Delaware, however, where the party remained a dominant organization, and whose leading figure, James A. Bayard, served as Madison's peace commissioner in Europe for most of the war. Bayard's legal and political protégé Louis McLane also supported the war and was unanimously elected as an officer to the voluntary militia that formed in New Castle County in 1812.[42] Unlike the Quaker-informed Federalism of Burlington's "peace party," Delaware Federalists supported vigorous military action, which helped them persist after the war without trimming their sails. By contrast, New Jersey Federalists, especially those with Quaker connections, suffered renewed connotations of treason for their opposition to war just as had happened during the Revolutionary War.

Ironically, tiny and conservative Delaware was the only state in the nation that maintained genuine two-party competition all the way into the 1820s. This balance made its newspapers essential sites for simplifying voter choice into a dichotomous us-them and good-bad decision. The 1822 gubernatorial race exemplifies the durable features of formal politics in Delaware. The election matched Republican Joseph Haslet, previously elected governor in 1811, against the New Castle resident James Booth, a long-standing judge, leading Federalist, and head of the conservative evangelical family discussed in the previous chapter. A Republican paper championed Haslet as the son of "that gallant Irishmen, Col. John Haslet," who commanded the Delaware Regiment of the Continental Army and died a martyr in the patriot victory at Princeton in December 1776. By contrast, it denounced Booth for joining the enemy during the war and "on all occasions since he has been the warm friend of our deadly foe Great Britain." If Haslet's connection to an Irish war-hero father aided his cause, his Presbyterianism apparently required defense, for the same paper insisted that the charges against him as a "sectarian" were unfair.[43]

The Republican paper attacked Booth on many grounds, but especially for having benefited from "ultra Federalists'" corrupt patronage that had awarded the Booth family lucrative government appointments for fifty years. One letter charged that Booth supported his large family from appointments to nine lucrative offices and other important posts went to his nephew and son-in-law. The paper decried such corruption and asked its readers to "recollect how constantly some men, not to say some families, have held on upon offices." The Republican paper warned successful Federalists, "stop gentlemen; the people have something to say to this."[44]

Booth failed to persuade his Republican neighbors in New Castle to support him. New Castle Hundred voters held fast to their typical partisan mode and favored the Republican over the local man by 165 to 100 votes, a steady 62 percent for the Republican candidate, matching the strong Republican voting majority in New Castle County overall. Haslet's margin in New Castle was crucial to offset Booth's much stronger support in Sussex County. In the end, the Republican Haslet secured the governor's chair with just a twenty-two-vote margin in the state. Delaware voters' allegiance to parties founded in the late 1790s remained strong even in the 1820s.

The consistency of partisan voting in Delaware and New Castle Hundred reflects the effectiveness of the state parties. Practically no cross-party voting occurred in the annual election of state assemblymen, nor did the percentage of votes in the triennial gubernatorial election change significantly from 1809 to 1824. As we have seen, New Castle Federalist James Booth carried no extra hometown votes in his narrow loss in 1822. In 1823, another gubernatorial election was held (Haslet was the third consecutive governor to die in office before completing his term), and local New Castle voters again cast 63 percent of their votes for the Republican candidate, who carried the state. This partisan balance reappeared at all levels of the 1823 election. Among twenty-two candidates for state senate, assembly, and levy court, the nearly three hundred voters in New Castle Hundred never strayed by more than four votes from the number given to the candidate at the top of the ticket.

Managing voters was essential to an effective party organization, but as attacks on both sides emphasized, parties retained an illegitimate aura well into the nineteenth century. Republicans overcame the unseemly novelty of demanding voter discipline by recasting party loyalty as a civic obligation. New Castle County Republicans carefully explained the principles underlying their nominating convention where delegates from every hundred gathered at the Red Lion Inn to select a countywide ticket. This process, and especially the complete acceptance of all its nominees, reflected the democratic political principle of "submission to the will of the majority." The Republican paper continued that the party ticket required absolute adherence even if one discovered a particular friend dropped by the nominating convention. The party creed was "Principles and Not Men," for to neglect the ticket, even if one did not vote for a Federalist, would aid our enemies who make "men and not measures" their "governing object."[45]

In the midst of regularly hard-fought elections and explosive rhetoric, New Castle Hundred voters played a remarkably consistent partisan role. From 1809 to 1823, local voter turnout ranged from 214 to 281, typically with 62 percent of votes cast for the Republican ticket. Consistent voting patterns reflected hard partisan work and genuine party commitments but also rested on the voting technology itself. Tickets were printed and distributed by each party in advance of the election, and these forms were then deposited in ballot boxes. Stray votes that broke from each ticket represented scattered individual alterations to the printed form. The expectation of absolute party discipline led one Republican election inspector to defend his reputation in 1823 by insisting that he used every effort in his power "to prevent any mutilation of the Democratic ticket."[46] What seems remarkable is that his district voted overwhelmingly Republican at a constant 177 to 29 ratio for all twenty-eight men on the ballot, with the exception of just two Republicans. These unfavored candidates received fifty-two and forty-seven fewer votes than their party colleagues (votes that did not go to their defeated Federalist opponents), yet still won by easy majorities in the countywide election. This modest departure from total party conformity triggered widespread criticism and prompted a strong public defense. This disciplined system with its expectation of absolute voter loyalty to the dictates of party was a far cry from the independent ideal of republican citizenry, but the growing sense of partisanship as a political virtue was essential to the institutionalization of modern political culture in the new nation. Among the most novel group identities in the postwar period was partisanship itself, a party identity that was especially palpable in early republican Delaware and would grow more powerful in coming decades throughout the Delaware Valley and the nation.

The early republican political trajectory of each town had different contours: the stifled third-party tradition in Easton that brought close attention to the area's Pennsylvania German voters, the Quaker-influenced conservatism of Burlington Federalism, and the competitive bipartisanship in New Castle that built upon ethno-religious connotations of each party. All of them, however, consciously defined electoral politics as a contest for only white men, and partisan identity in each place slowly became a marker not just in formal politics but for everyday life as well. People in each area crafted new political understandings from the distinct multicultural logic of their local circumstances, but all participated in a broader political formation with national scope. The growing commonalities of white masculine voters active on a national stage are evident in how local life engaged the three national political crises that are examined next.

The Missouri Controversy and the Politics of Race

Party politics in the early republic cannot be understood without placing it in local contexts, but that focus must be complemented by attention to national issues that penetrated communities. The Missouri Controversy is often treated as the first national crisis among a string of events that ultimately climaxed in the Civil War; however, it may be even more instructive to place that conflict and its controversial resolution in the context of Revolutionary local politics. The Missouri Controversy became explosive because it drew together several overlapping and often incompatible ideals about slavery and African Americans, the health of the young republic, the nature of partisan politics, and elected representatives' relationship to their constituents. In short, the Missouri Controversy reached into communities throughout the country in ways that had happened previously only in times of war.

The Missouri Controversy is generally judged significant due to its national implications, but regional forces also drove it and deserve exploration, especially the crucial role of Mid-Atlantic voters and politicians who inaugurated and resolved the conflict. The importance of the middle states in causing the Missouri Controversy is usually attributed to the key role played by two New York congressmen, Republican James Tallmadge and Federalist Rufus King. Tallmadge's February 1819 proposal to prohibit slavery in Missouri initiated the two-year controversy, while King, allied with Philadelphia Federalists and conservative newspapers, pushed the issue on its moral merits and with clear hopes for partisan gain.

Yet the crisis still might never have been more than a congressional spat had it not entered into broader public consciousness through a series of unusual public meetings, the likes of which had not been seen since the Revolutionary War, that first raised the issue of prohibiting slavery in territories applying for admission to the nation. The first of these popular meetings occurred in Burlington, New Jersey, on August 30, 1819. Their rapid spread and impact led a St. Louis newspaper to complain six months later that popular assemblies in "every doghole town and blacksmith's village in the northern states" manufactured the controversy.[47] The meetings proved incendiary because the national political parties had so carefully avoided serious attention to slavery in order to build nationwide support among white voters. Now, however, the issue had been unavoidably raised by a talented group of activists spurred by a moral vision and prepared to use mass meetings, committees of correspondence, and newspapers to put their case before the public.

Given the Republican stranglehold on politics at the national level, and especially in New Jersey where Republicans blocked a still active Federalist organization, it is not altogether surprising that Burlington people, with their decades-long connection to Quaker antislavery efforts, played an important role pushing the controversy outside party structures.[48] Three Burlington men in particular led the local opposition movement, and their differences from each other reveal the range of local people united by their opposition to the expansion of slavery. The first, Elias Boudinot, who chaired the initial August meeting, had been bitterly dismayed by American politics since Jefferson's election. To him, the rise of parties and their demand for strict loyalty had debased politics to a crude popularity contest that allowed slavery not just to persist but to strengthen. As his pioneering role in moral reform suggested, Boudinot did not reject political action per se; rather, he found partisanship and institutionalized parties detrimental to the best purposes of the nation.

This cast of mind propelled Boudinot to the forefront of antislavery activism during the Missouri Controversy. One widely distributed circular letter he wrote explained that their "respected assembly" acted upon "dictates of religion and morality" as well as those of "sound policy and national reputation." The meeting hoped to act "in concert with such gentlemen" as "feel an anxiety to prevent the numerous and appalling evils that must result from extending and perpetuating slavery amongst us."[49] Carefully emphasizing the respectable qualities of the campaign, Boudinot accepted popular mobilization in order to block the expansion of slavery to new states. Opposition to slavery had partisan implications that made it appeal to Federalists and gave Republicans pause, but the issue clearly extended beyond mere party calculations for Boudinot, who had largely rejected partisanship by 1819, and whose antislavery commitments stretched back to his founding of the New Jersey Abolition Society in 1788 and to positions he had taken in Congress in 1791.[50]

The second figure, Samuel Emlen Jr., may have been the most important local leader of Burlington's antislavery public meeting about Missouri. He represented an essential element of the successful Federalist machine in Burlington County, even though he never held a formal position in the party or ran for public office. Emlen's chief leadership positions were within the Society of Friends, where he served in many capacities as a member of its Meeting for Ministers and Elders and as clerk of the Burlington Monthly Meeting. As required of Quakers in good standing in the period, Emlen disdained elected office for himself but still participated in politics. As he explained to his father-in-law, the esteemed Public Friend William Dillwyn, antislavery success required a stronger commitment from representatives in Congress.[51]

Other active Burlington Federalists, such as William Griffith, the third local meeting organizer, must have eyed with glee the opportunity for partisan gain from the issue; yet, as we learned in Chapter 3, Griffith also had been a leader in the early New Jersey abolition movement. Antislavery had long been important to Federalist newspapers, which wielded it rapierlike to wound their Republican opponents by ridiculing the notion that Republicans, led by presidential slaveholders, could embody the highest ideals of the nation. As the *Trenton Federalist* explained, "We do not believe that slavery and republicanism have any connection with, but are directly opposed to each other." In a similar vein, the paper lampooned Jeffersonian Republicans' attempt to elect Madison with the claim that republicanism, equality, and liberty could be found in their purest form in Virginia. "Can this be liberty where the poor Africans' blood is mingled with his tears?"[52] Federalist newspapers used slavery and race to stigmatize Republicans as slaveholding hypocrites who employed democratic ideals only in self-interested ways.

The legality of slavery in territories entering the nation threatened to sunder party solidarities that were already weak almost everywhere. Ironically, while most New England and Mid-Atlantic Federalists were prepared to champion antislavery, the leaders of Federalism's most successful state party in Delaware were fundamentally committed to the support of white popular sovereignty that would extend slavery in places such as Missouri. This controversy threatened to destroy whatever coherence remained of the Federalist Party, yet Republicans also disagreed about how to deal with the issue, and they had much more to lose. Many Mid-Atlantic Republican newspapers broke with their party's congressional leadership that generally countenanced Missouri's admission as a slave state. The *True American*, for example, published strong antislavery pieces, and on an important related issue, which we will turn to in the final chapter, also favorably circulated a protest by free blacks announcing that all "respectable people of color" opposed African recolonization.[53] From a top-down perspective, Republicans were a proslavery party, but a local and regional view reveals a wider range of positions on the explosive question of African Americans' status, especially when they were "respectable" and free.

The ground swell of popular opinion against slavery in Missouri took several months to reach Easton. The first issue of a new hyperbolic antiparty (and short-lived) local paper, *The Mountaineer*, favorably reported on a local antislavery meeting chaired by Samuel Sitgreaves. Again, like Boudinot, Sitgreaves had been repelled from formal politics by Republican success, embraced moral reform, and had long been an active supporter of gradual emancipation. Most likely Sitgreaves took up the Missouri cause based on its moral and ethical merits, for he had become disgusted with Federalist moderates who had supported the dissident Republican DeWitt Clinton for president in 1812. He explained his "almost total Seclusion from all political Intercourse" to another unreconstructed Federalist in 1816 and his "Apathy of Despair" caused by "repeated occurrence of similar Apostacies" among his former Federalist colleagues.[54]

Whatever his internal motivations in championing antislavery in 1820, slavery and African Americans had little local presence in Easton. The town had no resident slaves that year and only seventy-two free blacks (3 percent of the total population) lived there. Whites in Easton addressed questions of slavery without confronting local people with an obvious reason to support slavery's legality.

Activists in Burlington also mobilized without a substantial local African American presence; the township's 17 slaves and 258 free blacks made up less than 10 percent of the total population in 1820. But New Castle offers a completely different racial setting for the issue. African Americans made up 24 percent of the local population, and a quarter of them were still enslaved. Slavery's persistence as a legal institution in Delaware, and the unavoidable black presence in New Castle, led local whites to an adamant defense of slavery. Nicholas Van Dyke Jr., a Federalist U.S. senator and New Castle resident, denounced slave restrictions on the floor of the Senate and lampooned those who suggested that the Declaration of Independence should be a guide for interpreting the Constitution. To deny Missouri citizens the right to make their own decision about slavery would "dissolve the bonds of social order." Such an expansion of national power into the "domestic concerns" of states would pervert the federal structure of the nation. Van Dyke, like all Delaware Federalists in Washington, voted against any restrictions on slavery.[55]

The Missouri Controversy loomed as more than a mere partisan division. Federalists in Burlington and Easton led the restriction of slavery movement, but Delaware Federalists bucked that trend. At the same time, the crisis also took shape as more than a simple sectional cleavage dividing north and south. Delaware Federalists in Washington opposed restrictions, but they did so against the explicit instructions of their Federalist-controlled state legislature.[56] The New Castle Federalist James Booth, for example, chaired a bipartisan local meeting in January 1820 that opposed the extension of slavery.[57] While slavery remained legal in Delaware, its declining significance in the state, especially for northernmost New Castle County, added another destabilizing dimension to the crisis. Neither sectional nor party lines effectively explains the problem of slavery's place in the nation during the Missouri Controversy.

Given the public meetings in the Delaware Valley that favored restriction and given that this position was explicitly supported by all three state legislatures, popular opinion in the region seems clear enough. Nevertheless, politicians from Burlington, Easton, and New Castle in the U.S. House and Senate ultimately opposed the restriction of slavery in Missouri. Nicholas Van Dyke took the strongest stand of them all, but Republicans Joseph Bloomfield of Burlington and Thomas J. Rogers of Easton both accepted the proslavery compromise that resolved the controversy in the Congress, a position that angered their constituents.

Bloomfield's place among the eighteen northern "dough faces" in Congress who voted to rescind restriction in March 1820 was especially surprising. He voted against strongly expressed local opinion and against the public position of the state's leading Republican newspaper. Only three New Jersey Republicans in Congress ignored the state legislature's 33-to-5 vote, advising its representatives to block slavery in Missouri.[58] Bloomfield had even founded and served as president of the New Jersey Society for Promoting the Abolition of Slavery. His controversial support for slavery caused the venerable Republican leader to fail to secure his party's all-important nomination for reelection. Indeed, only five of the eighteen northern congressmen who supported slavery in Missouri would be re-elected in their next races.

Although Thomas J. Rogers was the ultimate Republican Party loyalist, he acted with greater caution than Bloomfield on the Missouri issue. Rogers voted to maintain the restriction on slavery in March 1820 and thus campaigned effectively as an antislavery man in the fall election; however, when the Missouri issue came before the House of Representatives for the third consecutive year in March 1821, he decided to compromise. That key vote passed the House 87 to 81, with 18 northerners again voting with the majority. Rogers was among only four compromise supporters in the twenty-three-person Pennsylvania delegation. He buckled to partisan pressure to accept the compromise and defuse an issue that threatened to spur a Federalist revival. For instance, the Philadelphia banker Nicholas Biddle wrote Rogers to assure him that the party's "principal persons" and Philadelphia's Republican newspapers all favored compromise.[59]

Rogers understood the needs of the party leadership, but the antiparty tradition in Easton remained vibrant, and its vindictive newspapers, which largely existed to attack Rogers, pounced on his support for Missouri's admission as slave state as yet another example of his corrupt commitment to party dictates that ignored local opinion. The *Expositor* insisted that Rogers had claimed to oppose slavery before the voters, but then acted differently in Congress to gain favor with "the greatest and most discerning men in the union." Moreover, it slandered Rogers for joining forces with a slave trader "to undertake the business of a negro driver. What a sweet pair you would be to yoke up . . . the poor blacks and drive them to Missouri for sale!" The Republican machine nevertheless returned Rogers to Congress, leading the Easton paper to complain that he had succeeded by lying about his record on Missouri, where his support for a new slave state made "five Missouri negroes equal in the scale of our political union, with three Pennsylvania farmers."[60]

As the *Expositor* made plain, racial politics infused the Missouri Controversy even in places with a negligible black presence. While many Federalist leaders championed antislavery and had been key leaders of gradual emancipation societies, neither the Federalist nor the Republican Party could commit itself to support the political rights of free African Americans. White antislavery in this period intertwined with colonization plans to expel people of color from the country and rested upon a deep fear that blackness would corrupt the United States. The example of independent black Haiti clearly spurred Elias Boudinot to oppose slavery's western expansion. As he explained to his nephew, the growth of slavery meant "we shall become a second Hayti—If it is difficult to get rid of negro slavery now," the campaign would be impossible when the slave population had grown tenfold.[61] Even more disturbingly, the Easton newspaper's excoriation of Rogers explained its position not from any injustice toward slaves, but because it betrayed white equality and political privilege. Similarly, Delaware's Federalist congressman Louis McLane, whose father had helped found the Abolition Society of Delaware, delivered a speech in the House of Representatives that conveyed the dilemma of supposedly enlightened white Americans of his day. McLane personally opposed slavery as an unjust institution, but he saw no reasonable way to rid the nation of that corruption. Like his fellow Delaware Federalist Nicholas Van Dyke Jr., who had also acknowledged slavery as an evil, McLane could not accept immediate solutions that would "put the white and black population upon an equality." As McLane explained to his colleagues, such rash actions would "destroy the features of both [white and black] by the vain attempt to amalgamate one with the other!"[62]

Republican and Federalist elected officials from all three river towns agreed to exclude African American rights from becoming central to their partisan disagreements, whether through the adamant proslavery of Van Dyke or the quiet willingness to compromise exhibited by Rogers. It is no coincidence that Elias Boudinot and Samuel Emlen Jr., two key leaders of the initial public meeting in Burlington that protested slavery in Missouri, and Samuel Sitgreaves, who did the same in Easton, mostly avoided party affairs. Those active in the electoral arena knew full well that slavery was an untouchable partisan issue. Slavery and race were unavoidable subjects of public concern, but political action by white Americans almost always put concerns for the nation and the party before any consideration of black rights. As had occurred among delegates to the federal Constitutional Convention, white politicians who prized national stability above all would also resolve the Missouri Controversy.[63]

Presidential Politics and Local Politics

The presidential election of 1824, another national political crisis, dramatically revealed that partisan instability was not merely the result of local dissidents and parochial issues. The façade of the first party system had finally crumbled beyond any hope of preservation, setting in motion a sweeping transformation of American electoral politics. The Mid-Atlantic states from New York to Maryland played a key role in the creation of a new national political system during the partisan realignment of the 1820s and 1830s. As Richard P. McCormick has noted, "the Middle States held the balance of political power in the nation" during the formation of the second party system and served as the country's "balance wheel," which had to be accommodated by other sections of the country.[64] In part, this regional significance arose because it had no native son among the presidential candidates in the 1820s. Further, the Mid-Atlantic held an essential political prize: Pennsylvania and New York were the country's two most populous states and together awarded half the electoral votes needed to become president. Because these states and the rest of the Mid-Atlantic generally supported protective tariffs, the national economic policies favored by John Quincy Adams would seem to have had an advantage in carrying this key region.[65]

While the middle states lacked the sharp regional consciousness of New England or the South, Mid-Atlantic residents keenly understood their differences from other regions. As Louis McLane, the leading Delaware Federalist on the national stage, explained, he was a "Middle States Northerner," explicitly neither a southerner nor a Yankee.[66] Similarly, a formerly Republican New Jersey paper that favored John Quincy Adams warned of Pennsylvania's strong support for Andrew Jackson: "a middle state has thus been chained to the car of southern interests, and follows, like a captive king, in the retinue of Andrew Jackson and southern nabobs."[67]

In contrast to this geographic consciousness, partisan boundaries had become so fluid as to be almost pointless by the early 1820s. The dull reelection of President Monroe in 1820, standing against no organized opposition, underscored the meaninglessness of parties. Yet with no incumbent to return to office in 1824, that election's chaos made plain that effective party organizations were needed to organize local diversity into comprehensible national patterns. In 1824 the dependable caucus of Republican congressmen, which had successfully selected Madison and Monroe for the presidency, was attended by only 26 of 214 Republicans in Congress. The ensuing election featured four candidates who all claimed to be the legitimate choice of the Republican Party. In a sense, the national race had inherited the partisan uncertainty that had often characterized Pennsylvania elections and that had contributed to its vicious political infighting.

The 1824 election produced great controversy, of course, but its voter turnout was low and inconclusive. Andrew Jackson placed best with 99 electoral votes and almost 153,000 popular votes, versus John Quincy Adams's second-place showing of 84 electors and barely 114,000 direct votes. With no majority in the electoral college, the election went to Congress, where Henry Clay helped to forge an Adams presidency. Although discussion of this election usually focuses on its resolution in the U.S. House of Representatives, that outcome arose from partisan collapse at the state level throughout the country. In all three states considered here, the ordinary presidential selection process failed. Even in Delaware, where electors were still chosen by the legislature, state politicians divided so sharply that only a single elector, an Adams supporter, received a majority, while the two more dubiously selected electors supported Clay and Crawford. Tiny Delaware managed to cast its three electoral votes for three different candidates in 1824! A pro-Adams newspaper decried the "scene of bargaining and intrigue" that named electors who lacked majority support in the legislature as required by the state constitution. Such chicanery indicated to those who favored Adams that "the wishes of the people are now a-days of no more importance than an idle wind."[68]

The weak nomination of William Crawford and running mate Albert Gallatin by the congressional Republican caucus was not even supported by the New Castle County Republican machine and its main vehicle, the *American Watchman.* Unable to agree on a positive endorsement, the party's New Castle County convention endorsed legislative candidates pledged *against* their own party's caucus selection of Crawford. This decision largely reflected state Republican animosity toward Federalist congressman McLane, who strongly backed Crawford, and his allied *Delaware Gazette.* Although top-down partisan solidarity imploded, a certain party logic persisted. Delaware Republicans may have been uncertain about whom to support in the presidential race, but they knew whom they opposed, for partisan animosity persisted even as the national framework collapsed.

Delaware's long-dominant Federalists now suffered the kind of schism that had persistently plagued Pennsylvania Republicans. The Federalist *Delaware Recorder,* part of the anti-McLane faction in the state party, denounced the *Gazette'*s endorsement of Crawford as "prostitution to purposes of individual ambition," which ignored "devotion to Federal principles."[69] Whatever newspapers may have claimed, no clear-cut party identity existed in a race that pitted four self-proclaimed Democratic Republicans against one another. This partisan uncertainty affected popular interest, and turnout declined dramatically—parties played a powerful role in convincing voters to go to the polls.

In New Castle Hundred, a mere 181 votes were cast—100 fewer than the preceding election. The mainstream Republican paper blamed the low turnout on "dissatisfied" local voters who had formed a "malcontent" ticket. The paper lampooned their efforts against the official slate as that of spoiled children who decided, "if we can't have our way, that we'll kick up a bubbery."[70] Demands for party loyalty now rang false, however, given the disarray of partisan politics.

After years of remarkable consistency, local votes for Republican assembly candidates ranged widely in 1824. Republicans retained all seven legislative seats in the county, but the Republican paper blasted the perfidy of local voters. "We have long ceased to wonder at anything from the Federal hundred of New Castle."[71] Although New Castle Hundred may have become the scourge of the county party, local voter disaffection could not overcome persistent Republican majorities elsewhere. Partisan orthodoxy had been shattered, but the county-level machine still had enough inertia to carry the day in 1824.

The dependable New Jersey Republican state convention that had flawlessly managed presidential elections for two decades, with the exception of 1812, also suffered schism in 1824 and produced an official ticket that mixed Jackson and Crawford electors.[72] This awkward union was challenged by Adams-and-Jackson-only tickets that also claimed to be the proper choice of true Republicans. The *Newark Sentinel* bemoaned the multiple slates emerging from the party convention and reminded readers that solidarity behind one ticket had been "the rallying point of the Republican cause" since 1798. "The good of the whole" required all Republicans to accept the mixed Jackson-Crawford slate agreed upon at the official convention. Similar to cosmopolitan evangelicals' insistence upon Christian unity before denominational preference, Republican Party regulars decried "private wishes" that would create the "confusion and disorder" gleefully awaited by Federalists.[73]

Federalists welcomed Republican confusion, but they also lacked a clear candidate in 1824. While Adams might seem a quasi-Federalist given his family lineage, this was decidedly not the case, notwithstanding the anti-Adams press's insistence upon the direct connection between father and son. To conservative Federalists, John Quincy Adams loomed as the worst candidate of all. Timothy Pickering denounced the younger Adams as an "apostate" for accepting cabinet positions in Republican administrations. As the Federalist *Delaware Gazette* reminded its readers, Adams was a base "turncoat," and it claimed William Crawford as the best conservative candidate despite his endorsement by the rump congressional Republican caucus. The *Gazette*'s support for Crawford might seem to break from its strong Federalism; however, its political analysis remained consistent. As the paper noted a year before the election, Federalist policies had triumphed at the national level, even though its candidates, and especially the party name, had not. Supporting the status quo in national politics required no betrayal of values for moderate Delaware Federalists in the 1820s.[74]

Major Republican newspapers such as Delaware's *American Watchman* embraced John Quincy Adams as their candidate. Even more remarkably, the *True American*, long New Jersey's strictest party champion, rejected the convention's mixed support for Jackson and Crawford to strongly back Adams. As it reminded its readers, Adams deserved Republican support because he had broken with Federalism as early as 1808. The *True American* assured its readers that while favoring Adams might seem "novel . . . and though it may expose [us] to ridicule, to sneers, or to enmity, yet it is the most independent and most accountable" presidential choice. Adams had the proper experience and ability for effective leadership, while Jackson suffered from a character of "desperate violence."[75]

Burlington Township's presidential vote exemplifies the partisan fluidity of 1824. It remained a Federalist bastion and the stronghold of the machine headed by William Griffith and William Coxe Jr. Although their conservative wing of Burlington Federalism, which they styled the "Old Ticket," had lost total control over the county's assembly seats to dissident Federalists in 1823, the October 1824 state election sent all four of their candidates to the legislature. Although their weakest candidate won by a two-vote margin out of more than three thousand cast, the traditional Burlington Federalist organization regained county control just before the presidential election. Griffith received the most votes of any Burlington legislative candidate, and in the next month's popular election of presidential electors he organized Burlington Federalists in favor of Andrew Jackson. This most Federalist of towns gave their strongest support to Jackson in 1824.

Burlington voters faced a complicated choice. Jacksonian success may have arisen from its place on two tickets (the official Republican one as well as an all-Jackson independent ticket). With the long-standing surety of party guidelines gone, voters were uncertain and apathetic, and the presidential election drew fewer than half the voters who had participated in the previous month's state elections. Nevertheless, the local strength of each candidate (as judged by votes cast for his electors) indicates a remarkable shift in Burlington's political commitments. Jackson won handily with seventy-five votes, Adams placed second with fifty, while the Crawford men on the official Republican ticket, not surprisingly, received a mere seventeen votes from the Federalist town.[76] Jackson appealed to Burlington Federalists as an outsider to the old national system, which had in essence disenfranchised Federalists in the state and nation for the past two decades. Jackson was an attractive protest candidate to conservative Burlington voters in 1824.

Jackson not only carried Burlington Township, but also swept New Jersey's eight electoral votes, a remarkable victory that overcame major obstacles. While the Republican convention had chosen a mixed Jackson-Crawford slate, most Republican newspapers and elected officials publicly favored Adams. The upstart Jackson had carried the state without strong support within the once dominant Republican machine. The 1824 presidential election in Delaware and New Jersey revealed a significant partisan transition, and developments in Pennsylvania pointed to an even more sweeping realignment.

Pennsylvania's state Republican convention voted 124 to 1 in favor of Jackson in 1824, but this reflected a last-minute change by party insiders to accept popular demands rather than a deep commitment to the newcomer from Tennessee. To understand the disarray concealed by the apparent strength of Pennsylvania Jacksonianism, one needs to place the contest in the all-important context of the preceding gubernatorial election. The dominant group in the state Republican Party, known as "The Family," had its base in the populous eastern part of the state and planned to make Samuel D. Ingham the next governor. A U.S. congressman from Bucks County (whose district included Easton), Ingham had close ties to fellow congressman Thomas J. Rogers, the Easton newspaper editor and party leader. At the chaotic 1823 state convention, the initial leading gubernatorial candidates of western and eastern interests both lost to the unheralded John A. Schulze, a former Lutheran minister from Berks County. His principal supporter at the convention was Easton resident James Madison Porter, who led a dissident Northampton County delegation that broke with the official delegation led by Rogers. Porter thought of himself as an ardent Republican, but rejected party leadership by Rogers, Ingham, and The Family machine.[77] Schulze narrowly managed to get the party's nomination for governor in 1823 and then enjoyed a landslide victory over Independent Republican Andrew Gregg.

The Family's inability to nominate (and therefore elect) their preferred gubernatorial candidate in 1823 put them in a dubious position for the 1824 presidential race. The Family strongly favored John C. Calhoun for the country's top office and totally failed to predict Jackson's swift rise that combined rural and urban support in Pennsylvania.[78] Jackson inspired those who wanted something new, especially an option outside the stultifying control of corrupt insiders who had honed the close connections linking the party press, nominating procedures, and government patronage.

As we have seen in Delaware and New Jersey, partisan newspapers lost their strong sense of direction in the swirling uncertainty of the 1824 campaign, and this was even more evident in Pennsylvania. For example, Christian Jacob Hutter's *Easton Centinel* continued to publicize the virtues of Calhoun even after he had withdrawn from the presidential race.[79] Moreover, during the months of intrigue when the election went to the U.S. House, Hutter's paper barely covered the issue at all, waiting, it seems, to be sure of the winner. Nobody, after all, knew who would emerge victorious. Thomas J. Rogers, for example, had jumped from being a Calhoun champion to a Jackson man, but with Adams's election certified by Congress he rushed to assure the new president of his loyalty and boasted to an Adams ally in Washington that he could "answer for three presses himself."[80]

Party leaders of all stripes seemed incompetent in 1824 because the election's partisan implications were opaque. Republican papers allied with Rogers, such as the *Easton Centinel*, would ultimately condemn Adams's election, but they also called for restraint on the part of Easton's newly formed Hickory Club. While these local Jacksonians denounced Adams as a "liar" and "calumnator" whose election was an "execration of the republican people," the party counseled patience to assess the course of the new administration.[81] The Family's leadership of Pennsylvania's Republican Party derived its influence from success at the polls and the patronage this granted. They may have initially preferred Calhoun but now hoped to work amicably with Adams and had little experience as a party out-of-power. Republican insiders' familiarity with success via control of partisan newspapers and state nominating procedures encouraged them to ignore the popular support that had begun to build around Jackson as an outsider in 1824, a sentiment that would swell into a powerful wave of support beyond the old party leadership's ability to control in the next few years.

The 1828 presidential election began as soon as Adams was awarded the presidency in early 1825. His triumph led Jacksonians to fear for the country's future, and when Clay was named secretary of state, they denounced the deal as a "corrupt bargain" by insiders who overrode the clear choice of the people. Outraged by such machinations and convinced that representative government was fundamentally threatened, Jacksonians began preparing for the climactic 1828 campaign. Politically aware people understood that that contest held significance unmatched since the election of 1800.

Although less well-known than the famed Jacksonian denunciations of the corrupt bargain, Adams supporters had their own misgivings about the contested election that were as principled (and simultaneously self-serving) as those of the Jacksonians. As the pro-Adams Republican *True American* explained the 1824 election to its readers, Jackson's "plurality of the electorate" rested upon eighteen southern electoral votes gained from the three-fifths representation that the Constitution awarded based on their enslaved population. Without the additional votes provided by the enslaved enumeration, Adams would have placed first in the electoral college. The paper asked, "freemen of the nation, are you willing that General Jackson, a slave-holder, should be palmed upon you by the votes of masters for their slaves? We think not."[82] To Adams supporters, the presidency had properly gone to the people's choice. Unlike the case of the new president's father, who had lost his reelection bid in 1800 on the basis of slave representation in the electoral college, this time a close race had been honorably resolved.

In a period when the legitimacy of a permanently organized opposition only gradually became an accepted feature of the political landscape, electoral failure needed to be explained either by corruption (as Jacksonians charged) or through systemic failure (as Adamsites suggested). Confidence in popular sovereignty required that "the people" would always make the proper decision when given a fair chance. Opening suffrage to almost all adult white men and the increasingly direct election of presidential electors in the 1820s extended popular participation in voting further than ever before. But this opening was accompanied by deep misgivings about the corruption of mass party politics. In 1824, for the first time since Thomas Jefferson's election, the national electoral system was widely seen to suffer the kinds of abuse and chicanery that everyone knew existed at local and state levels.

The lumbering partisan realignment of the 1820s did not occur as a direct inheritance from the first to the second party system. Federalist Burlington, for example, supported Jackson in 1824 as the only outsider in the race, and emergent Jacksonianism had significant roots among Federalists throughout the Delaware Valley. Successful Federalists such as Louis McLane in Delaware, who had championed Crawford in 1824, now became an ardent Jackson man. In 1827, the old Federalist *Delaware Gazette* described the presidential candidates in extraordinary language for a conservative paper. It condemned Adams and his supporters for "arrogantly claim[ing] all the respectability of the country for their party." In fact, such claims only consisted of "apeing the manners of the European nobility," while we ally ourselves with "honest farmers, mechanics, and laborers, who . . . support their families by the fruits of their own labour." The formerly Federalist paper proclaimed that Jacksonians embraced the country's "bone and sinew," while Adams supporters' "wisdom consists in wealth, and [their] gentility in a clean shirt and a suit of broad cloth."[83]

Delaware's 1827 congressional race showcased partisan fluidity. The Federalist McLane spearheaded efforts to create a new Jackson party and carried much of Delaware's effective Federalist machine to Jackson. However, the failure of James A. Bayard Jr., McLane's legal partner and political ally, to win Delaware's lone seat in the U.S. House of Representatives in a direct statewide race indicated that Delaware Jacksonianism was more attune to national developments than the present partisan reality in the state. Bayard ran against New Castle's Kensey Johns Jr. for the open seat in Congress that had become vacant when the legislature elevated McLane to the U.S. Senate. Bayard and Johns were both sons of leading Delaware Federalists, whose names they inherited, but this next generation chose opposite sides at the onset of a new political era. Bayard backed Jackson as part of the McLane wing of the state Federalist Party, while Johns favored Adams and Thomas Clayton, McLane's bitter rival and also a former Federalist.

Amid the complexities of that congressional race, which included two other candidates who withdrew from the contest, the old partisan guidelines that had endured for so long in Delaware finally ended. Leaders and newspapers from both older parties backed both the Bayard-Jackson and the Johns-Adams slates; everyone recognized that the old partisan patterns had been swept aside. When the initial Republican congressional candidate withdrew from the race in favor of fellow Adams supporter Kensey Johns, the state's leading Republican paper found itself in the peculiar position of endorsing a longtime Federalist family for Congress. As the *American Watchman* explained, "the old names 'Democrat' and 'Federalist' are, for the present at least, entirely lost sight of in Delaware, where they have been adhered to with such tenacity. You hear of no party names here now but Adams-men and Jackson-men. An amalgamation of old parties has taken place."[84] Similarly, the *Delaware Gazette*, the venerable Federalist paper, backed Bayard-Jackson and broke from the regular nomination of its party for the first time. As it explained, the old party labels had passed, and "the name of Federal and Democrat will be lost sight of in this electioneering campaign. The appellation will be—Jackson and Adams. This is as it should be we cannot get along under any other head." Although nobody in the late 1820s knew what shape political parties might take in the future, "the terms Democracy and Federalism can no longer stand as the watchwords of party."[85]

In the midst of such partisan turmoil, one might expect New Castle voters to support Johns as a hometown candidate. However, the town and county both favored the Jacksonian Bayard, though not strongly enough to overcome Johns's strength in the two southern counties. Jacksonians in New Castle Town were singled out for abuse by papers that favored Johns and Adams. The Federalist *Delaware Journal* named George Read Jr. as one of the key boosters of the "miserable county ticket" with Bayard at its head, and Read and James R. Black were discounted as petty political chieftains who secretly moved the levers of the nomination process like "would-be-lords."[86]

Johns's victory over Bayard in 1827 set the political mold in Delaware for the upcoming presidential race. Because Delaware remained one of only two states where legislatures chose electors in 1828, party insiders closely controlled the presidency there. McLane had failed to create a winning Jacksonian coalition in 1827 and failed again the next year when Adams won all three of Delaware's electoral votes. Ironically, success in Washington and at the national level had left McLane vulnerable in his home state.

McLane moved faster than public opinion and the old party organizations in Delaware, but his political calculations were astute. For example, the Republican *American Watchman* failed as a partisan newspaper when it backed Johns-Adams. As the editors explained in its final issue, their defense of the Adams administration meant a loss of subscribers that forced them to sell the paper to Josiah F. Clement, also a Republican, but one who had favored Jackson. The renamed *Delaware Patriot and American Watchman* ardently supported Jackson.[87]

The realignment of partisan commitments led a Federalist-Jacksonian newspaper in Delaware to explain to "Federalists of New Jersey" how best to negotiate the transition before the 1828 election. Federalism "no longer exist[ed] as a party. You never can expect to act as a party again. However, in the dissolution of your party organization . . . you have a consolation which rarely happens to the conquered. Your principles are triumphant." This Federalist-turned-Jacksonian paper warned their colleagues in neighboring New Jersey not be swayed by "Eastern [i.e., New England] Federalists" who promote John Quincy Adams as our candidate. Remember, Jackson's central pledge to 'destroy that monster, Party.'" True Federalists, the Delaware paper insisted, could not back an apostate like Adams, who had ascended to the presidency as a Republican operative. The honorable course demanded support for the outsider, who would restore virtue by casting out corrupt partisanship.[88]

The 1824 presidential election in New Jersey had clearly pointed to "a general breaking up of the old parties of Federalists and Democrats."[89] Although Federalists had the most to gain from the destruction of the old party formation in their state, Republicans also carefully planned how to take advantage of the transition. New Jersey's major Republican paper staunchly backed Adams in 1824 and 1828, and it concentrated on attacking Jackson as central to its pro-Adams argument. Led by Samuel Southard, the state's former U.S. senator, who now served as Adams's secretary of the navy, most New Jersey Republican insiders favored Adams in 1828. Adams supporters throughout the country generally proved to be mediocre political organizers, but not in New Jersey where the effective state Republican organization supported the administration, largely because access to patronage had been the guiding light of partisanship there for more than a decade.[90]

The 1828 presidential race brought the first truly bipartisan statewide election to New Jersey since 1812, and the decision to support Adams or Jackson amounted to a new partisan formation there. Because no established newspaper in New Jersey supported Jackson, his backers founded new ones, such as the *Trenton Emporium*, to tout their candidate. Probably hoping to taint Adams with Burlington's staunch Federalism in the past, this West Jersey Jacksonian paper denounced Burlington as the center of pro-Adams electioneering, with its roads littered with anti-Jackson "Coffin Handbills" that portrayed the former general as a cruel and violent military leader.[91] The insurgent Jacksonian movement could not overcome the state political establishment, and, as in formerly Federalist Delaware, formerly Republican New Jersey cast all its electoral votes for Adams in 1828.

The embrace of Jackson by some former Federalists in New Jersey and Delaware may actually have improved Adams's standing in these states. Uncertain of what national party developments might mean, many local leaders and voters simply favored the opponent of their traditional enemies. Such logic played an especially important role in New Castle and Burlington, where partisanship from the first party system proved unusually durable. This political calculus was neither ignorant nor monolithic, as the change in presidential voting in Burlington between 1824 and 1828 demonstrates. In 1824 local voters had favored Jackson as the only candidate operating outside the party system that had effectively silenced Federalists at the state and national levels. However, Burlington voters would reject him in 1828. The Adams slate carried the day there with 59 percent of local votes, and Burlington County proved even more staunchly pro-Adams at 64 percent. Such strong pro-Adams support in Burlington was essential in a statewide race that his electors won with just 51 percent of the vote. Reversing its traditional opposition to Federalist voters in Burlington County, the (formerly) Republican *True American* praised Burlington voters for giving Adams his largest margin of victory in 1828.[92]

As the scholar Herbert Ershkowitz has argued, the 1828 election established a lasting pattern for New Jersey party politics that would hold fast into the 1850s and that in many respects persisted into the twentieth century. The immediate victors in this realignment were former Federalists, such as Garrett D. Wall, who in 1820 had been elected to the New Jersey legislature on a "union" ticket of Federalists and dissident Republicans, both of whom were excluded from patronage by the dominant Republican machine in the state.[93] Wall probably was the leading Jackson man in the state when he moved to Burlington in 1828, as an advantageous location for his legal practice. An Episcopal vestryman, Wall declined to serve when elected governor by the legislature in 1829, preferring federal appointments, and became a Jacksonian U.S. senator from New Jersey in 1835. Like McLane in Delaware, Wall was among the key leaders of Federalist Jacksonianism in the Delaware Valley. Pennsylvania had its leading conservatives in this tradition too. James Buchanan was the towering example of an ex-Federalist "amalgamator" who joined the Jacksonian movement, but in staunchly Republican Easton, the few remaining Federalists were too embittered by the vulgarity of popular politics to see General Jackson as a legitimate presidential candidate. Instead, a new generation of Northampton County conservatives, such as James Madison Porter, worked within the Democratic Party.

While Adams supporters in Delaware and New Jersey effectively controlled major parts of the older Federalist *and* Republican organizations in those states, the hegemonic (if internally divided) Republican machine in Pennsylvania took up the cause of Jackson and his running mate Calhoun in 1828. Of course, the mere eleven electoral votes for Adams from New Jersey and Delaware paled beside the twenty-eight that Pennsylvania held. The Jacksonian ground swell in Pennsylvania that had surprised party leaders in 1824 continued unabated, and rather than combat this new political force, Pennsylvania's Republican insiders joined the movement as latecomers.

Jacksonianism threatened to push conservative Republicans such as the Easton newspaper editor Christian Jacob Hutter in a direction that he abhorred. Once an active Quid, Hutter had been a late-Republican convert, and the populist edge of Jacksonianism disturbed him. His *Easton Centinel* cautiously accepted Jacksonianism, but this tepid support spurred Thomas J. Rogers to return to newspaper publishing after an absence of several years. Rogers's new vehicle, the *Delaware Democrat and Easton Gazette,* ran only during the critical eighteen-month election season in 1827 and 1828, its motto forcefully rejecting the corrupt 1824 election: "Liberty is Ruined by Providing any kind of Substitute to Popular Elections." Casting the Adams election as a "great evil" caused by an "Aristocratic" electoral system, the first issue of the paper proclaimed electoral reform a "*holy* undertaking" and the upcoming presidential contest a "great struggle between liberty and power, similar to that which terminated in 1800." Furthermore, Rogers emphasized the legitimacy of partisanship and "does not hesitate to say, he is a party man."[94] Jacksonianism surged forward on a populist impulse, to which partisan leaders such as Rogers yoked the fuller legitimization of political parties.

The fusion of populist rejection of the old parties with a persistent professional party organization marked a central way that the new political culture of the second party system built upon certain strands of Revolutionary identity politics and simultaneously pushed them in new directions. While The Family's coterie of Pennsylvania Republican leaders preferred Calhoun for president, they pragmatically supported Jackson in 1828. Jacksonians in Northampton County effectively linked their candidate to the Revolution, through both his own military service and their revival of an important Revolutionary ritual. The Hickory Pole connected their movement to Liberty Poles raised during the American Revolution and was a highly charged public expression around Easton, as they had been used locally in the Fries Rebellion of 1798–99. This connection helped give Jacksonians especially powerful ammunition against John Quincy Adams, who, of course, was linked by the opposition press with the "reign of terror" imposed by his father's administration. The Fries Rebellion remained a powerful local memory that bound together Revolutionary mobilization, Pennsylvania German solidarity, hatred of Adams, and the need to overcome distant "aristocratic" enemies at the center of power. As a letter to the *Easton Centinel* queried, "the question now strikes us, what is the reason that in 1776 the tories cut down the liberty poles, in 1799 the federalists cut them down, and in 1828 the Adams men cut down the Hickory polls even on the Sabbath day?"[95]

Easton Jacksonians not only wielded powerful rhetorical and historical arguments but also organized rank-and-file voters in large publicly announced committees of correspondence that listed more than three hundred members of the local Committee of Vigilance. Matching these names to local tax lists suggests that party leaders in Easton consciously included committee members from every economic rank. Forty-two percent of the town's taxpayers in 1830 were identified in the newspapers as Jacksonians, and they perfectly reflect the town's social structure, even at the lowest rank, where 36 percent of the committee was drawn from the bottom 39 percent of Easton taxpayers.

Because the Adams campaign organized so poorly in Easton, no complete profile of local Adams men can be attempted. Only six known Adams supporters can be identified in the 1830 tax list, and with four of them in the town's top taxpaying quintile, a sharp contrast between the lopsided presidential camps in Easton seems evident. Religious identity reinforces this contrast because the two Adams supporters whose religious affiliation can be identified were a Presbyterian elder and an Episcopalian vestryman, while the most significant religious affiliation among Jacksonians was Lutheran and Reformed. As with economic status, known Jacksonians came from every locally organized religious group and did so at rates matching the overall pattern of religious affiliation in Easton.[96]

Jacksonianism in Easton benefited from the scores of ordinary laborers who went there to build the massive canal network that made the town a prime example of the economic and physical transformations of the 1820s. Canals spread out from the Pennsylvania town in all directions. Anthracite coal from the northwest first arrived there via the Lehigh Canal in 1820, and six years later it carried more than 31,000 tons through the town.[97] Meanwhile, workers had begun digging the Morris Canal across northern New Jersey to link Easton with Newark and New York City, and the Delaware division of the Lehigh Canal worked its way south along the Delaware River, over the falls at Trenton, to Bristol, Pennsylvania (opposite Burlington), from whence the river flowed swiftly to Philadelphia. Development as a canal and early manufacturing center brought increasing social stratification to Easton, as demonstrated by a comparison with wealth distribution rates in New Castle and Burlington. As Easton became more fully integrated in the market economy and began early industrial development, its wealth distribution moved in a sharply inegalitarian direction. Rapid demographic and economic expansion in Easton included a growing separation between rich and poor, while the other towns' populations and wealth distributions remained quite consistent over the broad Revolutionary period.[98]

Canals not only changed the social structure of Easton but also helped to reshape its cultural landscape. As Josiah White, the Quaker proprietor of the Lehigh Canal commented, "the hands come from all nations and stranger to us."[99] Easton residents made similar observations about canal construction and the changes that accompanied it. For instance, Joel

Jones wrote to a business partner in Philadelphia about a black family who were forced from their "hovel" on the riverbank by the arrival of canal workers, presumably Irish, who erected a "shantee."[100] Poor blacks and new Irish laborers occupied the same physical space in the town, and long-term residents distinguished themselves from both ragged groups. Pennsylvania Germans in Easton increasingly understood themselves as both the oldest and best-established group in the area in the face of the canal-and-manufacturing-driven arrival of newcomers.

Canal laborers in Easton, like common sailors in New Castle, were a mobile segment of the population who rarely left written records even as they contributed significantly to the public life of these river towns. Canal boatmen, however, were a better-established group, as demonstrated by their increasing prominence in Easton's nineteenth-century tax lists. One of these men's experiences can be captured in unusual detail through his attempt to purchase local property, and these events help us to see how economic, political, and cultural forces each intersected with one another in important ways. In June 1828, Jacob Hartzel sent $102 to Thomas Cadwalader, the Philadelphia attorney for the Penn Estate, to purchase part of proprietary lot number 37 in Easton.[101] Hartzel was a long-term local boatman who appeared in the lowest rank of taxpayers in both 1814 and 1830. He had even less economic security than most boatmen, for his three children were listed among those needing aid from the state for their education in 1830. His attempt to purchase the lot might have closed swiftly, but five days after he sent his money to Cadwalader, the Philadelphia attorney received a letter from Isaac Wikoff, a wealthy druggist in Easton, who protested the purchase. Wikoff charged that Hartzel's father had once occupied the house on the lot, but due to the son's "very intemperate habits" it had been sold at a sheriff's auction where Wikoff purchased it. The druggist insisted that he had acted with benevolent intentions and permitted Hartzel to reside in the house and operate a tavern there, if he could "stay sober, keep a decent house and pay me moderate Rent." The arrangement collapsed, however, when Hartzel "became so perfectly worthless that I should lose both rent and [liquor] license if he continued in the tavern any longer." As a result, Wikoff felt "compelled to turn him out and as no one would rent him a house, I let him have a House adjoining, where he now resides a tenant of mine and owes me near two years Rent."[102]

When Cadwalader demanded clarification, Hartzel explained that he intended no "erroneous impression," but had gotten "a person unacquainted with the circumstances to write for me, as I am unable to write intelligibly myself." He conceded some of Wikoff's points, but added that Cadwalader's local agent assured him that because of his father's connection to the property, he possessed the right of first refusal. Hartzel closed with a passionate plea for fair play: "I need, I presume, scarcely trouble you with the circumstances which caused the sale of my property by the Sheriff. I am a poor man, and followed boating. Whatever money I had was lost by the death and failure of the estate of Mr. George Lerch in the year 1823. I am now clear of all debts, and if I can obtain this Lot it will give me a home for my wife & children. . . . I have suffered enough by misfortunes already and hope that you will not aid Mr. Wikoff to take this property unjustly from me."[103] Unmoved, Cadwalader later used Wikoff as his intermediary to communicate with Hartzel. After all, why should the attorney write directly to a semiliterate boatman? For his part, Wikoff thought so little of Hartzel that he supposed him to be "a mere fool in the hands of some designing person to extort from me."[104] Hartzel, however, was not easily put off and mobilized support from Easton's conservative Republican attorney James M. Porter. Writing in Hartzel's defense, Porter expressed "a strong leaning toward Mr. Hertzel's claim. . . . [I]t will give him a home in his old days, which he may need. . . . I hope you will not decide against the poor man who has struggled hard [for three years?] to raise the $100 to pay for it."[105]

Wikoff and Hartzel fell on opposite sides of the divide separating cosmopolitan and local interests in Easton and throughout the nation, both of which had growing influence as the broad Revolutionary era drew to a close in the 1820s. Cosmopolitans looked beyond petty local issues and expressed a kind of respectability that the boatman Hartzel, accused of drunkenness, poverty, and inability to support his children's formal education, could not muster. Wikoff, by contrast, mobilized literate and legal skill in this conflict as well as economic resources through banks in Philadelphia and Easton. Moral judgments about Hartzel's character emphasized his individual failure rather than growing class differences in early industrial Easton, and the growing economic interdependence of a credit-based economy meant that George Lerch's financial collapse would have consequences beyond his own household.

Hartzel and Wikoff both participated in wide-ranging social networks, but Wikoff's circles remain more easily accessible and visible today. Hartzel needed a local scribe and relied on the proprietor of a Philadelphia tavern, "where our [Easton] boatmen . . . generally stopped," to convey the deed that he hoped to acquire from Cadwalader.[106] The tavern was an important community institution that served myriad purposes, but its functions were increasingly circumscribed by the developments of the 1820s. The marginally literate Jacob Hartzel, with his Pennsylvania German ethnic name and of unknown religious affiliation, lost his bid to purchase a house lot in Easton to the elite Episcopal vestryman Isaac Wikoff. The property dispute was closed in Cadwalader's legal files with a draft for $102.25 on Wikoff's account at the Bank of the Northern Liberties.[107]

Not surprisingly, Wikoff supported Adams for president in 1828 and would be a Whig by 1832, but this political affiliation left him vulnerable to attack in Easton. The *Delaware Democrat* dismissed Wikoff as a "decided Federalist," while listing Hartzel as a member of the town's Jacksonian Committee of Vigilance.[108] The Jacksonian movement offered men like Hartzel the chance to strike back against local elites like Wikoff via electoral politics. A focus on economic and legal resources, as well as attention to conservative evangelical reform, often make it seem that cosmopolitans enjoyed unalloyed success in the period from the ratification of the federal Constitution through the construction of the Benevolent Empire, but those developments occurred alongside the powerful localism of Revolutionary mobilization and its institutionalization in partisan politics. An important part of Jacksonianism's attraction to laboring Pennsylvania German men such as Hartzel was that it allowed them to challenge and defeat cosmopolitan figures who were influential in most other areas of public life.

Christian Jacob Hutter's German-language *Northampton Correspondent* did not use ethnic appeals in the 1824 presidential contest but prominently employed them four years later when it insisted that "no German man should have to think what he has to do" when comparing the "Tennessee farmer" and the "aristocratic Adams." Relying on the old party labels, the paper insisted that Federalists believed that "big changes took place in the German counties of Pennsylvania in favor of the usurper [i.e., Adams]." But such impudent opinions rested on "the expectation that the Germans are really as dumb as they always described them . . . [and] are carried away by the pamphlets of lies against General Jackson." Federalists were surely mistaken to believe that "Germans [would] leave the party of virtue and freedom to believe the[se] lies." For, "in most of [Northampton's] townships, especially in the completely German ones, the Adams men are as scarce as white mice and we can therefore confidently rely on the belief that Northampton will maintain its good reputation in this most important election as the most important Democratic county in the state."[109] Northampton County and Pennsylvania voters overwhelmingly supported Jackson, who won the state by a fifty-thousand-vote margin, and in the midst of that landslide a newly sweeping use of ethnicity rallied partisans to the cause.

No genuine two-party competition occurred in Easton, Northampton County, or Pennsylvania in the 1820s—all lopsidedly favored Andrew Jackson. The Republican state organization of the early republic successfully transformed itself into the Democratic machine of the 1830s. Nevertheless, critical political changes occurred in the transition of the 1820s. Jackson may have carried the state twice in that decade, but the huge increase in voter turnout between the two presidential elections led to a much stronger Adams vote in 1828. The historian William Shade has calculated that the turnout of eligible voters in Northampton County rose from 21 to 63 percent between the two presidential elections, and its Adams vote jumped from a mere 3 percent in 1824 to 20 percent in 1828.[110] Adams still lost in dramatic fashion, but as Jackson became better known in Pennsylvania he fared more poorly in each election from 1824 to 1832.

On the central economic issue of tariffs, Pennsylvanians favored the protectionism that Adams forthrightly supported. Indeed, Delaware Valley Jacksonians also strongly supported protective legislation, while Jackson himself carefully avoided a definitive stand on the issue (and most others) during the 1828 campaign. The policy gap that separated the pro-development leaders of the state party from Jackson's increasing opposition to a strong government role in the economy led to conflict. The former Quid, Family leader, and Republican congressman from the Easton area, Samuel D. Ingham, was among the unexpected men that Jackson appointed to his cabinet in 1829, but their strong disagreements led to Ingham's resignation as secretary of the treasury two years later. The closest study of Pennsylvania politics in the period frustratingly described the state's strong support for the newcomer from Tennessee as "Jackson Madness," but Pennsylvania's embrace of Jackson was never the preferred route of the state's political leaders, who joined the movement only when they realized that it would win without them.[111]

Jacksonianism in the Delaware Valley

Policy questions did not decide the presidential election of 1828, nor did the weight of professional party organizations, nor did the partisan allegiances of cultural groups. These three major forces overlapped with one another, and their combination gave the politics of the late 1820s a new quality that departed from the older style of the Revolutionary period. Partisan newspapers increasingly employed ethnic, religious, and class identities to explain the partisan landscape of the 1820s. The pro-Adams *True American*, for example, lambasted a Jacksonian paper for expressing itself like an "old Scotch woman" whose shrieking prayers led her dog to squeal.[112] Such derogatory prejudice only occasionally appeared in print, but responses to such assertions were widespread. In celebrating the victory of 1828, the *Trenton Emporium* fused the abuse heaped on its partisans in a manner representative of most Jacksonian papers. Although they called us "dirty shirts" and accused us of being "Irishmen with a noggin of whiskey in one hand and a Jacksonian ticket in the other," now our enemies can see that we actually represent "that immense mass of our countrymen, the Farmers, the Mechanics, the plain men—who never dream of titled distinctions, or power or place for themselves or their families."[113] The *Delaware Democrat* offered similar reasons to "rejoice." Although the Adams aristocracy "insulted and abused the people by calling them the rabble, stupid Dutch, [and] turbulent Irish," the voters overcame such name-calling to elect Jackson.[114]

Pennsylvania German ethnicity was employed to support Jackson by the

Easton press, but downriver, in areas without a large Pennsylvania German population (and where Jackson would lose in 1828), different types of identity politics informed the campaign. Pro-Adams newspapers in Delaware and New Jersey closely examined Jackson's positions on racial issues. Although published in a slave state, the *Delaware Journal* pilloried the southerner on a score of issues, including his moral failure as a slave trader. After presenting evidence to show that Jackson sold slaves in 1800 and 1811, the paper queried, "what is now to be said for this manseller—this dealer in human flesh—this trader in women and children?" The same paper also denounced the "barbarity and brutal ignorance" of General Jackson's "horrible [military] victory" over Native Americans.[115] Newspapers from West Jersey, with its strong Quaker tradition, regularly targeted Jackson's slaveholding and his "desperate violence" as a military man.[116] Articles in defense of Native American rights, especially regarding the Cherokee conflict with the state of Georgia, also regularly appeared in New Jersey's anti-Jackson press.[117] Jackson's opponents often defended free blacks and Indian rights and questioned slavery, but his defenders easily turned these issues aside by reminding readers that the hero's Indian victories "gave peace and security to our frontier" and that martial and presidential leadership had been united by no less heralded a figure than George Washington. The Jackson press also used the racially informed attacks on their candidate to bolster his supposed connection to Jefferson, another man of the people, who also suffered campaign allegations charging him with "base intrigue with his negro slave."[118]

Instead of focusing on racially informed critiques, Jacksonians presented themselves as triumphing over other kinds of prejudice. A Delaware paper, for example, explained how the elitism of Adams cast the election into a struggle between good and evil by denigrating Jackson men as "the scum of the people" and "men without education," most of whom were assumed to be laborers and "foreigners used to war and oppression." Such people supposedly supported Jackson from "ignorance." Meanwhile defenders of the Adams administration supposedly counted themselves the "most enlightened, scientific, and genteel part of Americans" that alone possessed proper decision-making capabilities. Jacksonians invoked such allegations to rally ordinary Americans against "a few purse-proud aristocrats," and their powerful rhetoric shaped perceptions of them at the time and since.[119]

Obviously, an electoral system that prohibited free black men and all women from formal participation (not to mention political leadership) glaringly failed to engage all Americans, but the ways in which politics became a legitimate public concern for ordinary white men during and after the Revolutionary War represented a significant opening in American life. A broad consensus embraced popular partisanship for white men and made this an "Age of Egalitarianism" even as the accelerating market economy increased inequality among whites and a recommitment to slavery.[120] The abuses disguised by the political rhetoric of the second party system should not be ignored, but neither should we dismiss how parties institutionalized Revolutionary commitments for ordinary white male voters to play an important role in formal politics.

The inclusive and egalitarian impulse that both parties shared in the emerging second party system prompted them to resist, if not reject, moral reformers' claims to be the nation's best guides. Cosmopolitan evangelical reform was an important force in early national life, but not in the vigorously masculine world of popular partisan politics. Neither Adams nor Jackson could present themselves convincingly as evangelicals, due to both their own religious backgrounds and their pragmatic need to appeal to the diverse spiritual opinions of the electorate. Supporters of John Quincy Adams, for example, denied that their candidate's religious principles could be transformed by his entering a Unitarian church as his opponents charged. This was impossible, pointed out an Adams defender, who signed as "A Friend," for surely Quakers remain the same no matter what church they enter. "As well might it be said that because there are some white men who go to the African church that they must be Africans!"[121] The shift from religious to racial identity attempted to dispel concerns about his spirituality by employing the growing sense of the permanence of racial difference to imply that Adams's religious character was equally unchangeable.

Jackson's victory heralded a new era of American electoral politics, even though key features of the second party system were only dawning in the late 1820s.[122] The transitional nature of this decade allows us to see how central strains of Revolutionary identity politics informed the creation of a more modern system that was paradoxically defined by both an increasing populism and a more forceful professionalism in electoral life. The normalization of a national party system, which would only be fully accomplished in the 1840s, legitimized certain features of Revolutionary politics and discredited others. Yet even in the face of strengthening national norms, localist traditions persisted and continued to shape politics. Rather than separate the second party system from its local context as a national approach encourages or isolate it from its close relationship to the American Revolution as traditional periodization encourages, the new partisan formation is best understood within the context of transformed and ongoing Revolutionary values among ordinary people who increasingly relied on ethnic, racial, and class-based language to explain electoral politics.

Chapter 7
The Persistence of Local Diversity

Partisan politics and cosmopolitan evangelicalism each sought to reshape the nation by reforming local diversity into national unity. Both efforts had significant local support, yet they contrasted with one another and faced considerable opposition. These competing bids to define the nation spurred ongoing contests among localist and cosmopolitan forces that made national society and culture increasingly palpable in the 1820s. These struggles strengthened a new national consciousness around a more inclusive and egalitarian sense of the country than had existed in the colonial era, even as it made its own sharp distinctions between insiders and outsiders. National identity took shape in the Delaware Valley in close relationship to local traditions that it variously reconciled and coerced depending on the logic of local circumstances. This national formation remained so inchoate, however, that local diversity could not be ignored, much less swept aside or dismissed.

This final consideration of how the Delaware Valley's Revolutionary identity politics helped to create the nation by 1830 examines interrelated changes in each town at the onset of the Jacksonian era. We begin by considering how electoral politics and evangelicalism clashed with one another in the partisan realignment of the 1820s. Pennsylvania Germans weakened moral reform efforts in Easton, yet cosmopolitan inroads there contributed to growing local distinctions between Lutherans and German Reformed members. Next, we turn to the dramatic challenges faced by Burlington Friends in accommodating a strengthened national culture. Finally, we place the exclusion of African Americans from the promise of the nation in relationship to the changes that occurred for white ethnic and religious groups. The growing coherence of the nation intersected with the dynamic persistence of diverse local identities throughout the country. Their interrelationships can best be understood by examining how specific individuals and groups struggled to find their own place in the nation. While the distinct experiences of each group remind us of the importance of local particularity, their participation in a common process of creating the nation and responding to demands made in its name underscores the connections that bind together ethnicity, religion, race, and politics.

Just as evangelical reform disturbed many local people, the rising influence of national party politics challenged the concerns and interests of many people in these river towns. Local groups faced such national challenges in varied ways, and in Easton and Burlington, the strengthened national context caused local groups to split apart as never before. Unlike those two separations, African Americans in New Castle recommitted themselves to greater unity in the 1820s. Despite their important similarities and the necessity of comparative analysis, black racial identity and white ethno-religious identity carried different social consequences that had become even more evident by the close of the period. The near termination of an always-fragile hope for fuller black participation in American public life ended the broad Revolutionary era in the Delaware Valley.

Partisanship and Embattled Evangelicalism

Most partisan newspapers avoided close association with moral reform during the factionalized and personalist contest between Adams and Jackson in 1828. The press supporting both candidates had serious doubts about, and even outright hostility for, the validity of religion in the electoral context. This suspicion may have been simply a pragmatic decision because neither candidate had deep roots in either populist or cosmopolitan evangelicalism, yet partisan newspapers exploited almost any claim to advance their candidate regardless of plausibility. Clearly, most editors, the most engaged professional politicians of that period, felt that popular support for politicized religion was too unpredictable to aid their cause.

Evangelical leaders, nevertheless, made bold demands for a direct Christian political campaign to save the nation. Reverend Ezra Stiles Ely, a Philadelphia Presbyterian, instructed his congregation from the pulpit on July 4, 1827, to vote only for Christians and to bar infidels from office. "We are a Christian nation," he exclaimed, and, "we have a right to demand that all our rulers in their conduct shall conform to Christian morality." Ely had a dramatic plan: "I propose, fellow-citizens, a new sort of union, or, if you please, *a Christian party in politics.*"[1] This call gathered little support at the grassroots level and ultimately would splinter the solidarity of diverse groups that had drawn together in the Bible movement and other wings of early benevolent reform. Ely's call for a "Christian party in politics" and the Bible societies' comprehensive national campaign in the same years stemmed from a mistaken confidence that cosmopolitan evangelicals could represent the whole nation.

The popular writer Anne Royall derived her success in large part from her severe and sustained criticism of moral reform. She especially targeted Presbyterian and Congregational ministers as its manipulative leaders. Royall cast cosmopolitan reformers as consumed by petty morality and an unholy drive to secure donations from the common man. By contrast, on a journey from Philadelphia to Easton on the eve of Andrew Jackson's election, she found the dependable Americans whom she hoped would dismantle the Benevolent Empire. The "plain, honest, farmer-looking Germans" with their "sensible independence inspired me with a good opinion of the country."[2] She particularly praised Easton for its "freedom from priest-craft. I find no tracts nor pious education societies here." Instead, "they are Lutherans, who do not suffer those religious pirates to come amongst them." When she asked the Easton lawyer and congressman George Wolf (soon to be elected governor) why Pennsylvania Germans such as himself showed such little interest in evangelical reform, he supposedly responded, "'we put no more confidence in religious lies than we do in other lies.'" Such values led Royall to comment, "How often I have heard those Germans branded with the words ignorant and dull. But I find them the stay of Pennsylvania."[3]

Royall's praise for Pennsylvania Germans was a small part of her sustained assault on cosmopolitan reform and its bid to reshape American life. To her, the institutionalization of evangelical power threatened to reduce religion to mere commerce. Her condemnation of the Bible movement demonstrates the venom that informed opposition to religious reform by the late 1820s. "I hope to hear no more of the Bible, let it be seen and not heard. . . . [T]hese bible people wholly disregard its precepts. . . . Filling newspapers with Bibles, and crying 'bibles, bibles,' from the housetops, has no more title to the name religion than crying oysters in the streets, or advertising filberts."[4] Few opponents of evangelical reform adopted such scandalous language, but her hyperbole found a wide readership among people who shared her sentiments. Royall feared missionary "marauders" who "laid the whole country under contribution," and with that "money they get presses, and by presses they get money, and by both they get power."[5]

Partisan activists also doubted evangelical claims to represent all Americans. The Quaker-edited and pro-Adams *Trenton Federalist*, for example, published a letter by "A Lover of Toleration" that condemned Christian reformers because their "moral sense of the community has sanctioned aggression."[6] A New Jersey Jacksonian paper similarly opposed moral reform and reprinted a series of articles that rejected Reverend Ely's call for a Christian party in politics. It warned that this scheme by the "orthodox . . . to get the nation into their hands" should be feared and opposed because it required a dangerous unity of thought. If voters followed Ely, then they could vote only for a candidate who "thinks as they think, and professes as they think."[7] Signed by "Roger Williams," the article invoked the nation's diverse colonial origins, a theme with obvious resonance in the Delaware Valley where Quakers, Irish, Pennsylvania Germans, and African Americans all were influential. An antievangelical tone especially suited the vitriolic political style in Easton where a newspaper made fun of false

religious principles and advised those who walk to church to "talk as loud
as you can, so that others may know you are in the way of your duty."[8]

An unaligned Delaware newspaper caught in the throes of partisan uncertainty offered a particularly incisive assessment of how both religious
and partisan calls for national unity threatened local diversity by exploiting print culture. The *Delaware Register*, edited by ex-Republicans whose
paper had failed when it backed Adams in 1828, warned of the abuse of
power that allowed a handful of individuals to control tract societies and
partisan newspapers whose mass distribution led to inappropriate influence. "In this country few things are more to be dreaded, than organizations or institutions by which public opinion may be brought to bear
tyrannically against individuals or sects." When public opinion is "shocked
and stimulated by vast Associations, it is in danger of becoming a steady,
unrelenting tyrant, browbeating the timid, proscribing the resolute, silencing free speech, and virtually denying the dearest religious and civil
rights." The assault continued several issues later when the paper warned
that evangelical reform threatened to become "the handmaiden of
tyranny and oppression" via "a Union of Church and State."[9]

Americanization and Pennsylvania Germans in Easton

The unity that evangelical reformers and party organizers hoped to bring
to the nation in their separate ways fueled local conflicts and caused new
divisions to arise among varied groups in the Delaware Valley. Effective resistance to these nationalizing efforts often relied upon local political
practices and distinctive ethno-religious traditions that challenged all-
encompassing demands. Easton's Pennsylvania Germans accommodated
Anglo-American ways at varying rates in the early national period. As we
saw in Chapter 4, Lutherans' fuller engagement with non-German society
had been clear during Christian Endress's pastorate, when conflicts
erupted between the two local German congregations over language use,
control of their jointly owned building, and use of two burial lots in town.

The more selective ways in which Reformed members in Easton engaged Americanization informed their wariness of evangelical reform.
The East Pennsylvania Classis of the Reformed Synod, to which the Easton
congregation belonged, had a strongly Pennsylvania German orientation
even when compared to the other groups that made up the synod. Indeed,
its pointed opposition to moral reform in May 1829 shocked German Reformed leaders from outside the area. The public address of the classis
called into question the real purpose of evangelical reform and its institutional expression via Sunday schools, missionary societies, and, of course,
Bible societies. The classis warned that each had distinctive abuses. Sunday
schools could "entice young members from their own churches." Missionaries disrupted areas where settled pastors already worked "and make dis-

turbance[s] in peaceable churches." Finally, Bible societies could "degenerate into plans of speculation, merely to make money."[10] German Reformed members had good reasons to oppose the intrusion of evangelical reform around Easton, as it arrived with the creation of local Presbyterian and Episcopal churches in 1811 and 1819, which ended the exclusive presence of German churches in the town.

The Reformed critique of cosmopolitan evangelicalism built upon a strong denominational commitment that rejected the pan-Christian claims of Anglo-American reform. The classis noted that its own reform work was "exclusively to our own church. . . . As [the Reformed] institutions are constituted, they can never become injurious, but rather useful; for we are in connection with no other body, and least of all with the men who cherish such base designs."[11] This careful maintenance of denominational boundaries challenged a central premise of cosmopolitan reform that aspired to reshape the nation into a single spiritual body.

The East Pennsylvania Classis's bold opposition to a united American Christianity was especially striking because the official publication of the German Reformed Church favored an inclusive evangelical effort. The inaugural edition of the *Magazine of the German Reformed Church* plainly supported an assimilationist goal. Its prospectus admitted that its "special object is to improve the condition and promote the spiritual welfare of the German Reformed Church," but quickly added, "it is not intended, however, to be a mere sectarian work." Instead, "the general design of this work is to maintain the cause of true evangelical piety, in labouring to diffuse Christian knowledge."[12] As the first official Reformed Church publication printed in English, the *Magazine* called for accommodation with pan-Protestantism far in advance of Reformed sentiment in places such as Easton.

The magazine also gave unqualified praise to the Bible movement and allowed little room for legitimate dissent from the cause. As it observed, "in the controversy between the favourers and the opposers of Bible Societies there cannot be an innocent neutrality. . . . In this matter he that is not for Christ, is against him, and he, who gathereth not with him, scattereth." The magazine encouraged the German Reformed Church to join the evangelical union via Bible distribution that would further proper Christianity. "Contemplate a while the cruel, obscene, and disgusting mummery which constitute the worship of a heathen idol, and then compare with it the calm, solemn, and holy devotion of an assembly of pious Christians."[13] Those calling for the German Reformed Church to adopt more cosmopolitan values favored moral reform to make the nation more respectable, uniform, and Christian.

The magazine printed the address of the localist East Pennsylvania Classis only to condemn its narrow denominationalism. The conflict within the Reformed Church built on distinct local and cosmopolitan perspectives and on theological differences and centered, above all, on language use. As the English-language magazine complained, the classis had "extensively circulated" its declaration "by the German papers" and called upon "*all other German Editors . . .* to publish it." The circulation of antievangelical opinions in German made them more subversive from the Anglo-American perspective of the *Magazine of the German Reformed Church* and even tainted by "the appearance of evil."[14] By opposing evangelical reform in a Pennsylvania German idiom, the classis maintained a locally grounded ethno-religious identity that more cosmopolitan Reformed leaders thought should be left behind.

Despite the magazine's more accommodationist stance, it still maintained its own strong sense of Pennsylvania German ethnicity. Just as we saw how Lutherans in Easton found ways to retain ethnic meaning while participating more fully in Anglo-American society, the accommodationist faction among the German Reformed simply fashioned a different balance for ethnic self-understanding than did their localist brethren. The same issue of the magazine that criticized the East Pennsylvania Classis devoted its first stories to a biography of the sixteenth-century Palatine theologian "Henry" (not Heinrich) Bullinger and reprinted extracts from the missionary journal of Michael Schlatter, who had donated the Bible to Easton's Reformed congregation in the 1740s. The historical origins of the faith in central Europe, as exemplified by these men, remained central to the denominational identity of the German Reformed Church, even as some encouraged it to collaborate more fully with other American Christians.

The syncretic resolution of being both German and American is also apparent in the magazine's conflict with the classis. It was not a simple battle between backward people who spoke only German and their more educated and urbane English-speaking brethren. The magazine offered the "first appearance in an English dress" of the classis statement, but it presumed that the position would be "new to few of our readers," as it had been widely circulated in the German papers.[15] Both localists and cosmopolitans among the German Reformed in the 1820s were bilingual people whose language choices were not simply matters of technical competence.

The German Reformed disagreement about cosmopolitan evangelicalism occurred at the same time that a momentous division took place in the local religious practice of Pennsylvania Germans in Easton. Just as local Reformed members took a strong antievangelical position, the local Lutheran congregation decided to end its long-standing connection with the union church. A central fault line in sundering the shared building stemmed from the congregation's divergent participation in cosmopolitan reform. The split is itself an American story. As Pennsylvania Germans in Easton felt the need to band together less strongly in the early national period, they began to express their differences from one another more publicly. As much as the end of the union church acknowledged different ways that each congregation expressed its Pennsylvania German ethnicity by the early 1830s, their religious services and even the buildings in which they worshipped marked how thoroughly both had become American.

The grand new church that Lutherans built in Easton was the largest religious building in any of the three river towns when it was completed in 1832 and bespoke their central place in early national society (fig. 27). They had largely shed the inferior and peculiar connotations of their ethno-religious identity. Outsiders to Pennsylvania German areas may have still seen Lutheranism as odd and less American than other Protestant traditions, but in many areas Lutheranism was now an unapologetically dominant institution. Pennsylvania German religious and ethnic identity achieved the mixed blessing of becoming "normal," and ironically less recognizably distinct, in such areas. By 1833, Lutherans in Easton had created a Sunday school and a benevolent society and rented out its pews for the first time. Reverend John Peter Hecht continued Christian Endress's practice of preaching in both English and German, and, though American born, Hecht hardly disguised his German heritage, for he served as the professor of German at Easton's new Lafayette College.[16]

Easton's Reformed congregation was more hesitant about such a wholehearted embrace of Anglo-American models, but they were not a group of aging German peasants about to wither away as more modern and less distinctly ethnic Americans passed them by. After buying out the Lutheran interest and becoming the old union church building's sole owner, the Reformed congregation reshaped the building to exhibit their own achievements in strikingly public ways that announced their presence in the nation as both Pennsylvania Germans and Americans. By 1832 the Reformed congregation had added a new plaster interior and an imposing brick tower to the stone church building, topped by a tall steeple. Such potent changes in Easton's religious landscape were local examples of the more forceful expression of church architecture that occurred throughout the country in the early national period.[17] Although Quaker scruples prevented Burlington Friends from participating in the landscape sacralization movement, Episcopalians there and in New Castle both undertook major church-building projects in the period (figs. 4–5).

The transformation of Easton's sacral space coincided with changes in the leadership of the German Reformed congregation. Its assistant pastor by the end of the rebuilding year, Bernard C. Wolff, led prayers in English at the church's reconsecration in 1832. German Reformed members in Easton crafted a unique accommodation to the long-standing need for English preaching in their congregation by maintaining two pastors. Thomas Pomp continued to hold services exclusively in German until his death in

1852, while Wolff conducted English services, a local bilingual tradition that persisted into the 1870s.[18] Pennsylvania Germans in Easton had created and adopted many basic features of early national life, contributing to a syncretic process begun when their forebears crossed the Atlantic, and modified, discarded, and elaborated certain elements of their Old World culture and experience. By establishing themselves as equal citizens in the new nation, they helped make ethno-religious diversity central to national society, even as their assimilative accomplishments could also disguise Pennsylvania German distinctiveness.

Evangelicalism and the Separation among Burlington Friends

The division among Delaware Valley Quakers in the late 1820s was more profound than the dissolution of Easton's union church. The schism of the Society of Friends into separate Orthodox and Hicksite wings grew from divergent attitudes about Friends' proper relationship to cosmopolitan evangelicalism. The Orthodox group embraced moral reform, going even so far as to establish Quaker Bible and tract societies, while the Hicksites rejected such commitments and called instead for a renewal of distinctive Quaker piety's emphasis on the inward light as the bedrock of their identity, a commitment that refused affiliation with those who had become a people of the book by participating in the Bible movement.

As was commented upon at the time, the schism basically separated a much larger group of rural Hicksites from the more affluent and urban Orthodox. Although often cast as "separatists," Hicksites included approximately 70 percent of Quakers in the Delaware Valley. The Orthodox maintained control of the main Arch Street meetinghouse in Philadelphia, but outside the cosmopolitan metropolis, they were the majority in only three monthly meetings, one of which was Burlington. Given the close ties of Burlington Friends with their brethren in Philadelphia, their affluence, and the role of Burlington Friends in both the Quaker and non-Quaker Bible movements, the firm Orthodox commitment of Burlington Friends is not surprising.[19]

The careful accounting of the separation by William Allinson, the eldest son of the Quaker activist Samuel Allinson, reveals the bitter nature of the conflict and the motivations of its local Orthodox leaders. William began his account when he and his half-sister Elizabeth were among those assigned to a traveling committee to examine the "Infidelity and Insubordination" that threatened the Philadelphia Yearly Meeting in 1827. Interestingly, the Society of Friends confronted the same kinds of issues regarding representation that plagued the nominating conventions of early national political parties. Allinson reported that many Quarterly Meetings had sent "nearly double the number of Representatives [to the Yearly Meeting] in order to carry the point of choosing a clerk who should be subservient to their view."[20] Quaker meetings made decisions by consensus, but everyone knew that the clerk who recorded the sense of the meeting played a weighty role, perhaps even a decisive one, in times of conflict.

Allinson never doubted the propriety of his opposition to the wildly inappropriate demands of Hicksites. To him, these "conspicuous" members had adopted "speculative opinions and doctrines" and had become "puffed up in their minds and trust[ed] too much in their visionary views."[21] The growing conflict revolved around a central question of Quaker identity—how to balance individual conscience and group conformity, the personal inward light and the collective discipline of the Society.

While Allinson's travels as an Orthodox leader often led him to speak to hostile groups, his local meeting offered a protective harbor. Only three elders in the Burlington Preparatory Meeting joined with the Hicksites in 1828. All three were women, and all were born and raised outside the local meeting in more rural settings where Hicksite spirituality flourished.[22] Quakers in Burlington City were strongly Orthodox and maintained tight control by adjourning meetings when dissenting Hicksites attended.[23] Such decisions fueled the criticism that the Orthodox was a minority faction that relied on heavy-handed methods. Yet they felt that the "spirit of disaffection and opposition to the order and discipline of our society" required strident measures, even to the point of assigning door guards to their yearly, quarterly, and monthly meetings to "keep [them] select."[24]

Such actions led the first Monthly Meeting of Burlington Hicksite Friends at nearby Rancocas Township to explain that the schism had occurred because of "a party, who in various meetings for discipline, arrogate to themselves, the right of being alone judges of all business that comes before those meetings, however small may be their numbers." Moreover, this high-handed "party" was composed primarily of *men* who had "withdrawn and assembled together in some private place" whenever their "authority . . . has been questioned."[25] Because the three Burlington Preparatory Meeting elders who became Hicksites were women, issues of gendered authority likely shaped the local separation.

Burlington Preparatory Meeting was an Orthodox stronghold, but the Hicksite separation disrupted the larger monthly meeting.[26] Hicksites had overwhelming support in areas surrounding Burlington. Mt. Holly Monthly Meeting, which had separated from Burlington in 1776 to accommodate its many members, was just four miles to the east and had a particularly strong dissenting and antimaterialistic tradition exemplified by its most famous Friend, the eighteenth-century reformer John Woolman. The Hicksite movement swept Mt. Holly so thoroughly that its few remaining Orthodox members reorganized as a preparatory meeting within Burlington's jurisdiction. In the range of local responses to the separation, no community surpassed Burlington City for its staunch Orthodoxy. As early as 1813, leading local Quakers such as John Cox, who served as the long-term clerk of the Philadelphia Yearly Meeting, had warned family and friends of the dangerous ideas of Elias Hicks.[27]

Orthodox Friends in Burlington crafted their sense of Quakerism from a deep engagement with cosmopolitan reform. Burlington Friends had generously supported the New Jersey Bible Society, as we saw in Chapter 5, and this increasing commitment to the Bible as a central source of guidance diverged from the Hicksite commitment to the inward light. Margaret Allinson Parker, a leading Orthodox Friend in Burlington and another child of Samuel and Martha Cooper Allinson, began to participate in a women's Bible reading group in the late 1820s.[28] The deepening engagement with the Bible exemplified by Margaret Allinson Parker and her circle contributed to the divergence of Orthodox and Hicksite spirituality.

The crowning expression of cosmopolitan Orthodox Quakerism may have been the creation of the Bible Association of Friends in 1829, and Burlington leaders played a notable role in its formation. Indeed, John Cox and Samuel Emlen Jr. were the only non-Philadelphians among its forty founders, and a Burlington auxiliary sent delegates to its first annual meeting in 1830. As it had also done for non-Quaker Bible societies, the Burlington auxiliary made major financial donations to the movement, second only to Philadelphians in 1831.[29] The Bible Association of Friends was especially active in the early 1830s when it grew to twenty-one auxiliaries that stretched to Maine, Canada, Ohio, Indiana, Virginia, and North Carolina, and with the help of these local groups distributed nearly twenty-thousand texts before 1835.[30]

The Bible Association of Friends clearly modeled itself on the American Bible Society (ABS). It corresponded with ABS secretary John Nitchie and even praised the non-Quaker national Bible institution in print in 1831. Despite all these meaningful connections to cosmopolitan evangelical reform, the Quaker Bible group maintained an important sense of its distinctiveness. It allowed only Quakers to join the organization, and its celebration of the ABS also included a strong cautionary note about the limits of scriptural authority, for "much as we value that blessed book, we dare not call it the Word of God, or the Bread of Life."[31]

The cosmopolitan commitment of Orthodox Burlington Friends is well exemplified by Bible Association of Friends' member Stephen Grellet, a former Catholic from a noble family who fled the French Revolution and who had joined the Philadelphia Monthly Meeting in 1796. He became an extraordinarily active Public Friend, traveling throughout the United States and making four long European trips. His transatlantic and affluent social circle led him to become an Orthodox supporter. So, too, his Catholic upbringing may have furthered his acceptance of conservative evangelicalism's emphasis on the Bible and Jesus Christ as essential Christian unifiers rather than on the internalist spirituality of Hicksites.

failed effort to incorporate "The Sons of Benevolence of the Town of New Castle" demonstrates one facet of how the respectable black effort would be rejected. Its seven African American petitioners sought to create a legally recognized voluntary association for "suppressing vice and immorality, burying the dead, and taking care of the indigent and sick among their coloured brethren."[36] Six of the petitioners were long-term New Castle residents, and two of them, James Finney and Caleb Darby, had even achieved middling economic status in the third quintile of the local taxed population in 1826, a position held by just three of the town's twenty-five black taxpayers. Whatever the economic standing of the petitioners, only one of them possessed sufficient literacy to sign his own name. Joseph Manly, who also seems to have written the petition in his clear and steady hand, probably benefited from some formal education and, not coincidentally, was the youngest petitioner, the only one between the age of twenty-four and thirty-five in the 1830 census. What did this capable man, who was raising a young family in New Castle, think when the state legislature deemed it "inexpedient" to incorporate this black benevolent organization?[37]

Racial divisions may seem a constant and permanent source of conflict in early America, but this assumption takes too general a view and fails to note how much racial identity had changed in the years from 1770 to 1830 as nationalism provided a new sense of self-understanding with which other group identities interacted.[38] The meaning of blackness had begun to be uncoupled from slave status in the Revolutionary Delaware Valley through a rich combination of black action, gradual emancipation, Revolutionary ideology, and economic changes that made slavery less profitable. Together, these forces transformed the social context for black and white racial identities and the ethno-religious sensibilities that intersected with them as well.

The potential for a fundamental reimagining of race relations existed in the Revolutionary Delaware Valley, but white localists and cosmopolitans agreed almost unanimously to reserve full membership in the nation for whites alone. The American Colonization Society (ACS) was the most consistent and sustained effort among whites to improve the condition of African Americans in the country, but its solution to the "problem" demanded black resettlement in Africa. Its leadership included many prominent evangelical reformers such as Bible Society of Philadelphia (BSP) president William White, who served as ACS vice president, and Samuel Emlen Jr., the prominent Orthodox Quaker from Burlington. The varied branches of cosmopolitan reform shared a remarkably uniform vision, and reform activists participated in many different organizations within the movement. Samuel Bacon, for example, whose work organizing county auxiliaries for the BSP was discussed in Chapter 5, died in Africa, where he had gone to continue his missionary work a year after laboring in Northampton County.[39]

The call to deport free blacks from the United States enjoyed wide-spread popular support among white Americans. The Pennsylvania legislature resoundingly endorsed the aims of the ACS, and there seems little question that a broad consensus took shape among white Americans in the 1820s that included more direct hostility toward African Americans than that simply based on timeless racism. The first state constitutions of Pennsylvania and New Jersey had permitted African Americans with sufficient property to vote, and this racial inclusivity survived the earliest revisions of both documents. New Jersey terminated this possibility in 1808, as did Pennsylvania in 1837 when it decisively shut the door to African American voting. As one delegate at the state constitutional convention explained, "the people of this state are for continuing this commonwealth, what it has always been, a political community of white persons."[40] White hostility toward blacks was a persistent feature of early American society, but the need to explicitly exclude all free blacks from the polity, and especially the notion of the political community as one of "white persons," marked a novel response to the growing free black presence in a nation committed to popular sovereignty.[41]

Free blacks, and some of their radical white allies, rejected this racist nationalism. The struggle against early national society's growing racism led African Americans to recommit themselves to a shared group identity. Whereas Pennsylvania Germans and Quakers had begun to explore divergent ways of engaging the nation at the close of the broad Revolutionary period, the perilous situation of free blacks demanded renewed racial solidarity. This recommitment is especially clear when we consider how the black opposition to the ACS initially came from ordinary African Americans, rather than from black elites who often had ties to leading white sponsors of colonization. Like other cosmopolitan leaders, black elites could voice a distinct perspective from popular local opinion. At two Philadelphia mass meetings to discuss colonization in 1817, ordinary blacks adamantly opposed colonization proposals and forced their leaders to reverse an initial stance in favor of removal. The meetings galvanized the movement for a unified African American community, and the "spirit of 1817" became a rallying cry for black solidarity for the next forty years.[42]

In 1831 members of the Union Church of Africans (UCA) in New Castle County challenged ongoing ACS efforts to send free blacks to Africa. UCA members found such plans abominable and argued against them in a fundamentally American way. They declared the ACS strategy to be "at variance with the principles of civil and religious liberty, and wholly incompatible with the spirit of the Constitution and Declaration of Independence of these United States." The goal of colonization was "unrepublican" and aimed for "the total extirpation of our race from this country." The UCA even turned religion against the ACS by asking whether its "Christian benevolence" could not be used more advantageously for blacks within the United States. The African Christians knew all too well that the evangelical ideal of Christian unity and the national promise of the equality of "the people" faltered in the face of racial difference. Nevertheless, UCA members demanded equal status by denouncing the "prejudice" that blocked their "full enjoyment" of "rights in common with other Americans."[43] The famed abolitionist William Lloyd Garrison, who printed the UCA petition in 1832, simultaneously condemned the ACS for excluding African Americans from its definition of who belonged in the nation. He charged, "colonizationists artfully represent [free blacks] as alien and foreigners, wanderers from Africa—destitute of that *amor patriae*, which is the bond of union." In short, the ACS falsely insisted that free blacks were non-Americans, "cherishing no attachment to the soil [and] feeling no interest in our national society."[44]

Black cosmopolitan organizations demanded that the ideals of the Revolution be implemented for their people. Their public mobilization as "Free People of Colour" and even as "Africans" expressed an identity politics central to the Americanization process that is more frequently associated with white ethnic groups. The Convention for the Improvement of the Free People of Colour, for example, first met in Philadelphia in 1831 to respond to increasing attacks on free blacks and included delegates from New Castle, Burlington, and Easton.[45] Yet even as the Convention clung steadfastly to the view that the Declaration of Independence and the Constitution guaranteed "all the rights and immunities of citizenship . . . in letter and in spirit . . . to every freeman born in the country," they felt forced to make plans for possible emigration to Canada.[46] This was an option of last resort, reserved for when conditions became intolerable in the United States. The group maintained that free blacks needed better conditions in their "native land" and "reject[ed] all plans of colonization anywhere."[47]

By 1835 the organization decided to downplay public self-assertions that highlighted their racial identity. "After an animated and interesting discussion" the Convention recommended that "our people . . . abandon the use of the word 'colored,' when either speaking or writing concerning themselves; and especially to remove the title of African from their institutions, the marbles of churches, and [such]." The Convention chose pragmatic action in a period of increasing hostility marked by five major antiblack riots in Philadelphia beginning in 1834.[48] This violence forcefully demonstrated the deteriorating conditions for African Americans in the region since the founding of institutions such as the UCA. At this point some black leaders counseled removing the title "African" from the façades of their institutions, a decision that probably encouraged some individuals of African descent to downplay blackness itself.

At the same meeting at which the Convention decided to de-emphasize racial identity, they also demonstrated an ongoing engagement with evangelical reform by founding the American Moral Reform Society, an explicitly national effort fully consistent with cosmopolitan values. Nevertheless, it retained a distinctive style and political strategy as an organization for free people of color. Along with such standard reform tenets as commitment to education, temperance, and economy, this group also championed "universal liberty"—a position never trumpeted in quite the same way by white moral reformers. Even as this free black group advised a more mild-mannered public face, they adamantly denounced American inequality. They judged the United States without parallel in "the history of the nations" for the degradation caused by "*American slavery* and *American prejudice*," and they "refuse[d] to be . . . enchanted with the robe of American citizenship."[49]

The anticolonization efforts of the UCA and the work of the Convention for the Improvement of the Free People of Colour were opening salvos in a new struggle over the meaning of the nation that would ultimately lead to the Civil War. But the creation of these cosmopolitan black institutions also marked the conclusion of an earlier contest over Revolutionary identity politics. Black racial identity was one of a number of interrelated categories of self-understanding and public consciousness that underwent major changes from 1770 to 1830. African Americans, like female evangelical reformers, had created new independent institutions that insisted upon their right to participate in the public life of the nation.

The inclusive possibilities and the exclusive limits to the national culture taking shape in the 1820s appeared with shocking clarity for African Americans. While the Revolution had accelerated the speed with which slavery was outlawed in the states north of Delaware, gradual emancipation helped to make blackness (as opposed to slave status) the key indicator of exclusion from national equality. The demographic transition from slavery to freedom for the majority of African Americans in these towns was complete by 1800, and blacks in each of them quickly acted to attain full rights in a host of ways. Despite major efforts to conform to the respectable and evangelical tenets of national society, a growing antiblack racism and concomitant white commitment to violence forcefully blocked African American access to the inclusive promises of the nation.

Identities in the New Nation

> *I shall be like a traveler who has gone out beyond the walls of some vast city and gone up a neighboring hill; as he goes farther off, he loses sight of the men he has just left behind; the houses merge and the public squares cannot be seen; the roads are hard to distinguish; but the city's outline is easier to see, and for the first time he grasps its shape. Like that, I fancy I can see the whole future of the English race in the New World spread before me. The details of this huge picture are in shadow, but I can see the whole and form a clear idea of it.*
>
> —Alexis de Tocqueville[50]

None of the river towns examined here was a vast city, nor does this study share Tocqueville's confident claim to have seen the whole future and grasped its single shape. Moreover, his sense of the "English race" in the New World imagined a more homogeneous national society than that actually found in the Delaware Valley. Nevertheless, the French chronicler of American democracy provides more than just the pleasing image of climbing a hill outside these towns to try to achieve a closing broader prospect. Our effort to understand how the American Revolution shaped everyday life and politics for ordinary people has meant that many of our concerns have run parallel to those of the most famous visitor to the early United States.

The most significant shared Revolutionary experiences in New Castle, Burlington, and Easton arose from the tensions among and within a diverse range of cultural identities as they remade themselves in the transition from colonial to national status. The Revolutionary War stimulated new claims about the public importance of group identity in the Delaware Valley, which contributed to the difficulty its late colonial elites had managing the popular mobilization that led to war. Eventually, an anticolonial revolt swept established authorities from power in most of the Delaware Valley, and this mass movement claimed legitimacy by embracing popular sovereignty. The sense of "the people" that emerged in the multicultural Delaware Valley was grounded in the social perceptions of individuals who created a sense of themselves from multiple, and often conflicting, sources. The rejection of colonial authority led to fundamental changes in the region that were more closely tied to cultural identity than to economic forces or even to formal politics. The unspoken rules that governed everyday life were altered by the Revolutionary mobilization, and the postcolonial period required that a new sense of order be crafted to explain national society.

The often divisive and potentially radical claims of group interest advanced by the region's Revolutionary identity politics were frequently at odds with assertions about the primacy of the nation that were articulated with particular clarity by people with new types of partisan and evangelical commitments. These two broad bids to shape national authority shared some abstract goals and structural similarities with each other: both drew on a cosmopolitan breadth of vision, and both had many local champions. Yet they were ultimately incompatible with one another because they built upon such different premises. The conflict-oriented masculine culture of partisan politics had a more open embrace of ordinary white men, while the genteel and feminized culture of evangelical reform engaged nonwhites as central to its work. The tumult that ensued as local people participated in and confronted these cosmopolitan efforts, while simultaneously drawing upon religious, racial, and ethnic traditions, gave shape to the nation and extended the American Revolution into the first three decades of the nineteenth century.

By the Jacksonian era, certain key issues in the localist-cosmopolitan struggle central to the Delaware Valley's long-lived Revolutionary identity politics had been resolved. All successful actors in formal politics now embraced popular sovereignty for adult white men of nearly any social standing. This racialized democratization of partisan politics ended the lingering deferential ideals that elite formal politics could still convey. By reinforcing the local nature of partisanship, while also offering a broad national ideal, the modern political parties of the Jacksonian era successfully transcended the localism that often informed Revolutionary politics. Moreover, this transition occurred in the Delaware Valley with substantial changes for particular cultural groups, as Pennsylvania Germans, Scots Irish, and even respectable women created more public space for themselves in the new nation than they had achieved in the colonial period.

Despite an important inclusive impulse, this nationalization process should not be cast as purely egalitarian. Quakers gradually recovered from Revolutionary abuse, but never again achieved the prominence that they had enjoyed in the colonial Delaware Valley. The expansion of the franchise to include almost all white men also meant a comparative loss in status for white women, especially for the vast majority whose social circumstances barred them from achieving the respectability of their cosmopolitan sisters.[51] The Revolutionary transition had also opened the possibility of a more inclusive place for free blacks in the nation, but this closed as a result of the white consensus about what marked the limit of appropriate Revolutionary change. By the late 1820s a complex range of overlapping and often competing claims to participate in the nation's public life were muted by the successful assertion of white masculinity as the central unifying quality of the democratic majority.

The power of such majoritarian imperatives led Tocqueville to foreboding conclusions. His overriding fear of a tyrannical democratic majority led him to insist upon the limited utility of popular sovereignty for creating a just society. What restraints could be placed upon a majority whose actions were to be feared? Popular opinion could easily exceed "the bounds of justice and reason." Thus, to accept the majority's "total power" meant adopting "the language of a slave."[52] This juxtaposition of tyranny and slavery was neither casual nor myopic. Although Tocqueville did not develop his view of American racial inequality in detail, he unequivocally asserted that great revolutions in America "will be caused by the presence of the blacks upon American soil. That is to say, it will not be equality of social conditions but rather their inequality which may give rise" to destructive forces in a democracy.[53]

Tocqueville's warnings about democratic abuse fell short of the most enraged voice of American dissent to appear in print as the Jacksonian era emerged from the passing Revolutionary one. In a manifesto that resounded with the passion of a spokesman for a large subaltern class, David Walker, a free black born in North Carolina and living in Boston, denounced the hypocrisy of white Americans.[54] His *Appeal to the Colored Citizens of the World* shrewdly manipulated a national identity that had come to identify its subjects as exclusively white. Walker repeatedly used the term *American* to describe whites, and he warned that they would suffer direct violence unless they ended slavery: "This language perhaps is too harsh for the American's delicate ears. But Oh Americans! Americans!! I warn you in the name of the Lord . . . to repent and reform, or you are ruined!!!"[55] Walker presented Americans as the white oppressors of blacks throughout his work, which led him, like many evangelicals, to adopt an internationalist cosmopolitanism that critiqued nationalism as a parochial identity. At other points, however, Walker still claimed the nation, especially its Revolutionary and Christian ideals, as genuinely belonging to people of African descent. He explained, "this country is as much ours as it is the whites, whether they will admit it now or not, they will see and believe it by and by."[56] Walker quoted the Declaration of Independence at length in his closing pages and then demanded, "See your Declaration Americans!! Do you understand your own language? . . . 'ALL MEN ARE CREATED EQUAL!!' . . . Compare your own language . . . with your cruelties and murders."[57] While few black leaders adopted Walker's inflammatory public style, his outrage was widely shared among African Americans, and his central message, although not his confrontational stance, was the same as that adopted by the Delaware Valley's Convention for the Improvement of the Free People of Colour in the early 1830s.

The challenge to remember that early America was more than a white province has begun to be met by a growing number of careful studies about the central place of African Americans and Native Americans in creating that shared world of inequality. Real hurdles remain, however, in placing racial identity within a still broader ethno-religious context so that the historical interactions among a larger number of cultural groups can be understood. First, treating "race" as an isolated category of experience reifies that subject as a distinctive phenomenon. Second, the commonplace understanding of the United States as an immigrant society is still mostly associated with national developments from the 1830s to today, rather than extending to the colonial and founding era of the nation. Understanding how religion, race, and ethnicity shaped individuals' understandings of themselves and their society is essential to contend with the full range of lived experience in the Revolutionary Delaware Valley and will prove essential for us to come to terms with our own ongoing multicultural society.

The decades from 1770 to 1830 witnessed major transformations initiated by people who believed that human actions could improve the world.

For both good and bad, the changes wrought by the Revolutionary mobilization often ran beyond individual intentions and expectations. By adopting an intensive local comparative perspective, we have followed the interrelated trajectories of multiple groups across this period of rapid change. The central challenge here has been to recognize difference without esssentializing it as static or isolated from multiple social influences and, at the same time, to explain the place of difference within an integrated system of meaning shared by people with widely varied perspectives. In short, the analysis of cultural identity needs to assess both difference and commonality in order to explain how identities are contingently constructed in cultural systems. Such an inquiry gains urgency from our need to understand our own multicultural reality of global interconnection. But such grand aspirations need to have a foundation in close-to-the-ground details, and as a result, we have persistently examined the logic of local circumstances in three specific towns in order to carefully explain the subtle yet meaningful ways that cultural identities shaped personal perceptions and guided individual actions. To that end, I want to conclude with one more individual story, for despite the particularity of any specific example, it also speaks to broader themes of this study. Any of the groups discussed here could offer a fitting final example, but ultimately the Revolutionary transition of Pennsylvania Germans in the Delaware Valley proves to be an especially instructive place to close, as their substantial changes in the period remain largely unknown today.

Three generations of the male line in George Wolf's family offer a useful overview of the change over time traced in this book and underscore the necessity of tending closely to specifics when analyzing dynamic cultural identities. George Wolf's father and grandfather emigrated from Alsace-Lorraine and arrived in Philadelphia in 1751. They soon settled in newly established Northampton County and suffered Indian attacks during the wars of the mid-1750s. Like most central European immigrants to Northampton County in this period, their Americanization was hastened by conflict with Native Americans. At the same time, these immigrants also "Germanized," as their ethnic attachment came to have significance in Pennsylvania that it had never held in Europe. The German script on the family patriarch's will in 1779, for example, was heavily shaped by French linguistic influences. The eighteenth-century "German" southwest from whence most Pennsylvania Germans had come was itself an enormously mixed region of local Swiss, French, and German traditions.[58]

The father of our main subject had his own complicated ethnic identity. He acquired land in the "Irish Settlement" of Allen Township through a controversial purchase from the loyalist Andrew Allen (his brother James was discussed in Chapter 2), who rapidly liquidated his property to avoid confiscation by patriots under the state's punitive anti-tory legislation. Wolf successfully defended his rightful ownership before the court at Easton, and whether he colluded with the prominent loyalist, or genuinely secured the property before the enactment of the confiscation laws, he clearly profited from the changing fortunes wrought by the Revolution. As a result of this land acquisition, George Wolf was born and raised in a strongly Scots Irish township a few miles up the Lehigh River from Easton. He received a classical education in the local Presbyterian-run academy, headed by Robert Andrews, who had trained at Trinity College, Dublin, and later studied law in Easton under John Ross. Like his legal mentor, Wolf backed the insurgent Republican Thomas McKean in the governor's race of 1799 and supported Jefferson for president the next year. An influential bilingual attorney with the largest legal practice in early nineteenth-century Easton, Wolf took the centrist third-party option in partisan politics, supporting Ross's election to Congress as a Quid in 1804 and the successful reelection of McKean as a third-party candidate the next year. Wolf would later join the regular Republican Party, and with his nomination as the Republican candidate for the U.S. House of Representatives in 1824, 1826, and 1828, he won without facing any partisan opponents in the general elections.

George Wolf successfully transcended boundaries of ethnicity, politics, status, and religion in the Revolutionary Delaware Valley. He baptized seven children in the local Reformed congregation and had a funeral in the Lutheran church, where a Presbyterian minister delivered the eulogy. Backed by the powerful state party, Wolf enjoyed a stunning victory in the 1829 governor's race. Voters in Easton gave him nearly unanimous support (532 to 15), 90 percent of those in Northampton County favored him, and he carried the state with a comfortable 60 percent of the vote. His election would seem to be the capstone of a classic American success story.

But that easy success story is misleading in significant ways. Not only does it tend to suppress the ways that anti-Indian and antiloyalist violence were essential to his family's achievements and growing participation in American public life, such an account also glosses over the instability of partisan politics in which Pennsylvania German identity was both an asset and a liability. Wolf secured the party's gubernatorial nomination at a bitterly divided state convention, where he emerged as a last-minute compromise candidate. Although often portrayed as comfortably allied to The Family faction of the party headed by Samuel D. Ingham and George Mifflin Dallas at the state level and by Thomas J. Rogers at the local, in fact his distance from that group made him an acceptable figure to delegates suspicious of the eastern-based Family.[59]

Wolf can hardly have been the preferred candidate of Rogers, as they had sparred repeatedly in local contests.[60] Ironically, when Simon Snyder became the state's first Pennsylvania German governor in 1808, Wolf lost to Rogers his patronage position as clerk of Easton's orphan court. As an anti-Snyderite newspaper in the area noted sarcastically, "Hurra for the Tuetshe [Dutch] governor. He removes Teush and butts in de Irishers in de offices."[61] Of course, the partisan press had no interest in examining the powerful but often contradictory connections among ethnicity, religion, status, and political allegiance that remained fluid even as political newspapers strove to fix them with simple meanings that furthered their own agendas.

The unheralded success for a nonincumbent that Wolf achieved in the governor's race did not mark a simple Jacksonian realignment in Pennsylvania. In fact, Wolf ran much stronger at town, county, and state levels than Andrew Jackson had the previous year. Wolf's support for internal improvements and banking placed him at odds with what would soon emerge as key Jacksonian policies, and Wolf's dissent from prominent figures in the state party was equally pronounced. True to his third-party and antiparty commitments, he appointed his legal mentor John Ross, the old Quid congressman from Easton, to the state supreme court, a choice that shocked the Ingham-Rogers wing of the party.[62]

Wolf's election and Ingham's appointment to Jackson's presidential cabinet left both congressional seats in Easton's district without incumbents, leading to a special election in 1829. Nomination by the state party remained essential for victory, and, as had occurred so often before, the nominating meeting proved extremely contentious. Three separate Northampton delegations arrived all claiming to be the legitimate "Jacksonian" one. When convention officials chose to recognize one group, the excluded delegates joined forces and put forth their own candidates against those selected by the official process. As a letter in the *Easton Centinel* complained, "to crown all, the contending parties all profess to be Democrats, and to be governed by democratic usages."[63]

The long-dominant party was clearly in disarray when both its nominees lost. The local Jacksonian press still claimed a victory for "Democracy and Virtue" triumphing over "Federalism," but, in fact, their control was shaken. One-party dominance could not mask the ongoing disagreement among Pennsylvania Democrats who had inherited the internal rancor of their Republican predecessors. Moreover, the third-party option remained powerful. While Constitutional Republicans, Quids, and Independent Republicans had passed away, Pennsylvania Democrats now faced a new popular threat that they dubbed the "contemptible cloak of anti-masonry."[64]

Wolf's Pennsylvania German origins aided his victory, but also led to serious setbacks, most notably when his ethnic kinsmen withdrew their political support from him in 1835. Governor Wolf's most significant policy innovation was to enact a general education law that made state-supported schooling compulsory. To Wolf, this law would ensure that republican virtue could be extended to all people in the state and not just to the wealthy. The issue contributed to Wolf's undoing, and he lost his reelection bid in yet another hard-fought three-way governor's race, this one won by Joseph Ritner, who headed the Anti-Masonic ticket.

The public education law left Wolf vulnerable because it intruded on the religious and linguistic traditions of Pennsylvania Germans. Falling into patterns remarkably similar to the English-language Charity School controversy of the 1750s, ordinary Pennsylvania Germans firmly opposed government intrusion into realms customarily understood as under the control of family and church.[65] Pennsylvania German fear that government leaders aimed to expunge the ethno-religious sensibilities of their children remained consistent in these two schooling controversies, yet the context in which that fear expressed itself had changed remarkably. While only a handful of Pennsylvania German leaders joined the Charity School movement in the colonial period, all three candidates in the 1835 governor's race were Pennsylvania Germans. Indeed, since Simon Snyder's election in 1808, every Pennsylvania governor, save the single-term officeholder William Findley, had been of German descent. The overlapping forces that shaped the ascendance of Pennsylvania Germans such as George Wolf were obviously complex, but the Revolutionary mobilization played a central role by casting out an older order and creating space into which these former ethnic outsiders moved.

What, then, has the telling of such stories within stories about diversity in the Revolutionary Delaware Valley revealed? First, it leads us to understand the significance of the American Revolution in a new way, for in the Delaware Valley it triggered unexpected assertions about the validity, and even the necessity, of cultural diversity in the Revolutionary nation. The sudden demise of Anglo authority in the region led to a long transitional period in which fluid identities rooted in cultural differences shaped the politics and popular culture of postwar life. In many respects this Revolutionary experience was unique to the Delaware Valley, building on the demographic diversity of the region and the specific conditions of its late colonial society and wartime experiences. Residents of the Delaware Valley may have created and experienced this identity politics earlier and more forcefully than those in many other areas of the new nation, but it was a harbinger of things to come elsewhere. The ongoing central challenge of political life in the United States has been to maintain a common national identity for a diverse collection of citizen-strangers. Revolutionary ideals have provided important shared values for the nation, among the most important of which has been a deep commitment to resist those who have claimed natural superiority and privilege. The fragile balance between a diverse citizenry and the need for a humane social consensus in national public life has rightly been contested throughout American history. Alongside the egalitarian impulse of the Revolution that often expresses itself through local autonomy, we also need to preserve space for a necessary cosmopolitanism to help us transcend the isolationism that unalloyed localism can become. Regional culture is itself produced from the mediation of local and cosmopolitan extremes and needs to be maintained and fostered. Similarly, the mixed authority within a federal political structure when properly balanced gives free range to local action, while ensuring that individuals are protected from abusive local majorities. Localism and cosmopolitanism must be maintained in interactive equipoise if the fullest promises of the American Revolution are to be achieved. The changes that the upsurge in the Revolutionary Delaware Valley's identity politics helped to set in motion—and the potential for change that they still embody—is too important a legacy to cast aside.

It may seem odd to close this study with an observation by a French, Roman Catholic aristocrat who never chanced to visit any of these river towns, yet Tocqueville astutely targeted a central dilemma still faced by modern multicultural democracies. As he saw it, complacency, materialism, and conformity, rather than democracy or revolution, most threatened the future of the United States. The kind of social unrest that had swept Revolutionary France seemed unlikely to him to occur here. Rather, he feared that Americans "may finally become so engrossed in a cowardly love of immediate pleasures . . . that they will prefer tamely to follow the course of their destiny rather than make a sudden energetic effort necessary to set things right."[66] A belief in the potential for positive social change through human action had galvanized the Revolutionary struggle to end colonial rule, but by the 1820s, as today, such broad efforts were all but impossible for most Americans to imagine.

Revolutionary conflict in the Delaware Valley intensified people's awareness of the public importance of a diverse range of local identities, and their centrality to everyday life in the region helped to establish the conditions within which the nation was created there. This national identity rested upon values of respectability, whiteness, partisanship, and evangelical Protestantism that were broadly but not universally shared throughout the region and the nation. The partial reconciliation of these competing values contained the promise of Revolutionary ideals. The experiences, actions, and beliefs of particular people, at a particular time, in particular places created this broad cultural formation that persists today in modified form. For determining what it is to be American, and what it should mean, remains an ongoing challenge of national life.

Appendix

A Note on the Unit of Comparison: Towns, Townships, Hundreds, and Counties in the Delaware Valley

The question of what local unit to study has proved a vexing starting point for community studies of the Delaware Valley. While some have argued that the county provides the most appropriate unit for social analysis in this region, others insist that the rural township provides a better subject.[1] The focus in this book has primarily been on an even smaller administrative locality. The small urban centers of New Castle Town, Burlington City, and Easton Borough each shaded into more rural settlements that bore similar names. A tight focus on the small scale of these three centers permitted a detailed examination of a full range of local evidence that required less sampling of data, and, as a result, individuals' complex constellations of associations could be traced across religious, economic, demographic, and political lines. The pursuit of local experience in each place also required some flexibility because geographic mobility was a prominent feature of early American society, and no person's life was strictly circumscribed by town boundaries. While the inhabitants of three specific river towns are at this book's analytical center, its comparative approach allowed a broader assessment of developments throughout the Delaware Valley.

Anachronistic assumptions about the size of urban settlements often undermine awareness of the importance of small-town life in the early republic. Rather than isolated or insignificant hamlets, the three river towns examined here were substantial for their day. Easton's population of 1,045 in 1800 made it the fifth-largest urban center in Pennsylvania, and New Castle's population of 824 that year probably ranked it third in Delaware. New Jersey lacked a major city until after the turn of the century, a lack of concentrated population centers that meant that no newspaper was published in the state before the Revolution and contributed to no town-level data being published in the state's published 1800 census data. In the overwhelmingly rural landscape of early New Jersey, Burlington was a leading urban site. All three towns were important market, political, social, religious, and legal centers in Philadelphia's small-town hinterland.[2]

Burlington, Easton, and New Castle were chosen for study because each offered rich possibilities for understanding everyday life from 1770 to 1830. They were not dominant locales with strikingly unique roles such as nearby Wilmington, Delaware; Trenton, New Jersey; or Bethlehem, Pennsylvania. Rather, they were representative of dozens of similar places scattered throughout the region.[3] Had a town on the opposite bank of the Delaware River from each of the ones studied here been selected instead, it would not have altered the general argument of this book. Those alternative possibilities (Salem, New Jersey; Bristol, Pennsylvania; and Phillipsburg, New Jersey) simply lacked the richer sources available for the towns that were ultimately selected and allowed a broader tristate assessment of the Delaware Valley.

TABLE 1

CENSUS OVERVIEW FOR THREE DELAWARE RIVER TOWNS, 1790–1830

	Total Pop.	All Whites	All Blacks	Free Blacks	Slaves
1790[1]					
New Castle	NA				
Burlington	NA				
Easton[2]	1,262	1,239	23	15	8
1800					
New Castle Town	824	663	160	102	58
New Castle Hundred	1,614	1,217	395	220	175
New Castle total	2,438	1,880	555	322	233
Burlington Township	NA				
Easton Borough	1,045	1,004	41	37	4
1810					
New Castle Town	1,034	798	236	201	35
New Castle Hundred	1,306	942	364	225	139
New Castle total	2,340	1,740	600	426	174
Burlington Township[3]	2,419	2,204	215	211	4
Easton Borough	1,657	1,616	41	41	0
1820					
New Castle Town[4]	1,023	787	236	—	—
New Castle total	2,671	2,039	632	471	161
Burlington Township	2,758	2,483	275	258	17
Easton Borough	2,370	2,298	72	72	0
1830					
New Castle Town	1,010	779	231	208	23
New Castle Hundred	1,453	967	486	444	42
All New Castle	2,463	1,746	717	652	65
Burlington City	1,860	1,658	202	200	2
Burlington Township	808	806	2	2	0
All Burlington Township	2,668	2,464	204	202	2
Easton Borough	3,529	3,438	91	91	0

Source: Unless otherwise noted all figures were compiled from the manuscript schedules of the federal census on microfilm at the National Archives, Mid-Atlantic Repository, Philadelphia.

[1] No local schedules for the state of Delaware exist for 1790, nor do any survive from New Jersey until 1830.
[2] The local enumerator did not distinguish between Forks Township, Easton, and a third unidentified area in 1790.
[3] The census office published figures for Burlington Township and Easton Borough in 1810 and 1820. See U.S. Census Office, *Urban Statistical Surveys . . . in the Year 1810* (New York: Arno Press, 1976), 29, 35, and U.S. Census Office, *Urban Statistical Surveys . . . in the Year 1820* (New York: Arno Press, 1976), n.p.
[4] The New Castle statistics published for 1820 combined town and hundred entries. Figures for New Castle Town in 1820, without distinguishing between free blacks and slaves, are cited in Constance Jean Cooper, "A Town among Cities: New Castle, 1780–1840" (Ph.D. diss., University of Delaware, 1983), 61.

TABLE 2

WEALTH DISTRIBUTION FOR THREE DELAWARE RIVER TOWNS, 1772–1830:
PERCENTAGE OF TOTAL TAX PAID BY TOP AND BOTTOM SEGMENTS OF THE
TAXED SOCIAL STRUCTURE

New Castle, Del.	1776[1]	1798	1815	1826
	(n = 262)	(n = 147)	(n = 209)	(n = 222)
Top 10%	35	70	44	43
Bottom 20%	5	3	4	6
Burlington, N.J.	1774	1796	1814	NA
	(n = 233)	(n = 388)	(n = 648)	
Top 10%	33	40	40	
Bottom 20%	4	4	4	
Easton, Pa.	1772/74	1796	1814	1830
	(n = 74[2])	(n = 184)	(n = 378)	(n = 744)
Top 10%	52	33	57	67
Bottom 20%	1	3	1	1

Source: Tax analysis is based on all tax records for the years cited. The New Castle lists can be found under Assessment Records, Record Group 2535, New Castle County, microfilm, DHR. The Burlington lists can be found under New Jersey Tax Rateables, Burlington County, NJSA. The Easton lists can be found in the Northampton County Archives, Easton, Pennsylvania. There are some modest discrepancies in the total number of records here and in the religious data in Tables 3 through 5 because taxed institutions, of course, did not have religious affiliations.

Note: Taxable wealth distribution should not be accepted as a direct reflection of social structure for a variety of reasons. (The classic analysis of taxable wealth distribution, based on Chester County, Pennsylvania, just north of New Castle County, is James T. Lemon and Gary B. Nash, "The Distribution of Wealth in Eighteenth-Century America," *Journal of Social History* 2 [1968]: 1–24. Recent work has refined their analysis; see, especially, Paul G. E. Clemens and Lucy Simler, "Rural Labor and the Farm Household in Chester County, Pennsylvania, 1750–1820," in Stephen Innes, ed., *Work and Labor in Early America* [Chapel Hill: University of North Carolina Press, 1988], and Jack D. Marietta, "The Distribution of Wealth in Eighteenth-Century America, Nine Chester County Tax Lists, 1693–1799," *PH* 62 [1995]: 532–45. Also see Carole Shammas, "A New Look at Long-Term Trends in Wealth Inequality in the United States," *AHR* 98 [1993]: 412–31.) The type of property assessed ignores many liquid assets so that the actual wealth at the top of the social structure was significantly undercounted. Moreover, many people were too poor and too transient to be taxed, especially in places like New Castle with its strong local seafaring tradition, not to mention that in this approach enslaved individuals are counted as property rather than as contributing to the bottom of the social structure. Nevertheless, this type of data does offer a basic measure to assess change over time and to make comparisons among the three towns.

Two developments in Table 2 deserve fuller comment. First, the sharply inegalitarian spike that seems to occur in New Castle between 1776 and 1798 is probably misleading. This seems likely to be the result of the changing administrative boundaries of the tax assessment district. The 1776 list assessed the entire rural hundred, including the yet unincorporated town. The extreme inequality revealed in the 1798 town tax list probably placed a heavier burden on its wealthiest citizens than local officials were prepared to endorse, as the wealth distribution for New Castle Town in 1815 and 1826 reflects rates much closer to that of 1776 and is also more consistent with the pattern in Burlington, which showed little variation from 1774 to 1814. Ironically, the high-water mark of 70 percent of taxable wealth possessed by the top decile of taxpayers in New Castle in 1798 may well represent a more accurate depiction of the extremes separating rich and poor in these towns before local officials moved to protect the interests of their wealthiest citizens.

The second, and more certain, economic development suggested by this data is that Easton had high rates of social stratification. Its sharp inequality in the mid-1770s and in the two nineteenth-century tax lists can be attributed to quite different causes. Easton was still close to the frontier in the 1770s, as suggested by its hosting an Indian conference in 1777, and such conditions contributed to sharper inequality there than in the much more established colonial capitals of Burlington and New Castle. The data extracted from the 1796 Easton tax list is the most egalitarian of all eleven lists studied here, but this did not represent a lasting trend, for the Easton data in 1814 and 1830 show the most marked inequality of any of the towns (with the exception of New Castle in 1798, discussed earlier).

What explains the sharp trend of growing inequality in early national Easton versus relative socioeconomic consistency in Burlington and New Castle? The difference can be found in the major development of canals in Easton and its fuller participation in early industrial manufacturing. Unlike the older towns that lacked the essential natural resources to harness water power, Easton raced to develop a more market-based economy in a new world of factory production. As it grew by leaps and bounds in physical, demographic, and economic terms, Easton's wealth distribution moved in a sharply inegalitarian direction. The growing separation of rich and poor in Easton informed its inhabitants' strong commitment to Andrew Jackson and the emerging Democratic Party, which far outpaced such partisan attachments in Burlington and New Castle.

[1] This list is for New Castle Hundred, a larger rural area that included the town until its incorporation in 1798. The later three lists are for the town.
[2] These early lists are incomplete and mutilated, so data has been combined from two lists. Out of 102 combined records (repeated individuals were excluded), 74 include legible assessment values.

TABLE 3

BURLINGTON, NEW JERSEY:
RELIGIOUS AFFILIATION AND SOCIAL STRUCTURE, 1774–1830
(RAW NUMBER [% WITHIN CATEGORY])

Burlington City 1774
total number of records = 233
total known religious affiliation = 163
total unknown religious affiliation = 70

	QX	Q-fam	TotalQ	Epis	Mix	Misc./?	NRA
1Q top 10% (n = 23)	12 (52.1%)	1 (4.3%)	13 (56.5%)	8 (34.7%)	1 (4.3%)	1 (4.3%)	0 (0.0%)
1Q (n = 45)	21 (46.6%)	2 (4.4%)	23 (51.1%)	16 (35.5%)	1 (2.2%)	1 (2.2%)	4 (11.1%)
2Q (n = 46)	6 (13.0%)	5 (10.8%)	11 (23.9%)	7 (15.2%)	0 (0.0%)	2 (4.3%)	26 (56.5%)
3Q (n = 41)	17 (41.5%)	7 (13.1%)	24 (58.5%)	7 (17.0%)	0 (0.0%)	2 (4.8%)	8 (19.5%)
3/4Q (n = 15)	8 (53.3%)	1 (6.6%)	9 (60.0%)	2 (13.3%)	1 (6.6%)	0 (0.0%)	3 (20.0%)
4Q (n = 37)	6 (16.2%)	8 (21.6%)	14 (37.8%)	10 (27.0%)	0 (0.0%)	2 (5.4%)	11 (29.7%)
5Q (n = 49)	5 (10.2%)	7 (14.3%)	12 (24.4%)	19 (38.7%)	0 (0.0%)	0 (0.0%)	18 (36.7%)
Total 1774 (n = 233)	63 (27.0%)	30 (12.9%)	93 (39.9%)	61 (26.1%)	2 (0.9%)	7 (3.0%)	70 (30.0%)

Burlington Township 1796
total number of records = 386
total known religious affiliation = 234
total unknown religious affiliation = 152

	QX	Q-fam	TotalQ	Epis	Mix	Misc./?	NRA
1Q top 10% (n = 38)	14 (36.8%)	2 (5.2%)	16 (42.1%)	14 (36.8%)	2 (5.2%)	2 (5.2%)	4 (10.5%)
1Q (n = 77)	30 (39.0%)	7 (9.0%)	37 (48.1%)	24 (31.1%)	2 (2.5%)	2 (2.5%)	12 (15.6%)
2Q (n = 76)	18 (23.6%)	8 (10.5%)	26 (34.2%)	20 (26.3%)	1 (1.3%)	1 (1.3%)	28 (36.8%)
3Q (n = 82)	14 (17.0%)	6 (7.3%)	20 (24.3%)	21 (25.6%)	0 (0.0%)	8 (9.7%)	33 (40.2%)
4Q (n = 54)	15 (27.7%)	13 (24.0%)	28 (51.8%)	5 (9.2%)	0 (0.0%)	0 (0.0%)	21 (38.8%)
4/5Q (n = 43)	5 (11.6%)	7 (16.2%)	12 (27.9%)	6 (13.9%)	0 (0.0%)	3 (6.9%)	22 (51.1%)
5Q (n = 54)	7 (12.9%)	3 (5.5%)	10 (18.5%)	5 (9.2%)	0 (0.0%)	3 (5.5%)	36 (66.6%)
Total 1796 (n = 386)	89 (23.1%)	44 (11.3%)	133 (34.5%)	81 (21.1%)	3 (0.8%)	17 (4.4%)	152 (39.3%)

Burlington Township 1814
total number tax records = 645
total known religious affiliation = 338
total unknown religious affiliation = 307

	QX	Q-fam	TotalQ	Epis	Mix	Misc./?	NRA
1Q top 10% (n = 66)	25 (37.8%)	7 (10.6%)	32 (48.4%)	16 (24.2%)	2 (3.0%)	2 (3.0%)	14 (21.2%)
1Q (n = 123)	43 (34.9%)	13 (10.5%)	56 (45.5%)	33 (26.8%)	4 (3.2%)	3 (2.4%)	27 (21.9%)
2Q (n = 107)	34 (31.8%)	17 (15.8%)	51 (47.7%)	16 (14.9%)	0 (0.0%)	3 (2.8%)	37 (34.6%)
2/3Q (n = 25)	4 (16.0%)	3 (12.0%)	7 (28.0%)	5 (20.0%)	0 (0.0%)	0 (0.0%)	13 (52.0%)
3Q (n = 77)	11 (14.2%)	13 (16.8%)	24 (31.1%)	10 (12.9%)	1 (1.2%)	1 (1.2%)	41 (53.2%)
Botm. 1/2 (n = 313)	53 (16.9%)	44 (14.3%)	98 (31.3%)	20 (6.3%)	0 (0.0%)	6 (1.9%)	189 (60.3%)
Total 1814 (n = 645)	145 (22.5%)	91 (14.1%)	236 (36.6%)	84 (13.0%)	5 (0.8%)	13 (2.0%)	307 (47.6%)

Table 3 (CONT.)

Burlington Township 1830 Census
total number of records = 318
total known religious affiliation = 128
total unknown religious affiliation = 190

	QX	Q-fam	TotalQ	Epis	Mix	Misc./?	NRA
Total 1830 (n = 318)	58 (18.2%)	28 (8.8%)	86 (27.0%)	37 (11.6%)	0 (0.0%)	5 (1.5%)	190 (59.7%)

Source: The Burlington tax list data were all taken from manuscript records at the New Jersey State Archives in Trenton. No Burlington tax lists exist in the period under study after 1814. Unfortunately, the earliest surviving household schedules for the federal census in New Jersey are from 1830. Census data were compiled from microfilm records at the Philadelphia repository of the Federal Archives. Religious affiliations were determined from varied sources but especially the records transcribed in William Wade Hinshaw, comp., *Encyclopedia of American Quaker Genealogy* (Ann Arbor, Mich.: Edwards, 1938), vol. 2; George Dillwyn, "List of Persons Belonging to Burlington Particular Meeting, 1776," reprinted in *PMHB* 17 (1895): 116; and John E. Stillwell, *Historical and Genealogical Miscellany . . . New York and New Jersey* (Baltimore: Genealogical Publishing Company, 1970), 72–147.

Key to column headings for religious affiliation

QX   Exact match to Quaker record
Q-fam   Likely Quaker family connection
TotalQ Total Quaker affiliation (sum of the previous two categories)
Epis   Exact match to Anglican/Episcopalian record
Mix   Evidence of more than one religious affiliation (not significant in Burlington)
Misc./? Member of religious group without a regular organization in the town, or, possible, but inconclusive, name match
NRA   No known religious affiliation

Note: Explanation of quintile divisions (i.e., 1Q to 5Q): The data in all three Burlington tax lists prevented a meaningful division into five separate and equal quintiles. The creation of a mixed category allowed a more accurate grouping of specific individuals. This adjustment is most striking in the 1814 tax list, where the large number of identical tax rates necessitated grouping the entire bottom half of the tax list together as "Botm. 1/2." Also note that the highest quintile (1Q) includes data for the top decile, which also appears separately as "1Q top 10%."

TABLE 4

EASTON, PENNSYLVANIA:
RELIGIOUS AFFILIATION AND SOCIAL STRUCTURE, 1772–1830
(RAW NUMBER [% WITHIN CATEGORY])

Easton Township 1772/1774[1]
total number of records = 102
total known religious affiliation = 65
total unknown religious affiliation = 37

	Ref	Luth	Pres	Epis	Mix	Misc./?	NRA
1Q top 10% (n = 8)	2 (25.0%)	1 (12.5%)	0 (0.0%)	1 (12.5%)	1 (12.5%)	1 (12.5%)	2 (25.0%)
1Q (n = 16)	6 (37.5%)	1 (6.2%)	0 (0.0%)	1 (6.2%)	2 (12.5%)	1 (6.2%)	5 (31.2%)
2Q (n = 16)	5 (31.2%)	1 (6.2%)	0 (0.0%)	0 (0.0%)	3 (18.7%)	0 (0.0%)	7 (43.7%)
3Q (n = 13)	6 (46.1%)	4 (30.7%)	0 (0.0%)	0 (0.0%)	1 (7.6%)	0 (0.0%)	2 (15.3%)
4Q (n = 22)	4 (18.1%)	4 (18.2%)	0 (0.0%)	0 (0.0%)	3 (13.6%)	0 (0.0%)	11 (50.0%)
5Q (n = 14)	2 (14.2%)	1 (7.1%)	0 (0.0%)	0 (0.0%)	5 (35.7%)	0 (0.0%)	6 (42.8%)
No Tax Data (n = 21)	4 (19.0%)	3 (14.2%)	0 (0.0%)	0 (0.0%)	7 (33.3%)	1 (4.7%)	6 (28.5%)
Total 1772/74 (n = 102)	27 (26.4%)	14 (13.7%)	0 (0.0%)	1 (1.0%)	21 (20.5%)	2 (1.9%)	37 (36.3%)

TABLE 4 (CONT.)

Easton Borough 1796
total number of records = 184
total known religious affiliation = 104
total unknown religious affiliation = 80

	Ref	Luth	Pres	Epis	Mix	Misc./?	NRA
1Q top 10% (n = 18)	3 (16.6%)	7 (38.8%)	0 (0.0%)	1 (5.5%)	3 (16.6%)	2 (11.1%)	2 (11.1%)
1Q (n = 36)	6 (16.6%)	9 (25.0%)	0 (0.0%)	1 (2.7%)	6 (16.6%)	3 (8.3%)	11 (30.5%)
2Q (n = 37)	12 (32.4%)	6 (16.2%)	0 (0.0%)	0 (0.0%)	6 (16.2%)	0 (0.0%)	13 (35.1%)
3Q (n = 36)	13 (36.1%)	6 (16.6%)	0 (0.0%)	0 (0.0%)	2 (5.5%)	0 (0.0%)	15 (41.6%)
4Q (n = 37)	8 (21.6%)	8 (21.6%)	1 (2.7%)	0 (0.0%)	5 (13.5%)	0 (0.0%)	15 (40.5%)
5Q (n = 38)	9 (23.6%)	2 (5.2%)	0 (0.0%)	0 (0.0%)	1 (2.6%)	0 (0.0%)	26 (68.4%)
Total 1796 (n = 184)	48 (26.0%)	31 (16.8%)	1 (0.5%)	1 (0.5%)	20 (10.8%)	3 (1.6%)	80 (43.4%)

Easton Borough 1814
total number of records = 378
total known religious affiliation = 201
total unknown religious affiliation = 177

	Ref	Luth	Pres	Epis	Mix	Misc./?	NRA
1Q top 10% (n = 38)	6 (15.7%)	15 (39.4%)	2 (5.2%)	2 (5.2%)	8 (21.1%)	1 (2.6%)	4 (10.5%)
1Q (n = 77)	18 (23.3%)	23 (29.8%)	2 (2.5%)	3 (3.8%)	17 (22.1%)	1 (1.2%)	13 (16.9%)
2Q (n = 77)	13 (16.8%)	14 (18.1%)	3 (3.8%)	3 (3.8%)	7 (9.0%)	1 (1.2%)	36 (46.7%)
3Q (n = 73)	11 (15.0%)	14 (19.1%)	2 (2.7%)	1 (1.3%)	3 (4.1%)	1 (1.3%)	41 (56.1%)

	Ref	Luth	Pres	Epis	Mix	Misc./?	NRA
4Q (n = 54)	6 (11.1%)	10 (18.5%)	4 (7.4%)	3 (5.5%)	5 (9.2%)	0 (0.0%)	26 (48.1%)
4/5Q (n = 48)	5 (10.4%)	6 (12.5%)	1 (2.0%)	2 (4.1%)	2 (4.1%)	0 (0.0%)	32 (66.6%)
5Q (n = 49)	7 (14.2%)	8 (16.3%)	2 (4.0%)	0 (0.0%)	3 (6.1%)	0 (0.0%)	29 (59.1%)
Total 1814 (n = 378)	60 (15.8%)	75 (19.8%)	14 (3.7%)	12 (3.1%)	37 (9.7%)	3 (0.8%)	177 (46.8%)

Easton Borough 1830
total number of records = 744
total known religious affiliation = 275
total unknown religious affiliation = 469

	Ref	Luth	Pres	Epis	Mix	Misc./?	NRA
1Q top 10% (n = 74)	11 (14.8%)	16 (21.6%)	6 (8.1%)	2 (2.7%)	12 (16.2%)	1 (1.3%)	26 (35.1%)
1Q (n = 148)	19 (12.8%)	27 (18.2%)	13 (8.7%)	7 (4.7%)	20 (13.5%)	2 (1.3%)	60 (40.5%)
2Q (n = 148)	12 (8.1%)	23 (15.5%)	14 (9.4%)	13 (8.7%)	4 (2.7%)	3 (2.0%)	79 (53.3%)
3Q (n = 156)	9 (5.7%)	20 (12.8%)	8 (5.1%)	11 (7.0%)	4 (2.5%)	2 (1.2%)	102 (65.3%)
Bottom 2/5 (n = 292)	16 (5.4%)	20 (6.8%)	13 (4.4%)	7 (2.3%)	6 (2.0%)	2 (0.7%)	228 (78.0%)
Total 1830 (n = 744)	56 (7.5%)	90 (12.0%)	49 (6.6%)	38 (5.1%)	33 (4.4%)	9 (1.2%)	469 (63.0%)

TABLE 4 (CONT.)

Easton 1830 Census
total number of records = 578
total known religious affiliation = 235
total unknown religious affiliation = 343

	Ref	Luth	Pres	Epis	Mix	Misc./?	NRA
Total 1830 (n = 578)	50 (8.6%)	73 (12.6%)	42 (7.2%)	37 (6.4%)	31 (5.3%)	2 (0.3%)	343 (59.3%)

Source: Social structure data is derived from Easton Township and Borough tax lists, Northampton County Archives, Easton, Pennsylvania. Religious affiliation has primarily been identified from the following sources: Reformed church records for Easton from 1760 to 1852 have been translated and transcribed in Henry Martyn Kieffer, *Some of the First Settlers of "The Forks of the Delaware"*, new index (1902; Westminster, Md.: Family Line Publications, 1990); Presbyterian, Episcopal, and Lutheran typescript records at the Easton Area Public Library; additional Lutheran sources include 1770 and 1808 membership lists published in Barbara Fretz Kempton, *A History of St. John's Evangelical Lutheran Congregation of Easton, Pennsylvania, 1740–1940* (Easton, Pa.: Correll Company, 1940) as well as communion lists for 1816, 1817, and 1830 in the manuscript church records on microfilm at the Lutheran Seminary Archives.

Key to column headings for religious affiliation
Ref   German Reformed
Luth   Lutheran
Pres   Presbyterian (only sig. after 1810)
Epis   Episcopal (only sig. after 1810)
Mix   Evidence of more than one religious affiliation
Misc./? Member of religious group without pre-1830 organization in the town, or possible, but inconclusive, match
NRA   No known religious affiliation

Note: Explanation of quintile divisions (i.e., 1Q to 5Q): The highest quintile in each year (1Q) includes data for the wealthiest 10% (1Q top 10%), which also appear separately. In 1814 almost fifty individuals were taxed at the same rate (.125), requiring the creation of a boundary category labeled "4/5" group. In 1830, almost three hundred individuals cannot be meaningfully separated and are identified together as the "bottom 2/5" group.

[1] The Easton tax lists for the 1770s are mutilated and incomplete. To approximate a full record for a given year before national independence, data from 1772 and 1774 have been combined. Although there are a total number of 102 records in this combined list (repeated individuals are not counted twice), only 81 records have tax data, because the tax amount for 21 individuals was no longer legible. In this no tax data group, 15 individuals have a known religious affiliation and 6 do not.

Table 5

New Castle, Delaware:
Religious Affiliation and Social Structure, 1776–1830
(Raw Number [% within category])

New Castle Hundred 1776
total number of records = 262
total known religious affiliation = 93
total unknown religious affiliation = 169

	Epis	Pres	Mix	Misc./?	NRA
1Q top 10% (n = 27)	12 (44.4%)	3 (11.1%)	0 (0.0%)	0 (0.0%)	12 (44.4%)
1Q (n = 53)	22 (41.5%)	5 (9.4%)	2 (3.7%)	0 (0.0%)	24 (45.2%)
2Q (n = 57)	17 (29.8%)	3 (5.2%)	3 (5.2%)	0 (0.0%)	34 (59.6%)
3Q (n = 41)	10 (24.3%)	2 (4.8%)	0 (0.0%)	0 (0.0%)	29 (70.7%)
4Q (n = 46)	7 (15.2%)	1 (2.1%)	1 (2.1%)	0 (0.0%)	37 (80.4%)
4/5Q (n = 37)	7 (18.9%)	0 (0.0%)	0 (0.0%)	0 (0.0%)	30 (81.0%)
5Q (n = 28)	13 (46.4%)	0 (0.0%)	0 (0.0%)	0 (0.0%)	15 (53.5%)
Total 1776 (n = 262)	76 (29.0%)	11 (4.1%)	6 (2.3%)	0 (0.0%)	169 (64.5%)

TABLE 5 (CONT.)

New Castle Town 1798
total number of records = 147
total known religious affiliation = 92
total unknown religious affiliation = 55

	Epis	Pres	Mix	Misc./?	NRA
1Q top 10% (n = 15)	5 (33.3%)	4 (26.6%)	2 (13.3%)	0 (0.0%)	4 (26.6%)
1Q (n = 30)	6 (20.0%)	9 (30.0%)	7 (23.3%)	1 (3.3%)	7 (23.3%)
2Q (n = 29)	6 (20.6%)	8 (27.5%)	6 (20.6%)	1 (3.4%)	8 (27.5%)
3Q (n = 30)	10 (33.3%)	2 (6.6%)	2 (6.6%)	0 (0.0%)	16 (53.3%)
4Q (n = 29)	10 (34.4%)	5 (17.2%)	3 (10.3%)	0 (0.0%)	11 (37.9%)
5Q (n = 29)	9 (31.0%)	6 (20.6%)	1 (3.4%)	0 (0.0%)	13 (44.8%)
Total 1798 (n = 147)	41 (27.8%)	30 (20.4%)	19 (12.9%)	2 (1.3%)	55 (37.4%)

New Castle Town 1815
total number of records = 209
total known religious affiliation = 108
total unknown religious affiliation = 101

	Epis	Pres	Mix	Misc./?	NRA
1Q top 10% (n = 20)	5 (25.0%)	6 (30.0%)	7 (35.0%)	1 (5.0%)	1 (5.0%)
1Q (n = 40)	8 (20.0%)	14 (35.0%)	10 (25.0%)	2 (5.0%)	6 (15.0%)
2Q (n = 39)	9 (23.0%)	9 (23.0%)	5 (12.8%)	0 (0.0%)	16 (41.0%)
3Q (n = 33)	6 (18.1%)	7 (21.2%)	1 (3.0%)	0 (0.0%)	19 (57.5%)
bot. 1/2 (n = 97)	19 (19.5%)	7 (7.2%)	4 (4.1%)	7 (7.2%)	60 (61.8%)
Total 1815 (n = 209)	42 (20.0%)	37 (17.7%)	20 (9.5%)	9 (4.3%)	101 (48.3%)

New Castle Town 1826
total number of records = 222
total known religious affiliation = 98
total unknown religious affiliation = 124

	Epis	Pres	Mix	Misc./?	NRA
1Q top 10% (n = 19)	7 (36.8%)	0 (0.0%)	6 (31.5%)	0 (0.0%)	6 (31.5%)
1Q (n = 38)	12 (31.5%)	6 (15.7%)	11 (28.9%)	0 (0.0%)	9 (23.6%)
2Q (n = 39)	9 (23.0%)	10 (25.6%)	4 (10.2%)	0 (0.0%)	16 (41.0%)
3Q (n = 38)	10 (26.3%)	5 (13.1%)	1 (2.6%)	1 (2.6%)	21 (55.2%)
bot. 1/2 (n = 107)	18 (16.8%)	8 (7.4%)	1 (0.9%)	2 (1.8%)	78 (72.8%)
Total 1826 (n = 222)	49 (22.0%)	29 (13.0%)	17 (7.6%)	3 (1.3%)	124 (55.8%)

New Castle Town and Hundred 1830 Census
total number of records = 165
total known religious affiliation = 69
total unknown religious affiliation = 96

	Epis	Pres	Mix	Misc./?	NRA
Total 1830 (n = 165)	33 (20.0%)	23 (13.9%)	9 (5.4%)	4 (2.4%)	96 (58.1%)

Table 5 (cont.)

Source: New Castle tax lists for 1776, 1798, 1815, and 1826 are all at the Hall of Records, Dover, Delaware. Note that New Castle Town was incorporated in 1798, thus the figures for 1776 are for larger and more rural New Castle Hundred, which surrounded and included the settled town. Census data for 1830 was compiled from the household schedules on microfilm at the Philadelphia repository of the Federal Archives. Individual religious affiliation is drawn from many sources. The most important sources were the complete Anglican-Episcopal parish register in Christopher M. Agnew, ed., *God with Us . . . The Vital Records of . . . Immanuel Church, New Castle, Delaware* (New Castle, Del.: Immanuel Church, 1986), and Presbyterian pew and communion lists and financial records for New Castle at the Presbyterian Historical Society, Philadelphia. The Presbyterian records for the 1770s are incomplete.

Key to column headings for religious affiliation
Epis   Episcopalian (or Anglican)
Pres   Presbyterian
Mix   Evidence of more than one religious affiliation
Misc./?   Member of religious group without a regular organization in the town; or possible, but inconclusive, match
NRA   No known religious affiliation

Note: Explanation of quintile divisions (i.e., 1Q to 5Q): Only one of the four New Castle tax lists could reasonably be divided into five equal quintile parts. In the 1776 list, a border category between the lowest two quintiles is designated as 4/5Q. In the lists for 1815 and 1826 a large number of the poorest taxpayers were assessed at the same low rate and are grouped together as "bot. 1/2" (they represent 46% and 48%, respectively, of the total taxed inhabitants). The highest quintile in each year (1Q) includes data for the wealthiest 10% (1Q top 10%), which also appear separately.

Abbreviations

AAS	American Antiquarian Society, Worcester, Massachusetts
ABSA	American Bible Society Archives, New York City
AHR	*American Historical Review*
DH	*Delaware History*
DHR	Delaware Hall of Records, Dover, Delaware
DLR	David Library of the America Revolution, Washington Crossing, Pennsylvania
EAI	*Early American Imprints, Series I (Evans), 1639–1800* (New York: Readex Microprint Corporation, 1940)
EAI s	*Early American Imprints, Series II (Shaw-Shoemaker), 1801–1819* (New York: Readex Microprint Corporation, 1964–83)
FLP	Free Library of Philadelphia
Henry Mss.	Manuscript History of Northampton County, Pennsylvania, volumes by name, Historical Society of Pennsylvania, Philadelphia
HSD	Historical Society of Delaware, Wilmington, Delaware
HSP	Historical Society of Pennsylvania, Philadelphia
JAH	*Journal of American History*
JER	*Journal of the Early Republic*
MCEAS	McNeil Center for Early American Studies (formerly PCEAS)
NBM	New Brunswick Museum, Saint John, New Brunswick
NJH	*New Jersey History*
NJSA	New Jersey State Archives, Trenton, New Jersey
NoCC Misc. Mss.	Northampton County, Pennsylvania, Miscellaneous Manuscripts, volumes by date or name, Historical Society of Pennsylvania, Philadelphia
PA Arch.	*Pennsylvania Archives*

PCEAS	Philadelphia Center for Early American Studies (now MCEAS)
PH	*Pennsylvania History*
PHS	Presbyterian Historical Society, Philadelphia
PMHB	*Pennsylvania Magazine of History and Biography*
QCHC	Quaker Collection, Haverford College
RAH	*Reviews in American History*
WMQ	*William and Mary Quarterly*, 3rd series

Notes

Introduction

1. Alan Tully, *Forming American Politics: Ideals, Interests, and Institutions in Colonial New York and Pennsylvania* (Baltimore: Johns Hopkins University Press, 1994), especially chap. 7. Quaker and Anglican individuals came from a variety of national backgrounds, yet the public expression of both in the colonial Delaware Valley had overwhelmingly Anglo normative connotations.

2. Jack P. Greene, *Pursuits of Happiness: The Social Development of Early Modern British Colonies and the Formation of American Culture* (Chapel Hill: University of North Carolina Press, 1988), 137.

3. For an intensive assessment, see Wayne Bodle, "Themes and Directions in Middle Colonies Historiography, 1980–1994," *WMQ* 51 (1994): 355–88. For a recent study, see Gabrielle M. Lanier, *The Delaware Valley in the Early Republic: Architecture, Landscape, and Regional Identity* (Baltimore: Johns Hopkins University Press, 2005). A full exploration of a regionalist perspective should also look beyond early America; a useful starting point is "*AHR* Forum: Bringing Regionalism Back to History," *AHR* 104 (1999): 1156–1220.

4. The landmark study of the region remains James T. Lemon, *The Best Poor Man's Country: A Geographical Study of Early Southeastern Pennsylvania* (Baltimore: Johns Hopkins University Press, 1972), which argues that a "conservative defense of liberal individualism" defined the area from the onset and rejects the attention of "cultural determinists" to national and ethnic forces; see Lemon, xiii, xv. James A. Henretta challenged Lemon's thesis in "Families and Farms: *Mentalité* in Pre-Industrial America," *WMQ* 35 (1978): 3–32. In direct contrast to Lemon, Michael Zuckerman offers a stirring call-to-arms for Mid-Atlantic studies to focus on cultural diversity in "Puritans, Cavaliers and the Motley Middle," in Michael Zuckerman, ed., *Friends and Neighbors: Group Life in America's First Plural Society* (Philadelphia: Temple University Press, 1982), 3–25. The standard work on Pennsylvania pluralism, Sally Schwartz, *A "Mixed Multitude": The Struggle for Toleration in Colonial Pennsylvania* (New York: New York University Press, 1987), offers an optimistic view of tolerance based on mostly elite sources, yet presents many examples of ethnoreligious conflict and consciousness.

5. Jeanette Eckman, ed., *New Castle on the Delaware*, 3rd ed. (1936; New Castle, Del.: New Castle Historical Society, 1950), 65–68.

6. My introduction to this key expression of Quaker aesthetics was Patricia J. Keller, "*Of the best Sort but Plain*": *Quaker Quilts from the Delaware Valley, 1760–1890* (Chadds Ford, Pa.: Brandywine River Museum, 1996), 25n. Frederick B. Tolles first

framed the issue in his classic study *Meeting House and Counting House: The Quaker Merchants of Colonial Philadelphia, 1682–1763* (Chapel Hill: University of North Carolina Press, 1948). Also see Susan Laura Garfinkel, "Genres of Worldliness: Meanings of the Meeting House for Philadelphia Friends, 1755–1830" (Ph.D. diss., University of Pennsylvania, 1997), and Catherine C. Lavoie, "Quaker Beliefs and Practices and the Eighteenth-Century Development of the Friends Meeting House in the Delaware Valley," in Emma Jones Lapsansky and Anne A. Verplanck, eds., *Quaker Aesthetics: Reflections on a Quaker Ethic in American Design and Consumption* (Philadelphia: University of Pennsylvania Press, 2003), 156–88.

7. Sarah J. Purcell, *Sealed with Blood: War, Sacrifice, and Memory in Revolutionary America* (Philadelphia: University of Pennsylvania Press, 2002).

8. Gordon S. Wood calls for attention to a long Revolutionary chronology in *The Radicalism of the American Revolution* (New York: Vintage, 1991) and in his insightful "The Significance of the Early Republic," *JER* 8 (1988): 1–20. For stinging attacks on his book as essentially elitist, and for Wood's barbed response, see "Forum: How Revolutionary Was the Revolution?" *WMQ* 51 (1994): 677–716. Alfred Young has similarly called for a long Revolutionary period, albeit from a contrasting neo-Progressive perspective, in his "Afterword: How Radical Was the American Revolution?" in Alfred F. Young, ed., *Beyond the American Revolution: Explorations in the History of American Radicalism* (Dekalb: Northern Illinois University Press, 1993), 317–64.

9. The best of the rich scholarship about formal politics in the Revolution includes Bernard Bailyn, *The Ideological Origins of the American Revolution*, enlarged ed. (1967; Cambridge, Mass.: Belknap Press, 1992); Gordon S. Wood, *The Creation of the American Republic, 1776–1787* (1969; Chapel Hill: University of North Carolina Press, 1998); Edmund S. Morgan, *Inventing the People: The Rise of Popular Sovereignty in England and America* (New York: Norton, 1988); and Jack N. Rakove, *Original Meanings: Politics and Ideas in the Making of the Constitution* (New York: Knopf, 1996).

10. For a sense of social history's sweeping impact on colonial scholarship, see Jack P. Greene and J. R. Pole, eds., *Colonial British America: Essays in the New History of the Early Modern Era* (Baltimore: Johns Hopkins University Press, 1984). There have, of course, been major studies of the Revolution by social historians. Most importantly, Gary B. Nash, *The Urban Crucible: The Northern Seaports and the Origins of the American Revolution*, abridged ed. (1979; Cambridge, Mass.: Harvard University Press, 1986), and the varied essays in two volumes edited by Alfred F. Young, *Beyond the American Revolution* and *The American Revolution: Explorations in the History of American Radicalism* (Dekalb: Northern Illinois University Press, 1976). For an insightful early essay decrying the impasse of narrowly "idealist" versus rigidly "materialist" interpretations of the Revolution, see Robert E. Shalhope, "Republican and Early American Historiography," *WMQ* 39 (1982): 334–56.

11. The standard assessment of the "civic culture" of American nationalism is Philip Gleason, "American Identity and Americanization," in Stephen Thernstrom, ed., *Harvard Encyclopedia of American Ethnic Groups* (Cambridge, Mass.: Harvard University Press, 1980), 31–58. A cruder celebration of the "nonethnic" yet "English" origins of civic nationalism in the United States is Liah Greenfeld, *Nationalism: Five Roads to Modernity* (Cambridge, Mass.: Harvard University Press, 1992). Rogers M. Smith has challenged such views by probing how hierarchies of race, ethnicity, gender, and religion shaped federal citizenship laws in *Civic Ideals: Conflicting Visions of Citizenship in U.S. History* (New Haven, Conn.: Yale University Press, 1997).

12. I do not mean to ignore diversity within Europe and the many contestations there among ethnicity, religion, and polity. Ethno-religious conflict was clearly central to the early development of British identity. Consider, e.g., Daniel Defoe's view

of the "True-Born Englishman" as "a mixture of all kinds . . . that het'rogeneous thing. . . . in whose hot veins . . . mixtures quickly ran." On British identity forming against such diversity, see Linda Colley, *Britons: Forging the Nation, 1707–1837* (New Haven, Conn.: Yale University Press, 1992), 15–16.

13. Recent scholarship about changing conceptions of racial categorization has been quite fruitful but still suffers from scant attention to developments before the antebellum era as well as from a failure to consider how ethnic and religious categories intersect with racial ones. The best of the new work includes David R. Roediger, *The Wages of Whiteness: Race and the Making of the American Working Class* (New York: Verso Press, 1991); Joanne Pope Melish, *Disowning Slavery: Gradual Emancipation and "Race" in New England, 1780–1860* (Ithaca, N.Y.: Cornell University Press, 1998); and John Wood Sweet, *Bodies Politic: Negotiating Race in the American North, 1730–1830* (Baltimore: Johns Hopkins University Press, 2003).

14. Washington Irving, *The Sketch-Book of Geoffrey Crayon, Gent.* (1819–20; New York: Oxford University Press, 1996), 45.

15. Steven Watts, *The Republic Reborn: War and the Making of Liberal America, 1790–1820* (Baltimore: Johns Hopkins University Press, 1987), 184 (quote), and *The Romance of Real Life: Charles Brockden Brown and the Origins of American Culture* (Baltimore: Johns Hopkins University Press, 1994). On the anti-German animus of Brown's 1798 novel *Wieland*, see Sydney J. Krause, "Charles Brockden Brown and the Philadelphia Germans," *Early American Literature* 39 (2004): 85–119.

16. For a sophisticated study of colonial ethnicity, see Ned C. Landsman, *Scotland and Its First American Colony, 1683–1765* (Princeton, N.J.: Princeton University Press, 1985). Kathleen Neils Conzen, David A. Gerber, Ewa Morawska, George E. Pozzetta, and Rudolph J. Vecoli, "The Invention of Ethnicity: A Perspective from the U.S.A," *Journal of American Ethnic History* 12 (1992–93): 3–41, provides a useful conceptual framework. Although the English word *ethnicity* is of twentieth-century coinage, the term's Greek origins emphasized national distinctiveness, as did its use in fourteenth-century Scotland. Ethnic associations are too deeply rooted in human experience to be properly studied as only recent phenomena; see Anthony D. Smith, *The Ethnic Origins of Nations* (New York: Basil Blackwell, 1986), and John A. Armstrong, *Nations Before Nationalism* (Chapel Hill: University of North Carolina Press, 1982).

17. I have found the following approaches to cultural identity especially helpful: Benedict Anderson, *Imagined Communities: Reflections on the Origin and Spread of Nationalism*, rev. ed. (1983; London: Verso, 1991); Fredrik Barth, ed., *Ethnic Groups and Boundaries* (Boston: Little, Brown, 1969); Anthony P. Cohen, "Culture as Identity: An Anthropologist's View," *New Literary History* 24 (1993): 195–209; David A. Hollinger, *Postethnic America, Beyond Multiculturalism* (New York: Basic Books, 1995); Thomas C. Holt, "Marking: Race, Race-Making, and the Writing of History," *AHR* 100 (1995): 1–20; Joane Nagel, "Constructing Ethnicity: Creating and Recreating Ethnic Identity and Culture," *Social Problems* 41 (1994): 152–76; and Dror Wahrman, *The Making of the Modern Self: Identity and Culture in Eighteenth-Century England* (New Haven, Conn.: Yale University Press, 2004).

18. This paragraph borrows heavily from John E. Toews's insightful "Historiography as Exorcism: Conjuring up 'Foreign' Worlds and Historicizing Subjects in the Context of the Multicultural Debate," *Theory and Society* 27 (1998): 535–64.

19. On the rapidly changing nature of racial identity in this period, see Michael A. Morrison and James Brewer Stewart, eds., *Race and the Early Republic: Racial Consciousness and Nation-Building in the Early Republic* (Lanham, Md.: Rowman & Littlefield, 2002).

20. Gender, of course, played a crucial role in these changing relationships, but this study will not centrally examine that important dimension of group categoriza-

294 Notes to Pages 10–12

tion. For recent Delaware Valley studies that effectively prioritize gender, see Bruce Dorsey, *Reforming Men and Women: Gender in the Antebellum City* (Ithaca, N.Y.: Cornell University Press, 2002), and Margaret M. Mulrooney, *Black Powder, White Lace: The du Pont Irish and Cultural Identity in Nineteenth-Century America* (Hanover: University of New Hampshire Press, 2002).

21. The community study approach within social history transformed colonial scholarship, especially under the combined impact of a quadrumvirate of 1970 books about colonial New England: John Demos, *A Little Commonwealth: Family Life in Plymouth Colony* (New York: Oxford University Press, 1970); Philip J. Greven Jr., *Four Generations: Population, Land, and Family in Colonial Andover, Massachusetts* (Ithaca, N.Y.: Cornell University Press, 1970); Kenneth A. Lockridge, *The New England Town: The First Hundred Years, Dedham, Massachusetts, 1636–1736*, expanded ed. (1970; New York: Norton, 1985); Michael Zuckerman, *Peaceable Kingdoms: New England Towns in the Eighteenth Century* (New York: Knopf, 1970). A later comparative study is Christine Leigh Heyrman, *Commerce and Culture: The Maritime Communities of Colonial Massachusetts, 1690–1750* (New York: Norton, 1984). On community in the Virginia context, see Darrett B. Rutman, "The Social Web: A Prospectus for the Study of the Early American Community," in William O'Neil, ed., *Insights and Parallels* (Minneapolis, Minn.: Burgess, 1972), 57–89, which articulated the approach in Darrett B. Rutman and Anita H. Rutman, *A Place in Time: Middlesex County, Virginia, 1650–1750* (New York: Norton, 1984).

22. An early influential critique was Thomas Bender, "Wholes and Parts: The Need for Synthesis in American History," *JAH* 73 (1986): 120–36.

23. The leading example of early American historical ethnography is Rhys Isaac, *The Transformation of Virginia, 1740–1790* (New York: Norton, 1982). Like many other anthropologically inspired historians, Isaac draws heavily on Clifford Geertz's "thick description," especially his influential *The Interpretation of Cultures* (New York: Basic Books, 1973). For their more recent views of the relationship between history and anthropology, see Rhys Isaac, "On Explanation, Text, and Terrifying Power in Ethnographic History," *Yale Journal of Criticism* 6 (1993): 217–36, and Clifford Geertz, "History and Anthropology," *New Literary History* 21 (1990): 320–35. Other important critiques include James Clifford, *The Predicament of Culture: Twentieth-Century Ethnography, Literature, and Art* (Cambridge, Mass.: Harvard University Press, 1988); Pierre Bourdieu, *The Logic of Practice* (Stanford, Calif.: Stanford University Press, 1990); and Joan W. Scott, "The Evidence of Experience," *Critical Inquiry* 17 (1991): 773–97.

24. The classic work is Lee Benson, *The Concept of Jacksonian Democracy: New York as a Test Case* (Princeton, N.J.: Princeton, University Press, 1961). An effective critique is Richard L. McCormick, "Ethno-Cultural Interpretations of Nineteenth-Century American Voting Behavior," *Political Science Quarterly* 89 (1974): 351–77. For an effort at rehabilitation, see Ronald P. Formisano, "The Invention of the Ethnocultural Interpretation," *AHR* 99 (1994): 453–77. The review essays by Daniel Walker Howe and Robert P. Swierenga in Mark A. Noll, ed., *Religion and American Politics: From the Colonial Period to the 1980s* (New York: Oxford University Press, 1990), 121–71, make plain the powerful intersection of party politics and religion since the 1830s, a relationship for which we have a poor understanding in the preceding four decades of national life.

25. For rich assessments that are far from simply celebratory, see Amy Gutmann, ed., *Multiculturalism: Examining the Politics of Recognition*, 2nd ed. (Princeton, N.J.: Princeton University Press, 1994), especially the central essay by philosopher (and occasional Quebec politician) Charles Taylor, which places the origins of the "politics of recognition" in eighteenth-century concepts of the liberal individual; and

Kwame Anthony Appiah, *The Ethics of Identity* (Princeton, N.J.: Princeton University Press, 2005), which extends his humane critique from "The Multiculturalist Misunderstanding," *The New York Review of Books* 44 (October 9, 1997): 30–36.

26. For early American syntheses that make cultural diversity central to their analysis, see Alan Taylor, *American Colonies: The Settling of North America* (New York: Penguin Books, 2001), and Jon Butler, *Becoming America: The Revolution Before 1776* (Cambridge, Mass.: Harvard University Press, 2000).

27. The essential starting point for examining transatlantic diversity in colonial British America is Bernard Bailyn and Philip D. Morgan, eds., *Strangers within the Realm: Cultural Margins of the First British Empire* (Chapel Hill: University of North Carolina Press, 1991).

Chapter 1

1. On the region's cultural geography, see James T. Lemon, *The Best Poor Man's Country: A Geographical Study of Early Southeastern Pennsylvania* (Baltimore: Johns Hopkins University Press, 1972); Peter O. Wacker, *Land and People: A Cultural Geography of Preindustrial New Jersey: Origins and Settlement Patterns* (New Brunswick, N.J.: Rutgers University Press, 1975); Gabrielle M. Lanier, *The Delaware Valley in the Early Republic: Architecture, Landscape, and Regional Identity* (Baltimore: Johns Hopkins University Press, 2005); and Bruce Stutz's evocative and historically informed nonacademic book *Modern Lives, Modern Times: People and Places on the Delaware River* (New York: Crown, 1992).

2. See Amandus Johnson, *The Swedish Settlements on the Delaware, 1638–1664*, 2 vols. (1911; New York: Franklin, 1970); and several works by C. A. Weslager: *The Swedes and the Dutch at New Castle* (New York: Bart, 1987); *Dutch Explorers: Traders and Settlers in the Delaware Valley* (Philadelphia: University of Pennsylvania Press, 1961); and *New Sweden on the Delaware, 1638–1655* (Wilmington, Del.: Mid-Atlantic Press, 1988).

3. For a careful assessment of New Castle's eventual economic eclipse by nearby Wilmington, see Constance Jean Cooper, "A Town among Cities: New Castle, 1780–1840" (Ph.D. diss., University of Delaware, 1983).

4. The American Board of Customs systematically gathered standardized information on forty-one North American customs houses from 1768 to 1772. Customs 16/1, "Imports and Exports (American), 1768–1773," 226–28, 102, Public Records Office, Kew, England; James Shepherd and Gary Walton, *Shipping, Maritime Trade, and the Economic Development of Colonial North America* (New York: Cambridge University Press, 1972); John J. McCusker and Russell R. Menard, *The Economy of British America, 1607–1789* (Chapel Hill: University of North Carolina Press, 1985).

5. Duc de la Rochefoucault Liancourt, quoted in John A. Munroe, "The Philadelawareans," *PMHB* 69 (1945): 136.

6. Customs 16/1, 1772–73, 229–30.

7. Ibid., 243–48.

8. McCusker and Menard is the essential work on the colonial economy. For regional studies that discuss the West Indies connection, see Lemon, 27–31, and Paul G. E. Clemens, *The Atlantic Economy and Colonial Maryland's Eastern Shore* (Ithaca, N.Y.: Cornell University Press, 1980), 176–78. On postwar economic development, see Mary McKinney Schweitzer, "The Economy of Philadelphia and its Hinterland," in Catherine E. Hutchins, ed., *Shaping a National Culture, The Philadelphia Experience, 1750–1800* (Winterthur, Del.: Winterthur Museum, 1994), 99–119, and Diane Lindstrom, *Economic Development in the Philadelphia Region, 1810–1850* (New York: Columbia University Press, 1978).

9. Gravesend was the last port on the Thames for ships departing London. Edward C. Carter II, John C. Van Horne, Lee W. Formwalt, eds., *Journals of Benjamin Henry Latrobe, 1799–1820*, 3 vols. (New Haven, Conn.: Yale University Press, 1980), 3:39.

10. Simon Newman generously shared his database of tattooed sailors with me. For his assessment of the rowdy and masculinist culture of jack tar, see "Reading the Bodies of Early American Seafarers," *WMQ* 55 (1998): 59–82.

11. Patience Essah, *A House Divided: Slavery and Emancipation in Delaware, 1638–1865* (Charlottesville: University Press of Virginia, 1996); Darald D. Wax, "Africans on the Delaware: The Pennsylvania Slave Trade, 1759–1765," *PH* 50 (1983): 38–49, and "Quaker Merchants and the Slave Trade in Colonial Pennsylvania," *PMHB* 86 (1962): 143–59.

12. Runaway Advertisement, *Pennsylvania Gazette,* June 22, 1769, reprinted in Billy G. Smith and Richard Wojtowicz, *Blacks Who Stole Themselves* (Philadelphia: University of Pennsylvania Press, 1989), 92. Sidney Mintz and Richard Price, *The Birth of African-American Culture: An Anthropological Perspective*, rev. ed. (1976; Boston: Beacon Press, 1992); John Thornton, *Africa and Africans in the Making of the Atlantic World, 1400–1800*, 2nd ed. (1992; New York: Cambridge University Press, 1998); and Michael Gomez, *Exchanging Our Country Marks: The Transformation of African Identities in the Colonial and Antebellum South* (Chapel Hill: University of North Carolina Press, 1998) are essential starting points for studying African cultures in early America.

13. A "hundred" is the local administrative unit in Delaware, the equivalent of the more familiar "township" in Pennsylvania and New Jersey. New Castle Town would be incorporated from the more densely settled portion of New Castle Hundred in 1798. The discussion here and in the next two paragraphs is based on my analysis of the 1800 census manuscript for Delaware; for additional census data and a further explanation of the local administrative units, see the appendix.

14. For countywide census data, see Essah, tables 5–7, 77, 79. Ira Berlin, "Time, Space, and the Evolution of Afro-American Society on the British Mainland of North America," *AHR* 85 (1980): 44–78, provides an excellent framework for analyzing the intersection of region, demography, and black culture, although superseded in some ways by his magisterial *Many Thousands Gone: The First Two Centuries of Slavery in North America* (Cambridge, Mass.: Belknap Press, 1998).

15. Smith and Wojtowicz, 144–45. Also see David Waldstreicher, "Reading the Runaways: Self-Fashioning, Print Culture, and Confidence in Slavery in the Eighteenth-Century Mid-Atlantic," *WMQ* 56 (1999): 243–72.

16. Absalom Jones and Richard Allen had both been enslaved in colonial Delaware before becoming key leaders of independent African congregations in postwar Philadelphia; see Gary B. Nash, *Forging Freedom: The Formation of Philadelphia's Black Community* (Cambridge, Mass.: Harvard University Press, 1988), 66–70, 136–38.

17. Runaway Advertisement, broadside, August 19, 1799, reprinted in EAI, no. 48959.

18. Marianne S. Wokeck, *Trade in Strangers: The Beginnings of Mass Migration to North America* (University Park: Pennsylvania State University Press, 1999), chap. 5, especially 169–75. Among all North American ports, only Philadelphia and New York imported more Irish linen than New Castle in 1772; see Customs 16/1, 108.

19. On the Scots Irish concentration in New Castle, see John A. Munroe, *Colonial Delaware: A History* (Millwood, N.Y.: KTO Press, 1978), 162–67, quote 164.

20. On the difficulty in distinguishing between the Scots and Scots Irish in America, other than at an individual biographical level, see Ned C. Landsman, *Scotland and Its First American Colony 1683–1765* (Princeton, N.J.: Princeton University Press,

1985), 270. Marianne S. Wokeck uses the collective term *Irish,* emphasizing that it primarily refers to people of Scottish descent who had settled in northern Ireland, especially Ulster; see Wokeck, xxi, n. 2. Elizabeth I. Nyabakken has argued for crucial differences between Scots and Scots Irish commitments within Presbyterianism in "New Light on the Old Side: Irish Influences on Colonial Pennsylvania," *JAH* 68 (1982): 813–32. Most recently, Patrick Griffin has cautioned against treating the Scots Irish as a clearly delineated group with a common identity; see *The People with No Name: Ireland's Ulster Scots, America's Scots Irish, and the Creation of a British Atlantic World, 1689–1764* (Princeton, N.J.: Princeton University Press, 2001). Maldwyn A. Jones provides an introductory overview in "The Scotch-Irish in British America," in Bernard Bailyn and Philip D. Morgan, eds., *Strangers within the Realm: Cultural Margins of the First British Empire* (Chapel Hill: University of North Carolina Press, 1991), 284–313. A splendid collection that shows the diverse Irish immigrant experience in this period is Kerby A. Miller, ed., *Irish Immigrants in the Land of Canaan: Letters and Memoirs from Colonial and Revolutionary America* (New York: Oxford University Press, 2003); also see his *Emigrants and Exiles: Ireland and the Irish Exodus to North America* (New York: Oxford University Press, 1985).

21. Griffin, 2; Sally Schwartz, *"A Mixed Multitude": The Struggle for Toleration in Colonial Pennsylvania* (New York: New York University Press, 1987), 96, 200–203, 259.

22. *[Wilmington] Delaware Courant,* May 5, 1787.

23. *[Wilmington] Delaware Gazette,* October 10, 1787.

24. On Presbyterianism and eighteenth-century gentility in the region, see Ned C. Landsman, "Presbyterians, Evangelicals, and the Educational Culture of the Middle Colonies," in Nicholas Canny, Joseph E. Illick, Gary B. Nash, and William Pencak, eds., "Empire, Society, and Labor: Essays in Honor of Richard S. Dunn," special supplemental issue, *PH* 64 (Summer 1997): 168–82.

25. William Thompson Read, *Life and Correspondence of George Read* (Philadelphia: Lippincott, 1870), 51–59.

26. John Montgomery Forster, *A Sketch of the Life of the Rev. Joseph Montgomery* (Harrisburg, Pa.: private printing, 1879), 18, 31.

27. John E. Pomfret, *Colonial New Jersey* (New York: Scribner's Sons, 1973), 42–43.

28. Samuel Smith, *The History of the Colony of Nova-Caesaria, or New Jersey* (1765; Trenton, N.J.: William S. Sharp, 1890), 98–99.

29. J. William Frost provides a useful introduction in *The Quaker Family in Colonial America* (New York: St. Martin's Press, 1973). On women Public Friends, see Rebecca Larson, *Daughters of Light: Quaker Women Preaching and Prophesying in the Colonies and Abroad, 1700–1775* (New York: Knopf, 1999).

30. For a useful overview of the Quaker meeting structure in the mid-eighteenth-century Delaware Valley, see Richard Bauman, *For the Reputation of Truth: Politics, Religion, and Conflict Among the Pennsylvania Quakers, 1750–1800* (Baltimore: Johns Hopkins University Press, 1971), Appendix 1.

31. *[Wilmington] Delaware Gazette,* August 8, 1787; *Delaware Courant, and Wilmington Advertizer,* August 4, 1787.

32. For a detailed family genealogy, see R. Morris Smith, *The Burlington Smiths: A Family History* (Philadelphia: private printing, 1877), especially chaps. 1, 13, and 14; William E. Schermerhorn, *The History of Burlington, New Jersey* (Burlington, N.J.: Enterprise, 1927), 47; Samuel Smith, *History of . . . New Jersey.*

33. Thomas L. Purvis, "'High Born, Long-Recorded Families': Social Origins of New Jersey Assemblymen, 1703 to 1776," *WMQ* 37 (1980): 602, 618, 597.

34. Hanka Gorska, *Inventory of Historic Sites* (Philadelphia: Delaware Valley Regional Planning Commission, 1969), 174. Burlington's Library Company granted seasonal memberships to summer residents throughout the period.

35. New Jersey State Tax Rateables, box 8, Book 176 (1774), and Burlington County Abstracts, box 90 (1784), New Jersey State Archives, Trenton. Most tax records fail to distinguish the political unit of Burlington City from more rural Burlington Township, in which it was situated.

36. Paul G. E. Clemens, "Material Culture and the Rural Economy: Burlington County, New Jersey, 1760–1820" in Peter O. Wacker and Paul G. E. Clemens, *Land Use in Early New Jersey* (Newark: New Jersey Historical Society, 1995), 265–306, especially 271–72 and 284.

37. Julian Ursyn Niemcewicz, *Under Their Vine and Fig Tree: Travels through America in 1797–1799, 1805* (Elizabeth, N.J.: Grassmann, 1965), 225–26. Alan Taylor ably sketches affluent Burlington in the opening chapter of *William Cooper's Town: Power and Persuasion on the Frontier of the Early American Republic* (New York: Knopf, 1995).

38. Valerie Gladfelter, "Power Challenged: Rising Individualism in the Burlington, New Jersey, Friends Meeting, 1678–1720," in Michael Zuckerman, ed., *Friends and Neighbors: Group Life in America's First Plural Society* (Philadelphia: Temple University Press, 1982), 116–44, especially 125.

39. On Burlington Preparatory Meeting's inability to find poor Friends to be the recipients of charity, see "Account of the Receipts and Disposal of William Wright's Legacy" (1810), L.1.6.1., Quaker Collection, Haverford College. Barry Levy has convincingly shown increasing Quaker affluence in the eighteenth century in *Quakers and the American Family: British Settlement in the Delaware Valley* (New York: Oxford University Press, 1988), especially 182–83.

40. William Wade Hinshaw, comp., *Encyclopedia of American Quaker Genealogy* (Ann Arbor, Mich.: Edwards, 1938), 2, 214, 237; George Morgan Hills, *History of the Church in Burlington* (Trenton, N.J.: Sharp, 1876), 350; and John E. Stillwell, *Historical and Genealogical Miscellany . . . New York and New Jersey* (Baltimore: Genealogical, 1970), 96.

41. On the intensifying expectations for Quakers in good standing, see Jack D. Marietta, *The Reformation of American Quakerism, 1748–1783* (Philadelphia: University of Pennsylvania Press, 1984). On the Rogers family, see Stillwell, 83, and Hinshaw, II, 182.

42. Ellen G. Miles, *Saint-Memin and the Neoclassical Profile Portrait in America* (Washington, D.C.: Smithsonian Institution Press, 1994), 3.

43. Thomas Graeme, September 10, 1750, Penn Manuscripts, Pennsylvania Land Grants, 1681–1806, vol. 9, 125, HSP.

44. For a stinging denunciation of the proprietors and their alliance with the Iroquois, see Francis Jennings, *The Ambiguous Iroquois Empire: The Covenant Chain Confederation of Indian Tribes with English Colonies from its Beginnings to the Lancaster Treaty of 1744* (New York: Norton, 1984), 325–46 and 388–97. Anthony F. C. Wallace agrees that the Walking Purchase was a crude fraud but questions its significance for later events in *King of the Delawares: Teedyuscung, 1700–1763* (1949; Syracuse, N.Y.: Syracuse University Press, 1990), 251.

45. For a clear overview of Lutheran and Reformed cooperation, see Donald Herbert Yoder, "Lutheran-Reformed Union Proposals, 1800–1850: An American Experiment in Ecumenics," *Bulletin of the Theological Seminary of the Evangelical and Reformed Church* 17 (1946): 39–77. An essential source for Pennsylvania German colonial history is Charles H. Glatfelter, *Pastors and People: German Lutheran and Reformed Churches in the Pennsylvania Field, 1717–1793*, 2 vols. (Breinigsville, Penn.: Pennsylvania German Society, 1980–81); on Easton, see Glatfelter, 1:385–91.

46. The relatively small literature on Germans in early America is ably assessed in A. G. Roeber's impressive synthetic essay " 'The Origins of Whatever is Not English among Us': The Dutch-speaking and German-speaking Peoples of Colonial British America," in Bailyn and Morgan, eds., *Strangers within the Realm*, 220–83.

47. The best ethnic surname analysis of the 1790 census is Thomas L. Purvis, "The European Ancestry of the United States Population, 1790," *WMQ* 41 (1984): 85–101, part of a forum that includes a dissenting view. For the Northampton County estimate, see Thomas L. Purvis, "Patterns of Ethnic Settlement in Late Eighteenth-Century Pennsylvania," *Western Pennsylvania Historical Magazine* 70 (1987): 107–22. Additional work includes Forrest McDonald and Ellen Shapiro Mc-Donald, "The Ethnic Origins of the American People, 1790," *WMQ* 37 (1980): 179–99, which triggered significant opposition, including *WMQ* 37 (1980): 700–703.

48. Thomas Graeme to Thomas Penn, November 6, 1750, reprinted as appendix 13 in Dietmar Rothermund, *The Layman's Progress: Religious and Political Experience in Colonial Pennsylvania* (Philadelphia: University of Pennsylvania Press, 1961), 163.

49. Lawrence Henry Gipson, *The British Empire Before the American Revolution*, rev. ed. (New York: Knopf, 1958–70), 3:173–77; Charles H. Lincoln, *The Revolutionary Movement in Pennsylvania, 1760–1776* (Philadelphia: University of Pennsylvania, 1901), 47.

50. Ethan Allan Weaver, *The Forks of the Delaware* (Easton, Pa.: Eschenbach, 1900), ix.

51. Richard Smith, *A Tour of Four Great Rivers . . . in 1769* (New York: Scribner's Sons, 1906), 78.

52. James Burd quoted in Randolph Shipley Klein, *Portrait of an Early American Family: The Shippen Family across Five Generations* (Philadelphia: University of Pennsylvania Press, 1975), 147.

53. Smith, *Tour*, xiv–xv, 78–79.

54. A. D. Chidsey Jr., *A Frontier Village: Pre-Revolutionary Easton* (Easton, Pa.: Northampton County Historical and Genealogical Society, 1940), 245.

55. Georgian architecture and its intersection with vernacular traditions are examined in Henry H. Glassie, *Folk Housing in Middle Virginia: A Structural Analysis of Historic Artifacts* (Knoxville: University of Tennessee Press, 1975). For a study of its development in the Delaware Valley, see Bernard L. Herman, *Architecture and Rural Life in Central Delaware, 1700–1900* (Knoxville: University of Tennessee Press, 1987), especially 39–41.

56. *Philadelphia Monthly Magazine* 2 (July–September 1798): 113.

57. Quoted in Scott T. Swank, ed., *Arts of the Pennsylvania Germans* (New York: Winterthur and Norton, 1983), 29. For an example of half-timber construction from the period, see Gerald S. Lestz, *Lancaster County Architecture, 1700–1850* (Lancaster, Pa.: Historic Preservation Trust, 1992), 31.

58. Parsons to Samuel Rhoades, August 17, 1751, quoted in Chidsey, 83; also see Parsons to Benjamin Franklin, January 15, 1753, reprinted in Leonard W. Labaree, ed., *The Papers of Benjamin Franklin* (New Haven, Conn.: Yale University Press, 1959–present), 4:410.

59. Parsons to Richard Peters, 1754, quoted in Chidsey, 86–87. For additional examples of early Pennsylvania officials' hostility toward German immigration recorded by a local historian writing just after the period under study, see Israel Daniel Rupp, *History of Northampton, Lehigh, Monroe, Carbon, and Schuylkill Counties* (1845; New York: Arno Press, 1971), chap. 2. For a more extensive assessment of the outsider status of colonial Pennsylvania Germans, see Liam Riordan, "'The Complexion of My Country': The German as 'Other' in Colonial Pennsylvania," in Colin Calloway, Gerd Gemunden, and Susanne Zantop, eds., *Germans and Indians: Fantasies, Encounters and Projections* (Lincoln: University of Nebraska Press, 2002), 97–119.

60. Benjamin Franklin, *Observations Concerning the Increase of Mankind* (Boston, 1755), reprinted in *Franklin Papers*, 4:234. For other examples of Franklin's fear of German corruption, see *Franklin Papers*, 4:120–21, 5:21, 159.

61. *Franklin Papers*, 4:234.

62. Ibid., 4:479–80.

63. Uzal W. Condit, *The History of Easton, Pennsylvania* (Easton, Pa.: George W. West, 1885), 71–75.

64. The 61 percent figure combines Reformed, Lutheran, and mixed religious affiliation columns in Table 4 of the appendix.

65. See religious affiliation table in appendix for church sources; additional biographical data in Floyd S. Bixler, *The History with Reminiscences of Early Taverns and Inns of Easton* (Easton, Pa.: Northampton County Historical and Genealogical Society, 1931), 23.

66. Alan Tully, *Forming American Politics: Ideals, Interests, and Institutions in Colonial New York and Pennsylvania* (Baltimore: Johns Hopkins University Press, 1994), chap. 7, especially 285–309. On the "convergence" of religious consciousness and politics in colonial Pennsylvania, see Patricia U. Bonomi, *Under the Cope of Heaven: Religion, Society, and Politics in Colonial America* (New York: Oxford University Press, 1986), 168–81.

67. Tully, 416, 418.

68. For a masterful synthesis of colonial politics, see John M. Murrin, "Political Development," in Jack P. Greene and J. R. Pole, eds., *Colonial British America: Essays in the New History of the Early Modern Era* (Baltimore: Johns Hopkins University Press, 1984), 408–56. The best work on Delaware remains Munroe's general study *Colonial Delaware* and, for the later period, John A. Munroe, *Federalist Delaware, 1775–1815* (New Brunswick, N.J.: Rutgers University Press, 1954). On New Jersey, see Thomas L. Purvis, *Proprietors, Patronage, and Paper Money: Legislative Politics in New Jersey, 1703–1776* (New Brunswick, N.J.: Rutgers University Press, 1986).

69. Purvis, *Proprietors*, 72, 117–43. Larry R. Gerlach, *Prologue to Independence: New Jersey in the Coming of the Revolution* (New Brunswick, N.J.: Rutgers University Press, 1976), Appendix 1, 366. Purvis, "Social Origins of New Jersey Assemblymen," 597.

70. Smith, *The History of . . . New Jersey*, 488. Purvis, "Social Origins of New Jersey Assemblymen," 615, and his fuller analysis of Burlington assembly representatives in *Proprietors*, especially 72, 117–43, 237–38. An altogether less settled view of eighteenth-century New Jersey appears in Brendan McConville, *These Daring Disturbers of the Public Peace: The Struggle for Property and Power in Early New Jersey* (Ithaca, N.Y.: Cornell University Press, 1999). As McConville notes, West Jersey was far less prone to the unrest of East Jersey; see xi–xii, 19–20.

71. On Delaware-Pennsylvania relations, see Munroe, *Colonial Delaware*, especially 96–151, 234–35, and Gary B. Nash, *Quakers and Politics: Pennsylvania, 1681–1726* (Princeton, N.J.: Princeton University Press, 1968), especially 68–76, 82–83, and 235–36.

72. Although my interpretation differs sharply, I derive these figures from Wolfgang Splitter, "The Germans in Pennsylvania Politics, 1758–1790: A Quantitative Analysis," *PMHB* 122 (1998): Table 1, 50–51.

73. The most famous contemporary attack on Germans (accusing them of nefarious ties to the French and to Quakers) came from the Anglican clergyman and proprietary leader William Smith; see his anonymously published pamphlets *A Brief State of the Province of Pennsylvania* (London, 1755) and *A Brief View of the Conduct of Pennsylvania for the Year 1755* (London, 1756).

74. Parsons to James Hamilton and Benjamin Franklin, December 15, 1755, reprinted in *Franklin Papers*, 6:294.

75. Easton petition to Richard Peters, June 26, 1757, quoted in Stephen F. Auth, *The Ten Years' War: Indian-White Relations in Pennsylvania, 1755–1765* (New York: Garland, 1989), 81.

76. Parsons quoted in Paul A. W. Wallace, *Conrad Weiser, 1696–1760: Friend of Colonist and Mohawk* (Philadelphia: University of Pennsylvania Press, 1945), 472.

77. On the growing "racial" separation of Indians and Euro-Americans during the Seven Years' War and its aftermath, see Jane T. Merritt, *At the Crossroads: Indians and Empires on a Mid-Atlantic Frontier, 1700–1763* (Chapel Hill: University of North Carolina Press, 2003), chaps. 7–8, and Daniel K. Richter, *Facing East from Indian Country: A Native History of Early America* (Cambridge, Mass.: Harvard University Press, 2001), chaps. 5–6.

78. Richard White's influential study established this key concept; see *The Middle Ground: Indians, Empires, and Republics in the Great Lakes Region, 1650–1815* (New York: Cambridge University Press, 1991); as well as Nancy L. Hagedorn, "'A Friend to Go between Them': The Interpreter as Cultural Broker during the Anglo-Iroquois Councils, 1740–70," *Ethnohistory* 35 (1998): 60–80; and "Forum: The Middle Ground Revisited," *WMQ* 63 (2006): 3–96.

79. Francis Jennings has repeatedly emphasized the importance of this cross-racial alliance; see, e.g., *Empire of Fortune: Crowns, Colonists and Tribes in the Seven Years War in America* (New York: Norton, 1988), especially part III and chap. 17.

80. Samuel Parrish, *Some Chapters in the History of the Friendly Association for Regaining and Preserving Peace with the Indians by Pacific Measures* (Philadelphia: Friends Historical Association, 1877), 63n.

81. Thomas Willing to Robert Morris, November 1756, quoted in Schwartz, 224.

82. Governor Denny, July 11, 1757, quoted in Parrish, 69–70.

83. Johnson quoted in James H. Merrell, *Into the American Woods: Negotiators on the Pennsylvania Frontier* (New York: Norton, 1999), 266–67. Also see Johnson to the Commissioners for Trade, August 1, 1762, reprinted in James Sullivan, ed., *The Papers of Sir William Johnson* (Albany: University of the State of New York Press, 1921–65), 3: 847–48.

84. Amos W. Butler, ed., "Documents: A Visit to Easton," *Indiana Magazine of History* 32 (1936): 267, 268.

85. Ibid., 270.

86. On Moravian-Indian relations, see Merritt.

87. Job Chilloway's participation in colonial society can be traced in *Minutes of the Provincial Council of Pennsylvania* (Harrisburg, Pa.: Penn and Company, 1852), 9:754; "Minutes of the Committee of Observation and Inspection of Northampton County, Pennsylvania, 1774–1777," reprinted in *Two Hundred Years of Life in Northampton County, Pennsylvania* (Easton, Pa.: Northampton County Bicentennial Commission, 1976), 6:55; and William A. Hunter, "Documented Subdivisions of the Delaware Indians," *Bulletin of the Archaeological Society of New Jersey* 20 (1978): 37. Jane Merritt suggested Job's likely relationship to Wilhelm to me. For a spectacular example of the fluid nature of white-Indian boundaries in the Delaware Valley, see Marshall J. Becker, "Hannah Freeman: An Eighteenth Century Lenape Living and Working among Colonial Farmers," *PMHB* 114 (1990): 249–69.

88. The "sickening plummet" of Indian-white relations in eighteenth-century Pennsylvania is a principal theme of Merrell's brilliant *Into the Woods*, 37 (quote), 88–92 (Settlement Indians), 145 (Tatamy). William A. Hunter, "Moses (Tunda) Tatamy, Delaware Indian Diplomat," in Herbert C. Kraft, ed., *A Delaware Indian Symposium* (Harrisburg: Pennsylvania Historical and Museum Commission, 1974), 71–88; and Chidsey, 62. Only 2 of 184 people were taxed less than the "widow Tattemy" in 1796.

89. *Minutes of Conferences Held at Easton in August 1761* (Philadelphia: Franklin and Hall, 1761), 3. The typography of Franklin's printed treaties attempted to capture the rhythm of negotiations shaped by the exchange of material objects. For

careful facsimile reproductions, see Julian P. Boyd, ed., *Indian Treaties Printed by Benjamin Franklin, 1736–1762* (Philadelphia: Historical Society of Pennsylvania, 1938). An essential reference guide is Francis Jennings, ed., *The History and Culture of Iroquois Diplomacy* (Syracuse, N.Y.: Syracuse University Press, 1985).

90. *1761 Treaty Minutes,* 8.

91. *Franklin Papers,* 4:234.

92. Nancy Shoemaker, *A Strange Likeness: Becoming Red and White in Eighteenth-Century North America* (New York: Oxford University Press, 2004).

Chapter 2

1. Mary Beth Norton, *The British-Americans: The Loyalist Exiles in England, 1774–1789* (Boston: Little, Brown, 1972), 8.

2. On the centrality of religion to ethnic and national sensibilities, see Harry S. Stout, "Ethnicity: The Vital Center of Religion in America," *Ethnicity* 2 (1975): 204–24, and J. C. D. Clark's sweepingly revisionist *The Language of Liberty, 1660–1832: Political Discourse and Social Dynamics in the Anglo-American World* (New York: Cambridge University Press, 1994).

3. This figure is based on my higher count for Quakers; see appendix for more information and sources.

4. "Damages by the British in New Jersey, 1776–1782," vol. 2, Burlington County, reel 1, microfilm edition examined at DLR.

5. Cynthia Dubin Edelberg, *Jonathan Odell: Loyalist Poet of the American Revolution* (Durham, N.C.: Duke University Press, 1987); Moses Coit Tyler, *The Literary History of the American Revolution, 1763–1783,* 2 vols. (New York: Putnam's Sons, 1900), 2:98–129. Tyler identified Odell as "the most powerful and unrelenting of the Tory satirists," 98.

6. "To Britannia, in the year 1763," Odell Family Papers, folder 12, NBM.

7. Odell to Society for the Propagation of the Gospel [hereafter SPG], July 5, 1768, quoted in George Morgan Hills, *History of the Church in Burlington* (Trenton, N.J.: Sharp, 1876), 295.

8. Thomas Chandler, SPG report, quoted in Hills, 306–7.

9. New Jersey Provincial Congress, quoted in Hills, 309.

10. Edelberg, 41–43.

11. Third, fourth, and sixth stanzas of "Song for a Fishing Party Near Burlington," reprinted in Winthrop Sargent, ed., *The Loyal Verses of Joseph Stansbury and Doctor Jonathan Odell: Relating to the American Revolution* (Albany, N.Y.: Munsell, 1860), 9–10.

12. Odell to SPG, January 25, 1777, quoted in Hills, 316–18.

13. Margaret Hill Morris, *Private Journal Kept During the Revolutionary War* (1836; New York: Arno Press, 1969), 6. Subsequent citations are all to this edition, but see the useful biographical essay in John W. Jackson, *Margaret Morris, Her Journal with Biographical Sketch and Notes* (Philadelphia: MacManus, 1949).

14. Morris, 5.

15. The following discussion of early martial conflict in Burlington is based upon ibid., 6–12.

16. John W. Jackson, *The Pennsylvania Navy 1775–1781: The Defense of the Delaware* (New Brunswick, N.J.: Rutgers University Press, 1974), 56; also see chap. 6.

17. Morris, 33.

18. Ibid., 14, 21.

19. Ibid., 21, and "Journal of Sergeant William Young," *PMHB* 8 (1884): 260.

20. Morris, 23. Laurel Thatcher Ulrich has rightly emphasized that religion

helped give women a powerful voice to condemn unchristian behavior of both patriots and loyalists in "'Daughters of Liberty': Religious Women in Revolutionary New England," in Ronald Hoffman and Peter J. Albert, eds., *Women in the Age of the American Revolution* (Charlottesville: University Press of Virginia, 1989), 211–43.

21. While several major studies of Quakers include the Revolutionary period, two specialized monographs make it their central focus: Arthur J. Mekeel, *The Quakers and the American Revolution*, rev. ed. (1979; York, England: Sessions Book Trust, 1996), and William C. Kashatus III, *Conflict of Conviction: A Reappraisal of Quaker Involvement in the American Revolution* (Lanham, Md.: University Press of America, 1990). For an analysis of nonpatriot women that includes Quakers, see Judy Van Buskirk, "They Didn't Join the Band: Disaffected Women in Revolutionary Philadelphia," *PH* 62 (1995): 306–29.

22. Society of Friends, "The Testimony of the People Called Quakers," broadside dated 24/1m/1775, EAI, no. 14052.

23. Society of Friends, "An Epistle from the Meeting for Sufferings," circular letter dated 20/12m/1776, EAI, no. 43025.

24. "John Hunt's Diary [1770–1800]," reprinted in *Proceedings of the New Jersey Historical Society* 52 (1934): 177–93, 223–39; and 53 (1935): 27–43, 111–28, 194–209, 251–62. Quote for 22/1m/77 (1934): 224–25.

25. Burlington County figures from Mark Edward Lender, "The Enlisted Line: The Continental Soldiers of New Jersey" (Ph.D. diss., Rutgers University, 1975), 46.

26. Burlington Monthly Meeting Minutes [hereafter BMMM], 2/8m/1779. For patriot soldiers quartered in the meetinghouse, see BMMM, 5/8m/1782, and Burlington Preparative Meeting Minutes, 28/11m/1782, QCHC.

27. Charles Moore et al., to Samuel Preston Moore Jr., June 2, 1777, reprinted in John Jay Smith, ed., *Letters of Dr. Richard Hill and his Children* (Philadelphia: private printing, 1854), 241–42.

28. *Pennsylvania Ledger*, December 10, 1777, reprinted in Sargent, *Loyal Verses*, 15.

29. On Quaker patriots, see Kashatus.

30. Richard F. Hixson, *Isaac Collins: A Quaker Printer in 18th Century America* (New Brunswick, N.J.: Rutgers University Press, 1968). Collins moved his print shop from conservative Burlington to the patriot capital of Trenton after publishing his first thirteen issues.

31. For the charges against Carlisle, see BMMM, 1/4m/1776 and 6/5m/1776, QCHC. The disownment figure is from Lois V. Given, "Burlington City Friends in the Revolution," *Proceedings of the New Jersey Historical Society* 69 (1951): 196–211.

32. Thomas Paine, *Common Sense* (1776; London: Penguin, 1986), 82.

33. Burlington Monthly Meeting for Women Minutes [hereafter BMMW], 1/12m/77, QCHC.

34. For Buchanan and Haines as representatives at the same Quarterly Meeting, see BMMW, 5/5m/1777. For Barker's replacement as clerk, see BMMW, 6/4m/1789.

35. See, e.g., Mary P. Ryan, *Women in Public: Between Banners and Ballots, 1825–1880* (Baltimore: Johns Hopkins University Press, 1990); Linda K. Kerber, "Separate Spheres, Female Worlds, Woman's Place: The Rhetoric of Women's History," *JAH* 75 (1988): 9–39, and the forum "Beyond Roles, Beyond Spheres: Thinking about Gender in the Early Republic," *WMQ* 46 (1989): 565–85.

36. Society of Friends, *Rules of Discipline and Christian Advices of the Yearly Meeting of Friends for Pennsylvania and New Jersey* (Philadelphia: Sansom, 1797), v. Quaker domesticity is the central subject of Barry Levy, *Quakers and the American Family: British Settlement in the Delaware Valley* (New York: Oxford University Press, 1988). Also see Jean R. Soderlund, "Women's Authority in Pennsylvania and New Jersey Quaker Meetings, 1680–1760," *WMQ* 44 (1987): 748–49.

37. Morris describes the trip at 34–36.

38. Ibid., 5–6.

39. Ibid., 17.

40. Margaret Hill Morris's experience as an independent Quaker neutral falls outside the scope of the major assessments of women in Revolutionary America that generally emphasize them as patriots; see Cathy N. Davidson, *Revolution and the Word: The Rise of the Novel in America* (New York: Oxford University Press, 1986); Linda K. Kerber, *Women of the Republic: Intellect and Ideology in Revolutionary America* (1980; New York: Norton, 1986); Mary Beth Norton, *Liberty's Daughters: The Revolutionary Experience of American Women, 1750–1800,* rev. preface (1980; Ithaca, N.Y.: Cornell University Press, 1996); and the essays in Hoffman and Albert, *Women in the Age of the American Revolution.*

41. For a careful study of single women in colonial Philadelphia, see Karin Wulf, *Not All Wives: Women of Colonial Philadelphia* (Ithaca, N.Y.: Cornell University Press, 2000).

42. Morris, 25.

43. This Quaker influence thesis is conjectural, and no known evidence about the drafting of the constitution sheds light on this point. See Judith Apter Klinghoffer and Lois Elkis, "'The Petticoat Electors': Women's Suffrage in New Jersey, 1776–1807," *Journal of the Early Republic* 12 (1992): 159–93 and Larry R. Gerlach, *Prologue to Independence: New Jersey in the Coming of the American Revolution* (New Brunswick, N.J.: Rutgers University Press, 1976), 340–45, for a discussion that stresses the constitution's conservative whig qualities. A lack of local voting data prevents a full exploration of who actually did vote under the law, but for evidence that at least a handful of women did vote in Burlington, see Henry C. Shinn, "An Early New Jersey Poll List [October 9, 1787]," *PMHB* 44 (1920): 77–81.

44. Hunt, 227. This note, obviously added some years later, is in the margin of the entry for 26/9m/1777.

45. Samuel Allinson to Patrick Henry, 17/10m/1774, reprinted in Larry R. Gerlach, *New Jersey in the American Revolution, 1763–1783: A Documentary History* (Trenton, N.J.: New Jersey Historical Commission, 1975), 87–89.

46. Allinson and his neighbor William Dillwyn, brother of the prominent Public Friend George Dillwyn, expressed this view in their preface to Granville Sharp, *An Essay on Slavery* (Burlington, N.J.: Isaac Collins, 1773), xv, vii–viii. Allinson's antislavery efforts continued to the end of his life; see, e.g., Samuel Allinson to Martha Allinson, 1789 letters, Allinson Family Papers, folder 31, QCHC. Jean Soderlund splendidly reconstructs the movement in *Quakers and Slavery: A Divided Spirit* (Princeton, N.J.: Princeton University Press, 1985).

47. Samuel Allinson to William Livingston, 13/7m/1778, reprinted in Gerlach, *Documentary*, 383, 382. For additional Allinson-Livingston correspondence, see Carl E. Prince and Dennis P. Ryan, eds., *The Papers of William Livingston*, 4 vols. (Trenton, N.J.: New Jersey Historical Commission, 1979).

48. William Livingston to Samuel Allinson, July 25, 1778, reprinted in Gerlach, *Documentary*, 385.

49. This was a metaphorical claim. Gerlach, *Documentary*, 387, emphasis in original.

50. Harold Bell Hancock, "County Committees and the Growth of Independence in the Three Lower Counties, 1765–1776," *DH* 15 (1973): 269–78.

51. Quoted in John A. Munroe, *Colonial Delaware: A History* (Millwood, N.Y.: KTO Press, 1978), 248.

52. G. S. Rowe, *Thomas McKean: The Shaping of an American Republicanism* (Boulder: Colorado Associated University Press, 1978), 40.

53. George Read Sr., quoted in G. S. Rowe, "Thomas McKean and the Coming of the American Revolution," *PMHB* 96 (1972): 23.

54. Joseph Montgomery, *A Sermon Preached at Christina Bridge and New Castle* (Philadelphia: Humphries, 1775), 7–8. Montgomery's invocation of the simultaneity of continental patriot prayers resonates with Benedict Anderson's emphasis on such awareness as crucial for the development of nationalism; see Anderson, *Imagined Communities: Reflections on the Origin and Spread of Nationalism*, rev. ed. (1983; London: Verso, 1991).

55. The best study of the religious roots of Revolutionary ideology focuses on New England; see Nathan Hatch, *The Sacred Cause of Liberty* (New Haven, Conn.: Yale University Press, 1977). On the Mid-Atlantic, see Keith L. Griffin, *Revolution and Religion: American Revolutionary War and the Reformed Clergy* (New York: Paragon House, 1994). Patricia Bonomi offers a broad synthesis in *Under the Cope of Heaven: Religion, Society, and Politics in Colonial America*, updated ed. (1986; New York: Oxford University Press, 2003), 187–216. For other wide-ranging arguments, see the essays in Ronald Hoffman and Peter J. Albert, eds., *Religion in a Revolutionary Age* (Charlottesville: University Press of Virginia, 1994).

56. Montgomery, 9.

57. Ibid., 23.

58. Ibid., 11.

59. Ibid., 24–25.

60. Ibid., 11.

61. Ibid., 29–30.

62. Charles H. Metzger, "Chaplains in the American Revolution," *Catholic Historical Review* 31 (1945–46): 77.

63. Porter published his defense in the *[Philadelphia] Pennsylvania Gazette*, January 17, 1776.

64. "The Revolutionary War Diary of William Adair," *DH* 13 (1968): 154–65. Two outstanding studies of African Americans in the broad Revolutionary period are Sylvia R. Frey, *Water from the Rock: Black Resistance in a Revolutionary Age* (Princeton, N.J.: Princeton University Press, 1991), and Gary B. Nash, *Forging Freedom: The Formation of Philadelphia's Black Community* (Cambridge, Mass.: Harvard University Press, 1988). Other important work is collected in Ira Berlin and Ronald Hoffman, eds., *Slavery and Freedom in the Age of the American Revolution* (Charlottesville: University Press of Virginia, 1983).

65. Samuel Patterson to James Booth, undated letter, William Kent Gilbert Collection of Colonial and Revolutionary Documents of the State of Delaware, vol. 1, 56, Library of Congress, Manuscript Division.

66. The magisterial comparative study is David Brion Davis, *The Problem of Slavery in the Age of Revolution, 1770–1823* (Ithaca, N.Y.: Cornell University Press, 1975).

67. This is the principal theme of Charles Royster, *A Revolutionary People at War: The Continental Army and American Character, 1775–1783* (New York: Norton, 1979).

68. Thomas Montgomery appeared in the fourth quintile of New Castle Hundred taxpayers in 1776. Thomas Montgomery to Alexander Porter, letter, December 15, 1779, Slavery Collection, folder 3, HSD. Konstantin Dierks kindly shared this letter with me.

69. On the Delaware delegates at the Second Continental Congress, see Munroe, *Colonial Delaware*, 250–54.

70. Thomas Rodney to Caesar Rodney, letter from New Castle, July [2]4, 1776, quoted in Harold Bell Hancock, *The Loyalists of Revolutionary Delaware* (Newark: University of Delaware Press, 1977), 54.

71. Henry Hobart Bellas, ed., "Personal Recollections of Capt. Enoch Anderson,"

Papers of the Historical Society of Delaware 16 (1896): 20. Also see Len Travers, *Celebrating the Fourth: Independence Day and the Rites of Nationalism in the Early Republic* (Amherst: University of Massachusetts Press, 1997).

72. Thomas McKean to George Read Sr., letter, February 12, 1778, R. S. Rodney Collection, HSD.

73. Samuel Paterson to George Read Sr., letter, September 19, 1776, R. S. Rodney Collection, HSD.

74. Caesar Rodney to Thomas McKean and George Read Sr., letter, September 18, 1776, R. S. Rodney Collection, HSD.

75. Gunning Bedford to George Read Sr., letters, October 1 and November 2, 1776, R. S. Rodney Collection, HSD.

76. George Read Sr., to Gitty [Gertrude] Read, letter, December 6, 1776, R. S. Rodney Collection, HSD.

77. John McKinley to George Read Sr., letters, December 4, 7, 1776, R. S. Rodney Collection, HSD.

78. Caesar Rodney to George Read Sr., letter, January 23, 1777, R. S. Rodney Collection, HSD.

79. John Clark to Samuel Patterson, letter, June 24, 1777, reprinted in William Thompson Read, *Life and Correspondence of George Read* (Philadelphia: Lippincott, 1870), 317–19.

80. Bruce E. Burgoyne, trans. and ed., *A Hessian Diary of the American Revolution by Johann Conrad Döla* (Norman: University of Oklahoma Press, 1990), 77.

81. Caesar Rodney to Thomas McKean, letter, May 8, 1778, reprinted in George Herbert Ryden, ed., *Letters to and from Caesar Rodney, 1756–1784* (Philadelphia: University of Pennsylvania Press, 1933), 267–68.

82. Jacob Vandegrift petition to the General Assembly, October 30, 1781, quoted in Harold B. Hancock, ed., "Revolutionary War Material in the Hall of Records, 1775–1787" *DH* 17 (1976): 59–61.

83. Examination of Captain Moore, November 2, 1777, reprinted in *Delaware Archives*, 5 vols. (1911–10; New York: AMS Press, 1974), 3:1307–8.

84. Edward H. Tatum Jr., ed., *The American Journal of Ambrose Serle* (San Marino, Calif.: Huntington Library, 1940), 257, 259–60.

85. Ambrose Serle quoted in Clark, 203–4.

86. Tatum, 259–60.

87. The definitive study is Dee E. Andrews, *The Methodists and Revolutionary America, 1760–1800: The Shaping of an Evangelical Culture* (Princeton, N.J.: Princeton University Press, 2000). Rhys Isaac explores the similarities and the differences between the evangelical and patriot movements in late eighteenth-century Virginia in *The Transformation of Virginia 1740–1790* (New York: Norton, 1982), especially 264–69.

88. Ross had close connections with conservative Whigs. His brother George, a Philadelphian, signed the Declaration of Independence, and his sister Gertrude married George Read Sr. See Robert T. Conrad, rev. and ed., *Sanderson's Biography of the Signers* (Richmond, Va.: Harold and Murray, 1846), 548–49.

89. Undated letter [before fall 1777] from an anonymous spy, reprinted in Read, 323.

90. New Castle County, Court of Oyer and Terminer, quoted in Hancock, *Loyalist Delaware*, 71.

91. Loyalist Memorial of John Watson, reprinted in Harold Bell Hancock, "New Castle County Loyalists," *DH* 4 (1951): 334. [Cited hereafter as Hancock, "NCC."] Also see AO12/39/2, PRO, microfilm examined at DLR.

92. Loyalist Memorial of John Drake, reprinted in Hancock, "NCC," 346.

93. Tatum, 258.

94. Loyalist Memorial of Theodore Maurice, AO12/39/27–28, PRO, microfilm examined at DLR.

95. Wayne Bodle generously gave me a photocopy of the original from the PRO. It has also been reprinted in Hancock, *Loyalist Delaware*, 118–24.

96. The apparent Anglican dominance of late colonial New Castle is somewhat misleading due to incomplete Presbyterian records before 1791, which also inflates the unusually high 65 percent of all taxpayers without known religion affiliation in 1776. Because the administrative boundaries of New Castle Hundred in 1776 shrank considerably to those of New Castle Town in 1798, the previous discussion refers to changing percentages within each tax quintile and not to raw numbers. See the appendix for further data and sources.

97. Thomas McKean to John Adams, letters, September 28, November 15, 1813, and January 1814, reprinted in Charles Francis Adams, ed., *The Works of John Adams* (Boston: Little, Brown, 1856), 10:74, 81, 87.

98. Francis S. Fox, *Sweet Land of Liberty: The Ordeal of the American Revolution in Northampton County* (University Park: Pennsylvania State University Press, 2000), 53–56. For two early local historians' similar characterization of ethnic alignments, see Henry Manuscripts, Easton volume, 58–59, HSP, and Israel Daniel Rupp, *History of Northampton, Lehigh, Monroe, Carbon, and Schuylkill Counties* (1845; New York: Arno Press, 1971), 10.

99. Wallace Brown, *The King's Friends: The Composition and Motives of the American Loyalist Claimants* (Providence, R.I.: Brown University Press, 1965), 85–105, 142–49.

100. Stephen Brobeck identifies William Allen as "the wealthiest and most influential member" of the interrelated "Proprietary Gentry" of late colonial Pennsylvania. William and three sons all appear in Brobeck's twenty-two-person group. See Stephen Brobeck, "Revolutionary Change in Colonial Philadelphia: The Brief Life of the Proprietary Gentry," *WMQ* 33 (1976): 414, 416, 426–27.

101. "Diary of James Allen, Esq., Philadelphia, Counsellor-at-Law, 1770–1778," reprinted in *PMHB* 9 (1885): 176–96, 278–96, 424–41. The original is at the HSP, but my quotations are from the published version: October 14, 1775, 186; January 25, 1777, 285. I appreciate Greg Knouff's calling to my attention this source and several others in this section.

102. Little has been written about this early ethnic and immigrant society beyond their own *Historical Catalogue of the St. Andrew's Society, 1749–1881* (Philadelphia: St. Andrew's Society, 1881). I appreciate Tim Hanson's reference to this volume.

103. For brief biographies of Gordon, see Fox, *Sweet Land*, chap. 2, and A. D. Chidsey Jr., *A Frontier Village, Pre-Revolutionary Easton* (Easton, Pa.: Northampton County Historical and Genealogical Society, 1940), chap. 8. For a useful overview of the government structure and its offices, see Wayne L. Bockelman, "Local Government in Colonial Pennsylvania," in Bruce C. Daniels, ed., *Town and County: Essays on the Structure of Local Government in the American Colonies* (Middletown, Conn.: Wesleyan University Press, 1978), 216–37.

104. Charges to Grand Jury, June 1775, NoCC Misc. Mss., "Pleas and Prosecutions," HSP.

105. German-language newspaper publishers such as Christopher Sauer and Henry Miller exhibited a close understanding of English legal and political concepts, as demonstrated in Sauer's widely quoted 1764 article reminding his readers that German settlers possessed the full rights of Englishmen. However, the views of such men were not necessarily representative, and the fact that Sauer felt compelled to make such an argument to his literate audience suggests that his view was not widespread. Willi Paul Adams places German-language newspaper editors in a strongly Anglo-American context in "The Colonial German-Language Press and the

American Revolution," in Bernard Bailyn and John B. Hench, eds., *The Press and the American Revolution* (Worcester, Mass.: American Antiquarian Society, 1980), 151–228. For an intricate exploration of British and German legal and conceptual differences, see A. G. Roeber, *Palatines, Liberty, and Property: German Lutherans in Colonial British America* (Baltimore: Johns Hopkins University Press, 1993).

106. Vernon was a Quaker of British descent. NoCC Misc. Mss. (1758–1767), March 18, 1758, 19, HSP. For an insightful assessment of related issues, see John Murrin, "English Rights as Ethnic Aggression," in William Pencak and Conrad Edick Wright, eds., *Authority and Resistance in Early New York* (New York: New York Historical Society, 1988), 56–94.

107. On Pennsylvania German legal integration in Reading (the heavily German seat of adjacent Berks County), see Laura L. Becker, "The People and the System: Legal Activities in a Colonial Pennsylvania Town," *PMHB* 105 (1981): 135–49.

108. Henry Mss., "Easton," 57, 81, HSP.

109. The "Minutes of the Committee of Observation and Inspection of Northampton County, Pennsylvania, 1774–1777" have been carefully reprinted in *Two Hundred Years of Life in Northampton County, Pennsylvania*, 11 vols. (Easton, Pa.: Northampton County Bicentennial Commission, 1976), 6:33–78, December 21, 1774, 35. Cited hereafter as "Northampton Committee Minutes." The key study of such organizations is Pauline Maier, *From Resistance to Revolution: Colonial Radicals and the Development of American Opposition to Britain, 1765–1776* (New York: Knopf, 1972).

110. "Northampton Committee Minutes," May 22, 1775, 36–37.

111. Ibid., May 22, June 30, and July 20, 1775, 38–39, 41.

112. See appendix for religious affiliation data.

113. "Northampton Committee Minutes," August 2, 1776, 56.

114. *New England Journal,* July 20, 1776, quoted in John B. Stoudt, *The Liberty Bells of Pennsylvania* (Philadelphia: Campbell Press, 1930), 136. The parade was also reported in a Philadelphia German-language newspaper; Henry Miller's *Staatsbote,* July 10, 1776; see Henry Mss., "General," 161, HSP.

115. The names Kachlein and Arndt were spelled many different ways in surviving records (e.g., Kichline and Orndt), indicative of their status as ethnic outsiders and notably unlike local leaders in the other river towns. Information about Peter Kachlein is drawn from the pension application of his son; Peter Kachlein Jr., roll 1456, no. W2945, Revolutionary War Pension and Bounty-Warrant Files, National Archives, Washington, D.C., microfilm edition examined at DLR. [Hereafter cited as pension application.] Arndt information is drawn from the account in his family Bible, reprinted and translated in John Stover Arndt, *The Story of the Arndts* (Philadelphia: Stower, 1922), 11–22.

116. On the military losses, see H. M. M. Richards, "The Scots Irish in the British Military Prisons of the Revolutionary War," *Pennsylvania German Society* 32 (1924): 14. A copy of Arndt's muster roll appears in Peter Kachlein Jr.'s pension application. For the casualty list, see William Egle, ed., *Pennsylvania in the War of the Revolution, Associated Battalions and Militia, 1775–1783*, 2 vols. (Harrisburg, Pa.: Myers, 1890–92), 2:575–76. Some sources confuse Peter Kachlein Sr. with his son of the same name. The son would be prominent in postwar Easton.

117. "Northampton Committee Minutes," December 2, 1776, 62. On the close timing of the amnesty and Gordon's resignation, see Fox, *Sweet Liberty*, 18–19.

118. "Northampton Committee Minutes," November 19, 1776, 63.

119. Deposition of Andrew Sullivan [Sullamen?], February 6, 1778, NoCC Misc. Mss. (1767–78), 197, HSP.

120. Sullivan deposition, 197.

121. Allen, "Diary," June 6, 1777, and January 18, 1778, 28 and 432. Also see Fox, *Sweet Land,* 123.

122. Sullivan deposition, 197.

123. Naturalization oath quoted in Elmer E. S. Johnson, "The Test Act of June 13, 1777," *Pennsylvania German Society* 28–39 (1930): 18.

124. For an explicit complaint that the Test Act violated the naturalization oath, see the petition from two Northampton County men reprinted in Richard K. Mac-Master, *Conscience in Crisis: Mennonites and Other Peace Churches in America, 1739–1789* (Scottsdale, Pa.: Herald Press, 1979), 419–20. On the significance of the Test Acts for disenfranchising Quakers and conservatives, see Owen S. Ireland, *Religion, Ethnicity, and Politics; Ratifying the Constitution in Pennsylvania* (University Park: Pennsylvania State University Press, 1995).

125. For an excellent analysis of Revolutionary disaffection in Pennsylvania, see Anne M. Ousterhout, *A State Divided: Opposition in Pennsylvania to the American Revolution* (New York: Greenwood Press, 1987), for the Test Act specifically 161–63, 191–94.

126. Deposition of John Batt, August 18, 1777, NoCC Misc. Mss. (1767–78), 193, HSP.

127. "Northampton Committee Minutes," August 5, 8, 16, 1776.

128. Report of Field Officers, 3rd Northampton Battalion, August 5, 1776, *Records of Pennsylvania's Revolutionary Governments, 1775–1790,* Pennsylvania Museum and Historic Commission, Record Group 27 (54 microfilm reels), roll 10, frame 820, examined at DLR.

129. Worthington Chauncey Ford, ed., *Journals of the Continental Congress, 1774–1789,* 34 vols. (Washington D.C.: U.S. Government, 1907–34), 7:62–63.

130. "Northampton Committee Minutes," January 23, 1777, 68–69.

131. "Proceedings of a Treaty Held at Easton, January 30–February 6, 1777," reprinted in Paul H. Smith et al., eds., *Letters of the Delegates to Congress, 1774–1789, vol. 25, March 1, 1788–July 27, 1789 with Supplement, 1774–87* (Washington D.C.: Library of Congress, 1998), 603. These minutes were only recently rediscovered in the Scottish Public Record Office.

132. John Bull to Council, letter, January 31, 1777, *PA Arch.,* 1st series, vol. 5, 208.

133. "Proceedings of a Treaty Held at Easton," 602, 610, internal quotation marks added.

134. Ford, February 27, 1777, 7:166.

135. Isaac Sidman, pension application, no. s3,194.

136. Petition to the Pennsylvania Supreme Executive Council from the Second Battalion of Northampton Militia, October 1, 1781, *Records of Pennsylvania's Revolutionary Governments,* microfilm edition, roll 19, frame 17.

137. Abraham Horn, pension application, no. s39,718.

138. Daniel Labar, pension application, no. s49,308.

139. Isaac Sidman, pension application.

140. George Washington to James Sullivan, May 31, 1779, reprinted in Thomas C. Amory, *The Military Services and Public Life of Major-General John Sullivan* (1868; Port Washington, N.Y.: Kennikat Press, 1968), 104, emphasis in original. On Sullivan's campaign, see Colin G. Calloway, *The American Revolution in Indian Country: Crisis and Diversity in Native American Communities* (New York: Cambridge University Press, 1995); Isabel Thompson Kelsay, *Joseph Brant, 1743–1807* (Syracuse, N.Y.: Syracuse University Press, 1984); Barbara Graymont, *The Iroquois in the American Revolution* (Syracuse, N.Y.: Syracuse University Press, 1972); and the revisionist Joseph R. Fischer, *A Well-Executed Failure: The Sullivan Campaign against the Iroquois* (Columbia: University of South Carolina Press, 1997).

141. Washington quoted in Amory, 106.

142. Sullivan to Congress, September 30, 1779, quoted in Amory, 130–39.

143. Nicholas Fish, letter, quoted in David J. Fowler, *Guide to the Sol Feinstone Collection of the David Library of the American Revolution* (Washington Crossing, Pa.: David Library, 1994), item no. 1879.

144. E. A. Benians, ed., *A Journal by Thomas Hughes, 1778–1789* (New York: Cambridge University Press, 1947), 101. I appreciate Judy Van Buskirk's citation to this account. John M. Coleman, "The Treason of Ralph Morden and Robert Land," *PMHB* 79 (1955): 439–51.

145. Instructions to Pennsylvania Assembly, August 20, 1783, quoted in Henry Mss., "General," 168–70, HSP.

146. "Journal of Lieutenant Samuel M. Shute" and "Journal of Captain Daniel Livermore" reprinted in Frederick Cook, ed., *Journals of the Military Expedition of Major General John Sullivan* (Auburn, N.Y.: Knapp, Peck, and Thompson, 1887), 268, 180.

147. "Diary of Lieutenant James McMichael of the Pennsylvania Line, 1776–1778," reprinted in *PA Arch.*, 2nd series, 15:207, 204.

148. James Kirby Martin, ed., *Ordinary Courage: The Revolutionary War Adventures of Joseph Plumb Martin*, 2nd ed (St. James, N.Y.: Brandywine Press, 1999), 117, 118.

149. Israel Evans, *A Discourse Delivered at Easton* (Philadelphia: Bradford, 1779), 39.

Chapter 3

1. Jackson T. Main established this neo-Progressive framework in *Political Parties before the Constitution* (Chapel Hill: University of North Carolina Press, 1973). For thoughtful elaborations, see Edmund S. Morgan, *Inventing the People: The Rise of Popular Sovereignty in America* (New York: Norton, 1988), chaps. 10–11; and Richard Bushman, *The Refinement of America: Persons, Houses, Cities* (New York: Knopf, 1992).

2. Richard P. McCormick, *Experiment in Independence: New Jersey in the Critical Period, 1781–1789* (New Brunswick, N.J.: Rutgers University Press, 1950), 81–82, 92.

3. Peter Jaquett to Caesar A. Rodney, November 8, 1804, reprinted in Harold B. Hancock, "Loaves and Fishes: Applications for Office from Delawareans to George Washington," *DH* 14 (1970): 150–58, quote 151.

4. Jaquett, 151–52, 157.

5. Reprinted, along with a biographical essay, in John A. Munroe, "Timoleon's Biographical History of Dionysius, Tyrant of Delaware," *Delaware Notes* 31 (1958): 137, 114–15, 136–37. On the intense violence in the 1787 election that clearly extended divisions from the Revolution, see John R. Kern, "The Election Riots of 1787 in Sussex County, Delaware," *DH* 22 (1987): 241–63.

6. Merrill Jensen et al., eds., *The Documentary History of the Ratification of the Constitution* (Madison: Wisconsin State Historical Society, 1970–present), 2:77, 78. On New Castle's Presbyterian minister and Revolutionary politics, see John A. Munroe, "Parson in Politics," *DH* 23 (1988–89): 300–312, and H. Clay Reed, "The Delaware Constitution of 1776," *Delaware Notes* 6 (1930): 31, 99n. The situation here supports J. C. D. Clark's central point that modern political sensibilities have made us deaf to the fundamentally religious context of eighteenth-century popular sovereignty; see Clark, *The Language of Liberty 1660–1832: Political Discourse and Social Dynamics in the Anglo-American World* (New York: Cambridge University Press, 1994).

7. On Read's leading role among Delaware's delegates to the Constitutional Convention and during ratification, see John A. Monroe, "Delaware and the Constitu-

tion: An Overview of Events Leading to Ratification," *DH* 22 (1987): 219–38, and Jensen et al., *Documentary History of Ratification*, 3:39, 92–95 (on the election of New Castle County delegates to the ratifying convention).

8. Jensen et al., *Documentary History of Ratification*, 3:39.

9. The best recent anti-Federalist study is Saul Cornell, *The Other Founders: Anti-Federalism and the Dissenting Tradition in America, 1788–1828* (Chapel Hill: University of North Carolina Press, 1999).

10. Jensen et al., *Documentary History of Ratification*, 2:229–30, 646–48.

11. Ibid., 2:720–21.

12. Centinel, IX, [Philadelphia] *Independent Gazetteer*, January 8, 1788.

13. Voting data here and throughout the book is based on material compiled by the First Democratization Project at the American Antiquarian Society. I am especially indebted to Philip Lampi for his painstaking work building this material and for his rich knowledge of early national elections.

14. Joshua M. Wallace to Elias Boudinot, March 11, 1789, Wallace Papers, 6:110, HSP.

15. For an assessment of Kinsey as a justice by a near contemporary, see Lucius Q. C. Elmer, *The Constitution and Government of the Province and State of New Jersey . . . and Reminiscences of the Bench and Bar* (Newark, N.J.: Dennis and Co., 1872), 275–78.

16. On Kinsey's father, see Alan Tully, *William Penn's Legacy: Politics and Social Structure in Provincial Pennsylvania, 1726–1755* (Baltimore: Johns Hopkins University Press, 1977), 97–98.

17. For Ann Kinsey Wharton's marriage and Episcopal baptism, see, respectively, George Morgan Hills, *History of the Church in Burlington* (Trenton, N.J.: Sharp, 1876), 350, and John E. Stillwell, *Historical and Genealogical Miscellany . . . New York and New Jersey* (Baltimore: Genealogical Publishing Co., 1970), 96.

18. William Wade Hinshaw, comp., *Encyclopedia of American Quaker Genealogy* (Ann Arbor, Mich.: Edwards, 1938), 2:237, 214, and Stillwell, 96. On the long ties of Burlington Anglicans and Quakers, see Valerie Gladfelter, "Power Challenged: Rising Individualism in the Burlington, New Jersey, Friends Meeting, 1678–1720," in Michael Zuckerman, ed., *Friends and Neighbors: Group Life in America's First Plural Society* (Philadelphia: Temple University Press, 1982), 116–44.

19. For a convenient reprinting of the 1793 militia rolls, which the editor suggests can be used as a partial substitute for New Jersey's missing local census data, see James S. Norton, ed., *New Jersey in 1793* (Salt Lake City, Utah: private printing, 1973), 2–6, 52–53.

20. John Lawrence to Elias Boudinot, February 16, 1789, reprinted in Merrill Jensen and Robert A. Becker, eds., *The Documentary History of the First Federal Elections, 1788–1790*, 4 vols. (Madison: University of Wisconsin Press, 1976–1989), 3:81, 82n.

21. Richard P. McCormick, "New Jersey's First Congressional Election, 1789: A Case Study in Political Skulduggery," *WMQ* 6 (1949): 237–50.

22. Jensen and Becker, *Documentary History of the First Federal Elections*, 3:89–90.

23. Ibid., 1:233.

24. Owen Ireland, *Religion, Ethnicity, and Politics: Ratifying the Constitution in Pennsylvania* (University Park: Pennsylvania State University Press, 1995) and Robert L. Brunhouse, *The Counter-Revolution in Pennsylvania, 1776–1790* (1942; New York: Octagon, 1971).

25. [Philadelphia] *Pennsylvania Mercury*, September 13, 1788, reprinted in Jensen and Becker, *Documentary History of the First Federal Elections*, 1:273.

26. John Arndt to Tench Coxe, November 15, 1788, reprinted in Jensen and Becker, *Documentary History of the First Federal Elections*, 1:329.

27. [Benjamin Rush, probable author], "To the German Inhabitants of the State of Pennsylvania," November 13, 1788, reprinted in Jensen and Becker, *Documentary History of the First Federal Elections*, 1:339.

28. Rush to Tench Coxe, January 25, 1789, reprinted in Jensen and Becker, *Documentary History of the First Federal Elections*, 1:386.

29. Owen Ireland's careful analysis of ethno-religious partisanship has explained Pennsylvania ratification as a result of the electorate's decisive shift as Quakers (and others) who had been disenfranchised by the Revolutionary Test Acts were allowed to vote again beginning in 1786. This changed the balance of power away from radical Constitutionalists in favor of conservative Republicans. This assessment matches mine for Burlington County, New Jersey, where Quakers were very influential. However, as Ireland also notes, the voting data in Northampton County, Pennsylvania, does not fully support his argument. In particular, I see stronger ethnic solidarity between German Reformed and Lutherans in Northampton County, whereas he stresses their political divergence. Our difference arises largely from looking at church Germans in different areas of Pennsylvania (his primary focus is on Lancaster County), underscoring the need for a strong local focus. In addition to his book, cited earlier, see Owen S. Ireland, "The Ethnic-Religious Dimensions of Pennsylvania Politics, 1778–1779," *WMQ* 30 (1973): 423–48, and Wayne L. Bockelman and Owen S. Ireland, "The Internal Revolution in Pennsylvania: An Ethnic-Religious Interpretation," *PH* 41 (1974): 125–59.

30. Burlington Meeting Monthly Minutes [hereafter BMMM], 7/10m/1776, 3/3m/1783. Burlington Preparative Meeting Minutes, 30/8m/1804, QCHC.

31. The more conservative count of exact Quaker matches (compare columns "QX" and "TotalQ" in Table 3 in appendix) yields a less optimistic sense of Quaker persistence, with Friends' declining from 27 percent (1774) to 23 percent (1796) and 22 percent (1814). However, this apparent decline is probably the result of evidentiary bias because no local membership list comparable to George Dillwyn's complete record of 1776 exists later in the period.

32. Whereas 51 percent of the Quaker population appeared in the bottom half of the taxed population in 1774, only 41 percent ranked there in 1796, and by 1814 just 42 percent of Burlington Quakers appeared there. Although no household census records survive for anywhere in New Jersey before 1830, in that year, 51 percent of Quaker household heads were older than fifty, versus just 34 percent among non-Quakers. At the youthful end of the age scale in 1830, 21 percent of non-Quaker households were younger than thirty, versus only 10 percent of Quaker ones. See tables in appendix.

33. Samuel Allinson, "Reasons against War, and Paying Taxes for its Support," 13/6m/1780, 24–page manuscript, Allinson Family Papers, box 11A, 7, QCHC. Marietta judges Allinson's unpublished essay "the best pacifist effort of any to come out of the Revolution"; Jack D. Marietta, *The Reformation of American Quakerism, 1748–1783* (Philadelphia: University of Pennsylvania Press, 1984), 261.

34. The scriptural passage can be found in Matthew 22:21, Mark 21:17, and Luke 20:25.

35. Allinson, 20.

36. Ibid., 12.

37. For Allinson's continuity with earlier Quaker dissent, see John Woolman, *The Journal and Major Essays of John Woolman*, ed. Phillips P. Moulton (Richmond, Ind.: Friends United Press, 1971), 78–87. Allinson knew well the older Woolman, a leading Quaker reformer and fellow Burlington County resident.

38. Allinson, 22–23, citing Titus 2:14, emphasis in the original.

39. Allinson, 20.

40. Ibid., 16, 17.

41. On Allinson's manuscript and the Quaker overseers of the press, see Peter Brock, *The Quaker Peace Testimony, 1690 to 1914* (York, England: Sessions Book Trust, 1990), 192.

42. Joseph Budd to William Livingston, August 18, 1780, in William Livingston, *The Papers of William Livingston*, ed. Carl E. Prince and Dennis P. Ryan (Trenton: New Jersey Historical Commission, 1979–88), 4:43–44.

43. James Whitall to Samuel Allinson, [1786], Allinson Family Papers, box 3, folder 30C, QCHC.

44. Samuel Allinson to James Whitall, 1/11m/1786, Allinson Family Papers, box 3, folder 30B.

45. Ibid.

46. Domestic and marriage information is reconstructed from the 1776 membership list and Hinshaw.

47. On increased disownments for poor Quakers unable to attract marriage partners, see Barry Levy, *Quakers and the American Family: British Settlement in the Delaware Valley* (New York: Oxford University Press, 1988), 143–44, 236–56, tables 4, 7.

48. James Craft, "Extracts from Craft's Journal [1768–1785]," *Historical Magazine* 1 (1857): 302. The published journal misdates this entry as 1779; it should be 25/1m/1777.

49. Ibid., 3/1m/1779, [1m/]1780, 3m/1780.

50. The quotation is from BMMM, 4/3m/1782; also see 2/4m/1781.

51. On Burlington's move against alcohol, see BMMM, 1/12m/1788. Although Quakers made up 46 percent of the founding members of the Philadelphia Prison Society in 1787, the importance of Friends in early republican penal reform has not been analyzed in the major studies by David Rothman, *The Discovery of the Asylum: Social Order and Disorder in the New Republic* (Boston: Little, Brown, and Co., 1971), and Michael Meranze, *Laboratories of Virtue: Punishment, Revolution, and Authority in Philadelphia, 1760–1832* (Chapel Hill: University of North Carolina Press, 1996); for the statistic cited earlier, see Meranze, 143 n29. On Quakers' Indian policy, see Daniel K. Richter, " 'Believing That Many of the Red People Suffer Much for the Want of Food': Hunting, Agriculture, and a Quaker Construction of Indianness in the Early Republic," *JER* 19 (1999): 601–28. Anthony Wallace offers a more sanguine view of Quaker missions in *The Death and Rebirth of the Seneca* (New York: Vintage, 1969), 272–77. Obviously, Quaker engagement with Native Americans was not new in the early republic, but it took new shape from the changing wartime emphasis of the Society.

52. R. Laurence Moore, *Religious Outsiders and the Making of Americans* (New York: Oxford University Press, 1986), xi, xv, 19–20.

53. See Alan Tully, *Forming American Politics: Ideals, Interests, and Institutions in Colonial New York and Pennsylvania* (Baltimore: The Johns Hopkins University Press, 1994), chap. 7.

54. On the census as a tool of national order, see Benedict Anderson, *Imagined Communities* (1983; London: Verso Press, 1991), 163–70. The most important recent work on racial identity in early America includes Joanne Pope Melish, *Disowning Slavery: Gradual Emancipation and "Race" in New England, 1780–1860* (Ithaca, N.Y.: Cornell University Press, 1998); John Wood Sweet, *Bodies Politic: Negotiating Race in the American North, 1730–1830* (Baltimore: Johns Hopkins University Press, 2003); and Michael A. Morrison and James Brewer Stewart, eds., *Race and the Early Republic: Racial Consciousness and Nation-Building in the Early Republic* (Lanham, Md.: Rowman & Littlefield, 2002).

55. For a not wholly satisfying attempt to track ethnic population based on statis-

tical projections from surname analysis, see "The Population of the United States, 1790: A Symposium," *WMQ* 41 (1984): 85–135. On religious census data beginning in 1850, see Roger Finke and Rodney Stark, *The Churching of America, 1776–1900: Winners and Losers in Our Religious Economy* (New Brunswick, N.J.: Rutgers University Press, 1992), especially 6–13.

56. The Constitution of the United States of America, article 1, section 2. Paul Finkelman, "Slavery and the Constitutional Convention: Making a Covenant with Death," in Richard Beeman, Stephen Botein, and Edward C. Carter II, eds., *Beyond Confederation: Origins of the Constitution and American National Identity* (Chapel Hill: University of North Carolina, 1987), 188–225.

57. The early figures compare Easton and New Castle Town and Hundred in 1800 with Burlington City and Township in 1810, the earliest year for which local summary data survives for New Jersey towns. Complete surviving local household census data for all three towns begins only with the 1830 census. For more details, see the appendix.

58. Alongside the classic study of early abolition, Arthur Zilversmit, *The First Emancipation* (Chicago: University of Chicago Press, 1967), also see Richard S. Newman, *The Transformation of American Abolitionism: Fighting Slavery in the Early Republic* (Chapel Hill: University of North Carolina Press, 2002). The best local study is Jean R. Soderlund, *Quakers and Slavery, A Divided Spirit* (Princeton, N.J.: Princeton University Press, 1985). I also benefited from Dee Andrews, "The First Emancipation, 1780–1810," unpublished paper, delivered at a conference in honor of Richard S. Dunn, May 1996.

59. Quoted in Zilversmit, 82.

60. For local manumission certificates, see Clement Alexander Price, ed., *Freedom Papers: 1776–1781* (Burlington, N.J.: Burlington County Historical Society, 1984), 26, 38.

61. *Cases Adjudged in the Supreme Court of New Jersey; Relative to the Manumission of Negroes* (Burlington, N.J.: Neale, 1794), 26–27.

62. William Griffith, *Address of the President of the New Jersey Society for Promoting the Abolition of Slavery* (Trenton, N.J.: Sherman & Mershon, 1804), EAI, s no. 6903, 4, 5.

63. Doron Ben-Atar and Barbara Oberg, eds., *Federalists Reconsidered* (Charlottesville: University Press of Virginia, 1998), especially Paul Finkelman, "The Problem of Slavery in the Age of Federalism," 135–56.

64. Griffith, *Address*, 5; *Trenton Federalist*, December 23, 1800, The *Trenton Federalist* also ran announcements for the New Jersey Abolition Society; see, e.g., January 5, 1802. The conservative *New Jersey State Gazette* also ran antislavery pieces; see, e.g., July 9, 1799.

65. Griffith, *Address*, 6, 9.

66. Minutes of the Acting Committee of the Society for the Abolition of Slavery, HSD; see, e.g., 21/10m/1801.

67. [Wilmington] *Delaware Gazette*, September 8, 19, 1789.

68. [Wilmington] *Delaware Gazette*, September 23, 1789.

69. Society of Friends, *Rules of Discipline, and Christian Advices of the Yearly Meeting of Friends for Pennsylvania and New Jersey* (Philadelphia: Sansom, 1797), EAI, no. 32162, 38.

70. NoCC Misc. Mss. (1778–97), 47, 79–81.

71. Ibid., 53.

72. Molly Evans's case appears repeatedly in the Minutes of the Acting Committee of the Society for the Abolition of Slavery; see especially 21/9m/1802, 24/9m/1802, and 20/6m/1803.

73. [Wilmington] *Delaware Gazette*, September 19, 1789.

74. The classic exploration of this relationship is Edmund S. Morgan, "Slavery and Freedom: The American Paradox," *JAH* 59 (1972): 5–29, but also see François Furstenberg's provocative, "Beyond Slavery and Freedom: Autonomy, Virtue, and Resistance in Early American Political Discourse," *JAH* 89 (2003): 1295–1330.

75. *The Constitution of the New Jersey Society, for Promoting the Abolition of Slavery* (Burlington, N.J.: Neale, 1793), n.p.

76. [Wilmington] *Delaware Gazette*, September 23, 1789.

77. Miscellaneous Petitions, January 15, February 10, 1816, and January 24, 1809, Legislative Papers, DHR. I first became aware of them from Constance Jean Cooper, "A Town Among Cities: New Castle, 1780–1840" (Ph.D. diss., University of Delaware, 1983), 312–13.

78. These figures combine data for New Castle Town and Hundred. See the appendix for additional information and sources.

79. The Robert Vonjoy in the census and Robert Vanjoy in the tax list are undoubtedly the same person. See appendix for statistical data and sources.

80. Samuel Sitgreaves to Thomas Bradford, letter, December 31, 1788, NoCC Misc. Mss. (1778–97), 273.

81. Matthew S. Henry, manuscript notes for a history of Northampton County, "Easton" volume, 44, 55, HSP. Floyd S. Bixler, *Reminiscences of the Early Taverns and Inns of Easton* (Easton, Pa.: Northampton County Historical and Genealogical Society, 1931), 15–16.

82. Rayner W. Kelsey, ed., *Cazenove Journal, 1794* (Haverford, Pa.: Pennsylvania History Press, 1922), 18.

83. Gary J. Kornblith and John M. Murrin, "The Making and Unmaking of an American Ruling Class," in Alfred F. Young, ed., *Beyond the American Revolution: Explorations in the History of American Radicalism* (Dekalb: Northern Illinois University Press, 1993), 27–79.

84. Sitgreaves denied the charge and defended his "genuine Republican Principles" as aiming for a more just tax system. Samuel Sitgreaves to [unknown], letter, Philadelphia, January 6, 1790, Dreer Autograph Collection, vol. 6, Sitgreaves folder, HSP.

85. Henry Mss., "Easton," 47–51. Henry conducted interviews with members of long-settled local families in the 1840s. Interpreting his presentation of this material raises numerous challenges. I never accepted his research uncritically and relied directly upon it only when corroborated by other evidence. For a period sketch of this clothing style, see Julian Ursyn Niemcewicz, *Under Their Vine and Fig Tree, Travels through America in 1797–1799, 1805* (Elizabeth, N.J.: Grassmann, 1965), fig. 48. For a detailed study, see Ellen Gehret, *Rural Pennsylvania Clothing* (York, Pa.: Liberty Cap Press, 1975), and for a more elite (and lavishly illustrated) focus, see Linda Baumgarten, *What Clothes Reveal: The Language of Clothing in Colonial and Federal America* (Williamsburg, Va.: Colonial Williamsburg Foundation, 2002). I appreciate Kathryn Wilson's suggestions about interpreting this material; see her "Fashioning Difference: Women's Dress in Nineteenth-Century Philadelphia" (Ph.D. diss., University of Pennsylvania, 1996).

86. Pennsylvania German women's importance for ethnic folkways is supported by A. G. Roeber, *Palatines, Liberty, and Property: German Lutherans in Colonial British America* (Baltimore: Johns Hopkins University Press, 1993), especially 4–5, 233–35, and Joyce Goodfriend, *Before the Melting Pot: Society and Culture in Colonial New York City, 1664–1730* (Princeton, N.J.: Princeton University Press, 1992).

87. Henry Mss., "Easton," 50–51. For an analysis of similar violence by German women in New York, see Philip Otterness, *Becoming German: The 1709 Palatine Migration to New York* (Ithaca, N.Y.: Cornell University Press, 2004), 129–31, 164–65.

88. Donald A. Shelley, intro., *Lewis Miller: Sketches and Chronicles* (York, Pa.: Historical Society of York County, 1966), 92. I benefited from translations and interpretive suggestions by Jeffrey Fear, Christine Hucho, and Madelon Kohlerbusch.

89. Steven M. Nolt has made a major contribution to the study of Pennsylvania Germans in the postwar period in *Foreigners in Their Own Land: Pennsylvania Germans in the Early Republic* (University Park: Pennsylvania State University Press, 2002), which persuasively examines how this group increasingly understood their ethnic distinctiveness as central to being American. For an argument about Pennsylvania Germans' ambivalence toward slave emancipation based on their own uncertain ethno-racial status, see Owen S. Ireland, "Germans against Abolition: A Minority's View of Slavery in Revolutionary Pennsylvania," *Journal of Interdisciplinary History* 3 (1973): 685–706.

90. The best introduction to Pennsylvania German material culture is Scott Swank, ed., *Arts of the Pennsylvania Germans* (New York: Norton and Winterthur, 1983).

91. The most complete analysis is Paul Douglas Newman, *Fries's Rebellion: The Enduring Struggle for the American Revolution* (Philadelphia: University of Pennsylvania Press, 2004). Other important works include the special issue of *Pennsylvania History*, *PH* 67 (2000) dedicated to the Fries Rebellion; Kenneth Keller, *Rural Politics and the Collapse of Pennsylvania Federalism* (Philadelphia: American Philosophical Society, 1982); William W. H. Davis, *The Fries Rebellion, 1798–99* (1899; New York: Arno Press, 1969); and Peter Levine, "The Fries Rebellion: Social Violence and the Politics of the New Nation," *PH* 40 (1973): 241–58.

92. See the useful overview essay by Alan Taylor, "Agrarian Independence: Northern Land Rioters after the Revolution," in Young, ed., *Beyond the American Revolution*, 221–45, as well as Thomas P. Slaughter, *The Whiskey Rebellion: Frontier Epilogue to the American Revolution* (New York: Oxford University Press, 1986), and Robert Gross, ed., *In Debt to Shay's: The Bicentennial of an Agrarian Rebellion* (Charlottesville: University Press of Virginia, 1993). Terry Bouton has begun to explain the powerful economic forces that shaped political conflict in late eighteenth-century Pennsylvania in "A Road Closed: Rural Insurgency in Post-Independence Pennsylvania," *JAH* 87 (2000): 855–87, and "Tying Up the Revolution: Money, Power, and the Regulation in Pennsylvania, 1765–1800" (Ph.D. diss., Duke University, 1996).

93. *Trenton Federalist*, December 24, 1798.

94. James Morton Smith, *Freedom's Fetters: The Alien and Sedition Laws and American Civil Liberties* (Ithaca, N.Y.: Cornell University Press, 1956), 35–36.

95. Testimony of Jacob Eyerley, in Thomas Carpenter, *Two Trials of John Fries* (Philadelphia: Woodward, 1800), 47, 48. For a hyperbolic attack that blamed Eyerley for the rebellion, see [Philadelphia] *Aurora, and General Advertiser*, December 13, 1799, as well as Davis, *Fries Rebellion*, chaps. 4–5.

96. Carpenter, 41, 58, 60.

97. Philip Slough, deposition, Rawle Family Papers, series 1, box 5, folder 10, HSP.

98. [Philadelphia] *Aurora, and General Advertiser*, February 12, 1799. Annals of Congress, 5th Congress, 3rd session, 1799, 2955, online edition, http://memory.loc.gov/ammem/amlaw/lwac.html.

99. Testimony of Jacob Eyerley, in Carpenter, 49, 50.

100. Manuscript facsimile reproduced and translated in Davis, *Fries Rebellion*, xii and 12–13. William O'Reilly generously provided another translation and enriched my analysis. Henry's account is in the Henry Mss., "General," 178–79.

101. Richard Peters, in Carpenter, 80, 81.

102. William Barnett, March 23, 1799 testimony, Rawle Papers, box 5, folder 8, HSP.

103. Ibid., and John Fries, April 6, 1799, examination, Rawle Papers, box 5, folders 8 and 9, HSP.

104. Testimony of John Barrett, in Carpenter, 31.

105. [Philadelphia] *United States Gazette*, March 28, 1799.

106. Testimony of William Barnett and John Mohollon [*sic*], in Carpenter, 30–31, 45.

107. Henry Mss., "General," 180–81. On the role of language, see Birte Pfleger, "'Miserable Germans' and Fries's Rebellion: Language, Ethnicity, and Citizenship in the Early Republic," *Early American Studies* 2 (2004): 343–61.

108. James Craft Diary, vol. 1, 14/3m/99, 21/3m/99, 28/3m/99, 31/3m/99, HSP.

109. On the joint effort of local leaders and the external military force, see Samuel Sitgreaves's letter to William Henry, April 1, 1799, reprinted *PMHB* 23 (1899): 410–11.

110. Tom Smith quoted in Edward C. Carter II, John C. Van Horne, and Lee W. Formwalt, eds., *The Journals of Benjamin Henry Latrobe, 1799–1820*, 3 vols. (New Haven, Conn.: Yale University Press, 1980), 3:16.

111. [Philadelphia] *Aurora, and General Advertizer*, April 11, 1799, quoted in Paul Douglas Newman, "Fries's Rebellion and American Political Culture," *PMHB* 109 (1995): 65n.

112. Carpenter, 18.

113. Ibid., 41–42.

114. Ibid., 4.

115. Ibid., 15.

116. Ibid., 17. On Rawle in New York during the war, see Judith L. Van Buskirk, *Generous Enemies: Patriots and Loyalists in Revolutionary New York* (Philadelphia: University of Pennsylvania Press, 2002), 27–28, 34–35.

117. Carpenter, 121.

118. A. Reeder to John Arndt, May 9, 1799, Rawle Papers, box 5, folder 12, HSP.

119. Quoted in Newman, "Fries's Rebellion," 69.

120. Newman, *Fries's Rebellion*, epilogue.

121. Alexander Graydon, *Memoirs of His Own Time* (1811; Philadelphia: Lindsay & Blakiston, 1846), 390, and more generally 391–95.

122. [Easton] *American Eagle*, October 17, 1799. On the critical Northampton vote, see Sanford W. Higginbotham, *The Keystone in the Democratic Arch: Pennsylvania Politics, 1800–1816* (Harrisburg: Pennsylvania Historical and Museum Commission, 1952), 26–27, and Harry Marlin Tinkom, *The Republicans and Federalists in Pennsylvania 1790–1801: A Study in National Stimulus and Local Response* (Harrisburg: Pennsylvania Historical and Museum Commission, 1950), 238–39.

123. The Bible inscription appears in John Stover Arndt, *The Story of the Arndts* (Philadelphia: Stower Company, 1922), 11–22. For additional information, see "Some Arndt (Orndt) Family Data," *Pennsylvania German Society Proceedings* 15 (1906): 402–15.

124. This is the principal theme of Aaron Spencer Fogleman, *Hopeful Journeys: German Immigration, Settlement, and Political Culture in Colonial America, 1717–1775* (Philadelphia: University of Pennsylvania Press, 1996).

125. [Easton] *American Eagle*, August 8, 1799.

126. Jacob Arndt Jr., affidavit, April 14, 1799, Rawle Papers, box 5, folder 10, HSP. The accusation that corrupt political leaders improperly "sold" rights was a frequent idiom of Pennsylvania Germans in Northampton County during the Revolution, especially in condemning distant patriot elites in Philadelphia.

127. [Easton] *American Eagle*, August 29, 1799.

128. Ibid., October 10, 1799.

129. Ibid., October 18, 1800.

130. *Trenton Federalist,* December 23, 1799.

131. Rudolph J. Pasler and Margaret C. Pasler, *The New Jersey Federalists* (Rutherford, N.J.: Farleigh Dickinson University Press, 1975), 86–88.

132. Carl E. Prince's classic *New Jersey's Jeffersonian Republicans: The Genesis of an Early Party Machine, 1789–1817* (Chapel Hill: University of North Carolina Press, 1964) mistakenly identified Bloomfield as breaking from Federalist ranks in 1797, when he had actually begun this transition several years earlier; see Prince, 36–37. Pasler and Pasler's study also places his departure in early 1797; see 77–78.

133. Joseph Bloomfield, "Republican Meeting: 20 Sept 1800," EAI, no. 36856. William Griffith was well-known for his extended newspaper series that attacked the 1776 state constitution, republished as *Eumenes: Being a Collection of Papers* (Trenton, N.J.: Croft, 1799), EAI, no. 35570; on his role in the 1800 legislative race, see Pasler and Pasler, 95–99.

134. John Black, *Address to the Federal Republicans of Burlington County* (Trenton, N.J., 1800), EAI, no. 36771, 15, 31.

135. Black, 13, 22, 39.

136. Ibid., 32.

137. *Address to the Federal Republicans of the State of New Jersey* (Trenton, N.J., 1800), 6–7, 30–31.

138. Griffith, *Eumenes,* 33 and postscript (women), 35, 37n (immigrants).

139. The earliest surviving Burlington Township election returns were reported in the *Philadelphia Gazette,* October 18, 1800; for the hostile party labels, see *The Federal and New Jersey State Gazette,* October 21, 1800.

140. Patriotic Society of Newcastle County, Constitution, August 30, 1794, and circular, reprinted in Philip S. Foner, ed., *The Democratic-Republican Societies, 1790–1800: A Documentary Sourcebook* (Westport, Conn.: Greenwood Press, 1976), 319, 320, 324. I also examined original copies at the HSD. The standard work remains Eugene Perry Link, *Democratic-Republican Societies, 1790–1800* (1942; New York: Octagon Books, 1973).

141. Patriotic Society of Newcastle County, "Address to the People of the United States," January 8, 1795, reprinted in Foner, 330.

142. John A. Munroe, *Federalist Delaware, 1775–1815* (New Brunswick, N.J.: Rutgers University Press, 1954), 155–56.

143. Henry Hobarrt Bellas, *A History of the Delaware State Society of the Cincinnati* (Wilmington, Del.: HSD, 1895), published as *The Papers of the Historical Society of Delaware,* vol. 8, 26, 25.

144. [Wilmington] *Delaware and Eastern Shore Advertizer,* September 17, 1794, quoted in Munroe, *Federalist Delaware,* 199–200.

145. John A. Munroe, "Senator Nicholas Van Dyke," *DH* 4 (1951): 206–26.

146. [Wilmington] *Mirror of the Times,* September 17, 1800.

147. Testimony of George Read Jr., in Samuel H. Smith, ed., *Trial of Samuel Chase,* 2 vols. (1805; New York: Da Capo Press, 1970), 1:208.

148. Testimony of Gunning Bedford in Smith, *Trial,* 1: 284.

149. Carter et al., 3: 38. Read's careful preservation of the construction correspondence may make this the best documented American house from the early republic; the surviving papers are mostly in the Richard S. Rodney Collection, HSD.

150. Eliza Wolcott, "George Read (II) and His House" (MA thesis, University of Delaware, 1971), 8.

151. James A. Bayard to Richard Bassett, January 3, 1801, reprinted in Elizabeth Donnan, ed., *Papers of James A. Bayard, 1796–1815, Annual Report of the American His-*

torical Association for the Year 1913, vol. 2 (Washington, D.C.: U.S. Government Printing Office, 1915), 117, cited hereafter as *Bayard Papers*.

152. James A. Bayard to Alexander Hamilton, August 11, 1800, reprinted in *Bayard Papers*, 114, 115.

153. James A. Bayard to Richard Bassett, February 16, 1801, reprinted in *Bayard Papers*, 127. Useful recent studies include John E. Ferling, *Adams vs. Jefferson: The Tumultuous Election of 1800* (New York: Oxford University Press, 2004), on Bayard 185–95, and Bruce Ackerman, *The Failure of the Founding Fathers: Jefferson, Marshall, and the Rise of Presidential Democracy* (Cambridge, Mass.: Harvard University Press, 2005).

154. See David Waldstreicher, *In the Midst of Perpetual Fetes: The Making of American Nationalism, 1776–1820* (Chapel Hill: University of North Carolina Press, 1997) for a splendid exploration of the centrality of local conflict to early nationalism.

155. [Philadelphia] *Aurora, and General Advertizer*, March 13, 1801. Simon Newman generously shared this citation with me.

156. Henry Mss., "Easton," 63–64.

157. [Trenton] *True American*, March 17, 1801.

158. Ibid.

159. Ibid., March 17, March 24, 1801.

160. Ibid., October 13, 1801.

161. Peter Jaquett to Caesar A. Rodney, November 8, 1804, reprinted in Hancock, "Loaves and Fishes," 154.

162. Munroe, *Federalist Delaware*, 209–11, 102–3.

163. [Trenton] *True American*, October 13, 1801.

164. *Trenton Federalist*, October 18, 1802.

Chapter 4

1. Nancy L. Rhoden, *Revolutionary Anglicanism: The Colonial Church of England Clergy during the American Revolution* (New York: New York University Press, 1999).

2. J. I. Good and William J. Hinke, comps. and trans., *Minutes and Letters of the Coetus of the German Reformed Congregations in Pennsylvania, 1747–1792* (Philadelphia: German Reformed Publication Board, 1903), 381. Also see H. N. J. Klein, *The History of the Eastern Synod of the Reformed Church in the United States* (Lancaster, Pa.: Eastern Synod, 1943), 81–82. The colonial German Reformed Church operated under control from Amsterdam.

3. Armin George Weng stresses the German significance in the Church's new official name in "The Language Problem in the Lutheran Church in Pennsylvania, 1742–1820," *Church History* 5 (1936): 361.

4. These contrasting aspects of evangelicalism get splendidly divergent treatment by Nathan O. Hatch, *The Democratization of American Christianity* (New Haven, Conn.: Yale University Press, 1989) and Jon Butler, *Awash in a Sea of Faith* (Cambridge, Mass.: Harvard University Press, 1990), chap. 9.

5. Rhys Isaac, "Evangelical Revolt: The Nature of the Baptists' Challenge to the Traditional Order in Virginia, 1765–1775," *WMQ* 31 (1974): 345–68.

6. John E. Latta, *Christ's Ministers, Watchmen for Souls* (Hartford, Conn.: Hudson and Goodwin, 1809), 4.

7. John E. Latta, *A Sermon* (Wilmington, Del.: Porter, 1822), 6, 8–9, emphases in original.

8. No Delaware local census data survives for 1790. For county statistics, see Patience Essah, *A House Divided: Slavery and Emancipation in Delaware, 1638–1865* (Charlottesville: University Press of Virginia, 1996), table 7, 79.

9. Edward C. Carter II, John C. Van Horne, and Lee W. Formwalt, eds., *The Journals of Benjamin Henry Latrobe, 1799–1820*, 3 vols. (New Haven, Conn.: Yale University Press, 1980), 3:41–42.

10. Nora Beeson, ed., *Pavel Svinin's Traveling across North America, 1812–1813* (New York: Abrams, 1992), 46–47.

11. [John F. Watson], *Methodist Error; or, Friendly Christian Advice, to Those Methodists, Who Indulge in Extravagant Emotions and Bodily Exercises*, rev. ed. (Trenton, N.J.: Fenton, 1819), 28–29n.

12. Jeffrey Bolster emphasizes the biracial nature of seamen's work prior to the 1850s in *Black Jacks: African American Seamen in the Age of Sail* (Cambridge, Mass.: Harvard University Press, 1997); on black spiritual leadership among common seamen, see ibid., 122–26. Also see Marcus Rediker, *Between the Devil and the Deep Blue Sea* (New York: Cambridge University Press, 1987); Peter Linebaugh and Marcus Rediker, *The Many-Headed Hydra: Sailors, Slaves, Commoners and the Hidden History of the Revolutionary Atlantic* (Boston: Beacon Press, 2000); and Mechal Sobel, *The World They Made Together: Black and White Values in Eighteenth Century Virginia* (Princeton, N.J.: Princeton University Press, 1987).

13. The minister paraphrased the biblical injunction in Matthew 6:24 and Luke 16:13.

14. For a classic analysis of role-reversing humor, see Lawrence W. Levine, *Black Culture and Black Consciousness: Afro-American Folk Thought from Slavery to Freedom* (New York: Oxford University Press, 1977), especially 300–308.

15. Pauline Maier, "The Revolutionary Origins of the American Corporation," *WMQ* 50 (1993): 51–84.

16. For a brief comparison of different African Methodist churches, see Will B. Gravely, "African Methodisms and the Rise of Black Denominationalism," in Russell E. Richey, Kenneth E. Rowe, and Jean Miller Schmidt, eds., *Perspectives on American Methodism* (Nashville, Tenn.: Kingswood Books, 1993), 108–26.

17. Lewis V. Baldwin, *The Mark of a Man: Peter Spencer and the African Union Methodist Tradition* (Lanham, Md.: University Press of America, 1987), 11–12. Baldwin's scholarship has been indispensable to me. His most detailed work is *"Invisible" Strands in African Methodism: A History of the African Union Methodist Protestant and Union American Methodist Episcopal Churches, 1805–1980* (Metuchen, N.J.: American Theological Library Association, 1983).

18. Deed (1805), New Castle County, Recorder of Deeds, Book C-3, 226–30, microfilm reel 1A, Delaware Hall of Records, Dover, Delaware.

19. *Minutes Taken at the Several Annual Conferences of the Methodist Episcopal Church* (New York: Totten for Hitt and Ware, 1812), 23; and *Minutes Taken at the Several Annual Conferences of the Methodist Episcopal Church* (New York: Totten for Hitt and Ware, 1813), 32. Gary Nash made many incisive comments that improved my analysis throughout this section.

20. Articles of Association (1813), New Castle County, Recorder of Deeds, Book M-3, 470–473, microfilm reel 4A, DHR. The Articles have also been reprinted as an appendix to Baldwin, *Mark*, 73–79.

21. Articles, no. 6.

22. Baldwin, *Invisible*, 48–52; Gravely, 120–21.

23. *Minutes* (1812), 23, and *Minutes* (1813), 32.

24. An excellent secondary literature now exists on black religion and the emergence of free black communities in the broad Revolutionary era. Essential work includes Ira Berlin, *Many Thousands Gone: The First Two Centuries of Slavery in North America* (Cambridge, Mass.: Belknap Press, 1998), part III; Sylvia R. Frey, *Water From the Rock: Black Resistance in a Revolutionary Age* (Princeton, N.J.: Princeton University

Press, 1991); Leslie M. Harris, *In the Shadow of Slavery: African Americans in New York City, 1626–1863* (Chicago: University of Chicago Press, 2003); James Oliver Horton, *Free People of Color: Inside the African American Community* (Washington, D.C.: Smithsonian Press, 1993); Gary B. Nash, *Forging Freedom: The Formation of Philadelphia's Black Community* (Cambridge, Mass.: Harvard University Press, 1988); and Shane White, *Somewhat More Independent: The End of Slavery in New York City, 1770–1810* (Athens: University of Georgia Press, 1991).

25. Daniel Coker, *A Dialogue between a Virginian and an African Minister* (Baltimore: Edes for James, 1810), 41–43.

26. Baldwin, *Invisible*, 50–55, and *Mark*, 31. The UCA split into the African Methodist Union Protestant and the Union African Methodist Episcopal denominations in the 1850s.

27. On the African Union Church in New Castle, see New Castle County, Recorder of Deeds, Book S-3, 274–75 and Book T-3, 514–15, microfilm, DHR.

28. Articles, no. 6.

29. Peter Spencer, comp., *The African Union Hymn Book* (Wilmington, Del.: Porter, 1822), 3, Union Theological Seminary, New York City.

30. Nash, *Forging Freedom*, 67–70, 127–29, 266 table 12, 192. Also see Julie Winch, *A Gentleman of Color: The Life of James Forten* (New York: Oxford University Press, 2002).

31. *African Union Hymn Book*, 3–4.

32. The best, but by no means exhaustive, starting point for tracing the origins of Christian hymns is John Julian, *A Dictionary of Hymnology*, rev. ed. (1892; London: Murray Press, 1915). A more recent guide that addresses some of the gaps in Julian is Edna D. Parks, *Early English Hymns: An Index* (Metuchen, N.J.: Scarecrow Press, 1972). While drawn mostly from twentieth-century hymnals, including one compiled by the AME, Samuel J. Rogal, *Guide to the Hymns and Tunes of American Methodism* (Westport, Conn.: Greenwood Press, 1986) is quite useful. Interestingly, Rogal complains about the retention of English songs well into the twentieth century.

33. [Watson], 28–29, emphasis in original. Eileen Southern, *Music of Black Americans*, 2nd ed. (New York: Norton, 1983) remains the standard survey of African American musical traditions; on early religious singing among Afro-Christians, see 35–41, 75–88. The major work on African American church music is Jon Michael Spencer, *Black Hymnody: A Hymnological History of the African American Church* (Knoxville: University of Tennessee Press, 1992). Both of these fine studies lack deep analysis due to their broad chronological scope.

34. [Watson], 30–31, 133. On African cultural survivals, see Sterling Stuckey, *Slave Culture: Nationalist Theory and the Foundations of Black America* (New York: Oxford University Press, 1987).

35. *African American Congregational Singing: Wade in the Water* (Smithsonian/Folkways compact disc SF40073, 1994).

36. For examples of white congregational singing of Watts hymns, as arranged by the mid-eighteenth-century Philadelphia Presbyterian James Lyon, see *America Sings, vol. 1, The Founding Years, 1620–1800* (Vox Records 5350, 1976).

37. Gravely, 121.

38. *African Union Hymn Book*, 110–11, hymn 99, stanza 5.

39. Ibid., 10, hymn 5, stanza 2.

40. Ibid., 70, hymn 57, stanza 3.

41. On the significance of Christianity for Revolutionary era slave resistance, see Frey, especially chaps. 8–9, and James Sidbury, *Ploughshares into Swords: Race, Rebellion, and Identity in Gabriel's Virginia, 1730–1810* (New York: Cambridge University Press, 1997). Also note the rejection of this connection in Douglas R. Egerton,

Gabriel's Rebellion: The Virginia Slave Conspiracies of 1800 and 1802 (Chapel Hill: University of North Carolina Press, 1993), especially 179–81.

42. *African Union Hymn Book*, 14–16, hymns 8 and 9.

43. Ibid., 119, hymn 107, stanzas 1, 4. On alternative black explanations of the slave trade in African and African American oral traditions, see William D. Piersen, *Black Legacy: America's Hidden Heritage* (Amherst: University of Massachusetts Press, 1993), 4–14.

44. *African Union Hymn Book*, 119, hymn 107, stanza 3. David Grimsted discusses a similar sentiment in "Anglo-American Racism and Phillis Wheatley," in Ira Berlin and Ronald Hoffman, eds., *Slavery and Freedom in the Age of the American Revolution* (Charlottesville: University Press of Virginia, 1983), 338–444, quote 355–56.

45. On differences among free blacks in this period, see Julie Winch, *Philadelphia's Black Elite: Activism, Accommodation, and the Struggle for Autonomy, 1787–1848* (Philadelphia: Temple University Press, 1988), especially 34–48.

46. My emphasis on the double identity of African Americans draws, of course, on W. E. B. DuBois's classic assessment of the "double consciousness" of black Americans in *The Souls of Black Folk* (1903; Millwood, N.Y.: Kraus-Thompson Limited, 1973), 3–4.

47. Elmer T. Clark, J. Manning Potts, and Jacob S. Payton, eds., *The Journal and Letters of Francis Asbury*, 3 vols. (Nashville, Tenn.: Epworth and Abbington Press, 1958), 1:31, 115–16. Asbury recorded visiting Burlington twenty-five times from November 1771 to June 1815, twelve trips to New Castle from April 1772 to May 1791, and he never visited Easton.

48. Ibid., 1:75.

49. Ibid., 1:610, 651; 2:235.

50. For examples of such double entries, see James Craft Diary, 26/1m/00, 16/3m/00, 23/3m/00, 13/4m/00, HSP.

51. Craft, 12/6m/00.

52. S. W. Lynd, *Memoir of the Rev. William Staughton* (Boston, Mass.: Lincoln and Edmands, 1834), 51–52.

53. Ibid., 94. William Staughton, *A Discourse Occasioned by the Sudden Death of Three Young Persons by Drowning* (Philadelphia: Ustick, 1797); William Staughton, *Divine Condescension* (Burlington, N.J.: Ustick, 1804). On the press of Stephen Ustick, see Nelson B. Gaskill, *Imprints from the Press of Stephen C. Ustick . . . 1794–1836* (Washington, D.C.: Banta Press, 1940).

54. Elizabeth Booth, *Reminiscences* (New Castle, Del.: for the author, 1884), 10, 79, 87.

55. The best general interpretations of Quaker life in the Delaware Valley are Frederick B. Tolles, *Meeting House and Counting House* (1948; New York: Norton, 1963); Barry Levy, *Quakers and the American Family* (New York: Oxford University Press, 1988); and Jack D. Marietta, *The Reformation of American Quakerism, 1748–1783* (Philadelphia: University of Pennsylvania Press, 1984).

56. Thomas Colley, *An Apology for Silent Waiting Upon God* (Burlington, N.J.: Ustick for Allinson, 1805), 29, 4.

57. George Withy, *A Sermon Preached at Friends' Meeting-House, Burlington, New Jersey, on the 10th of the Fifth Month 1822* (Philadelphia, 1822), 1, 12, 14. This pamphlet, which I located at the AAS, purports to be a transcription recorded and printed without the consent of the speaker.

58. For useful introductions, see Margaret Hope Bacon's foreword to *Wilt Thou Go on My Errand? Three Eighteenth-Century Journals of Quaker Women Ministers* (Wallingford, Pa.: Pendle Hill, 1994), 1–18, quote on 1; Mary Maples Dunn, "Saints and Sisters: Congregational and Quaker Women in the Early Colonial Period," reprinted

in Janet Wilson James, ed., *Women in American Religion* (1978; Philadelphia: University of Pennsylvania Press, 1980), 27–46; Rebecca Larson, *Daughters of Light: Quaker Women Preaching and Prophesying in the Colonies and Abroad, 1700–1775* (New York: Knopf, 1999); and, for earlier origins, Phyllis Mack, *Visionary Women: Ecstatic Prophecy in Seventeenth-Century England* (Berkeley: University of California Press, 1992). Jean Soderlund has cautioned that an emphasis on autonomy distorts how early American Quaker women saw themselves within a family context in "Women's Authority in Pennsylvania and New Jersey Quaker Meetings, 1680–1760," *WMQ* 44 (1987): 722–49.

59. R. L. Bisset to Margaret Morris, letter, June 2, 1802, reprinted in John Jay Smith, *Letters of Dr. Richard Hill and his Children* (Philadelphia: private printing, 1854), 321.

60. Karin Wulf, *Not All Wives: Women of Colonial Philadelphia* (Ithaca, N.Y.: Cornell University Press, 2000), 202. Wulf offers a fascinating assessment of the symbolic significance of tax lists as marks of civic membership and concludes that gender replaced property as the "crucial determinant of membership in the polity" as a result of the Revolutionary transformation; see 200–210, quote 205. The most effective statement of the negative effects of the Revolution on women remains Joan Hoff Wilson, "The Illusion of Change: Women and the Revolution," in Alfred F. Young, ed., *The American Revolution: Explorations in the History of American Radicalism* (DeKalb: Northern Illinois University Press, 1976), 383–445.

61. In 1796, 47 percent of Burlington's taxpaying women were Quakers versus a 35 percent rate among the entire taxed population. In 1814, 41 percent of taxed women were Quakers versus a 37 percent overall rate. See appendix.

62. William Wade Hinshaw, comp., *Encyclopedia of American Quaker Genealogy* (Ann Arbor, Mich.: Edwards Inc., 1938), 2:196.

63. Martha Barker to Grace Buchanan, letter, 4/12m/1781, Martha Barker folder, Howland Collection, box 1, QCHC. Barker drew on two familiar scriptural passages here, Songs 8:7 and 2 Corinthians 3:2, but the "power of love" was her own formulation, which seems to convey what Carroll Smith-Rosenberg has described for a later period as a female world of love and ritual in *Disorderly Conduct: Visions of Gender in Victorian America* (1975; New York: Oxford University Press, 1985), 53–76.

64. The index to the Burlington Preparative Meeting of Ministers and Elders, Minutes, 1808–1839, QCHC, lists thirty-eight women versus just twenty-three men. Burlington Men's and Joint Preparatory Meeting Minutes, 1799–1814, 2/12m/1802 and 30/12m/1802, QCHC.

65. Reprinted in Smith, *Letters of Dr. Richard Hill*, 440.

66. Julian Ursyn Niemcewicz, *Under Their Vine and Fig Tree, Travels through America in 1797–1799, 1805* (Elizabeth, N.J.: Grassman, 1965), 51.

67. *The Friend*, 5/4m/1834, 202, and 29/3m/1834, 193–95.

68. Anne Royall, *Mrs. Royall's Pennsylvania, or Travels Continued* (Washington, D.C.: for the author, 1829), 105.

69. I am indebted to Rose Beiler for numerous suggestions about eighteenth-century Germany and Pennsylvania Germans. On the close cooperation of these churches, see the learned assessment by Donald Herbert Yoder, "Lutheran-Reformed Union Proposals, 1800–1850: An American Experiment in Ecumenics," *Bulletin of the Theological Seminary of the Evangelical and Reformed Church* 17 (1946): 39–77. For a strong study of a southwest German community, see David Sabean, *Property, Production, and Family in Neckarhausen, 1700–1870* (New York: Cambridge University Press, 1990).

70. These examples of close cooperation are discussed in Steven M. Nolt's excellent *Foreigners in Their Own Land: Pennsylvania Germans in the Early Republic* (Univer-

sity Park: Pennsylvania State University Press, 2002), 11–12, 113–14, and 120–21 (translation from article in the *Evangelisches Magazin,* January–March 1814).

71. The 1774 agreement is translated and reprinted in Barbara Fretz Kempton, *A History of St. John's Evangelical Lutheran Congregation of Easton, Pennsylvania, 1740–1940* (Easton, Pa.: Correll, 1940), 278–79.

72. A. Spaeth, H. E. Jacobs, G. F. Spieker, eds. and comps., *Documentary History of the Evangelical Lutheran Ministerium . . . 1748–1821* (Philadelphia: General Council of the Evangelical Lutheran Church, 1898), 137 [hereafter cited as *Lutheran Documentary History*].

73. Charles H. Glatfelter's *Pastors and People: German Lutheran and Reformed Churches in the Pennsylvania Field, 1717–1793,* 2 vols. (Breinigsville, Pa.: Pennsylvania German Society, 1980–81) is the essential starting point for all studies of eighteenth-century Pennsylvania German religion. He observed that Lutherans and Reformed people were "so numerous and close that the two should be studied together"; see Glatfelter, 1:xii. Although lacking full citations, Abdel Ross Wentz, "Relations between the Lutheran and Reformed Churches in the Eighteenth and Nineteenth Centuries," *Lutheran Church Quarterly* 6 (1933): 300–327, provides a useful overview.

74. Reprinted in Kempton, 32–33.

75. Theodore G. Tappert and John W. Doberstein, *The Journals of Henry Melchior Muhlenberg,* 3 vols. (Philadelphia: Muhlenberg Press, 1942–58), quotes from 3:376; on "Easttown," see, e.g., 1:416, 635; 2:145, 448–52, 691; 3:344–45, 685.

76. The small scale of new immigration to Easton is suggested by the paucity of entries in the Naturalization Docket (1802–12), Northampton County Court House, Easton, Pennsylvania.

77. Don Yoder, "Father Pomp's Life Story," translation of Nicholas Pomp's 1810 manuscript autobiography, Nicholas Pomp, vertical file, Lancaster Theological Seminary, Lancaster, Pennsylvania. Further biographical information about both men can be found in Henry Harbaugh, *The Fathers of the German Reformed Church in Europe and America* (Lancaster, Pa.: Sprenger & Westhaeffer, 1854–72).

78. Glatfelter, 2:462–63. On Hermann's role in the Free Synod, see Franklin P. Watts, "The Free Synod Movement of the German Reformed Church 1822–1837" (Doctorate of Sacred Theology, Temple University, 1954), especially chap. 6.

79. John B. Frantz, "Revivalism in the German Reformed Church in America to 1850" (Ph.D. diss., University of Pennsylvania, 1961), 150 (quoting Thomas Pomp, *The Weekly Messenger,* July 1841), 162–63, 141–42. Eight regional classis groups made up the intermediary organizational structure of the German Reformed Church in the Pennsylvania Synod.

80. *Lutheran Documentary History,* 178. Lutheran-Anglican cooperation was long-standing, especially under the Hanover kings and the shared work of Halle-based Lutherans and the Church of England through the Society for the Propagation of Christian Knowledge; see A. G. Roeber, *Palatines, Liberty, and Property: German Lutherans in Colonial British America* (Baltimore: Johns Hopkins University Press, 1993), 114.

81. B. M. Schmucker, quoted in Arthur C. Repp, *Luther's Catechism Comes to America* (Metuchen, N.J.: Scarecrow and American Theological Library Association, 1982), 268n. On Endress's test and ordination, see *Lutheran Documentary History,* 320.

82. The quote is from an 1851 sermon reviewing the congregation's history when the language of worship remained controversial. Reprinted in Kempton, 228–47, quote 235.

83. Reprinted in Kempton, 44–45.

84. William Fries Endress, *Endress Im Hof: A Genealogical History of the Endress Family* (New York: Knickerbocker Press, 1926), 50–51.

85. *Luther's Shorter Catechism* (Easton, Pa.: Weygandt, 1805). Also see Repp, 108–9.

86. Repp, 70–78.

87. Useful reference works on American religious traditions include Peter W. Williams, *America's Religions: Traditions and Cultures* (New York: Macmillan, 1990), and Charles H. Lippy and Peter W. Williams, eds., *Encyclopedia of the American Religious Experience: Studies of Traditions and Movements*, 3 vols. (New York: Charles Scribner's Sons, 1988).

88. Kempton, 36.

89. Easton Reformed consistory, letter, June 26, 1810, to the Lutheran congregation, translated by W. J. Heller, St. John's Lutheran Church, microfilm records (XCh394), Genealogical Collection, HSP.

90. Arbitration testimony of Philip Odewelder and Peter Schneider, NoCC Misc. Mss., "Pleas and Prosecutions," vol. 66, HSP. Unless otherwise noted, the following discussion is based on documents in this volume.

91. On the 1763 purchase, see Tappert and Doberstein, 1: 630, and Henry Mss., "Easton," 29, HSP.

92. The 1802 deed and the 1811 arbitration agreement are reprinted in Kempton, 269–76.

93. *Lutheran Documentary History*, 358. The German Reformed Synod faced a similar case from Philadelphia beginning in 1805; see *Acts and Proceedings of the Coetus and Synod of the German Reformed Church in the United States, 1791–1816* (Allentown, Pa.: Zion's Reformed Church, 1930), 38–39, 41, 44.

94. *Lutheran Documentary History*, 479.

95. The Northampton classis quoted in Watts, "Free Synod," 40. Also see Nolt, chap. 4.

96. Charles E. Schaeffer, *A Repairer of the Breach: The Memoirs of Bernard C. Wolff* (Lancaster, Pa.: Historical Society of the Evangelical and Reformed Church, 1949).

97. *Lutheran Documentary History*, 541.

98. Repp, 166–67.

99. On union churches as obstacles to the Lutheran General Synod, see Yoder, "Union Proposals," 61; Nolt, 115–16; and Christa R. Klein, "Lutheranism," in Lippy and Williams, eds., *Encyclopedia*, 3:436. On the "ethnically defined ecumenism" of a Lutheran pastor who served a congregation immediately adjacent to Easton, see Nolt, 121–24.

100. The best general introduction is Scott T. Swank, ed., *Arts of the Pennsylvania Germans* (New York: Norton and Winterthur, 1983), viii. A broad sample of Pennsylvania German material culture appears in Beatrice B. Garvan, *The Pennsylvania German Collection* (Philadelphia: Philadelphia Museum of Art, 1982). Don Yoder's recent work on paper ephemera is especially valuable for its dazzling range; *The Pennsylvania German Broadside: A History and Guide* (University Park: Pennsylvania State University Press, 2005).

101. Swank, x, viii, ix.

102. Essential studies include Donald A. Shelley, *Fraktur-Writings or Illuminated Manuscripts of the Pennsylvania Germans* (Allentown: Pennsylvania German Folklore Society, 1961); Frederick S. Weiser and Howell J. Heaney, *Pennsylvania German Fraktur of the Free Library of Philadelphia*, 2 vols. (Breinigsville, Pa.: Pennsylvania German Society and Free Library of Philadelphia, 1976); and Klaus Stopp, ed., *The Printed Birth and Baptismal Certificates of the German Americans*, 6 vols. (East Berlin, Pa.: Russell D. Earnest Associates, 1997). All note some Old World connections in *fraktur* work but agree that Pennsylvania German practice was highly innovative.

103. My introduction to Spangenberg came from Monroe H. Fabian, "The Easton Bible Artist Identified," *Pennsylvania Folklife* 22 (1972–73): 2–14. I am indebted to William O'Reilley for translating this inscription.

104. In addition to Fabian, details about Spangenberg's life can be gleaned from his Revolutionary War pension, no. W3196, microfilm reel 2251, Revolutionary War Pension and Bounty-Warrant files, National Archives, Washington, D.C., examined at DLR.

105. Frederick S. Weiser, "Fraktur," in Swank, ed., *Arts of the Pennsylvania Germans*, 230–65, 263, fig. 260.

106. Stopp, 1:29.

107. Pomp/*Ehre Vater taufschein*, Brenner Collection, 1133, FLP; reproduced in Weiser and Heaney, vol. 2, fig. 361.

108. The Streit/*Ehre Vater taufschein* is reproduced in Swank, 237, fig. 226.

109. On the emphasis on birth, see Corine Earnest and Russell Earnest, *Fraktur: Folk Art and Family* (Atglen, Pa.: Schiffer, 1999), 36–37, and note the title of Stopp's work.

110. For an introduction to Pennsylvania German popular spirituality, see Richard E. Wentz, ed., *Pennsylvania Dutch Folk Spirituality* (New York: Paulist Press, 1993).

111. Jesse Oberly confirmation certificate (1827), Borneman Collection, 557, FLP. Also reproduced in Weiser and Heaney, vol. 2, fig. 523. On the growing importance of confirmation certificates as well as Victorian and nationalist styles, see Yoder, *Broadside*, 229–36, 240–43.

112. This is Nolt's principal theme in *Strangers in Their Own Land.*

113. Earnest and Earnest, 153, 150. Maria Steiner *taufschein*, Borneman Collection, 261, FLP, also reproduced in Weiser and Heaney, vol. 1, fig. 113.

114. Figure cited in Yoder, *Broadside*, 229.

115. Shelley, 24.

116. The Stopp collection includes some twelve hundred variants of printed certificates; for Easton examples, see vol. 2, 78–95.

117. Christina Kerkendal *taufschein*, Borneman Collection, 58, FLP; reproduced in Weiser and Heaney, vol. 1, fig. 114, with emphasis on the same comparison.

118. Weiser and Heaney, 1:xxv.

119. For a detailed assessment of church Germans' baptismal beliefs, see Frederick S. Weiser, "The Concept of Baptism among Colonial Pennsylvania Lutheran and Reformed Church People," *Lutheran Historical Conference* 4 (1970): 1–45, especially 34–35. Also see Yoder, *Broadside*, 232–33.

120. Charles Henry Wharton, *A Letter to the Roman Catholics of the City of Worcester* (Philadelphia: Aitken, 1784), 15; George M. Hills, *History of the Church in Burlington* (Trenton, N.J.: Sharp, 1876), 316–18, 342–43.

121. Wharton, *Letter*, frontispiece, 18, 12, 37.

122. Ibid., 17, 36.

123. Ibid., 17, 17–18n. I have rearranged the order of this quote.

124. Charles H. Wharton, *A Short and Candid Inquiry into the Proofs of Christ's Divinity* (Philadelphia: Ormod and Conrad, 1796), 5–6.

125. Quoted in Charles H. Wharton, *A Concise View of the Principal Points of Controversy between the Protestant and Roman Churches* (New York: Clayton and Kingsland for Longworth, 1817), v.

126. Charles H. Wharton, *A Sermon on the Relations of the Christian Ministry* (Philadelphia: Aitken, 1785), 23–24.

127. William Henry Williams, *The Garden of American Methodism, The Delmarva Peninsula, 1769–1820* (Wilmington, Del.: Scholarly Resources, 1984). The most thorough study is Dee E. Andrews, *The Methodists and Revolutionary America,*

1760–1800: The Shaping of an Evangelical Culture (Princeton, N.J.: Princeton University Press, 2000).

128. John E. Latta, "Standing Committee of Missions of the General Assembly of the Presbyterian Church in the USA: A Report by Their Missionary," November 18, 1806, Presbyterian Historical Society, Philadelphia.

129. Latta, "Missionary Report."

130. William Thompson Read to James Booth Jr., letter, March 26, 1806, folder 1806–August 1817, Rodney Collection, HSD.

131. Latta, "Missionary Report."

132. Latta, *Christ's Ministers*, 5, 7.

133. John E. Latta, *An Affectionate and Earnest Address of the Minster to the People Under His Care* (Wilmington, Del.: Peter Brynberg, n.d. [post-1800]), 23, 24.

134. Latta, "Missionary Report."

Chapter 5

1. Bible Society of Delaware [hereafter BSD], *Constitution, Address, and First Annual Report* (Wilmington, Del.: Porter, 1816), 11. On the assimilating force of evangelicalism, see Harry Stout, "Ethnicity: The Vital Center of Religion in America," *Ethnicity* 2 (1975): 204–24.

2. Samuel J. Mills and John L. Schermerhorn, *Communications Relative to the Progress of Bible Societies in the United States* (Philadelphia: Philadelphia Bible Society, 1813), 4.

3. [William White], "An Address of the Bible Society Established at Philadelphia" (Philadelphia: Fry and Krammerer, 1809), 4, 9, 10. Bible Society of Philadelphia [hereafter BSP], Record Group 12.239, folder 3, American Bible Society Archives [hereafter ABSA], New York City. Also see the constitution appended to BSP, *First Report* (Philadelphia: Fry and Kammerer, 1809), 31, BSP, Annual Reports, 1809–30, PHS.

4. White, "Address," 5–6.

5. BSP, *First Report*, 5.

6. BSP, Minutes, vol. 2 (typescript 1812–19), April 21, August 18, and October 20, 1817, PHS.

7. *Documentary History of the Evangelical Lutheran Ministerium . . . 1748–1821* (Philadelphia: General Council of the Evangelical Lutheran Church, 1898), 1809 convention, 397, 405.

8. George Adams Boyd, *Elias Boudinot: Patriot and Statesman, 1740–1821* (Princeton, N.J.: Princeton University Press, 1952) remains the standard work; for a concise discussion of Boudinot's importance for the Bible movement, see Paul C. Gutjahr, *An American Bible: A History of the Good Book in the United States, 1777–1880* (Stanford, Calif.: Stanford University Press, 1999), chap. 1.

9. Elias Boudinot, *The Age of Revelation, or the Age of Reason Shewn to be an Age of Infidelity* (Philadelphia: Dickens and Maxwell, 1801), xii, xx.

10. Ibid., xxi.

11. Boudinot donated a copy of *Age of Revelation* to the Burlington Library Company, of which he was a trustee and member, but in a sample of 229 records from 1813 to 1829 the book was never borrowed. Borrower Records, Burlington Library Company.

12. Boudinot, *Revelation*, xv, xvi.

13. Elias Boudinot, *The Second Advent* (Trenton, N.J.: Fenton and Hutchinson, 1815), iv, 7.

14. Boudinot, *Second Advent*, 262.

15. Elias Boudinot, *A Star in the West, or a Humble Attempt to Discover the Long Lost Tribe of Israel* (Trenton, N.J.: Fenton, Hutchinson, and Dunham, 1816), i, 25, 78–79, 72, 79. For an early example of the missionary effort produced by this commitment, see *The Gospel According to St. John (In the Mohawk Language)* (New York: D. Fenshaw for the American Bible Society, 1818).

16. For a dismissive discussion of Boudinot's place in what would become a major discourse on Indians-as-Jews in the nineteenth century, see Richard Slotkin, *Regeneration through Violence* (Middletown, Conn.: Wesleyan University Press, 1973), 360–62.

17. New Jersey Bible Society [hereafter NJBS], Minutes of Meetings (1809–69), folder 1, 59, 70–71, 91–93, Record Group 12.110, ABSA.

18. NJBS, Minutes, 121, 122.

19. Elias Boudinot, "Address of the NJBS to the Public" recorded in the manuscript NJBS, Minutes, 75, 82–83, 87, 90.

20. NJBS, *First Report of the Managers* (Trenton, N.J.: n.p., 1810), 15.

21. On Emlen's role, see NJBS, Minutes, 93, and on the donation, see NJBS, *Second Report* (Trenton, N.J.: Sherman, 1811), 10–11.

22. On Collins's NJBS service, see *A Plan for the Establishment of a Bible Society in the State of New Jersey* (New Brunswick: Ambrose Walker, [1809]), n.p.

23. *Extracts from the Report of the Reverend Samuel Bacon* (Philadelphia: Fry, 1820), 11, appended to BSP, *Eleventh Annual Report* (Philadelphia: Fry, 1819) located in BSP Annual Reports, PHS.

24. Burlington Preparatory Meeting for Women, Minutes, n.d. (written between the entries for 28/5m/1812 and 30/7m/1812), QCHC.

25. NJBS, *Fourth Report of the Board of Managers* (Trenton, N.J.: Sherman, 1814), 4, 10; Eric M. North, "The Great Challenge: Distribution in the United States, Part I, 1816–1870," American Bible Society Historical Essay 14 (unpublished typescript, 1963), 21; ABSA.

26. NJBS, Minutes, "List of Subscribers and Donors," 2.

27. NJBS, *Fourth Report*, 4.

28. BSD, *Constitution, Address, and First Annual Report* (Wilmington, Del.: Porter, 1816), n.p.

29. Ibid., 11.

30. Ibid., 18.

31. Ibid., 19.

32. Ibid., n.p. Latta served on the committee that drafted this address. Given its similarity to his other publications and his leading role in the BSD, he must have been the principal author.

33. Ibid., n.p.

34. Ibid., 19.

35. Boudinot, "Address," 84.

36. The pioneering work is Kenneth Lockridge, *Literacy in Colonial New England* (New York: Norton and Company, 1974). Also see John Perlmann and Dennis Shirley, "When Did New England Women Acquire Literacy?" *WMQ* 48 (1991): 50–67, and Ronald J. Zboray, *A Fictive People: Antebellum Economic Development and the American Reading Public* (New York: Oxford University Press, 1983), especially 196–201.

37. BSD, Record of Minutes and Treasurer's Record Book (1813–70), December 13, 1813, HSD.

38. On the formation and early years of the BFBS, see Leslie Howam, *Cheap Bibles, Nineteenth-Century Publishing and the British and Foreign Bible Society* (New York: Cambridge University Press, 1991), 3–18, quote 3.

39. John Owen, *The History of the Origin and First Ten Years of the British and Foreign Bible Society*, 3 vols. (London: Tilling and Hewes, 1816–20), 1:2–5. The Burlington Quaker and Bible activist Samuel Emlen Jr. received a copy from his father-in-law, the Quaker Public Friend William Dillwyn, who traveled widely among British Friends; see the inscription in the copy at the Rare Book and Manuscript Library, University of Pennsylvania.

40. Owen, 1:38–39, 43, 41. An account of Steinkopf's work was printed in Burlington; see Karl Friedrich Adolf Steinkopf, *Letters Relative to a Tour on the Continent* (Burlington, N.J.: Allinson at Lexicon Press, 1815).

41. John Nitchie to Richard D. Hall, letter, December 14, 1821, John Nitchie Letterbooks, Agent and Accountant Records, ABSA.

42. Quoted in Howam, 12–13.

43. Boudinot, "Address," 87. For congressional opposition to Bible society petitions, see "Report #84," *State Papers* (Washington, D.C.: Davis, 1815–16) and "Report 52," *State Papers* (Washington, D.C.: Davis, 1817).

44. Boudinot, "Address," 89. For additional invocations of this passage (Isaiah 11:9), see BSP, *First Report*, 11; *Tenth Report*, 34, and below.

45. NJBS, Minutes, August 31, 1814, 167.

46. Elias Boudinot, *An Answer to the Objections of the Philadelphia Bible Society* (Burlington, N.J.: Allinson, [1815]), 6.

47. Ibid., 7.

48. Ibid., 10, 11, 13.

49. BSP, Minutes, vol. 2, February 15, 1819, 133.

50. Peter J. Wosh, *Spreading the Word: The Bible Business in Nineteenth-Century America* (Ithaca, N.Y.: Cornell University Press, 1994), 120–21, 43.

51. *Constitution of the American Bible Society* (New York: Hopkins, 1816), 13, 14.

52. Ibid., 16, 16–17.

53. NJBS, *Sixth Report* (Trenton, N.J.: Sherman, 1816), 4.

54. NJBS, *Ninth Report* (Trenton. N.J.: Sherman, 1819), 6.

55. Wosh, 11, 260.

56. Gutjahr, *American Bible*, 37.

57. NJBS, *Ninth Report*, 11–12.

58. *ABS Constitution*, 14.

59. BSP, *Tenth Report*, 33–34.

60. BSP, Minutes, vol. 1, January 20, 1818, 110.

61. BSP, *Eleventh Report*, 32.

62. BSP, *Twelfth Report* (Philadelphia: Fry, 1820), 5–7.

63. *Extracts from the Report of the Reverend Samuel Bacon* (Philadelphia: Fry, 1820), 5–6, all emphases in original, attached to the BSP, *Twelfth Report*, PHS.

64. *Extracts from Bacon*, 8–9.

65. Ibid., 19. The order of the quote has been reversed.

66. [Easton] *Mountaineer*, January 7, 1820.

67. J. K. Paulding, *Letters from the South*, 2 vols. (New York: Eastburn, 1817), 1:136–37.

68. Anne Royall, *The Black Book; or a Continuation of Travels*, 2 vols. (Washington, D.C.: for author, 1828), 1:163. Also see Steven M. Nolt, *Foreigners in Their Own Land: Pennsylvania Germans in the Early Republic* (University Park: Pennsylvania State University Press, 2002), especially chaps. 3 and 5.

69. [Easton] *Mountaineer*, April 7, 1820.

70. Ibid., April 13, 1821.

71. The other founding officer of the Northampton Bible Society was William Kennedy who lived across the Delaware River in Greenwich, New Jersey. He was also

a Federalist, reinforcing the political conservatism of the local Bible movement; see [Easton] *Mountaineer*, October 6, 1820.

72. BSP, *Ninth Report* (Philadelphia: Fry, 1817), and [Easton] *Mountaineer*, February 18, 1820.

73. BSP, *Thirteenth Report* (Philadelphia: Fry, 1821), 21.

74. Samuel Sitgreaves to Susan Sitgreaves, letter, December 14, 1818, Sitgreaves Collection, Cathedral Rare Book Library, Washington National [Episcopal] Cathedral, Washington, D.C. A photocopy of this letter and other material was kindly sent to me by Margaret Shannon.

75. The profile discussed in this and the following paragraph builds on fragmentary surviving evidence that yielded just sixteen names of NBS leaders who can be located in the town's 1830 tax list. Key sources include the local newspapers cited earlier as well as the [Easton] *Mountaineer*, March 23, 1821; [Easton] *Northampton Whig*, April 26, 1831; and NBS, *Sixth Annual Report* (Easton, Pa.: Hutter, 1825), Historical Pamphlet Collection, Marx Room, Easton Public Library.

76. *Documentary History of the Evangelical Lutheran Ministerium*, 565.

77. Twenty-two people were found in both the 1816 BSD membership list (BSD, *First Annual Report*, 20–22) and the 1815 town tax list. The annual meeting advertisement appeared in the [Wilmington] *Delaware Gazette*, September 30, 1828. The bipartisanship of New Castle's Bible movement contrasted with the 78 percent Federalist membership in Burlington. The comparison with Easton is somewhat strained because of its fragmented surviving records and the later formation of its Bible society. Nevertheless, its first two officers had both been active Federalists.

78. The specific religious affiliations of New Castle BSD members were ten Presbyterians, six Episcopalians, five with mixed affiliation, and a single person with no known religious affiliation. For overall data, see the tables in the appendix. On the success of Presbyterianism, see John M. Murrin, "Religion and Politics in America from the First Settlements to the Civil War," in Mark A. Noll, ed., *Religion and American Politics: From the Colonial Period to the 1980s* (New York: Oxford University Press, 1990), 25–26.

79. The best recent studies of the early national transformation of gender roles and moral reform are Bruce Dorsey, *Reforming Men and Women: Gender in the Antebellum City* (Ithaca, N.Y.: Cornell University Press, 2002) and Anne M. Boylan, *The Origins of Women's Activism: New York and Boston, 1797–1840* (Chapel Hill: University of North Carolina Press, 2002).

80. William White quoted in Owen, 2:531, 532.

81. Nitchie to Hall, letter, December 14, 1821.

82. NJBS, *Ninth Report*, 11–12; BSP, Minutes, vol. 2, April 19, 1819, 134.

83. New Castle Female Bible Society [hereafter NCFBS], Minutes and Records, vol. 1, February 1822, PHS, Philadelphia. On the leaders of female reform groups, see Anne M. Boylan, "Women in Groups: An Analysis of Women's Benevolent Organizations in New York and Boston, 1797–1840," *JAH* 71 (1984): 499n.

84. In *Reforming Men and Women*, Dorsey emphasizes that women in evangelical families were not merely drawn into the cause by husbands and fathers and stresses the fluidity of gender categories rather than the rigid totality of "separate spheres."

85. On the donation of Bibles to the Union Line, see BSP, Minutes, vol. 2, August 18, 1817, 104.

86. Charles H. Lyle, "Selected Entries, George Read II Accounts, Book B, Volume 6, 1814–1820" (unpublished typescript, September 1981, HSD), 4, 6.

87. Elizabeth Booth, *Reminiscences* (New Castle, Del.: for the author, 1884), 6–7.

88. I have been unable to locate a copy of Elizabeth Booth's hymn collection, *The Christian Pilgrim*.

89. Booth, *Reminiscences*, 92n.

90. NCFBS, Minutes and Records, vol. 1, March 1822, April 1823.

91. Ibid., vol. 2, July 25, 27, 1823.

92. Ibid., April 12, 1825.

93. Ibid., vol. 1, August 1825. David Paul Nord discusses the "differential pricing" policies that combined both giving and selling texts in *Faith in Reading: Religious Publishing and the Birth of Mass Media in America* (New York: Oxford University Press, 2004).

94. NCFBS, Minutes and Records, vol. 2, undated [August 1830] transcription of letter.

95. Ibid., April 1, 3, 1822.

96. Ibid., April 10, 1824.

97. Ibid., April 8, 1826.

98. [Trenton] *True American*, November 9, 1822.

99. NCFBS, Minutes and Records, vol. 2, April 8, 1826. The reference to India was not merely fanciful as Elizabeth Booth's friend Charlotte White went there as a missionary for three years around 1815. See Booth, *Reminiscences*, 74.

100. Paulding, 1:80, 228.

101. On the NCFBS integration with other Bible societies in the state, see NCFBS, Minutes and Records, vol. 2, April 11, 1823.

102. Sabbath School Society, Minutes and Records, 1820–41, PHS.

103. New Castle Sunday School Union, Constitution and By Laws (1827), 5–6, 6–7, copy located in the Institution Collection, AAS.

104. NCFBS, Minutes and Records, vol. 2, April 12, 1825.

105. John Nitchie to John Neilson, letter, May 25, 1825, John Nitchie Letter books, Agents and Accountant Records, box 2, folder 4, ABSA.

106. NCFBS, Minutes and Records, vol. 2, October 20, 1826.

107. Nitchie to E. W. Gilbert, letter, October 22, 1825, John Nitchie Letter books, box 2, folder 4, ABSA.

108. Nitchie to E. W. Gilbert, letter, October 11, 1826, John Nitchie Letter books, box 2, folder 6, ABSA. Also see [Wilmington] *American Watchman and Delaware Advertizer*, December 31, 1824.

109. BSD, Minutes, May 13, 1817, October 14, 1823.

110. E. W. Gilbert to John Nitchie, letter, December 15, 1826, Corresponding Secretary, Incoming Correspondence (1826–30), ABSA.

111. BSD, Minutes, October 19, 1824, October 18, 1825, October 17, 1826, October 15, 1827.

112. Nitchie to John Neilson, letter, September 25, 1827, and Nitchie to E. W. Gilbert, letter, December 1, 1827, John Nitchie Letter books, box 2, folder 7, ABSA.

113. BSP, *Proceedings of the Philadelphia Bible Society* (Philadelphia: Clark and Raser, 1827), 3.

114. *Address of the Managers* (Philadelphia: Clark and Raser, 1827), 12–13.

115. BSP, *Twentieth Report* (1828), 11.

116. BSP, *Twenty-First Report* (1829), 5, 7, 6, and BSP, *Twenty-Second Report* (1830), iv.

117. BSP, *Twentieth Report*, 11.

118. *Address of the Managers*, 10.

119. North, 131.

120. NCFBS, Minutes and Records, vol. 1, October 1829.

121. BSD, *Sixteenth Report* (Wilmington, Del.: n.p., 1829), 1.

122. David Paul Nord, "The Evangelical Origins of Mass Media in America, 1815–1835," *Journalism Monographs* 88 (1984): 19. For additional details about Bible

production, see Gutjahr, *American Bible,* chap. 1, and Paul Charles Gutjahr, "Battling for the Book: The Americanization of the Bible in the Publishing Marketplace, 1777–1860" (Ph.D. diss., Iowa University, 1996), 110–27. On the book trade generally, see the exemplary study by Rosalind Remer, *The Creation of an American Book Trade: Philadelphia Publishing in the New Republic, 1790–1830* (Philadelphia: University of Pennsylvania Press, 1996).

123. Nord, *Faith in Reading,* 9.

124. Female Bible Association of Easton, eleventh annual report, printed in the [Easton] *Northampton Whig,* April 26, 1831.

125. BSD, *Sixteenth Report,* 4, 5.

126. Ibid., 7.

127. ABS, *Fourteenth Annual Report* (1830), quoted in Gutjahr, "Battling for the book," 72–73.

128. See Jon Butler, *Awash in a Sea of Faith: Christianizing the American People* (Cambridge, Mass.: Harvard University Press, 1990), chap. 9.

129. Nord, *Faith in Reading,* 84.

130. On early local particularism in the Bible movement, see Wosh, chap. 3; for later changes, chaps. 5–6.

Chapter 6

1. Insightful assessments that caution against too quick an embrace of party are Richard Hofstadter, *The Idea of a Party System: The Rise of Legitimate Opposition in the United States, 1780–1840* (Berkeley: University of California Press, 1969), and Ronald P. Formisano, "Deferential-Participant Politics: The Early Republic's Political Culture, 1789–1840," *American Political Science Review* 68 (1974): 473–87.

2. The basic shape of this historiographic progression has moved from the class-based view of Progressive historians exemplified by Arthur Schlesinger Jr., *The Age of Jackson* (Boston: Little, Brown, 1945), to the ethnocultural thesis presented in Lee Benson, *The Concept of Jacksonian Democracy* (Princeton, N.J.: Princeton University Press, 1961), and an institutional view of parties as primarily "electoral machines" in Richard P. McCormick, *The Second American Party System* (Chapel Hill: University of North Carolina Press, 1966). Sean Wilentz, "On Class and Politics in Jacksonian America," *RAH* 10 (1982): 45–63, remains a useful general assessment. Harry L. Watson offers an apt synthesis of the period in *Liberty and Power: The Politics of Jacksonian America* (New York: Noonday, 1990), which, along with Charles Sellers, *The Market Revolution: Jacksonian America, 1815–1846* (New York: Oxford University Press, 1991), stresses broad economic differences as the key to understanding Jacksonian society and politics.

3. The contentious arguments over interpreting the Revolution's legacy for the new nation are on clear display in "Forum: How Revolutionary Was the Revolution? A Discussion of Gordon S. Wood's *Radicalism of the American Revolution,*" *WMQ* 51 (1994): 677–716.

4. John A. Munroe has treated Delaware effectively in several works; for this period, see *Federalist Delaware, 1775–1815* (New Brunswick, N.J.: Rutgers University Press, 1954). The literature on the Jeffersonian triumph is immense, but the pioneering work remains by Noble E. Cunningham; see, e.g., *The Jeffersonian Republicans in Power: Party Operations, 1801–1809* (Chapel Hill: University of North Carolina Press, 1963). The label used to identify Jeffersonian Republicans varies: "Democratic-Republican" and "Democratic" were also employed at the time and in subsequent scholarship. *Republican* refers here to the dominant presidential party of

Jefferson, Madison, and Monroe from 1800 to 1824. The term *first party system* is also used here for the sake of clarity, but see Ronald P. Formisano's astute "Federalists and Republicans: Parties, Yes—System, No," in Paul Kleppner, Walter Dean Burnham, Ronald P. Formisano, Samuel P. Hays, Richard Jensen, and William G. Shade, eds., *The Evolution of American Electoral Systems* (Westport, Conn.: Greenwood Press, 1981), 33–76.

5. My analysis of election data is heavily indebted to the First Democratization Project at the American Antiquarian Society, which has compiled most surviving newspaper election results for the country from 1789 to 1825. I have benefited enormously from Phillip J. Lampi's generosity and intensive knowledge of this material.

6. *Delaware Gazette*, September 2, 1816. The order of the quote has been reversed.

7. One of the Persecuted, "Federal Prosecution," broadside filed after the *Mirror of the Times*, September 22, 1804, AAS. References to the "wild Irish" invoked the language of the leading Massachusetts Federalist, and nativist, Harrison Gray Otis; see David Hackett Fischer, *The Revolution of American Conservatism* (New York: Harper and Row, 1965), and Edward C. Carter II, "A 'Wild Irishman' under Every Federalist's Bed: Naturalization in Philadelphia, 1789–1806," *PMHB* 94 (1970): 331–46.

8. [Wilmington] *American Watchman*, October 3, 7, 1818. Practically every issue in the fall election season contained an appeal for Irishmen to vote Republican.

9. *New Castle Argus*, May 21, 1805.

10. On the long-term stability of ethno-religious patterns in Delaware politics, see Munroe, *Federalist Delaware*, 239–41, and McCormick, *Second Party System*, 147–54.

11. An older set of studies on early national politics in Pennsylvania sketches the essential issues, but they badly need updating. Among the best of this scholarship is Sanford W. Higginbotham, *The Keystone in the Democratic Arch: Pennsylvania Politics, 1800–1816* (Harrisburg: Pennsylvania Historical and Museum Commission, 1952), which suffers from a state-and-nation framework inattentive to enormous local variations within Pennsylvania. The most promising new work is Andrew Shankman, *Crucible of American Democracy: The Struggle to Fuse Egalitarianism and Capitalism in Jeffersonian Pennsylvania* (Lawrence: University Press of Kansas, 2004).

12. Shankman's *Crucible of Conflict* provides the best assessment of divisions among Pennsylvanian Jeffersonian in this period; also see his "Malcontents and Tertium Quids: The Battle to Define Democracy in Jeffersonian Philadelphia," *JER* 19 (1999): 43–72, and Noble E. Cunningham Jr., "Who Were the Quids?" *Mississippi Valley Historical Review* 50 (1963): 252–63.

13. Samuel Sitgreaves to Matthew Carey, letter, September 4, 1809, S-Si (1809) folder, Lea and Febiger Papers, HSP. Samuel Sitgreaves to John Arndt, letter, September 1, 1808, Manuscript Division, Library of Congress. Margaret Shannon at the Washington National Cathedral generously supplied me with a photocopy of the original. Samuel D. Ingham would later be a prominent Pennsylvania Republican leader, and later still a member of Jackson's cabinet, but in 1806 he was elected to the state legislature as a Quid.

14. *American Eagle*, September 14, 1805. I appreciate my colleague Richard Blanke's translation of the supplement.

15. *American Eagle*, August 10, 1805.

16. Higginbotham, 99–100.

17. Jeffrey L. Pasley, "From Print Shop to Congress and Back: Easton's Thomas J. Rogers and the Rise of Newspaper Politics," unpublished conference paper (revised August 2000). The author generously shared a copy with me.

18. [Easton] *Northampton Farmer*, December 21, 1805.

19. Abraham Horn, broadside, September 30, 1808, NoCC., Misc. Mss (1797–1851), 189, HSP.

20. *Northampton Farmer*, September 13, 1806.

21. Horn, broadside, September 30, 1808. Abraham Horn was a perennial candidate for office who experienced mixed success: elected coroner in 1794 and to the assembly in 1798, he lost assembly races in 1796 and 1800 and also lost his bid to become sheriff in 1799. Reconstructing his early political career comes from brief newspaper comments; see *Eastoner Bothe*, October 22, 1794; *American Eagle*, August 8, 1799; and, most importantly, the letter signed "Minority" in *American Eagle*, October 18, 1800. Other than the broadside discussed here, few details of his life are known. In the 1814 Easton tax list he appears as a land surveyor in the second quintile of taxed wealth, but in 1818 he successfully applied for a Revolutionary veterans' pension, which required proof of poverty. His economic situation further worsened by 1820, forcing a move to Philadelphia, yet he received a Reformed burial in Easton in 1826. Abraham Horn, pension application, "Revolutionary War Pensions," S39, 718, microfilm version examined at DLR. Three of Horn's five sons in the 1830 Easton tax list were in the bottom half of taxable wealth, while two others placed in the second quintile.

22. The parallel texts of the bilingual broadside are nearly identical, although the German is somewhat more fluid in style and at points uses stronger pejorative language. It also includes an erroneous additional attack on Snyder for opposing the state constitution that does not appear in the English text. I am indebted to William O'Reilley's translation and assessment of the German text. All quotes are from the English version.

23. In addition to his Quid newspapers, C. J. Hutter also published a nonpartisan bilingual paper in Easton, *The People's Instructor*. It seems all but certain that his press issued Horn's bilingual broadside.

24. The foregoing paragraph is drawn from election season issues of both Easton newspapers. For the *Pennsylvania Herald*, see August 10, 17, 31, 1808; October 4, 1809; for the *Northampton Farmer*'s attacks on Hutter, see August 27, September 3, 1808.

25. *Herald*, October 3, November 9, 1808.

26. [Allentown, Pa.] *Der Unabhangige Republikaner [Independent Republican]*, July 27, 1810. I have relied upon Christian Lieb's translation of selected issues of this paper.

27. *Der Unabhangige Republikaner [Independent Republican]*, July 5, 1811.

28. Robert Traill, letter, September 11, 1815, reprinted in Uzal W. Condit, *The History of Easton, Pennsylvania* (Easton, Pa.: George G. West, 1885), 73–75.

29. *Newark Centinel*, October 25, 1808. Also see Rudolph J. Pasler and Margaret C. Pasler, *The New Jersey Federalists* (Rutherford, N.J.: Farleigh Dickinson University Press, 1975).

30. *Trenton Federalist*, September 28, 1807.

31. Elias Boudinot to Timothy Pickering, letter, June 3, 1808, reel 28, 335, Pickering Papers, Massachusetts Historical Society (microfilm edition).

32. Charles H. Wharton to Joshua M. Wallace, letter, June 10, 1808, Wallace Papers, vol. 6, 139, HSP.

33. Griffith quoted in Fischer, *Revolution of American Conservatism*, 329.

34. Boudinot to Pickering, letter, June 3, 1808, reel 28, 335; William Coxe Jr. to Pickering, letter, April 27, 1808, reel 28, 312, Pickering Papers (microfilm edition).

35. For two examples of Federalists' sustained wooing of the Quaker vote, see *Trenton Federalist*, September 19, 1808 and November 29, 1824. For a Republican appeal to Quakers to switch their partisan allegiance, see [Wilmington] *Mirror of the Times*, February 5, 1806, reprinted from the [Trenton] *True American*.

36. [Burlington] *Rural Visiter, A Literary and Miscellaneous Gazette*, 30/7m/1810. Allinson's family history and the Quaker dating style of the paper suggest that it had a Quaker audience.

37. *Trenton Federalist*, August 17, 1807.

38. *United States Gazette*, September 9, 1812. The best general study remains Donald H. Hickey, *The War of 1812* (Urbana: University of Illinois Press, 1989).

39. For descriptions of this critical election, see Prince, 173–81, and Pasler and Pasler, *New Jersey Federalists*, 142–49. Unfortunately, no election returns exist for the contests in Burlington County.

40. See, e.g., Walter Ray Fee, *The Transition from Aristocracy to Democracy in New Jersey, 1789–1829* (Somerville, N.J.: Somerset Press, 1933).

41. William Coxe Jr. to Richard S. Coxe, letter, December 22, 1813, file 2, Richard S. Coxe Papers, Special Collections, Rutgers University Library.

42. John A. Munroe, *Louis McLane: Federalist and Jacksonian* (New Brunswick, N.J.: Rutgers University Press, 1973), 42–46, 54–55.

43. [Wilmington] *American Watchman*, September 27, 1822.

44. For attacks on Booth, see [Wilmington] *American Watchman*, September 27 and October 1, 1822.

45. [Wilmington] *American Watchman*, October 3, 1818 and September 26, 1818.

46. Samuel H. Black of Pencader Hundred in [Wilmington] *American Watchman*, October 31, 1823.

47. *St. Louis Enquirer*, February 5, 1820, quoted in Glover Moore, *The Missouri Controversy 1819–1821* (Lexington: University of Kentucky Press, 1953), 81.

48. Moore's study, *Missouri Controversy*, remains the standard work. On the movement's Delaware Valley origins, see chap. 2, "Burlington County, New Jersey, Starts a Crusade," 65–83.

49. Elias Boudinot, printed circular, Burlington, November 5, 1819, vol. 44, 267, Pickering Papers (microfilm edition).

50. Albert F. Simpson, "The Political Significance of Slave Representation, 1787–1821," *Journal of Southern History* 7 (1941): 320.

51. Emlen quoted in Moore, *Missouri Controversy*, 67–69, 134.

52. *Trenton Federalist*, August 17, 1807, September 19, 1808. On Federalist antislavery, see Paul Finkelman, "The Problem of Slavery in the Age of Federalism," in Doron Ben-Atar and Barbara Oberg, eds., *Federalists Reconsidered* (Charlottesville: University Press of Virginia, 1998), 135–56.

53. [Trenton] *True American*, November 29, 1819.

54. [Easton] *Mountaineer*, January 7, 1820. Sitgreaves to Timothy Pickering, April 18, 1816, reel 44, 151, Pickering Papers (microfilm edition).

55. *Speech of Mr. Van Dyke . . . delivered in the US Senate, Jan. 28, 1820*, 2–3, 11, pamphlet at AAS.

56. Munroe, *McLane*, 103–4. On regional divisions within the south, see William W. Freehling, *The Road to Disunion: Secessionists at Bay, 1776–1854* (New York: Oxford University Press, 1990), especially chap. 8.

57. Moore, *Missouri Controversy*, 221.

58. Fee, 239–41.

59. Nicholas Biddle to Thomas J. Rogers, February 22, 27, 1821, quoted in Moore, *Missouri Controversy*, 163; also see 162, 188.

60. [Easton] *Expositor*, September 10, 1822, October 15, 1822.

61. Elias Boudinot to Elias E. Boudinot, letter, December 15, 1819, reprinted in J. J. Boudinot, *The Life, Public Services, Addresses and Letters of Elias Boudinot*, 2 vols. (New York: Da Capo, 1971), 2:173.

62. Louis McLane speech to the Sixteenth Congress, quoted in Moore, *Missouri Controversy*, 304.

63. The changing significance of race with the implementation of universal white manhood suffrage in the first decades of the nineteenth century has begun to receive careful analysis. Among the best recent explorations are James Banner Stewart, "The Emergence of Racial Modernity and the Rise of the White North, 1790–1840," *JER* 18 (1988): 181–236 [includes responses]; Alexander Saxton, *The Rise and Fall of the White Republic: Class Politics and Mass Culture in Nineteenth-Century America* (New York: Verso, 1990); and David R. Roediger, *The Wages of Whiteness: Race and the Making of the American Working Class* (New York: Verso, 1991). Unfortunately, this attention to the mutability of race has not been matched by parallel work on its intersection with ethnicity.

64. McCormick, *Second American Party System*, 104, 171.

65. A useful overview is Robert V. Remini, *The Election of Andrew Jackson* (New York: Lippincott, 1963); on the importance of New York and Pennsylvania, see 135–48.

66. Munroe, *McLane*, 105.

67. [Trenton] *True American*, October 25, 1828.

68. [Wilmington] *American Watchman*, November 12, 1824.

69. The Republican [Wilmington] *American Watchman* reported on the Federalist conflict in detail; see December 7, 1824.

70. [Wilmington] *American Watchman*, October 5, 1824.

71. [Wilmington] *American Watchman*, October 12, 1824; for election results, see November 5, 1824.

72. *Trenton Federalist*, October 25, 1824.

73. *Newark Sentinel*, November 2, 1824.

74. [Wilmington] *Delaware Gazette*, October 15, 1824, and June 3, 1823.

75. For the editor's long explanation that mostly condemned Jackson, see [Trenton] *True American*, September 18, October 2, 16, 1824.

76. Some Jackson electors actually received ninety-two local votes. Because this additional support came from the seventeen voters who favored the official Republican slate, they have not been included in the previously mentioned tally that argues that Jackson's key local backing came from Federalists. The return can be found in the *New Jersey Mirror*, November 10, 1824.

77. On the 1823 convention and election, see Philip Shriver Klein, *Pennsylvania Politics, 1817–1832: A Game without Rules* (Philadelphia: Historical Society of Pennsylvania, 1940), 132–49. The dizzying factionalism among Pennsylvania Republicans defies easy categorization. Klein's statewide focus leads him to present a closer alliance between Porter and The Family than our perspective permits. On Porter as a marginal figure in the state party, see Jean E. Friedman and William G. Shade, "James M. Porter: A Conservative Democrat in the Jacksonian Era," *PH* 42 (1975): 189–204.

78. Kim T. Phillips, "The Pennsylvania Origins of the Jacksonian Movement," *Political Science Quarterly* 91 (1976): 489–508.

79. *Easton Centinel*, February 18, 1825. Hutter had formerly been the great Quid enemy of the Rogers-led Republican Party in Northampton County, as discussed earlier, but by the early 1820s the old antagonists had joined forces to support The Family faction of the state party. This union was the source of endless comment by the ongoing antiparty and third-party papers in Easton, the *Expositor* and the *Mountaineer*.

80. Charles Francis Adams, ed., *Memoirs of John Quincy Adams* (Philadelphia: Lippincott, 1875), 6:496.

81. *Easton Centinel,* February 25, 1825.

82. [Trenton] *True American,* September 20, 1828. Similar accounts appear in [Wilmington] *Delaware Journal,* June 5, 1827, and the [Wilmington] *American Watchman,* which reprinted figures from the *New York Observer* to derive an Adams victory from free popular vote projections; see December 21, 1824.

83. [Wilmington] *Delaware Gazette,* September 18, 1827.

84. [Wilmington] *American Watchman,* September 21, 1827.

85. [Wilmington] *Delaware Gazette,* September 4, 7, 24, 1827.

86. [Wilmington] *Delaware Journal,* September 25, 28, 1827.

87. [Wilmington] *American Watchman,* January 15, 1828; [Wilmington] *Delaware Patriot,* January 18, 1828.

88. [Wilmington] *Delaware Gazette,* July 25, 1828.

89. *Trenton Federalist,* November 11, 1824.

90. On the effectiveness of Adams's organization in New Jersey, see Remini. On the importance of patronage to Republicans, see Carl E. Prince, *New Jersey's Jeffersonian Republicans: The Genesis of an Early Party Machine, 1789–1817* (Chapel Hill: University of North Carolina Press, 1964), and Herbert Ershkowitz, *The Origins of the Whig and Democratic Parties: New Jersey Politics, 1820–1837* (Washington, D.C.: University Press of America, 1982).

91. *Trenton Emporium,* October 4, 1828.

92. [Trenton] *True American,* November 7, 1828.

93. Ershkowitz, 93, 108; on Wall, see 101.

94. [Easton] *Delaware Democrat,* May 4, 1827.

95. *Easton Centinel,* October 3, 1828. The *Delaware Democrat* ran similar pieces September 25 and October 2, 16, 1828. On the ongoing power of the Fries Rebellion in local political culture, see Paul Douglas Newman, *Fries's Rebellion: The Enduring Struggle for the American Revolution* (Philadelphia: University of Pennsylvania Press, 2004), epilogue.

96. Jacksonians actually had fewer people of unknown religious affiliation than the overall figure in the town (57 percent versus 63 percent). This led Jacksonian Lutheran, Reformed, and Presbyterian support to be slightly higher than in the population at large. Jacksonians also had unusual strength among the small number of Methodists in town; five out of the seven known local Methodists were Jacksonians.

97. Norris Hansell, *Josiah White, Quaker Entrepreneur* (Easton, Pa.: Canal History and Technology Press, 1992), 50. For a concise introduction to canals on the Delaware, see the classic study by George Rogers Taylor, *The Transportation Revolution, 1815–1860* (White Plains, N.Y.: Sharpe, 1951), 38–42.

98. For wealth distribution statistics and sources, see appendix.

99. Quoted in Peter Way, *Common Labour: Workers and the Digging of North American Canals, 1780–1860* (New York: Cambridge University Press, 1993), 65.

100. Joel Jones to Thomas Cadwalader, letter, October 9, 1829, Cadwalader Collection, HSP.

101. Hartzel to Cadwalader, letters, June 10 and 23, 1828, correspondence 1826–31, box 10, Thomas Cadwalader Papers, Cadwalader Collection, HSP. All following citations are from this folder, but also see related material in the Penn Estate Correspondence and Wikoff-Hartzel Dispute folders.

102. Wikoff to Cadwalader, letter, June 28, 1828.

103. Hartzel to Cadwalader, letter, July 5, 1828.

104. Wikoff to Cadwalader, letter, July 5, 1828.

105. Porter to Cadwalader, letter, September 15, 1828.

106. Hartzel to Cadwalader, letter, July 1, 1828.

107. Wikoff to Cadwalader, letter, November 26, 1828.

108. [Easton] *Delaware Democrat*, November 29, 1827, and September 28, 1828.

109. [Easton] *Northampton Correspondent*, October 3, 1828. I have relied on translations by Christian Lieb.

110. William G. Shade, "Pennsylvania Politics in the Jacksonian Period: A Case Study, Northampton County, 1824–1844," *PH* 39 (1972): 315, 317.

111. Klein, 352, 355–60.

112. [Trenton] *True American*, October 30, 1824.

113. *Trenton Emporium*, November 29, 1828.

114. [Easton] *Delaware Democrat*, November 21, 1828.

115. [Wilmington] *Delaware Journal*, October 17, 31, 1828. This critique of Jackson's leadership of Indian wars cited Elias Boudinot as a key authority.

116. [Trenton] *True American*, October 16, 1824, and September 20, 1828.

117. For a partisan defense of Indians, see *Trenton Federalist*, February 20, 1824, and the [Trenton] *New Jersey Gazette*, January 9, 1830, and 25/12m/1830. For a defense of Jacksonian Indian warfare, see Easton's *Democrat and Argus*, December 15, 1831.

118. [Wilmington] *Delaware Patriot*, February 2, 1828.

119. [Wilmington] *Delaware Patriot*, July 29, 1828.

120. Lee Benson demolished the celebratory claim that Jacksonians deserve credit for the egalitarian triumph of the period. Although much abused, his classic work demands attention; see especially 329–38. For reassessments, see the defense by Ronald P. Formisano, "The Invention of the Ethnocultural Interpretation," *AHR* 99 (1994): 453–77, and more critical comments by Daniel Feller, "Lee Benson and the Concept of Jacksonian Democracy," *RAH* 20 (1992): 591–601.

121. [Wilmington] *Delaware Journal*, October 10, 1828.

122. For a clear, quantified assessment of the second party system's gradual formation in two distinct phases from 1824 to 1852, see William G. Shade, "Political Pluralism and Party Development: The Creation of a Modern Party System, 1815–1852," in Kleppner et al., eds., *Evolution*, 77–111.

Chapter 7

1. I first learned of Ely's sermon from Bruce Allen Dorsey, "City of Brotherly Love: Religious Benevolence, Gender, and Reform in Philadelphia, 1780–1844" (Ph.D. diss., Brown University, 1993), 309–15. Also see Anthony F. C. Wallace, *Rockdale: The Growth of an American Village in the Early Industrial Revolution* (1972; New York: Norton, 1980), 297.

2. Anne Royall, *Mrs. Royall's Pennsylvania, or Travels Continued* (Washington, D.C.: for the author, 1829), 98.

3. Ibid., 103–4, 104.

4. Anne Royall, *The Black Book; or a Continuation of Travels*, 2 vols. (Washington, D.C.: for the author, 1828), 1:223.

5. Royall, *Black Book*, 1:163–64. Almost every page of this volume attacked evangelical reform; see 163–247.

6. *Trenton Federalist*, 15/12m/1828. This paper began using a Quaker dating style in the late 1820s.

7. [Mt. Holly] *New Jersey Chronicle & Herald*, September 10, 1830.

8. [Easton] *Weygat Gridiron*, August 11, 1826.

9. [Wilmington] *Delaware Register*, October 3, October 24, 1829.

10. "Address of the *Classis* of East Pennsylvania," reprinted in the *Magazine of the*

German Reformed Church, September 1829, 279. Steven M. Nolt notes that this critique was itself part of an Americanization process in *Foreigners in Their Own Land: Pennsylvania Germans in the Early Republic* (University Park: Pennsylvania State University Press, 2002), 102–7.

11. "Address of the *Classis*," 279, 280.

12. "Prospectus," *Magazine of the German Reformed Church*, November 1827, 1.

13. "Bible Societies," *Magazine of the German Reformed Church*, November 1827, 4, 5; also see 17.

14. "Address of the *Classis*," 280.

15. Ibid.

16. John W. Richards, "Sermon, 1851," reprinted in Barbara Fretz Kempton, *A History of St. John's Evangelical Lutheran Congregation of Easton, Pennsylvania, 1740–1940* (Easton, Pa.: Correll Co, 1940), 236. For biographical information, see *St. John's Lutheran Church, Memorial Volume* (Easton, Pa.: Church Council, 1882), 3, 4.

17. On the new force of religious architecture, see Richard L. Bushman, *The Refinement of America: Persons, Houses, Cities* (New York: Knopf, 1992), especially part II, and Jon Butler, *Awash in a Sea of Faith: Christianizing the American People* (Cambridge, Mass.: Harvard, 1990), chap. 9.

18. Charles E. Schaeffer, *A Repairer of the Breach: The Memoirs of Bernard C. Wolff* (Lancaster, Pa.: Evangelical and Reformed Church, 1949), 28–35; Henry Martyn Kieffer, *Some of the First Settlers of "The Forks of the Delaware" and Their Descendents, Being a Translation from the German of the Records Books of the First Reformed Church of Easton, Penna. from 1760 to 1852* (1902; Westminster, Md.: Family Line Publications, 1990), 55.

19. The "Orthodox" label is something of a misnomer because this group fashioned a more novel accommodation to Anglo-American culture than the Hicksites. J. William Frost presents a clear overview in "Years of Crisis and Separation," in John M. Moore, ed., *Friends in the Delaware Valley: Philadelphia Yearly Meeting, 1681–1981* (Haverford, Pa.: Friends Historical Association, 1981), 77–78. The best book-length examinations are H. Larry Ingle, *Quakers in Conflict* (Knoxville: University of Tennessee Press, 1986), and Robert W. Doherty, *The Hicksite Separation* (New Brunswick, N.J.: Rutgers University Press, 1967); also see Bruce Dorsey, "Friends Becoming Enemies: Philadelphia Benevolence and the Neglected Era of American Quaker History," *JER* 18 (1998): 395–428.

20. William Allinson, "Memorandum of Procedure of Sundry Meetings," two manuscript volumes, 4m/1827–5/2m/1828, QCHC, vol. 1, 4m/1827.

21. Allinson, "Memorandum," vol. 1, 8/5m/1827.

22. Minutes, Meeting for Ministers and Elders, 1808–1839, Burlington Preparatory Meeting, QCHC. William Wade Hinshaw, comp., *Encyclopedia of American Quaker Genealogy* (Ann Arbor, Mich.: Edwards, 1938), 2:236, 264, 278.

23. See, e.g., Burlington Men's Monthly Meeting Minutes [hereafter BMMM], microfilm edition, reel 13, 4/2m/1828, QCHC, and Burlington Women's Monthly Meeting Minutes [hereafter BMMW] microfilm edition, reel 103, 4/2m/1828, QCHC.

24. BMMW, 7/4m/1828 and 5/5m/1828; and BMMM, 7/4m/1828 (quote).

25. Minutes, Burlington Monthly Meeting of Hicksite Friends (Rancocas), 4/2m/1828, microfilm edition, Friends Historical Library, Swarthmore College. The order of this quotation has been rearranged.

26. *The Friend* 4 (1831): 199. A similar assessment can be found in BMMM, 7/4m/1828.

27. John Cox letters to Richard and Abigail Mott, Richard Mott Papers, box 2,

folder 2 (1809–19), QCHC. Also see Susanna Parrish Wharton, comp., *The Parrish Family* (Philadelphia: Buchanan Company, 1925).

28. Mary Allinson to Margaret H. Hilles, letter, 27/1m/[1827?], Howland Collection, box 1, folder 2, QCHC.

29. Edwin B. Bronner, *Sharing the Scriptures: The Bible Association of Friends in America, 1829–1979* (Philadelphia: Bible Association of Friends, 1979); *Constitution and Address of the Bible Association of Friends in America* (Philadelphia: Conrad, 1829), 9; *First Annual Report of the Bible Association of Friends in America* (Philadelphia: William Brown, 1830), 3; *Second Annual Report of the Bible Association of Friends in America* (Philadelphia: William Brown, 1831), 16. The *Constitution* and *Annual Reports* are all held at the QCHC.

30. Frost, "Years of Crisis," 81.

31. On its ties to the ABS, see Bronner, 6, 15–16, quote 16n, and *First Annual Report of the Bible Association of Friends*, 11–12.

32. Benjamin Seebohm, ed., *Memoirs of the Life and Gospel Labours of Stephen Grellet*, 2 vols. (London: A. W. Bennett, 1860), 2:148, 208, 214–15.

33. On the importance of British connections for the Orthodox, see Doherty, 73–75, and Frost, "years of Crisis," 79.

34. Ann Dillwyn Alexander to Samuel Emlen, letter, 25/2m/1828, Howland Collection, box 1, folder 1, QCHC.

35. For anti-Catholic reform attention in the other towns, see NBS, *Sixth Annual Report* (1825), 4; and NCFBS, Minutes, vol. 2, April 10, 1824.

36. "An Act to Incorporate the Sons of Benevolence in the Town of New Castle," Petitions Negroes, Legislative Papers, 1830, Record Group 1111, DHR. I became aware of this petition from Harold B. Hancock, "Not Quite Men: The Free Negroes in Delaware in the 1830s," *Civil War History* 17 (1971): 320–31.

37. "Act to Incorporate the Sons of Benevolence in the Town of New Castle."

38. On the connections among black nationalism, antislavery, and colonization, see David Waldstreicher, *In the Midst of Perpetual Fetes: The Making of American Nationalism, 1776–1820* (Chapel Hill: University of North Carolina Press, 1997), chap. 6, epilogue; and the classic assessment for a slightly later period by George Fredrickson, *The Black Image in the White Mind* (New York: Harper and Row, 1971).

39. Ronald G. Walters, *American Reformers, 1815–1860* (New York: Hill and Wang, 1978), 78.

40. Quoted in Leon F. Litwack, *North of Slavery: The Negro on the Free States, 1790–1860* (Chicago: University of Chicago Press, 1961), 77. Also see Christopher Malone, "Rethinking the End of Black Voting Rights in Antebellum Pennsylvania: Racial Ascriptivism, Partisanship and Political Development in the Keystone State," *PH* 72 (2005): 466–504.

41. For other assessments of increasing northern racism in the 1820s, see Fredrickson; Malone; Gary B. Nash, *Forging Freedom: The Formation of Philadelphia's Black Community* (Cambridge, Mass.: Harvard University Press, 1988), especially 246–79; and Thomas P. Slaughter, *Bloody Dawn: The Christiana Riot and Racial Violence in the Antebellum North* (New York: Oxford University Press, 1989).

42. Julie Winch, *Philadelphia's Black Elite; Activism, Accommodation, and the Struggle for Autonomy, 1787–1848* (Philadelphia: Temple University Press, 1988), 34–48; and Julie Winch, *A Gentleman of Color: The Life of James Forten* (New York: Oxford University Press, 2002), chaps. 8–9.

43. UCA petition, reprinted in William L. Garrison, *Thoughts on African Colonization*, 2 vols. (1832; New York: Arno Press, 1968), 2:36–40.

44. Ibid., 1:4.

45. Peter Spencer, the UCA minister in Wilmington, Delaware, was an officer of

the organization; *Minutes and Proceedings of the First Annual Convention of the People of Colour* (Philadelphia: Committee of Arrangements, 1831), 9. None of the local delegates appear in the 1830 census for those towns; *Minutes of the Fifth Annual Convention for the Improvement of the Free People of Colour in the United States* (Philadelphia: Gibbons, 1835), 20–21.

46. *Minutes . . . First Annual Convention of the People of Colour*, 4–5, the order of this quote has been rearranged.

47. *Minutes and Proceedings of the Third Annual Convention for the Improvement of the Free People of Colour* (New York: By Order of the Convention, 1833), 23.

48. For a rich assessment of these riots, which stresses that black elites and their institutions were its main targets, see Emma Jones Lapsansky, "'Since They Got Those Separate Churches': Afro-Americans and Racism in Jacksonian Philadelphia," *American Quarterly* 32 (1980): 54–78.

49. *Minutes . . . Fifth Annual Convention for the Improvement of the Free People of Colour*, 31, 26, 21, 23, emphasis in original.

50. Alexis de Tocqueville, *Democracy in America*, 12th ed., ed. J. P. Mayer (1835–40; 1848; New York: HarperCollins, 1969), 408.

51. Key arguments about the Revolution's negative consequences for women include Joan Hoff Wilson, "The Illusion of Change: Women and the American Revolution," in Alfred F. Young, ed., *The American Revolution: Explorations in the History of American Radicalism* (DeKalb: Northern Illinois University Press, 1976), 383–445; and Susan Juster, *Disorderly Women: Sexual Politics in Revolutionary New England* (Ithaca, N.Y.: Cornell University Press, 1994).

52. Tocqueville, 251. Also see François Furstenberg, "Beyond Slavery and Freedom: Autonomy, Virtue, and Resistance in Early American Political Discourse," *JAH* 89 (2003): 1295–1331.

53. Tocqueville, 639.

54. David Walker, *Appeal to the Coloured Citizens of the World*, ed. Sean Wilentz (1829; New York: Hill and Wang, 1995). Walker's text exemplifies what James Scott describes as the "hidden transcript" of resistance by an oppressed group. James C. Scott, *Domination and the Arts of Resistance* (New Haven, Conn.: Yale University Press, 1990), especially chap. 8.

55. Walker, 40.

56. Ibid., 55.

57. Ibid., 75, emphasis in original.

58. This biographical discussion primarily draws on Henry J. Steele, "The Life and Public Services of Governor George Wolf," *Pennsylvania German Society* 39 (1930): 1–25, and Clara A. Beck, *Kith and Kin of George Wolf: Governor of Pennsylvania, 1829–1835* (Easton, Pa.: Correll, 1930).

59. Philip Shriver Klein depicts Wolf as an Ingham ally in *Pennsylvania Politics, 1817–1832: A Game Without Rules* (Philadelphia: Historical Society of Pennsylvania, 1940), 270–73, 286–87, 294–98.

60. See Rogers's attack on Governor Wolf in an undated letter in the Dreer Collection, HSP.

61. The [Easton] *Mountaineer* reprinted the quote on March 24, 1820, as an attack on Rogers, but claimed the *Easton Centinel* had originally printed it in 1809.

62. Rogers testified at Ross's unsuccessful impeachment trial; Thomas J. Rogers, letter, February 16, 1832, Dreer Collection, HSP.

63. *Easton Centinel*, October 9, 1829.

64. Ibid., October 23, 1829.

65. For an analysis of the Charity School controversy, see Liam Riordan, "'The Complexion of My Country': The German as 'Other' in Colonial Pennsylvania," in

Colin Calloway, Gerd Gemunden, and Susanne Zantop, eds., *Germans and Indians: Fantasies, Encounters and Projections* (Lincoln: University of Nebraska Press, 2002), 97–119.

66. Tocqueville, 645.

A Note on the Unit of Comparison

1. James T. Lemon adopts a multiple-county perspective in *The Best Poor Man's Country: A Geographical Study of Early Southeastern Pennsylvania* (Baltimore: Johns Hopkins University Press, 1972), xvi. For a critique, see Lucy Simler, "The Township: The Community of the Rural Pennsylvanian," *PMHB* 106 (1982): 41–68.

2. Easton's population rank is cited in Mark Allen Hornberger, "The Spatial Distribution of Ethnic Groups in Selected Counties in Pennsylvania, 1800–1880" (Ph.D. diss., Pennsylvania State University, 1974), 164. On the modest size of urban settlements in early Delaware, see John A. Munroe, *Federalist Delaware, 1775–1815* (New Brunswick, N.J.: Rutgers University Press, 1954), 21–24. On New Jersey towns, see Dennis P. Ryan, "Six Towns: Community and Change in Revolutionary New Jersey, 1770–1792" (Ph.D. diss., New York University, 1974); Peter O. Wacker and Paul G. E. Clemens, *Land Use in Early New Jersey: A Historical Geography* (Newark, N.J.: New Jersey Historical Society, 1995), population density maps for 1784 and 1810, 41; and Peter O. Wacker, "The New Jersey Tax-Ratable List of 1751," *NJH* 107 (1989): 35, 36. No local census manuscripts survive for New Jersey until 1830.

3. Frederick Tolles called attention to the need to study the "small town existence in the Middle Colonies" in his review essay "The Historians of the Middle Colonies," in Ray Allen Billington, ed., *The Reinterpretation of Early American History* (San Marino, Calif.: Huntington Library, 1966), 76–77.

Index

Acknowledgments

This book reaches back into my own distant past. I began work on it at the University of Pennsylvania, where I benefited from relationships with a remarkable range of colleagues and with the vibrant city of Philadelphia. This book could never have been completed without Richard S. Dunn's supportive guidance and the egalitarian camaraderie that his spirit and determination lent to the Philadelphia Center for Early American Studies (now the McNeil Center). Another absolutely unrepayable debt I owe is to Michael Zuckerman and his endlessly challenging contrarian brilliance. I especially value the intellectual and personal rewards of friendship with Max Page, Kathryn Jay (née Johnson), Nick Breyfogle, Paul Howard, Ann Little, John Bezís-Selfa, Rosanne Adderley, Alison Isenberg, Marc Stein, Ed Baptist, Karim Tiro, Rose Beiler, Marian Winship, and Beth Clement. Thanks especially to Max, John, Alison, and Karim, who improved this book by reading portions of the manuscript. If one's peers are especially important to our development as scholars, I was twice blessed with all the early Americanists who were at the Philadelphia Center while I claimed it as my turf. I especially learned there from Tom Humphries, Roderick Mc-Donald, Simon Newman, Konstantine Dierks, Dallett Hemphill, Judy Van Buskirk, Cami Townsend, Greg Knouff, Susan Klepp, Leslie Patrick, Ed Larkin, Cynthia Van Zandt, William O'Reilley, Billy Smith, and Wayne Bodle. I also benefited from careful readings of Chapter 2 by Greg and Francis S. Fox. Owen Ireland was a very generous reader of the manuscript for the University of Pennsylvania Press, and I was fortunate to have Bob Lockhart as my gentle editor at the Press. Dan Richter improved the entire work with his careful and insightful comments.

Much of the evidence on which this book rests has been preserved in local and state historical societies, from the august Historical Society of Pennsylvania to one-room collections such as the Marx History Room at the Easton Public Library. They keep alive our ability to know the past, and most of them persevere with small budgets and decreasing public funding. Among the many staff people who made me feel at home in their collections, I especially thank David Fowler, formerly at the David Library of the American Revolution; Constance Cooper at the Historical Society of Delaware; Dan Jones at the New Jersey State Archives; Ann Upton, Diana Franzunoff Peterson, and Emma Lapsansky-Werner at the Quaker Collection, Haverford College; John Petersen at the Lutheran Theological Seminary; Mary F. Cordato at the American Bible Society Library and Archive; Joel Sartorius at the Free Library of Philadelphia; Jim Green, Phil Lapsansky, and John C. Van Horne at the Library Company of Philadelphia; and Nancy Burkett, John B. Hench, Joanne Chaison, Caroline Sloat, Philip J. Lampi, S. J. Wolf, and Marie E. Lamoureaux at the American Antiquarian Society, with its stunning combination of material and human wealth.

Since leaving the Delaware Valley, I have settled on the eastern frontier at the University of Maine, where I have been fortunate to join a splendid History Department. William TeBrake and Scott See have served as exemplary chairs committed to maintaining a department culture that values professionalism and collegiality in equal measure. My debts to colleagues are numerous: Scott stands out not only as a chair but also as a reader of chapters and a steadfast friend; Martha McNamara also gave insightful comments on several chapters and her rich friendship; and Richard Blanke kindly translated several German documents for me. My work as a scholar and a teacher would also be sharply limited without the ready support of my department's office staff, Suzanne Moulton and Ulrike Livingston. This book has been strengthened by what I learned from undergraduate and graduate students at Orono. In particular, doctoral candidate Scott Lanzendorf did yeoman's service to compile and analyze tables in the appendix, and Christian Lieb translated many Pennsylvania German newspapers. Many outside my department have also enriched this study, especially the participants in our interdisciplinary faculty writing group. Of course, I owe an important debt to the interlibrary loan office of Fogler Library and especially to Mel Johnson, reference librarian *extraordinaire*. Finally, I thank Ben Friedlander for his rewarding engagement with this book and as a collaborative, interdisciplinary teacher. His blue editing pencil has done its best to curb my desire to present many more details.

Research grants and fellowships necessitate their own fundamental gratitude. The University of Pennsylvania awarded me fellowships that allowed me to discover the rewards of academic life both in the classroom and, thanks to the Roy F. Nichols Fellowship, as a scholar. I also enjoyed generous awards from the Andrew F. Mellon Foundation and the Pew Program in Religion and American History, which gave me the opportunity to share my work with Jon Butler. A host of smaller grants also critically sustained this project: Mini-Grant Award from the New Jersey Historical Commission; Gest Fellowship from the Quaker Collection, Haverford College; Bird & Bird Research Stipends from the History Department, University of Maine; Research Fellowship from the David Library of the American Revolution; Faculty Research Fund Award from the Office of Research and Sponsored Programs, University of Maine; Joyce A. Tracy Fellowship from the American Antiquarian Society.

This book has been improved by comments received at many conferences, first at the Pennsylvania Historical Association in October 1994, where John B. Frantz pointed me in profitable directions. Since then I have also benefited from comments by Philip D. Morgan, James Henretta, Alison Olsen, Randall K. Burkett, Graham Hodges, and Aaron Fogelman. An early version of Chapter 2 was published as "Identity and the American Revolution: Everyday Life and Crisis in Three Delaware River Towns," *Pennsylvania History* 64 (Winter 1997): 56–101; I appreciate William Pencak's solicitation of it. An earlier version of part of Chapter 4 was improved by suggestions from Gary Nash and published as "Passing as Black/Passing as Christian: African-American Religious Autonomy in Early Republican Delaware," in *Empire, Society, and Labor: Essays in Honor of Richard S. Dunn*, special supplemental issue, edited by Nicholas Canny, Joseph E. Illick, Gary B. Nash, and William Pencak, *Pennsylvania History* (Summer 1997): 207–29. Small parts of Chapters 1 and 2, much revised here, also appeared in "'The Complexion of My Country': The German as 'Other' in Colonial Pennsylvania," in *Germans and Indians: Fantasies, Encounters, Projections*, edited by Colin G. Calloway, Gerd Gemünden, and Susanne Zantop (Lincoln: University of Nebraska Press, 2002), 97–119.

My deepest thanks are to friends and family who have kept me mindful of things beyond early America. The Barry and O'Boyle families have enriched life from my earliest years, and Dean Goldfein has been a dear friend for almost as long. I'd be fatter and duller without my trio of mountain biking pals with whom I try to keep up (Mark Condon, Eric Pandiscio, and John Gause), and I'd be slimmer and duller without friends who define the pleasures of neighborhood (Tanya Baker and Jamie Heanes, Landis Greene and Bruce Norelius, Martin and Lesa O'Connell, and Phoebe Gause). My dedication of this book to my parents is a small testament to their generosity in all things. My brother Sean and his family have strengthened me by their creativity and humanity. One family member, Me Me Riordan, has read more drafts of this book than anyone other than I. What more could an academic nephew ask? But saving the most important expression of gratitude for last, my wife, Susan Thibedeau, and our splendid sons, Cormac and Declan, have contributed an endless supply of loving distraction.